An Environmental History of Medieval Europe

How did medieval Europeans use and change their environments, think about the natural world, and try to handle the natural forces affecting their lives? This groundbreaking environmental history examines medieval relationships with the natural world from the perspective of social ecology, viewing human society as a hybrid of the cultural and the natural. Richard Hoffmann's inter-disciplinary approach sheds important light on such central topics in medieval history as the decline of Rome, religious doctrine, urbanization and technology, as well as key environmental themes, among them energy use, sustainability, disease and climate change. Revealing the role of natural forces in events previously seen as purely human, the book explores issues including the treatment of animals, the 'tragedy of the commons', agricultural clearances and agrarian economies. By introducing medieval history in the context of social ecology, it brings the natural world into historiography as an agent and object of history itself.

RICHARD C. HOFFMANN is Professor Emeritus and Senior Scholar in the Department of History, York University, Canada. As a pioneer in the environmental history of pre-industrial Europe, he is widely known for his contributions to medieval studies, environmental studies and historic fisheries.

D0781115

Cambridge Medieval Textbooks

This is a series of introductions to important topics in medieval history aimed primarily at advanced students and faculty, and is designed to complement the monograph series *Cambridge Studies in Medieval Life and Thought*. It includes both chronological and thematic approaches and addresses both British and European topics.

For a list of titles in the series, see
www.cambridge.org/medievaltextbooks

AN ENVIRONMENTAL HISTORY OF MEDIEVAL EUROPE

RICHARD C. HOFFMANN

CAMBRIDGE
UNIVERSITY PRESS

CAMBRIDGE
UNIVERSITY PRESS

University Printing House, Cambridge CB2 8BS, United Kingdom

One Liberty Plaza, 20th Floor, New York, NY 10006, USA

477 Williamstown Road, Port Melbourne, VIC 3207, Australia

4843/24, 2nd Floor, Ansari Road, Daryaganj, Delhi - 110002, India

79 Anson Road, #06-04/06, Singapore 079906

Cambridge University Press is part of the University of Cambridge.

It furthers the University's mission by disseminating knowledge in the pursuit of
education, learning and research at the highest international levels of excellence.

www.cambridge.org
Information on this title: www.cambridge.org/9780521700375

First published 2014
Reprinted 2015

A catalogue record for this publication is available from the British Library

Library of Congress Cataloging in Publication data
Hoffmann, Richard C. (Richard Charles), 1943–
An environmental history of medieval Europe / by Richard C. Hoffmann.
pages   cm. – (Cambridge medieval textbooks)
Includes bibliographical references.
ISBN 978-0-521-87696-4 (hardback) – ISBN 978-0-521-70037-5 (paperback)
1. Human ecology – Europe – History – To 1500.   2. Nature – Effect of human
beings on – Europe – History – To 1500.   3. Social ecology – Europe – History – To
1500.   4. Europe – Environmental conditions – History – To 1500.   5. Europe –
Social conditions – To 1492.   6. Civilization, Medieval.   I. Title.
GF540.H64   2013
304.2094′0902–dc23
2013035617

ISBN 978-0-521-87696-4 Hardback
ISBN 978-0-521-70037-5 Paperback

CONTENTS

———————— • ————————

FIGURES

———— • ————

MAPS

———————— • ————————

PREFACE

Some might judge foolhardy the very notion of approaching medieval European history as if nature mattered. Yet the historiographic space between J. Donald Hughes's *Pan's Travail: Environmental Problems of the Ancient Greeks and Romans* (1994), and John Richards's *The Unending Frontier: an Environmental History of the Early Modern World* (2003) calls for at least a temporary span cobbled together by one familiar with the hazards of practising and teaching medieval and environmental history alike. The construction grew from original research and writing in these fields, but equally from trying to assimilate books, articles, conference papers, and conversations of colleagues in many disciplines into topics for discussion in graduate and senior seminars and eventually into lectures for undergraduates in History at York University, Toronto. Performances of able students at all levels showed what more could be made of these materials and the struggles of others indicated where approaches had to be rethought. Thus reconsidered and revised, the lectures became the core of this textbook, the substance of which was completed in September 2012.

The book is perhaps wishfully directed at two audiences, students of the Middle Ages and students of environmental history from both historical and palaeoscientific backgrounds. It therefore surely says some things one set of readers may find too elementary and another set still too alien, only to incite reversed opinions elsewhere. Patience can be a difficult virtue for readers and author alike, but an interdisciplinary enterprise must bring diverse expertise into a shared space where all can contribute. The book explores topics that are defined by general medieval history – the decline of Rome, the role of religious doctrine, the problem of the fourteenth century – by economic and social research with clear ecological implications – agricultural clearances and agrarian economics, tenurial rights, technology, urbanization – and by environmental studies – social metabolism, climate change, sustainability, the 'tragedy of the commons', biodiversity, the roots of today's environmental crisis. Evidence and findings rest on administrative, legal, religious, and literary texts; on artistic, practical, and discarded material objects; and on biological, geological, pedological, atmospheric, genetic, and chemical data sets. Coverage aspires to be inclusive, summoning up examples from various lands of western Christendom and, where appropriate, observing differences as closely as commonalities. Space and ignorance, however, thwart this ambition, leaving ample opportunity for more expert scholars and scientists to correct errors, omissions, and misconceptions. I anticipate the better-informed will take issue with assertions here made and within a brief span in academic time undertake to replace this initial assemblage of medieval environmental tales with more definitive syntheses and elegant recognition of diversities.

That what follows bears any historical weight or analytical substance is in no small measure due to the generous information, ideas, and criticisms of Ellen Arnold, Cristina Arrigoni Martelli, Steven Bednarski, Connie Berman, Steve Carpenter, Tom Cohen, Petra van Dam, Dagomar Degroot, Anton Ervynck, Piotr Górecki, Barbara Hanawalt, Bernd Herrmann, Stuart Jenks, Suzanne Jenks, Richard Keyser, Lisa Kiser, Tim Newfield, Kathy Pearson, Christie Peters, Tom Prinsen, Alasdair Ross, Linnéa S. Rowlatt, Martin Schmidt, Bradley Skopyk, Paolo Squatriti, Peter Szabo, Vickie Szabo, Richard Unger, Andrew Watson, and others I blush to have neglected. Elements of the published book were possible with help from Terence Barry, Peter Durrant, Della Hooke, Tim LeGoff, Rosa Orlandini, Oliver Rackham, Rosemary Ryan, William TeBrake, and Iain Wallace. Carolyn King has again turned my inchoate sketches and ideas into effective original maps and diagrams. At Cambridge University Press, Michael Watson initiated our discussions and sold to his colleagues my approach to the topic, Elizabeth Friend-Smith patiently shepherded author and manuscript through its drafts, and Chloe Dawson helped resolve many practical problems. I am grateful to all.

That I think of myself as an environmental historian is due to the example and suasion of my late colleague Elinor Melville, who remains deeply missed. That I even pretend to think as an environmental historian I owe to the example, instruction, and unfailing collegial support of Verena Winiwarter. My appreciation of the simultaneous strength and fragility of natural forces and the need for humility in approaching them was taught by time in and on waters great and small and by sharing the ways of a gardener, Ellen, who has for nearly a half-century mostly managed to keep my feet on the ground.

What is mistaken in this book is my own doing. I hope others will take up the questions it tries to raise, mend its faults, and enrich our understanding with their own better-founded answers to the dynamic interactions of medieval Europeans and their natural world.

King City, Ontario

Frontispiece: Nature and culture at Waterford, Ireland, 1372

INTRODUCTION: THINKING ABOUT MEDIEVAL EUROPEANS IN THEIR NATURAL WORLD

———————— • ————————

How much were medieval Italians themselves responsible for the food shortage that by late spring 1347 was affecting about half the population of Tuscany, for the onset that summer in Sicily and Genoa of an epidemic which would in a few years kill half or more of the European population, or for the buildings smashed and hundreds of deaths in Venice and further northeast in an earthquake of January 1348? Ought those events be related to unsurpassed flooding across central Europe in July 1342, and the crash of English grain yields to 40 per cent of normal in 1348–52?

Did the spread of an exotic animal, the rabbit, in thirteenth-century England and the Low Countries have anything to do with the simultaneous extirpation of native wild boar from Britain? And the arrival of an exotic fish, the common carp, in France at the very time that native salmon were vanishing from streams of coastal Normandy? Was any of this change to biodiversity connected to medieval classification of the beaver as a fish?

Why would a ninth-century abbot at the Carolingian royal abbey of Fulda in eastern Franconia and early fourteenth-century Cistercian monks at Lubiąż on the Oder river both assert that, more than a hundred years earlier, their respective blessed founders had established holy cloisters in a howling wilderness? The monks at Lubiąż kept chests full of charters from the 1170s–1190s which described the hamlets then on the site and commissioned the new abbey to care for those Christian souls. The soil beneath the very foundation stones of Fulda preserves remains of a royal hunting lodge and peasant huts.

Why, then, a half-millennium fiction of 'deserts' in damp and well-wooded central Europe?

What induced Londoners around 1300 to burn 'sea coal' despite its hateful stench but stop grumbling by century's end? That was not the outcome for folk at Troyes who around 1208 were cursing the stinking *merderon* ('shit hole') in a closed off urban arm of the Seine.

Why did King Offa II of Mercia (757–96) put what must have been hundreds of people to work digging a shallow ditch and mounding the earth beside it for more than a hundred kilometres parallel to his frontier with Welsh princes whose men could easily walk or ride over this 'dyke'? Did this activity bear any relationship to the construction in 1177 of the 400 metre Bazacle at Toulouse, which diverted the Garonne to drive a dozen mills – and put twice as many ship mills out of commission? Water from upland streams, channelled and controlled by complex techniques and local rules of Arab origin, greened thousands of hectares around Valencia year-round, offering consumers melons, sugar, even cotton, while other Mediterranean rivers fed the Tuscan Maremma and lagoons at the mouth of the Tiber, both commonly acknowledged as sources of debilitating or deadly *mal'aria*, the evil of the marsh. By the years around 1300 Dutch, Saxon, and East Anglian dwellers on drained land or marsh pastures along southern shores of the North Sea also knew to fear recurring fevers of the ague. An anonymous English poet wrote:

> A man may a while
> Nature begile
> By doctrine and lore
> And yet at the end
> Wil Nature home wend
> There she was before.[1]

Do such images belong to your vision of medieval Europe? Perhaps they should.

This book engages a different kind of medieval history. It takes a new look at information from the European experience between roughly 500 and 1500CE, some familiar to most

---

[1] C. Sisam and K. Sisam, eds., *The Oxford Book of Medieval English Verse* (Oxford: Clarendon Press, 1970), 554.

medievalists and much familiar to some, and reads it from a novel point of view, namely as evidence of relations between two dynamic entities, human society and the natural environment. This introduction begins to frame the Middle Ages with conceptual tools meant to help understand familiar medieval narratives in another way. History roots in time and place – establishing situations, telling stories, comparing stories, linking stories. Environmental history brings the natural world into the story as an agent and object of history. This is medieval history as if nature mattered.

Such is by no means the customary perspective and practice of traditional history, medieval or otherwise, which has been devoted to the evolution and interaction of humans and human cultures in time. After the modern historical discipline removed supernatural actors from its scholarship, only humans remained as its objects and agents. The non-human provided mere scenery and stage properties for the human story, whether conceived as an object of humane scholarship or of social science. Traditional historians consider human activities in both material and symbolic culture: acts of war or sexual congress; mechanical or artistic artefacts; ideas of kinship, justice, or the divine. They argue over the priority of material and ideological forces, but none denies structural linkages between, for instance, racism and slavery, misogyny and patriarchy, profit motives and class. All this comprises a cultural sphere of causation, where the interplay of human reason, emotions, goals, and actions operates with autonomy, determined by nothing outside that sphere.

Historical and interdisciplinary study and understanding of medieval Latin Christendom share the overarching modernist approach to this historic culture. Probably most medievalists try to approach it from within, using especially verbal artefacts, texts, to recapture and recapitulate the words, thoughts, and ideas of medieval people. What present-day anthropologists call an 'emic' perspective refers to the culturally specific participant's point of view, that is, how a medieval human agent perceived and conceived a course of action. The enterprise necessarily rests on that tiny share of the cultural acts performed by a small proportion of medieval people who committed to writing and other intentional elements of symbolic culture selected fragments of their lives, desires, expectations, and knowledge of themselves, their fellows, and their material surroundings. Whatever lay outside their cultural awareness does not exist. The contrasting 'etic' approach takes an observer's point of view, remaining 'culturally neutral' with respect to the original event/actors, though not, of course, the observer's own culture, source of her categories. It asks of medieval texts and other remains questions that may have been far from the maker's conscious intent – e.g. racial stereotypes in a romance, tree species in a manuscript illumination – or even beyond his capability – e.g. performance theory. It calls upon such concepts as subaltern theory or a supply curve for labour, and exploits modern technologies – ultraviolet lights, dendrochronology, etc. – outside any medieval cultural competence or imagination to make medieval people, their works and experiences understandable in present-day terms.

Studied by these means the civilization of medieval Latin Christendom may be crudely typified by certain dominant cultural features, all essential to its character though not all unique to it. Formative was an often uncomfortable blend of older antique Mediterranean and northern barbarian traditions and practices, and then an increasingly self-conscious identification with Latin, i.e. Roman, Christianity. These variously provided paradigms for symbolic cultures, high and popular, and notably the key but sharply limited role of Latin literacy. Pre-eminent subsistence strategies rested more or less heavily on cultivation of cereal grains, but always included some elements of local and interregional exchange. Diverse and fragmented landholding and military elites, often joined by claimants to supernatural authority, contested for political power. Even before the end of the first millennium CE this decentred sociocultural community had established a broad territorial range across all three great regions of western Eurasia – Mediterranean, Atlantic maritime, and continental – joining Sicily to Scandinavia and the Carpathians to Iceland as never before. These peoples absorbed, imitated, conquered, or defied their closest neighbours for a millennium until around 1500 they burst forth on to the rest of the world. Taken collectively, such shared, though never uniform, historical attributes differentiated Latin Christendom from its sibling co-heirs to classical Mediterranean civilization, namely Byzantium and the *Dar al-Islam*, for all that they occasionally provide insightful comparisons. While a view from notably al-Andalus, Russia, or the eastern Mediterranean may occasionally appear below, those must be secondary to the attempt to establish both commonalities and diversities across the Latin west.[2]

Among all those products of an autonomous, autopoetic cultural realm, human ideas have, of course, their own histories. One such idea distinguishes between humans and other things of *this* world, calling the latter 'nature', that which is not 'human', not 'culture'. A conceptual dichotomy between culture and nature is commonly thought characteristic of western modernity, but can also be traced in other settings, including, in some ways, medieval Christendom.

Modern thinking consigns to the realm of science this world apart from humans, an autonomous sphere of material things subject to its own causality. Some such 'laws of nature' are physical, like that Newton described as gravity or Einstein's relation of energy to matter. Chemical laws govern the combustion of carbon to CO_2 and the hydrocarbon cellulose to CO_2 and water, both with the emission of heat. Atmospheric chemistry explains how water, nitrogen, and carbon cycle between solid, liquid, and gaseous states. Processes of plate tectonics shape and shake continents. Geographers study spatial relationships in terms of regions at various scales. Living nature comprises individual organisms and genetically distinctive sets called species, with physiological and behavioural attributes evolving over time in patterned ways. Every organism lives by exchanging energy and

---

[2] A case can be made to include Byzantium (Balkans, Aegean, Asia Minor?) in an environmental history of medieval Europe, but it fails to compel. The relationship of both Byzantium and the societies of classical Islam to the Christian west is best acknowledged as one of cognates, co-heirs of classical Mediterranean culture, each going in its own direction. By analogy, the history of China does not encompass Korea or Japan, nor is Canada's story that of the United States. Developing that thesis is not, of course, the task of this book. That certain kinds of Byzantine texts document and derive from the same classical experience and mentality as some later western ones is true, though more reflective of a broader Mediterranean culture and physical environment (which would therefore include southwest Asia and North Africa) than anything especially connected to a transcultural 'medieval' millennium.

Just as diagnostic are the quite separate scholarly communities who for the past century have pursued the histories of medieval western Christendom and medieval Byzantium. Though both rightly acknowledge and study intercultural contacts and engagements between medieval Latin and Greek Christians, the two scholarly groupings otherwise deal with different and distinctive bodies of sources to explore different kinds of questions. Even had Byzantinists treated most of the issues that this book will explore, which is by no means evident, their findings, as those on contemporary Baghdad, would have to be handled as comparative rather than integral topics.

materials with its environment, a process called metabolism. The ecological principle recognizes the interconnectedness of living and non-living things through various relationships (predator–prey, competition), processes (photosynthesis, decomposition), and cycles (water, carbon, nitrogen). Each set of closely interacting living and non-living things is called an ecosystem; at larger scale, less closely linked ecosystems form a landscape, ecological counterpart to the geographers' region. Metabolic analysis traces flows of matter and energy between and through organisms and communities at all scales, and helps identify questions of sustainability, asking how long those inputs and effluents can continue to flow without harming the recipient and its surroundings.

Since René Descartes and the Scientific Revolution of the seventeenth and eighteenth centuries this 'natural sphere of causation' is recognized as autonomous, meaning it is not evidently controlled by supernatural entities or forces nor by human wishes, emotions, mental constructions, historical time, or cultural preferences. It is, however, understandable to humans *only* through cultural representations, namely ways humans are able to think and communicate about it, from the basics of language ... to science itself.

How then is nature to be connected to culture and placed into time as a protagonist in a human story? How is environmental history possible? For traditional history the question is moot. Its nature is but a backdrop to human affairs, having no or insignificant actual effects on them. On the other hand, a cultural tradition reaching from the ancient Greeks to twentieth-century geopolitics and such commentators as Jared Diamond holds natural forces responsible for human history itself. Environmental determinism asserts that natural conditions actually dominate, with climate especially argued to shape human physiology, psychology, and social organization. Greco-Roman ideas that tropical and temperate zones produced peoples of different temperaments were also known in the Middle Ages; later writers proposed that the need to manage floodwaters compelled formation of elaborate bureaucratic states. Early twentieth-century racist reasoning and climatic 'explanations' for European rule over 'lesser races' put geographical and other environmental determinisms in a bad odour not yet dissipated. This position is neither inherently adhered to nor promoted by environmental historians, simply because past experience has too often disproved its denial of human agency.

Most recent intellectual fashion has been the reverse stance, in the not unrelated positions of cultural determinism and constructivism. The former simply treats cultural stereotypes – Greek sailors, American ingenuity, the superiority of capitalism – or cultural processes – strategies of court politics, the radicalization of revolutions – as sufficient causes for changing material conditions. In scholarly terms it adheres to pioneering sociologist Emile Durkheim's injunction that social phenomena have social explanations. The latter, notably twentieth-century, paradigm argues that all humans can know, use, or encounter is necessarily and simply a cultural construct. Nature, science, mythology, and everything purportedly known outside human consciousness is but an artefact of that consciousness. The non-cultural is unknowable and thus without meaning in human history. At most, one could trace the evolution of human ideas about the non-human but never really test these against any external reality. Constructivism has real importance for environmental history, for historians, like other modern environmental thinkers, must acknowledge the power of culture in shaping human perceptions and human actions in the past as in the present. But in its extreme this antidote to environmental determinism is antithetical to environmental history (and any other engagement with non-human phenomena). It asserts as impossible what is, in fact, done by ordinary people, historians, and even medievalists all the time. But all three of these approaches continue to treat nature and culture as the two distinct and separate entities graphically represented in Figure 0.1.

Another frame of reference is needed to consider how humans actually operate with regard to the world of nature and thus how historical scholarship can explore, identify, compare, and begin to

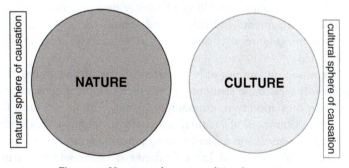

Figure 0.1 Humans and nature: traditional separation

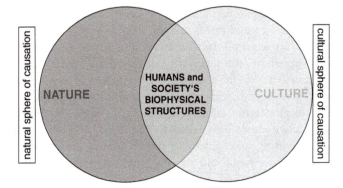

Figure 0.2 Humans and nature: an interaction model: society as hybrid

explain what individuals and groups have there experienced and done in the immediate and the more distant past. Such a tool or heuristic model was developed in discourse on present-day environmental relations by the school of social ecology in Vienna. It subsumes simpler, more limited, and more ambiguous ideas offered by some American environmental historians during the 1980s. What is hereafter referred to as the interaction model acknowledges the reality, autonomy, and *inter*relationship of both nature and culture (Figure 0.2). It establishes human society, human artefacts, indeed even human bodies, as *hybrids* of the symbolic and the material, for human organisms and material cultures necessarily exist simultaneously in both the cultural and the natural spheres. Humans and their biophysical structures, while inherently cultural in quality, are unavoidably subject to the natural realm and its laws, whether humans are aware of them or not. Material culture is conjoined with symbolic culture while at the same time its objects, living and non-living, participate in flows of energy and materials with the natural environment. Individuals and whole societies thus have metabolisms (Figure 0.3) and cease to exist if those cannot be maintained.

Of course, humans not only interact with the natural sphere, they consciously seek to use elements of it for their cultural purposes and in so doing, they modify it, consciously or not. The model dubs this process 'colonization' of a natural ecosystem, imagining an ancient or medieval peasant (Latin *colonus*) turning a natural savannah or woodland into a cultivated field. In a colonized ecosystem, selected natural processes are guided to operate for human ends set, it is vital to

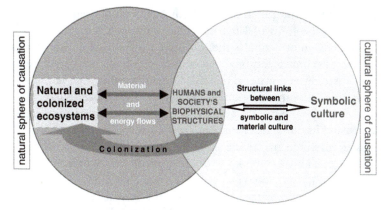

Figure 0.3 Humans and nature: biophysical structures as ecosystem compartments linked to symbolic culture

emphasize, by culture itself. Colonization, however, never completely replaces natural with anthropogenic and controlled processes, so it can have *un*intended as well as planned consequences. Other human interventions may themselves be wholly unconscious but no less transformative, as when infected Roman soldiers carried malaria into the Rhine delta.

Seen another way (Figure 0.4), material nature, living and non-living, and human communications (symbolic culture) join in an inter*active* and reciprocal relationship mediated by human material life. As already remarked, humans experience elements of the natural

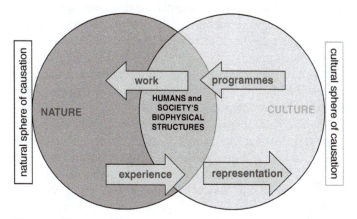

Figure 0.4 Humans and nature: connecting experience, thought, and action

world directly but can grasp it only through cultural representation, mainly in the form of language. Once absorbed into the cultural sphere, this information is there subject to its autonomous actions and may become a part of a new cultural construct, a programme to do something of a material quality. The programme itself has, however, no environmental impact, no effect on the natural sphere, until human work there modifies the existing flows of energy and materials. Work and its outcomes then become subject to autonomous natural causation, which may itself alter subsequent human experience of nature. As culture responds – in no a priori way – to represented experience and as natural processes are themselves affected by human work, reciprocal change rolls through the interactive system. The process is recursive; causes turn into effects which turn into further causes. Over time culture and nature co-adapt; they engage in co-evolution.

The interaction model encompasses the dynamic attributes of both nature and human culture and helps pinpoint the kinds of relationships arising in their conjunction. It imparts a temporal dimension to the particular operations of cultural and natural processes while preserving the autonomy, indeed the mutual indeterminacy, of both causal spheres. As a heuristic device the model provides a means of organizing the evidence of the past to pose and answer relational questions about the interplay of humans and their environment without predetermining those answers.

The most recent thinking about the interaction model is aware of criticism that it reifies what are indeed cultural constructs, culture and nature, and thus situates their interplay in timeless and undifferentiated space. Hence we move beyond the heuristic to acknowledge that the generalized interaction in fact occurs in specific times and places where (at least theoretically) identifiable human individuals and groups with particular cultural programmes (intentions) and practices (skills, techniques, routines) worked at and thus changed together with particular places possessed of their own natural attributes. Hybridity and co-adaptation thus come in observable and explicable form as 'socio-natural sites', small or large, where people operate *in* the natural sphere and give those sites a hybrid quality. At the small end of a scale the ground located between the Morzyna stream and a wooded outlier of the Sudety mountains in Silesia, where a late twelfth-century peasant named Głąb 'first cleared that place which is now [about 1268] called the Great Meadow or in Polish *Wiela*

Łąka',[3] was and is a socio-natural site. So, too, is the Arno flood plain at Florence, where the inundation of November 1333 destroyed mills, bridges, and other facilities, killed more than three hundred people, and caused the communal government both to initiate reconstruction and to regulate land use in hopes of avoiding a repetition. Ascending the scale, Offa's Dyke is also a socio-natural site, as are those vast expanses of upland England and central Spain turned into sheep pastures in response to late medieval demand for high-quality woollen fabrics. The concept of socio-natural sites reminds especially the generalizing historian – as this one must be – that environmental history occurs locally and that part of the task is to discriminate among the local and the larger forces which have shaped it.

Encompassed or identified within the interaction model are the three overarching themes encountered together or separately in most works which can be understood as environmental history, whether or not the original authors were aware of it. In no a priori or hierarchical order, environmental historians ask about environmental influences, about attitudes towards nature, and about human impacts on the natural world. Exploring environmental influence on human condi-tions and activities would assess what, if any, issues or outcomes in a particular historical situation can reasonably and demonstrably be traced to forces arising in the natural sphere. In a medieval setting, for instance, had the wet weather conditions already setting in during 1314 any meaningful effects on the tactics and results of the combat between Scots and English along the damp valley of the Bannockburn on 24 June of that year? Likewise, to what extent were the demo-graphic crash of the mid-fourteenth century and its immediate con-sequences driven by biological interaction of human bodies and a disease best called the 'Black Death'? Most such questions arise from human experiences, but some recent environmental history research has sought to establish natural events or conditions of the medieval past – volcanic eruptions come to mind – and then considered their possible and probable effects on human societies or thought. The risk, of course, is falling into the reductionist trap of environmental determinism.

---

[3] As described in the late thirteenth-century *Liber fundationis Claustri Sancte Marie Virginis in Heinrichow*, Book 1, chapter 7, and translated in P. Górecki, *A Local Society in Transition: the Henryków Book and Related Documents*, Studies and Texts 155 (Toronto: Pontifical Institute of Mediaeval Studies, 2007), 123.

The interest of many historians, literary scholars, and others in identifying ideas about the natural world held by past individuals, social groups, or entire cultures likewise pertains to the enterprise of environmental history. Such research may seek fundamental general assumptions about how nature was understood to work as the 'other' for human society, asking, for instance, whether it was thought to be inherently threatening (a fatalist attitude), tending towards a benign stability or partnership with humans, easily damaged by improvident human activities, or in need of regular human management. More easily ascertained, given appropriate sources, may be specific notions about how the natural world is identified, configured, or operates. Medieval lawyers, and philosophical theologians, for instance, articulated divergent understandings of differences between humans and animals and thus the right of humans to dispose of beasts. The further question then arises about the connection, if any, between such ideological phenomena in the cultural sphere and human activities in the material realm. To what extent did, for example, experiences of medieval miners influence Albert the Great's ideas about minerals or, continuing around the process depicted in Figure 0.4, Albert's ideas or those of scholarly alchemists shape programmes and work underground? At the extreme, some might think such wholly immaterial ideas as the one-footed human races or the theology of redemption to be so exclusively elements in an autonomous medieval culture as to fall outside the hybrid zone of environmental history. But humans can only act on the basis of representations and their representations are shaped in part by the theoretical concepts they hold.

Human impacts on the environment come perhaps first to the mind of modern readers and have quantitatively dominated more recent periods of historical interest – acid rain, global warming, extinctions resulting from human historical agency – while emerging more slowly as a topic for the Middle Ages. Medieval research can approach and has proceeded from either side, whether seeking effects on biodiversity of medieval agricultural clearances or asking how much the Black Death was rooted in prior economic and social conditions. Here the scholar's risk lies in perceiving as human effects what may be incidents in processes of long-term natural change. As will be remarked below, environmental historians have had to learn that nature is and was itself not simply stable or even consistently equilibrating at all scales of analysis. The interaction model was developed to remind students of an inherently reciprocal relationship between two overlapping autonomies.

Just as the three themes of influence, ideas, and impacts will recur in chapters to follow, so will several of the paradigms which environmental historians have employed to organize their questions and evidence into what they offer as likely forms of answers. Some topics lend themselves to being approached as a question of 'pollution', trying to learn how, why, and with what effects humans were releasing 'poison' into the environment. It is perhaps the issue most ordinary people now see as typically 'environmental' and can apply also in the more distant past. Medieval cities and manufacturing processes were obviously potential sources of toxic effluents. So, too, could be convents. But this chemical, medical, and inherently technological approach misses many other aspects of medieval Europeans in their natural surroundings. Ecological balance underlies another family of questions, asking what caused disturbance to past natural systems or what natural systems may have been disturbed by certain human or, indeed, natural changes. Ascertaining the effects of woodland clearances, introduction of migratory sheep, or a drier climatic regime draws on ecology, climatology, resource science, and agronomy for potential answers. This paradigm is central to issues of ecological equilibrium or collapse which have been applied to medieval societies. Related but distinct is the area of resource use and sustainability, which today arises from physics and resource economics to ask how people make use of their natural surroundings, whether this use pattern can or could continue, and what bounding conditions applied in the past as in the present. It refers not only to acquisition of resources – as fuel from a managed woodland or forage from a hay meadow – but also to use of the environment for processing wastes. At what size or density of human habitation did certain diseases become endemic? 'Conviviality' expresses paradigmatic questions of values and equity in environmental relations: how are and were humans part of nature? How ought people live on the earth? Francis of Assisi may have engaged those questions rather differently from either his own local bishop or his still pagan contemporaries in Old Prussia or Lithuania. In all historical study, paradigms set the parameters for the information needed from the past and thus for the kinds of evidence historians seek on which to base their analyses and tell their stories. A *Life* of Francis may convey much about his feeling for animals but little about their use for draught power; an English demesne account does the reverse.

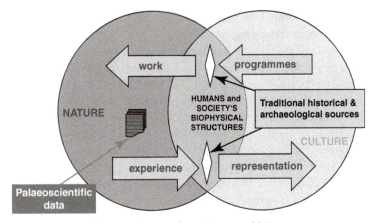

Figure 0.5 Sources for environmental history

Some such stories fit together into a larger narrative; others will not. Acknowledging diversity is important to understanding.

The sources from which environmental history is to be written can and must themselves be placed into the interaction model to connect it to the critical method that lies behind every truth-claiming statement about the past (Figure 0.5). Traditional history uses verbal (written or oral) and material remains (artefacts, structures, etc.) from the past as its source of information about that which produced them. Medievalists are well aware of the critical methods developed to test the authenticity of medieval texts and to establish their credibility as descriptions and simultaneously products of past consciousness. A charter established as a medieval forgery can tell the alert reader as much, but different, information as a fully authentic one; so can a mythic or misinformed or purposely slanted narrative, be it literary or historiographic. Archaeology as a historical discipline attends to material remains, but otherwise poses comparable critical tests and pursues the same large purpose – understanding past human experience.

All traditional historical sources are products of a culture *and* simultaneously exist (or once existed) in the material realm. They can be construed as material results of past symbolic culture, whether depicting or simply recognizable as evidence of representation, of programme, or even of cultural processes with little bearing on the hybrid zone of human–nature interaction. (A liturgical manuscript may participate in the natural world only in the physicality of its vellum, pigments, and perhaps splashes of candle wax.) But as every medieval history student was once taught, traditional sources were always made to serve past purposes, not subsequent historians' questions, and always function as potentially distorting lenses between the present observer and the past. The historical discipline has, however, no other access to the past it would study.

Many societies lacked cultural grounds for purposeful written descriptions of environmental issues, concepts, or conditions, so like many economic, social, and other historical themes, these must be learned by reading 'against the grain' to see what the creator had simply assumed, had refused to acknowledge, or had attempted to conceal. This narrowly constricted role of the written record prevailed in most semi-literate pre-modern societies around the world. For all the long-perfected investigative skills of medievalists in many disciplines, honest scholars have to admit their inability to reconstruct many of the most interesting aspects of past environmental relations from the surviving records of any given past society, and notably those of medieval western Christendom. Knowledge of the rations of monks at Bede's Lindisfarne is inaccessible to a present student, as are the methods whereby conquering Hungarians assessed and allocated the resources of the Pannonian basin.

Modern palaeosciences can reconstruct aspects of past environments from surviving natural features, identifying data and drawing inferences from tree rings, ice cores, isotopic analysis of organic items, animal bones, and other objects surviving and recovered from the past and reasonably believed to provide 'proxy data' about conditions under which those natural objects came to be or came to survive. For instance, differences in diet between elite and common women and men in sixth- to eighth-century Swabia have been inferred from variations in the proportions of strontium and calcium in their skeletons, and the trend of annual temperatures in fourteenth-century Greenland has been established from the changing balance between two isotopes of oxygen in annual layers of the ice core. Counting and correlating the annual rings in medieval oak objects enables precise dating of the artefact and, with variations in the width of the rings, fluctuations in annual weather conditions where the tree had grown. Unlike all other historical evidence, palaeoscientific data is not itself a product of past human culture although, like other history, it is a product of present-day human culture. Reference to even such conceptually simple, if skilled and tedious, palaeoscience as treating the pollen of cereal grains and arable weeds as a proxy for changes in land under the plough or under trees re-emphasizes, as has already been seen in the interaction model, in the characteristic themes, and in the prevalent paradigms, the essentially interdisciplinary quality of environmental history.

Regular collaboration with the natural sciences, as with the social and humanistic disciplines familiar in interdisciplinary medieval studies, does not, however, make environmental history in general or that of medieval Europe in any way the less history. Its purpose is not to ascertain general laws for cultural evolution, but to explore human experience with the natural world in a particular part of the past, namely, in this instance, that of western Christendom between the breakdown of classical Mediterranean civilization and the emergence of 'modernity', however the latter may be defined.

Cultures of the Middle Ages (then) and of Medieval Studies (now) combine to establish how this book proceeds. As chapter 3 will detail, environmental awareness rarely entered the demonstrable consciousness of medieval people and thus even less into their texts. This has encouraged an equivalent disregard for the natural world on the part of Medieval Studies. Conversely, the new subdiscipline of environmental history has only slowly gained awareness of pre-industrial times. Fortunately, besides the isolated contributions of self-conscious students of medieval environmental history, many findings of economic and social historians, historians of science, historical geographers, archaeologists, and palaeoscientists need only be recast into a mode of telling stories in which the medieval world of nature is a genuine protagonist, not merely a passive stage set for exclusively human agents.

The first task is to establish characteristic features of European nature and human relations with it before medieval times and in the critical period of metamorphosis from a subcontinent subsumed or subservient to classical Mediterranean civilization to a self-centred and autonomous culture identifiable as western Christendom. To this end chapter 1 first relates how post-glacial Europe acquired distinctive regional physical and climatic characteristics, but remained by nature neither static nor pristine. From Pleistocene hunter-gatherers to Iron Age cultures both Greco-Roman and barbarian, Europeans adapted to and modified their ecosystems. Classical Mediterranean civilization established long-lasting practices for exploiting characteristic land forms and annual weather patterns in harmony with what became influential cultural values. Roman imperialism spread these forms and their impacts on the natural world into Europe's interior. There they also affected the different adaptations of northern peoples who struggled to come to terms with maritime and continental climates and broad biotopes alien to crops and conventions conceived elsewhere. But the eventual slow breakdown of classical civilization helped set in motion cultural discontinuities on both sides of Roman frontiers, and together with atmospheric and pathogenic pressures of no obvious human origin shaped complex changes during early medieval times. These are detailed in chapter 2. Time-honoured human relations with foodstuffs, domestic plants and animals, and the land itself gave way to new. Different patterns barely to be detected in the exiguous record of the sixth, seventh, and early eighth centuries gain some shape in regional case studies, and are then thrown into harsh relief by the spotlight of a high literate culture revived by an alliance of Carolingian dynasts and Christian religious authorities. Suddenly, long-obscure innovations in ideological expectations and institutional practice affecting people and land appear clearly and as programmatic for a future.

Chapters on the formation and evolution of central linkages between medieval Europeans and their natural surroundings follow. Chapter 3 tries to pull together historical treatments and evidence of large-scope medieval ideas about the natural world and proper human relations with it, arguing for a problematic gap between the representations of nature which prevailed in medieval high culture on the one side and evident empirical experiences of and work in nature on the other. While several highly abstract ways of thinking attracted learned attention then and now, only some texts claiming to reflect practical experience and manipulation of nature do seem to emerge and co-evolve with practice over the course of the medieval millennium. In contrast, chapter 4 demonstrates how cultural expectations of food expressed by both medieval social power and human numbers drove a long process of forming the traditional European landscapes which prevailed until quite recently and in many places remain largely visible today. From Carolingian times to the early fourteenth century, cultural pressures to consume and hence to produce both cereal grains and domestic livestock lay behind woodland clearances, intensification of agricultural land use, and drainage of wetlands. General cultural bias against less than fully sedentary agropastoralism and ubiquitously tenacious struggles between seigneurial initiatives and peasant risk aversion had effect everywhere, as is revealed by the contrasted foodways and production systems of the newly irrigated landscapes of Muslim al-Andalus. Prestigious display motivated men of power to other forms of landscape modification, too. But environmental consequences of both typical and anomalous new anthropogenic ecosystems, colonizations of the natural sphere, were also plain, even to some contemporary observers already in central medieval centuries.

Chapters 5 and 6 turn to the medieval use, management, and sustainability of colonized local ecosystems. The former focuses on primary biological production systems, namely those natural or artificial arrangements which rested on capture of solar energy by green plants. It establishes key elements of material and energy flows tapped by traditional European handling of arable agriculture, livestock, woodlands, and wildlife, and identifies the environmental impact of these practices. The second of these paired chapters treats the nonliving environment and first the energy basis of a characteristically low-energy civilization. Medieval western Christendom relied mainly on biochemical energy from green plants to fuel human and animal muscle work or to burn as biomass from wood or charcoal. Under certain circumstances, fossil fuels and movements of water and air provided essential supplements. In later medieval centuries mining and fabrication of metals gained a larger place in material culture and also in the pollution and destruction of natural systems. Resurgent urbanization created new kinds of human environments with a peculiar inability to maintain themselves except by metabolic exchanges of energy, materials, and waste with surrounding ecosystems. Hence medieval cities early established distinctly urban 'ecological footprints'.

Questions of sustainability, overshoot, and collapse in medieval resource use turn attention to institutional aspects of who controlled resources and authorized, limited, or prohibited their use. Chapter 7 addresses human possession and use of medieval nature through legal notions of ownership, usufruct, and regulatory rights and practices. Conflicting claims of seigneurs and subject communities with common rights frame a whole category of struggles where, however, the modern stereotypical 'tragedy of the commons' played little part. A new configuration of protagonists gained importance in later medieval centuries as princes and their officers, in other words the state, intervened in relations between user groups and all sorts of resources. Rhetorical appeals to the public good might serve to protect a resource or to allocate it among competitive users.

Natural forces emphatically retained their own strong dynamic in medieval Europe, driving changes to which humans had to respond in culturally shaped ways (chapters 8 and 9). Both the natural phenomena and cultural consequences now spark scholarly interest. Quite without human intent or understanding, medieval Europeans experienced acute and large-scale epidemic events and a shifting pattern of long-term endemic diseases, both with significant effects on material lives and symbolic cultures. Like disease, natural forces manifest in earth's geology and atmosphere have gained new recognition as drivers of human experience and histories. Now understood as resulting from slow movement of tectonic plates, earthquakes and volcanic eruptions suddenly took lives and possessions, compelling social and intellectual responses. In some respects more perceptible to well-attuned interdisciplinary scholars now than to people then, medieval Europeans went through changes in atmospheric conditions at both the short term (weather) and the long (climatic change). Both gradual and catastrophic occurrences are to be traced at continental scale and in local and regional examples. Environmental risks, shocks, and gradual changes affected people following diverse cultural practices in varying ecological circumstances differently.

Where, then, do medieval environmental relations end? Chapter 10 relates determinist interpretations of a fourteenth-century 'ecological crisis' from both environmental and anthropogenic perspectives and more recent scholarly views stressing a path-dependent (contingent) relationship among medieval ecosystems, unpredictable natural shocks, and social responses to them. Nevertheless, from a material culture standpoint much speaks for a continuity of European experience with the natural world all the way from the break in late antiquity to the establishment of a fossil energy system during the late eighteenth and nineteenth centuries. Yet coincident with fourteenth- to sixteenth-century dynamics in the natural sphere were autonomous transformations in relevant European cultural patterns, some mainly symbolic and others very much in the hybrid zone of developing technology. Both the symbolic and the material explain the largely unintended, indeed unimagined, impact of the massive encounter with the extra-European world which Europeans initiated at the close of the fifteenth century. After the Columbian voyages, no humans and no Europeans experienced the natural sphere as they had before. While much nevertheless remained unaltered (limited energy sources, the immanence of spirit, the centrality of agriculture), coincident natural and cultural mutations reset key features of European environmental relations at a scale comparable to the late antique discontinuity which had delineated a medieval European from a classical Mediterranean civilization. Narrative arcs contained within European culture and its own natural world would thereafter be transcended.

LONG NO WILDERNESS

—————— • ——————

A long past of continual dynamic changes naturally shaped Holocene (post-glacial) Europe, where medieval history took place. European regions acquired distinct physiographic, climatic, and biological features, but pristine European nature was neither static nor wholly stable.

Nor was the Europe inherited by the Middle Ages in any way pristine. From the Neolithic to the age of classical Mediterranean civilization successive human cultures had repeatedly affected and transformed European landscapes. Even Pleistocene and post-Pleistocene hunters deployed fire to make game more accessible. Subsequent agricultural adaptations (arable and pastoral) further opened European woodlands and in the Mediterranean established practices which would remain fundamental through and beyond the Middle Ages. Environmental effects of classical Mediterranean antiquity are not wholly agreed among present-day scholars, who notably debate questions of deforestation while plausibly linking hunting to loss of biodiversity. Classical Greeks and Romans made the environment an object of tacit and self-conscious thought, leaving to future generations of the learned a cultural legacy of ideas and knowledge and allowing some present-day inference of their assumptions, representations, and programmes for human action. North of the Alps Iron Age 'barbarians' worked to wrest their own livelihoods from a different configuration of land forms, soils, climate, and biota.

Both natural and cultural forces had thus shaped the material and symbolic heritage to which a new European civilization, one later called medieval, would gradually accede as its classical Mediterranean forebear disintegrated. This chapter aims to set out essential features of those antecedent processes and conditions.

NATURAL DYNAMICS IN HOLOCENE EUROPE

For millennia before the Middle Ages dynamic natural forces had continually changed and shaped the face of western Eurasia.

As elsewhere in the northern hemisphere, successive Pleistocene readvances of glacial ice carved European landscapes even far south of the glacial front. The latest retreat of the ice caps, which set in about fourteen thousand years ago (henceforth abbreviated as 14kya), had comparable wide-ranging effects. At its greatest extent, ice some 2 kilometres thick covered Europe north of a line from Dublin to Berlin to Moscow, while barely 600 kilometres to the south another ice cap and related valley glaciers filled the entire arc of the Alpine mountain system, from the Pyrenees across the Alps and into the Apennines, Carpathians, and northern Balkans. Across the intervening polar desert, melt-water streams cut through soils picked up and deposited by winds off the ice. In winter Atlantic pack ice reached northern Portugal. As the ice locked up much of the planet's water, normal sea level was 125 metres below the present, Britain was joined seamlessly to the continent, and the Mediterranean and Black Sea were cut off and reduced to salt lakes. With permafrost even in Provence and temperatures there averaging below 10°C, only the southernmost parts of Spain and the Balkans offered refuge for cold-sensitive plants and animals. To the north hardy herd animals and megafauna (from cave bears to woolly mammoths to giant beaver) grazed on the tundra, pursued by small bands of hunter-gathers. These physiologically modern humans had entered Europe during an earlier interglacial and by the onset of the most recent advance, about 28kya, fully replaced their Neanderthal predecessors. Meanwhile their contemporaries in warmer and then damp southwest Asia (the 'Fertile Crescent') were achieving the first known permanent settlements and monumental structures.

The millennia of global warming that melted back the ice were not uninterrupted. The end of a sharply cold interval roughly 10kya is conventionally taken as the division between the Pleistocene and the Holocene, until now the most recent period in planetary history. Early Holocene cultures of southwest Asia were by then already responding to the drying of their regional climate by domesticating local plants and animals. Elsewhere the great melt raised sea levels, probably by more than a hundred metres between 12kya and 5kya. The rising Mediterranean cut Sicily off from the Italian peninsula and overtopped a rock sill at the Bosporus so the lake to the north expanded by 30 per cent to became the Black Sea. Flooding of what became the southern North Sea severed Britain from the continent, while the Baltic and Norwegian fjords turned from freshwater lakes into marine embayments. Local coastline changes would continue.

When unimaginable weights of melt water flowed to the sea from ice caps on land, even the earth's crust responded in a process called isostatic rebound. Northern lands relieved of the burden of ice rose some hundreds of metres, while newly flooded southern coasts were suppressed by a few metres. More locally important tectonic effects in Mediterranean Europe derived from the continued northward movement of the African continental plate, which has for some 70 million years pressed against Europe's southern margin to raise the Alps and related mountain chains. Most of the northern shore of the Mediterranean has been lifted a metre or two since the last glacial maximum, a movement that came in fits and starts punctuated by frequent earthquakes from Portugal to Asia Minor and accompanied by continental Europe's only recent volcanic activity. Prehistoric and historic eruptions of Vesuvius and Etna strongly affect regional resources and their use by humans.

The onset of the Holocene effectively completed Europe's gross physical makeup. Subsequent human and natural history there played out in a small peninsular projection of the Eurasian land mass. Especially students based elsewhere need to remember that the western and central European terrain directly involved in medieval western Christendom covers less than 6 million square kilometres, so less than 5 per cent of the earth's surface or a third that of Russia and barely more than half that of Brazil, Canada, China, or the United States. Unlike those continental states, Europe's comparatively small space is surrounded and deeply penetrated by the sea; no point west of the present European Union's eastern boundary is more than 650 kilometres from salt water. Though the vast majority of medieval Europeans knew of the sea only by hearsay, that relative proximity influenced how they lived in even their inland landscapes.

Five distinct physiographic provinces with characteristic land forms extend as roughly east–west bands across Holocene Europe (see Map 1.1). On its southern margin the Mediterranean basin comprises the sea and a narrow, mountainous coastal strip. Mediterranean Europe

Map 1.1 Europe's land forms and principal geographic regions

contains relatively few and small areas of level ground. Bedrock lies close to the soil surface in much of its abrupt relief. Young and highly folded mountains of the Alpine system bound the entire northern shore of the Mediterranean, extending from the Pyrenees to the Caucasus with only a few major breaks to ease regular or large-scale passage. From the foot of the Pyrenees the European plain sweeps north and eastwards into Russia, extending under and beyond the English Channel, North Sea, and Baltic. Although morainic hills punctuate some northern reaches and long slow-moving rivers flow west or north across its commonly deep soils, nowhere on the plain does its gentle relief exceed 300 metres. But the plain is interrupted along its southern margin by plateaux and hills of old igneous and metamorphic rocks, roots of a mountain system eroded down long before the Alps began to rise. This geology makes for more rugged relief of 300–1,500 metres and concentrations of metallic minerals – for cultures that recognize and use such material. The plain's northern edge similarly laps along Europe's northwestern uplands, the old, glaciated, shield-like topography of the northern British Isles and Scandinavia, with its characteristically interrupted relief and drainage as well as more potential mineral deposits. But life on all this terrain is shaped as much by patterns of atmospheric circulation that also emerged during the early to mid-Holocene.

Most of Europe lies in the earth's north temperate zone, where westerly winds prevail. Its post-glacial climate (large-scale weather) and weather (climate at small scale) are formed by the interplay of three large air masses: the warm and dry 'Bermuda (also Azores) high'; the moderate and wet 'Icelandic low'; and the cold, dry 'Siberian high'. Driven by solar radiation and global oceanic circulation, the strength and movements of these atmospheric structures shape the long periods and short-term events of winds, temperatures, and precipitation over Europe. Warm and moist conditions prevailed at the start of the Holocene. Then after a short cooler, wetter interval, at roughly 8kya the general 'Atlantic Climatic Optimum' set in, bringing mean annual temperatures some 2–3°C above late twentieth-century norms. This warmest part of the Holocene lasted some two millennia (to approximately 5.7kya or about 3500BCE). As the Atlantic Optimum slowly passed, mean temperatures tended towards twentieth-century values, but humidity, seasonality, and regional variations gained distinctive importance. During 3500–2600BCE Mediterranean conditions became more arid, especially with warmer and drier summers. The so-called 'Sub-Boreal' of northwestern Europe (*c.*4000–600BCE) was cooler and drier, but punctuated by century-scale wet spells. Two of the seven readvances that Alpine glaciers made before Roman times occurred during the late Sub-Boreal. But during the last pre-Christian millennium a gradual warming and drying trend (sometimes called the 'Sub-Atlantic') set in to culminate *c.*200BCE to 200CE as the 'Roman Climatic Optimum'. By then the modern Sahara desert had fully replaced a hitherto humid landscape south of the Mediterranean.

By the mid-Holocene, therefore, climate and physiography together came to define the three principal geographic regions in Europe: Mediterranean, Atlantic (or maritime), and continental (as in Map 1.1). Distinctions between and seasonal variation within these regions established basic conditions of life for plants, animals, and humans in classical and medieval times, as they still do today. Imperial Roman soldiers and medieval Italian wool merchants alike complained of the cold and damp British Isles, whose residents now look eagerly forward to holidays on warm, dry Mediterranean shores. Medieval German armies entered Italy to crown their king 'Holy Roman Emperor' only to perish of unfamiliar heat and diseases.

Mediterranean Europe is not directly influenced by the Atlantic Ocean, for the mountains and plateaux of the Iberian peninsula, assisted in some seasons by the Alps, divert the dominant westerly flow of oceanic air. Hence this is a region of two distinct seasons, warm dry summers and cool wet winters. At sea level a normal Mediterranean summer day reaches temperatures at or above 25°C under fair skies. Near-drought conditions prevail as evaporation exceeds precipitation. In contrasting winter, storms from the Mediterranean bring rain and normal daily highs not or barely reaching 10°C. Lowland frost is, however, unusual and brief.

In Atlantic or Maritime Europe a flow of oceanic air warmed by the Gulf Stream affects the climate year round. At low altitudes this extends as far east as Poland, but the Alps keep maritime circulation from reaching Hungary and the Balkans. Relatively stable sea temperatures moderate seasonal extremes compared with the same latitudes elsewhere. Winter frosts are intermittent but steady lowland freezing does not occur, so normal January temperatures stay above the freezing point as far east as Denmark and the upper Rhine valley. More eastern areas experience at least a month of means below freezing. Summers, reciprocally, are cooled, so that normal July means below

20°C prevail from the Loire to central Poland. Atlantic Europe is distinctively humid, with more precipitation more evenly distributed than south of the Alps. With no large western mountains to cause major rain shadows, damp maritime air penetrates well inland year round.

Breezes from neither the Mediterranean nor the Atlantic moderate conditions in Continental Europe. Regions so defined include the Spanish *meseta* plateau and generally all areas east of a line drawn roughly from the Gulf of Bothnia past the present-day Czech Republic to somewhere south of Vienna. Climatic extremes prevail there: cold winters with January means below freezing and hot summers at or above 20°C. Precipitation, low and diminishing eastwards, occurs year round, but frozen winter water is inaccessible to plants and animals, so seasonally replicating ice age conditions. Species that could do well in natural or colonized ecosystems of the Mediterranean or maritime west might not survive here. But likewise northern adaptations might have trouble with Mediterranean summer droughts.

Post-glacial changes in surface geology and climate opened Europe to repopulation by plants and animals that had survived in more southerly refugia and drove ecological adjustments in southern areas too. Botanical communities formed vegetative zones adapted to climatic and altitudinal conditions and sheltered characteristic fauna. Retreat of the ice and ice-front tundra left new land, mostly with rich and deep rock flour soils or even deeper wind-borne loess, to be settled first by such pioneer plants as grasses and sedges, then later by more sensitive and water-demanding shrubs and trees. Ever so slowly by human standards, plant species and associations expanded northward and upward. Tundra gave way to boreal woodland varieties such as spruce, birch, alder, or pine, and this to the characteristic trees of a mixed deciduous woodland. Soil type and water supply favoured pine, elm, and hazel in some areas, elsewhere and later communities of oak, linden, alder, and ash. Over time and taken collectively, the Holocene continental mainland developed diverse, mostly deciduous, woodlands. In the west conifers gain importance only with rising altitude in the Alps (to a lesser degree in the central uplands) or at higher latitudes towards and beyond the Baltic. Greater dryness and climatic extremes favour conifers, so in Continental Europe more entered the woodland mix and came to dominate, especially in the north. Southeast towards the Black Sea littoral emerged a parkland zone, often called wooded steppe, and then semi-arid true steppe country with very few trees. Steppe grasses also predominate on much of the semi-arid Spanish *meseta*. Farthest to the west, British woods, cut off by salt water before some species arrived in the vicinity, remained less diverse.

The Pleistocene megafauna disappeared with the glaciers, and the great herds of reindeer and horses moved north and east with the tundra and steppe. Woodland herbivores, deer and wild pig, became keystone species across Europe, along with fewer bison and aurochs (the wild ancestor of European cattle). Various smaller fur-bearers, rodents and their predators, were common. At the apex dined bear (an omnivore) and wolf. Likewise freshwater fishes with high temperature requirements spread slowly northwestwards through temporary ice-front lakes or linked watersheds, while anadromous cold-water salmon, trout, and others entered newly ice-free rivers along the Atlantic and connected waters.

The mid-Holocene onset of warming and especially drying in Mediterranean Europe gradually killed off there such northern trees as linden and elm. Since about 3000BCE what are now thought characteristic Mediterranean plant communities formed, comprising species well adapted to survive dry summers but intolerant of winter cold. A hard freeze kills olive trees, for instance. Hence, while a northward progression of east–west vegetative zones typifies northern Europe, altitudinal zonation prevails in the Mediterranean. Up to 800–1,000 metres open pine and oak savannah woodlands dominate or, where subject to aridity, fire, or grazing pressures, the 7 metre brush called *maquis* or even lower spiny shrubs, *garrigue*. Higher and more humid terrain supported deciduous woods – oak, elm, beech, chestnut – up to 1,300 metres, and higher still, mountain forest with pines, firs, and junipers, to a tree line at about 2,500 metres.

An abundance of ecological niches meant the Mediterranean region generally exhibited a high diversity of species, but its thin, often infertile, soils, and the sea into which they fed rather few nutrients, sustained comparatively low biological productivity. Wild herbivores included sheep, goat, cattle, donkey, pig, and deer, all prey in the mid-Holocene for such native carnivores as lion, leopard, wolf, and bear. Many, but not all, of these wild animals would still inhabit the woodlands, hills, and mountains of medieval Europe.

Fundamental ecological structures, the networks linking non-living and living elements of European environments, were established by the retreat of the ice to mountain remnants, the formation of circulation patterns over an open and ice-free Atlantic, and the subsequent return of plants and animals to the landscapes of Europe. Yet at neither large nor small scale was any of this entirely permanent or in equilibrium. Natural drivers of environmental change, climatic, tectonic, and biological, continued to operate. Ensuing mid-to late Holocene variability, including that during the Middle Ages, would take place within this framework of slowly evolving structures and short-term disturbances. In sum, and to this point observing no impacts from human activities, the 'pristine' nature taken over by medieval Europeans already had a long and dynamic history.

CULTURAL ADAPTATIONS AND IMPACTS UP TO THE ROMAN CLIMATIC OPTIMUM

Of course the Europe inherited by the Middle Ages was in no way pristine. Since deep human prehistory Europeans both adapted to their natural surroundings and actively modified them in ways people had intended, ways they found surprising, and ways of which they remained seemingly quite unaware. As with the natural sphere, some human interventions from even before classical Mediterranean civilization established what would be long-effective patterns of environmental relations.

Physically modern humans (*Homo sapiens*) inhabited Europe throughout the latest glacial readvance, living on the tundra as Palaeolithic hunter-gatherers by predation on megafauna and especially herd animals. Their stone and bone artefacts reveal specialized adaptations. Their cave paintings not only rank among the earliest known cultural representations of things of nature, they are also thought to be vehicles for manipulation of the game by supernatural means. As the ice retreated and with it the tundra ecosystem, a new Mesolithic culture advanced with the woodland, hunting its more solitary herbivores and gathering more plants and seasonal aquatic resources (shellfish, etc.). The landscape mosaic encouraged local cultures to co-adapt with local diversities: human use of fire to manage landscapes for game created open 'parkland' woods and in northwestern Britain even anthropogenic steppe grasslands. While especially coastal Mesolithic communities were nearly sedentary and rich in artefacts, there is no evidence to suggest that European hunter-gatherer populations pressed dangerously against the carrying capacity of their local ecosystem adaptations.

Arrival and adoption in Europe of humankind's first great ecological revolution, the agropastoral way of life now labelled 'Neolithic', is less simply explained than it is described and its significance emphasized. New cultural elements originating in southwestern Asia's 'Fertile Crescent' during the Pleistocene–Holocene transition (12.5–7kya) included agriculture (wheat, barley, certain legumes), domesticated animals (sheep, goat, cattle, pig, donkey), polished stone tools, and pottery. These earliest farmers used digging sticks to work the earth in temporary fire-cleared plots (so-called 'swidden' agriculture), which both fit and perpetuated an open woodland landscape.

The Neolithic cultural complex entered Europe by 7kya (5000BCE), roughly the time when the Atlantic Optimum was cooling into the Sub-Boreal. Its diffusion and adoption is now thought to have been driven less by subsistence needs than by symbolic culture, involving prestige items of consumption (meal, bread, beer, ceramics) and display of human dominion over nature (domesticated beasts). This hypothesis is based on the piecemeal and differential local adoption of Neolithic cultural elements. While the earliest farmers along Mediterranean shores and on loess soils in the Danube and Seine basins kept most of the original package, Mesolithic communities enjoying rich coastal resources along the Baltic, North Sea, and in Britain accepted pottery and polished stone tools a millennium earlier than they did farming.

Agropastoral ecosystems constituted an ecological revolution, a fundamental change in the relationship of humans to the natural world. Their creation is the quintessential human colonization of nature (see Introduction) prior to the age of fossil fuels. Agriculture transforms natural organisms and ecological connections into anthropogenic systems meant to serve human needs. While natural forces and metabolic processes continue, they are diverted to ends defined by culture. With the Neolithic, humans now worked to manage the soil and selected plants to gain high productivity from a system destabilized by its low biodiversity, ideally one food chain capped by humans. Obtaining more calories through more and on-going expenditure of energy (work) shifted social relations in human communities, too. The seasonality of raising crops altered appeals to the supernatural from a concern for wildlife to caring for the sun, rain, and fertile soil. The Neolithic Revolution in Europe further changed a broad range of surrounding natural conditions: cleared parcels never grow back to the same species mix as natural woodlands; clearings and abandoned fields offered more edge habitat favoured by, for example, deer. But the Neolithic was only the first step towards formation in Europe of fully agrarian societies.

During the millennia while most Europeans were accepting agriculture, other innovations of southwest Asian origin also began to shift their relations with non-living aspects of the environment. Palaeolithic peoples had already mined selected flint deposits and their successors added some special shiny stones, pure gold and 'native' copper. Salt they obtained by mining or boiling the water from brine springs, burning much wood to do so. Pure copper was decorative, but alloyed with tin made bronze, prettier, more easily moulded, and sharper. That Asian discovery spread along the Mediterranean from about 2000BCE, though remaining always an elite material. Copper and tin ores occurred only in highly localized surface deposits along the uplands, where simple pits and shafts demanded timber for props. Iron, a harder metal, whose working began in Anatolia, reached the central Alps around 1000BCE, but the so-called bog ores (naturally formed clumps of hydrous iron oxide) occurred in small quantities nearly everywhere. Its use, especially for weapons, spread rapidly. In general, metalworking had greater environmental impact than did mining, from both its demand for fuel and its toxic emissions. Although the European cultural periods labelled 'Bronze Age' (c.2000–750BCE) and (Pre-Roman) 'Iron Age' (750–1BCE) are named after metals, they are more essentially to be characterized as increasingly stable agrarian societies, typically developing relatively fixed settlements, organized field systems, use of draught animals (donkey, ox) and of horses for riding and light draught, social stratification, territorialized communities, and some degree of regional specialization. Literate Iron Age cultures also provided Europe's first historical records.

Early urbanization was a further cultural and ecological innovation from early fourth-millennium BCE Asia. It spread into Mediterranean Europe by the early Iron Age, though north of the Alps only after 200BCE. Such early concentrations of human populations served specialized purposes – in Europe mainly cult and political protection – while reflecting social stratification. If the town dwellers were not themselves farmers – and many were – they had to depend on a flow of food and other materials from the surrounding area. Like

agroecosystems and metallurgy, urban environmental consequences
will become a continuing theme for the Middle Ages.

Natural and cultural diversities of mid-Holocene Europe evolved
together, creating differentiated landscapes and mosaics of microecologies. Field archaeology and verbal references establish by the Bronze
Age distinctions of land use that much later Latin writers would call
ager, *saltus*, and *silva*. *Ager* denoted cultivated fields, mostly semi-
permanent objects of plough culture for grain production and fallow
pasture, located close to settlements. *Saltus*, 'scrub' or 'waste' pasture,
further provided a land reserve for future arable, which much of it had
also perhaps earlier been. In 'woodland', *silva*, a community harvested
wood as fuel and raw material, gathered wild food, dye, and medicinal
plants, and grazed cattle and pigs. Such multiple-use wastes and
woodlands were not, therefore, uncolonized by humans, just serving
different cultural purposes. Surviving markers or other distinctive
boundaries indicate division of terrain and hence its 'possession' by
humans.

Local and regional distinctions both reflected and promoted prehistoric diversity, sometimes as an adaptive strategy. While primitive
wheat varieties had dominated Neolithic Europe, the Bronze Age saw
more cultivation of barley in the northwest, spelt along the Alps, and
rye in eastern Europe. Discontinuous settlement areas along the
Mediterranean encouraged movement of peoples and cultures, but
also specific uses of local resources. Bronze and early Iron Age farmers
in central Italy, the territory soon known as Latium around the
emerging town of Rome, learned that their limestone, lava, and tufa
soils and irregular relief meant that some plots were suited to orchards,
others to cereals or olives, and others to seasonal grazing of livestock.
Short-term variability of weather, water supply, and seismic activity
warned against reliance on any single crop. These particulars had to be
learned by human users, sometimes through processes of trial and
error. Early Neolithic clearances for fields in upland Britain became
moorland and peat bogs under later wetter conditions; Bronze Age
clearances for pasture in Denmark strained local wood supplies to the
point that some pasture was left to grow back as trees. The adaptive
and thus interactive processes were incomplete by the Iron Age, but
perhaps further along in the Mediterranean basin than to its north.

Interactions between natural dynamics and human colonization of
natural ecosystems had both intended and unintended consequences
in prehistoric Europe. Fragmentary archaeological evidence affirms

human use of the natural sphere, but without written record wider cultural relationships and programmes remain unvoiced and thus no more than inferential. Then quite abruptly in Greco-Roman antiquity, Mediterranean agricultural adaptations and much else besides become illuminated. From the sixth and the second century BCE respectively, literate Greek and Roman writers depicted their cultures (actually selected fragments thereof) with a wealth of detail unmatched in Europe before the thirteenth and fourteenth centuries CE. But by classical antiquity certain relationships had changed from pre-Roman times in the west and, most importantly, Greco-Roman antiquity was distinctly part of a Mediterranean civilization with some cultural imperatives different from those of the north.

ENVIRONMENTAL PRECEDENTS AND LEGACY OF CLASSICAL MEDITERRANEAN CIVILIZATION

The world of classical Greece and Rome centred around the Mediterranean, where shared cultural elements antedated the imperial polity assembled by Roman conquests in the first century BCE. All around what the Romans called *Mare Nostrum* ('our sea') they found and encouraged self-governing 'city-states' (Greek *polis*, Latin *civitas*) comprising a rural district (*chora, pagus*) of farmers integrated around a central place (*urbs*) serving cult and security functions. Local rule remained with heads of leading families who, if acquiescent, easily assimilated to a Roman peace. Some 50–60 million people at home around the Mediterranean in the second century CE lived mainly from harvesting the flow of solar energy through the biomass production of domesticated plants under human control and management. Their adaptation to typical Mediterranean climatic and physiographic conditions set both the scene and precedents for subsequent medieval resource use there. Medievalists also need brief familiarization with classical energy systems, cultural understandings of the natural world, and the impact this urbanizing culture had on its surroundings.

Like all agroecosystems, that typical of the Mediterranean before modern times resulted from human colonization of natural ecosystems to meet human needs. The total biological productivity of agroecosystems is always less than that of intact natural systems, but a greater proportion is concentrated in the intended crop. The energy stored there is, in turn, 'exported' to human consumption, so agroecosystems require, over time, large subsidies of energy and plant nutrients. Risks to stability and sustainability are inherent; the key question is how societies handled them.

Mediterranean Europe acquired its Neolithic agricultural complex from southwestern Asia during the sixth and fifth millennia BCE. At first this comprised cereal grasses, legumes, and 'ovicaprids' (a collective term for sheep and goats, closely related herbivores often indistinguishable in archaeological contexts). Intensive hand labour by humans maintained the system until draught animals (oxen, donkey) and a simple plough arrived by the early Bronze Age. European communities equipped with these technologies practised rainfall-dependent 'dry farming', different from the flood and irrigation systems by then used in Mesopotamia and Egypt.

Climate, soils, and relief set preconditions for agricultural practice. Crop plants had to be adapted to the rainy cool winter and the hot dry summer: annual cereals seeded in autumn grow through the winter and spring to mature before the summer drought; perennial grasses, vines, olives, and other trees go dormant or otherwise adapt to dry heat. In the coastal and plateau areas best for human agricultural use, Mediterranean soils are often light, though some are clays. Broken relief further contributes to local diversity.

Grain, olives, and vines have formed the ruling trinity of Mediterranean crops since pre-classical times, providing an equally ancient staple diet of bread, oil, and wine. Less stereotypical legumes from field or garden could provide important supplements. Grain crops, wheat and barley, native to and domesticated in southwest Asia, were reared on ploughed fields (*ager*) in a two-year cycle, alternating crop and fallow. Resting the field one year in two and ploughing the weeds under hoarded two years of precious water for the grain. Bare fallow leaves the soil surface open during the winter rains, both absorbing water and risking erosion. Cereals planted in the autumn were harvested in May or June. Olive trees, native to a broad area along and east from the Mediterranean, provide food and lighting. Tolerant of thin and arid soil, they are sensitive to frost, so on the north they tidily mark a natural boundary of Mediterranean agriculture, which mostly coincided with that of the Roman world. As olives take ten to fifteen years to bear fruit (and then can last many human generations), secure peace is a prerequisite for investment. The grape vine was also a native Mediterranean plant, with deep roots to survive drought in poor soils. Purposeful production calls for seasonally intense labour to yield the wine that served as beverage and another source of calories. Vines and olives might be grown beside vegetables in gardens, but especially when raised for family subsistence were often interplanted in the grain fields as *cultura mixta*. All three were also specialized market crops in the Roman Mediterranean, where Athens had long profited from oil exports and Roman Italy and southern Gaul developed commercial viticulture.

Livestock played a secondary role in classical Mediterranean culture and agriculture, being reared for output of materials (meat, dairy, fibre, leather) and draught energy. Ovicaprids remained most numerous, but pig produced the Romans' favourite meat. Cattle had a smaller part, mainly as the primary draught animal (supplemented by donkeys), while horses had little place in Roman agriculture. A major technical problem inhibited stock rearing in the Mediterranean, as summer forage was sparse in agricultural areas long cleared of most woodlands and subject to summer drought. The typical response even before good written records was vertical transhumance, a semi-annual movement of livestock and their keepers (*not* whole settlements) to summer pastures in the mountains. This practice moved the animals to forage at the price of depriving the arable land of their manure and the risk of overgrazing upland woods and turning them to grass, *maquis*, or *garrigue*. Transhumance compounded the problem of fertility maintenance in Mediterranean dry farming, an issue that much worried Roman agricultural writers.

Agriculture was a principal source of environmental risk and impacts in the classical Mediterranean world, chief among them soil depletion due to erosion and other forms of soil exhaustion. Contemporaries and others feared the collapse of agricultural productivity, though debates falter from lack of data, both then and now. No serial quantitative accounts from any Roman agricultural enterprises survive. Roman agricultural writers, among the first anywhere to put down in ordered form some elements of agricultural experience, recommended precise knowledge of soils and careful selection and application of manures and other soil improvers. Ditching and terracing of agricultural land were advised – and evidently practised – to prevent and repair soil loss. A long tradition among modern writers points to the extended mouths of the Po and Tiber, Italian valleys clogged with sediment, and especially the arid North African wastelands where Roman agriculture once thrived, as evidence of Roman misuse and environmental destruction. More recent scholarly dissenters retort that floods, erosion, and deposition always were and still are aspects of the dynamic and diverse, not static or uniform, Mediterranean environment. They criticize literary references as mythic rhetoric, while adducing archaeological and geophysical evidence that most Mediterranean erosion dates to the Pleistocene or to much later, especially medieval, times; that Roman examples were highly localized and soon, in some instances repeatedly, repaired; and that the warm, dry Roman Climatic Optimum meant less, rather than more, soil loss.

Soil depletion in the classical Mediterranean was further associated with environmental damage from overgrazing and deforestation. Literary texts and common practice affirm livestock using uncultivable land and the distinctive foraging behaviours of cattle, swine, sheep, and, always infamously omnivorous, goats. Historical effects of grazing pressure are always a problem to demonstrate, although the arrival of transhumants at the first flush of the upland growing season would surely nip off much new growth and especially inhibit regrowth of trees in cutover areas.

Debate over human deforestation of the Mediterranean, which will resurface in future chapters, has its origins in and about the classical period. Ancients, and here most relevant, the Romans, long stand accused of overusing and misusing their woodlands, so they ceased to exist and/or to provide natural habitats and landscapes as before. Again, incidental literary references to once-wooded domains provide the main support, while the place of wood in the Roman economy offers good explanations. Wood was an essential fuel and raw material: 90 per cent of Roman wood harvests went for domestic and institutional heating and most of the rest to metallurgy and potteries. Fuel wood came from small-scale local suppliers, and that for Rome itself from a radius of some 200 kilometres around the city. To construct buildings and ships, expert lumbermen tracked down large timbers in forested mountain areas close to water-borne transport routes. Whole lowland and foothill woodlands had, moreover, been cleared for agricultural use and wetland swamps drained and cut. Consequences included more irregular hydraulic regimes, aridization, erosion, and a rising price for wood.

Dissenting scholars see things differently, not denying classical use of wood or certain signs of scarcity, but setting the evidence in a longer and critical perspective. Dating and scale matter. Historic changes to Mediterranean woodlands pale beside the prehistoric ones, as the main distribution of cultivated land, pasture, and woodland was established before the classical period and endured through it into modern times. Romans and others cut trees but did not generally destroy woodlands, even in central Italy, where pollen profiles from volcanic lakes show open woodland species continuously from the sixth millennium BCE through Roman times and beyond. But being subject to regular human use, Mediterranean woods had long been not pristine old-growth ecosystems but rather parts of managed landscapes. This included some local use of coppice (see chapter 5) for sustainable fuel production from natural regrowth. Documented local clearances and crises resulted, in this view, from local intensification or the high cost of transporting selected timber to a building site. Nor does it preclude regrowth of trees on subsequently abandoned farmland. *Systemic* failure of classical Mediterranean adaptations remains, therefore, unproved.

Wood fuel and the high cost of moving timber signify the place of energy and technology in classical Mediterranean culture. For Romans and their predecessors human labour provided the essential energy source. Hands wielding spades and hoes turned much soil and with iron sickles cut the grain and grapes, the one for threshing with a flail and the other to be crushed under foot. Small peasant farms employed one or two slaves, and the vast Roman plantations in Italy, Sicily, southern Spain, and North Africa dozens and hundreds of human beasts of burden. Animal energy provided an essential but limited supplement: an ox or donkey could pull the simple light ard (*aratrum*) to crumble the soil surface, perhaps haul a roller to crush the grain, and draw a cart. Overland transport was costly, so most bulk goods moved by water and cultural leaders promoted local self-sufficiency in basic foodstuffs. Mechanical technologies, too, ran mainly on muscle power. Grinding of grain to meal or flour began with a mortar and pestle; then came a hand quern and about 600BCE the rotary quern. A horse (faster than an ox) could rotate a larger stone than could a kitchen slave. Water mills appeared first in Roman towns from the first century CE but spread little. Men or beasts pressed grapes and olives. Rowed vessels outcompeted ungainly sailing craft.

Human and animal muscles carried out the Romans' purposeful modifications of their physical environment. Terraces and drainage works were most important and widespread. In the Tiber marshes from the very beginnings of Rome itself, then later in central Italy, along the lower Rhône, even in Britain, Romans created new agricultural land with reliable supplies of water for their familiar crops.

Terraces made the ubiquitous slopes more workable and prevented erosion. Irrigation works had more limited compass, with small areas managed for horticulture across the Empire, but large-scale enterprises confined to North Africa and Iberia. There catchment dams and cisterns with both surface and underground conduits supported intensive commercial agriculture, mainly for export to Italy and luxury demand elsewhere. All these works required regular laborious maintenance to be sustainable.

Classical antiquity was a literate culture and its elites long continued to claim an ideological connection with agricultural activities. This moved some Romans to compose manuals of agricultural practice. Surviving works of Cato (*c.*160BCE), Varro (37BCE), Columella (*c.*60CE), and others provide more information on overall purposes, managerial intent, and traditional knowledge of farming than is otherwise available in Europe for another 1,500 years. For all their skewed perspectives and very large omissions, the Roman agronomists offer one important avenue into classical thinking about the natural world.

Ancient Greco-Roman environmental thought was largely enmeshed in religious-philosophical-scientific speculation, manifest in several idea complexes, not a single package. By the late Republic and early Empire the Roman writers who would be the most influential for the Middle Ages had absorbed most of what their Greek teachers could offer, both their various schools of philosophy and their general departure from what by then seemed crude personifications of natural forces as Olympian gods in favour of a general intellectualized, indeed secularized, approach that was nevertheless compatible with the performance of civic cults. A mythic value remained to the Olympians as a way to refer to features and powers of that which was not 'culture', *nomos/cultura* being a concept coined by Greek thinkers and *physis/natura* the contrasted principle, quality, or process. Classical thinkers did not conceive 'nature' itself as an entity. Meanwhile at a more immediate, popular, and local level, unnamed domestic deities (*lares et penates*), hearth gods, and their outdoor counterparts, nameless, not fully realized deities or spirits of household, fields, springs, and woodlands, collectively embodied an immanent spiritual presence deemed protective of basic human and natural relationships. At both levels a wise and pious person showed respect with small and ceremonial sacrifices. The intimate connection of supernatural power with things of nature was further manifest in divination from, for instance, the flight of birds or entrails of a sacrificed ox, in veneration of certain groves, springs, and mountains, and in a seasonal round of festivals marking liminal steps in the annual agropastoral cycle. Classical theories of environmental determinism rested on the same sense of superior powers residing in nature as interpreted first medically, then geographically, even astrologically. The medical theory of humours traced health and bodily functions to the balance or imbalance among elements of air, fire, earth, and water, which late Greek writers then connected to climatic influences on whole societies.

The philosophical religion which prevailed among most Mediterranean social and cultural elites into and beyond the second century CE focused on right personal behaviour (ethics) and understanding the nature, origins, and purpose of the universe (metaphysics). Thinkers speculated on a single divinity behind all the personifications and local cults. Plato (427?–347BCE) and his followers privileged the immaterial Idea or Soul contrasted to the material world, for which they showed some disrespect, though acknowledging its creation by divine forces. Aristotle (388–322BCE) encouraged more empirical study of the world, being less certain of its divine causation and more interested in nature itself. His disciple Theophrastus (371–287BCE) identified natural processes and formed the concept of habitat. Roman naturalist Pliny the Elder (23–79CE) compiled such reported observations into a thirty-seven-volume *Natural History*.

Different classical ideas of philosophical and religious quality converged around an ordered plan of nature, while disputing the implications of this teleology. Some writers conceived a natural world in balance as a comfortable place meant for human beings; others saw in it a rough and crude starting point for human development by improving nature itself. Theophrastus offered domestication of animals and drainage of wetlands as proof that culture rightly moulds nature, just as Stoic philosophers, Roman politician and moralist Cicero (103–43BCE), and the geographer Strabo (64BCE–24CE) asserted that humans were indeed perfecting the natural space. Only some pastoral poets – but among them the Roman civic seer Virgil (in his *Eclogues* of 37/30BCE) – held that civilization corrupted nature and natural humans alike. At a more pragmatic level the dominant position was that reflected in the land ethic of Greek and early Roman subsistence farmers as voiced by, among others, the agronomists: care for the soil; not use but misuse of the land damaged its fertility and threatened its yields; special measures of fertilizing, fallowing, and physical infrastructures would maintain the crucial balance. Classical culture possessed, therefore, some kind of awareness that, for all the ultimate reality of the pure and immaterial Platonic Form or Idea, Mediterranean agriculture and the civilization it supported did rest on a physical infrastructure, what would now be called an anthropogenic ecosystem, that required maintenance for all to survive.

But other elements in classical Mediterranean culture pushed in contrary directions and drove what are now seen as significant anthropogenic losses of biodiversity. Discursive Greco-Roman sources depict and approve human use of plants and animals but evidence mythic taboos against overexploitation. Literature of the hunt (*Cynegetica*) describes only an elite recreation, with ritual displays of a ruler's power over nature at the cultural apex. Records of practice, however, show widespread commercial hunts and fisheries supplying game meat, hides and other animal parts, birds for food and plumage, local fresh and preserved fish. Military units hunted for food, as training exercises, and to destroy predators and vermin seen as competitors to human use. Wild animals on private land were the property of the landowner; those of unoccupied land or public water that of the state. Animals, preferably large, fierce, and exotic ones, put on show or goaded to fight other beasts or men in the arena gave prestige to the sponsor and entertainment to the audience. Their huge numbers – one triumph of Emperor Trajan in 107CE killed 11,000 – depended on an organized supply chain from Rome's frontier provinces. No more opposition was voiced to this than to human gladiatorial combats. Nor did known writers see habitat loss as among the consequences of agricultural clearances, erosion, or other human environmental impacts.

While complaints about fewer beasts or poor hunting could be mere literary convention, extirpations and extinctions are incontrovertible. Lion, hyena, and leopard had vanished from Mediterranean Europe by the first century BCE and bear populations in both the Balkans and the Apennines were much reduced. Elimination of all the now proverbially 'African' animals – lion, elephant, zebra, etc. – from areas north of the Sahara was complete by the fourth century CE. Besides these purposely targeted 'trophy' organisms, pursued on cultural grounds beyond all reasonable expenditure of energy, economic pressures took their toll on other biota. Capture and export of sturgeon from the Rhône delta to Roman markets, for example, caused steady shrinkage in their average size and eventual near disappearance from the archaeological record.

Ecological links between wild animal populations and the cultural prerogatives of Roman arenas and markets are at one level a side-effect of classical civilization's establishing in Europe two pre-eminent cultural innovations with great and wide environmental impact. These were urbanization and Romanization.

Classical urbanization created in Europe a new anthropogenic landscape form with distinctive ecological features. Concentrations of humans reached an unprecedented scale: fourth-century BCE Athens was the first European settlement to reach a population of 100,000; Rome at its peak about 150CE held 1,200,000 people on only eighteen square kilometres. As ancient cities always served mainly cult and administrative functions, their inhabitants long retained close connection to agriculture, but some commerce and manufactures arose mainly to serve those local urban populations (in contrast to the medieval urbanism treated in chapter 6 below). Chief environmental features of classical urbanism were the local removal of land from natural physical cycles by hardening the ground surface, replacing vegetative cover with brick and stone, concentrating many humans and their wastes, and imposing very anthropogenic city plans. The resultant artificial ecosystem had to divert output from a larger urban-centred landscape to meet its metabolic needs. Water supply was critical in the seasonally arid Mediterranean: emulating the aqueducts Greek cities had built since the sixth century BCE, from 312 Rome looked farther afield, eventually to create a network of overland and underground infrastructure with a sixty-kilometre radius. Food, initially drawn from citizen farms in the immediate vicinity, came greater distances as tribute and through publicly managed grain trades. From 58BCE Roman governments distributed free grain first from Sicily, then as a tribute or tax from Egypt. Human waste products, garbage and sewage, flowed from regularly cleaned streets and underground sewers into the local river and dump sites within and without city limits. In sum, material and energy flowed from elsewhere into an ancient city, where it was mostly consumed and the waste dumped. Ancient cities were in ecological terms largely 'parasitic' and 'sinks' for the now useless remains of their imports.

Romans especially spread urban life across their entire Empire, establishing internally self-governing *civitates* by absorption around the Mediterranean and introducing them especially in western parts to the north. Under Roman rule urban populations increased greatly, though the largest concentrations remained in the east. A half-dozen regional capitals there surpassed the 100,000 mark and a dozen or so in the next tier may have approached it. At the other end of the spectrum hundreds of little places with only 10,000 inhabitants still had their own local senates and municipal officials who sought to ape as best they could the forum, arches, arenas, and other emblems of civilized society. Some such sites – Augsburg, Barcelona, Florence – would survive or revive as nodes in much later medieval urban landscapes; others would decay to insignificance.

Cities were, however, but one aspect of Romanization, the physical spread of Latins and their cultural norms, as Roman veterans received land in the provinces and as local elites around and beyond the Mediterranean emulated and adopted Roman ways. Romans brought Mediterranean tastes for wheat, wine, temples, games, theatre, costume, aqueducts, and artistic motifs. They introduced vines to central and northern Gaul, even Britain, and chestnuts and walnuts north of the Alps. Broken jugs (*amphorae*) of Italian wine are found as far afield as Ireland and the Baltic, reflecting an annual export in the first century BCE of some hundred thousand hectolitres. Mediterranean values were carved on the land of Gaul and Iberia in rectilinear surveys for a 709 metre north–south grid (*centuriation*).

As Romanization played out during the Climatic Optimum, the lower Rhône valley provides a good example of local change. Roman conquest in 125–121BCE of a mixed population of Gauls and long-settled Greek colonists was followed by rapid acceleration of settlement. The agricultural population grew three-fold in the next two centuries and by a factor of six around the initial Roman colonies and soon expanding cities of Arles and Orange. In the first century CE the regional government actively encouraged development in the lagging upland fringes. Land on well-drained light soils, where most Romans settled, was shifted from mixed grain subsistence farming to commercial production of olives and vines. Wooded uplands and heavy lowland soils were then cleared, drained, and irrigated for more cash crops. The new grape and olive varieties, wineries and presses, perhaps even the wheat fields, were meant to yield surpluses for seaborne export to Rome.

Urbanization and Romanization together had effects resembling those attributed to present-day globalization. Cultural homogenization of taste and thus consumption norms increased the pressure of demand

against the natural sphere. Access to markets pushed regional specialization and interregional exchange, so further modifying local ecosystems. Classical civilization at its peak sustained diversity within the
larger Mediterranean pattern, but also exported that Mediterranean
pattern to parts of Atlantic maritime Europe. Certain classical cultural
features, environmental problems, and solutions would endure for the
Middle Ages and others break down, give way, and be replaced.

'BARBARIAN' ADAPTATIONS: THE IRON AGE IN NORTHERN EUROPE

A different ecological heritage came to early medieval western
Christendom from its second demographic and cultural progenitor,
peoples whom Greeks and Romans called 'barbarians'. The term
marked cultures which were not 'civilized' by Mediterranean behavioural standards, and those who lived to the north were plainly not, in
part from their interaction with different environmental conditions,
those of maritime and continental Europe. As previously mentioned,
different seasonalities there prevailed. While both enjoyed year-round
precipitation, the west winds off the Atlantic moderated the temperature extremes encountered further east.

Maritime and continental Europe together are further distinguished from the Mediterranean by their large areas of plains
and hills. Landscapes come in bigger units than are typical in the
Mediterranean. Large rivers run north or west across the
region to the Baltic and North seas, the English Channel, and Bay
of Biscay. Only along the southern edge does the Danube flow in
the opposite direction towards the Black Sea, which is also fed by
rivers from the eastern steppe region. Variety here does not come
from the Mediterranean's close mutual proximity of small land forms.
Diversities rather arise from differences of soil and drainage, in particular different areas of glacial action or periglacial deposits, where loess
occurs, and from the fact that the latter deep soils were not glaciated
and lie upon very different kinds of bedrock. Moves of more than
twenty kilometres in many areas of northern Europe encounter new
soil types to which local cultivators must adapt their practices, though
always within the larger pattern of more maritime conditions to the
west and continental further east.

In this part of Europe the Bronze Age–Iron Age transition began
around 700BCE and along the Baltic was still going as late as 300BCE.

As that cultural shift occurred, semi-sedentary agrarian societies emerged across the entire region. These peoples organized themselves into what they conceived as tribal groups, which moved around rather little and lived primarily by farming. Elites were warriors but the great mass of the population was independent free farmers. Those along the north slopes of the Alps and spreading out into Gaul and the British Isles were fair-skinned, bulky, ruddy people, said the Greeks (who were none of these). The Greeks called them *keltoi* (Celts) and the Romans would pick up that name, too. By the first century BCE Romans became further aware that on the other side of the Rhine and Danube there lived people not quite the same as the Celts (though the Romans also likely confused them). These the Romans called *Germani* (Germans). Celt and German were not native names but applied by Mediterranean cultures to certain barbarians whom they encountered north of their Mediterranean. (The cultural communities that much later Greek speakers would call *Sklavenoi* then lived further to the northeast of the Carpathians; they remained unknown to literate Mediterranean civilization prior to the sixth century CE.)

Whether *Keltoi*, *Germani*, or future *Sklavenoi*, these early Iron Age northern peoples were developing cultural features as essentially rural societies without towns. They lived in dispersed clusters of farmsteads, a handful of households in loose proximity in the woodland, separated from other such clusters by woodland of greater density. The farms remained semi-mobile. When numbers in a cluster grew too great, some people moved to form satellite settlements a distance away. Likewise, since dwellings were made of wood and human use depleted both local woodland and soil, after a generation or so farmers commonly abandoned their dilapidated houses and rebuilt elsewhere. Such moves might be only a few hundred metres or as much as ten kilometres. So the societies were not regularly mobile but moved only as necessary.

Northern barbarian peoples lived and moved about in a realm that was mostly wooded and more or less damp throughout the year. Hence their structures of living were in the first place adapted to dwelling among trees and secondly adapted to the particularities of climate and moisture in Atlantic and continental Europe. Woodland adaptations included the practice of what can be called either alternating fallow agriculture or infield–outfield. In this arrangement trees were cleared near the settlement to form arable land and that arable was farmed each year until it became exhausted. Then the parcel was left to go back to pasture and new arable was cleared nearby. Much later on the first patch might again be put to arable use, but only after a long cycle had left significant brushwood growing on it and restored most of the soil's fertility. Farmers probably also tried to maintain fertility on existing arable land, for Pliny attributed to the barbarians use of marl as a soil improver and archaeological field surveys find scatterings of broken pottery and other materials that would have come from farm or household waste. These anthropogenic traces in the soil are a major surviving marker of many such settlements and their fields.

An indigenous cultural understanding of the world these people were colonizing has been inferentially linked to the assemblage of land-based resources being used to support some kind of extended family unit. For this ill-defined concept of 'land', 'tenure', and 'holding' the Germanic term was *hube* or *hoba*, which a later linguistic shift made into the modern German word *Hufe*, which translates as 'hide'. 'Hide' in this instance is not the skin of an animal but rather denotes a vaguely normative unit of land that is being used, seemingly thought of as 'this spot pertains to us'. So the primary distinction that barbarian cultures held of the world around them lay between the small colonized part belonging to each family unit and the rest, open to all, belonging to none.

The resources of each household and *hube* supported practices we may call mixed farming. Although arable was important, so too was livestock, significantly more so than in stereotypical Mediterranean agriculture. Northern peoples showed greater preference for cattle and pig and less for the sheep and goats favoured by southerners. Cattle and pig are well adapted to open woodlands and woodland edges. The cattle browse on leaves and other herbage while omnivorous pigs root from the deep soil the many things they like.

Barbarian material culture rested primarily on wood. Habitations were made from logs or more commonly vertical planks set into the soil. So too were fortifications. Over wide areas of northern Europe stone is difficult to obtain and work, while wood was abundant. Building settlements and clearing land around the farmsteads opened up the woodland, forming edge habitat where sun-loving berries and various fruit trees multiplied. As domestic animals used the woodland for pasture, it was further opened up. This changed the species composition in the woodland. During the Bronze Age and Iron Age most of the woods of central and western Europe shifted towards a dominance of beech, which more than some previous species favours a more open situation. What some have believed to be the pristine deep woods of central Europe, full of beeches, have rather resulted from the ways in which humans and their livestock have exploited those woodlands since the Bronze Age.

Equally critical were adaptations to the climate and moisture regimes of the north. The cereal grains first domesticated in southwest Asia and long used in the Mediterranean needed a chilled period before the seeds would germinate. This is one reason why those regions plant in the autumn and the grain sprouts in and grows through the cool winter for an early summer harvest. In the post-Neolithic north those cereals of southern origin were transformed, semi-accidentally one presumes, into forms that do not require the chill. The new varieties could instead be planted in drying and warming spring soils, grown through the summer, and harvested at its end. Thus northern cultures developed with spring grains that suit year-round moisture, namely barley and oats. Also in northern agriculture rye tends to supplant wheat, enjoying a greater tolerance for wet soil, for the frozen winter soils encountered in continental areas, and in some places further to the west, for soils with certain chemical characteristics.

In another adaptation to climatic moisture regimes, while Bronze Age and Iron Age barbarian agriculturalists seem to have used symmetrical ploughs (ards) resembling those of the Mediterranean, they developed ways of handling this equipment to help manage water on their fields. Rather than just crumbling the surface and leaving it behind the track of the plough, they manipulated the tool to pick up some of the soil and move it somewhat to one side. Then by ploughing in a concentric path round and round a parcel they could push the soil in a predetermined direction. Used consistently over time the practice produces a slightly domed cross section, called ridge-and-furrow, with the soil in the middle of the parcel being higher and drier than that on the periphery, which would be marginally wetter. The ploughman gained some insurance: in an especially dry year the plants down in the furrow might still yield and in a wet year those a bit higher could do better. Ploughing those furrows also channelled runoff, making it possible in the high precipitation zones of northern Europe to drain some excess water from the field. Mediterranean farmers rarely wished to move precious water off their fields, but in the north a waterlogged soil threatened germination.

Northern agriculturalists also developed – and the evidence is most common for maritime Europe – a garden culture that focused on cool-season plants – cabbages, onions, roots, some of the legumes that will grow in the coolish winters of the west – and made these, too, a part of their subsistence diets. All these practices had to be learned.

At two geographical margins of northern Europe, the far northwest of the continent and farthest southeast along the shores of the Black Sea, there was less natural woodland and greater commitment to livestock. In northwestern coastal areas from the Jutland peninsula around to the Rhine delta were fresh and salt marshes, few trees, and since the fifth century BCE an emphasis on rearing cattle. On the other extreme of the eastern wooded steppe or parkland, animals could remain outside through the winter because the snow was rarely too deep for them to forage, and people kept larger mixed herds. But those societies remained sedentary. Only still further east in the open steppe did nomadic adaptations occur, communities which actually moved with their animals from one zone of pasturage to another. The nomadic adaptation is characteristic not of Europe but rather of areas to Europe's east that can be thought of as central Asia, for all the occasional importance of nomads' incursions into European history.

After centuries in which northern peoples lived in such conditions, developing and using such techniques, it is clear that by the start of the Roman Iron Age and far away from any defended Roman frontier, central European woodland ecosystems were not primeval. No longer purely natural, their shape and components derived from ways in which they had long been used by humans and their domestic animals. It is also clear that by the start of the Roman Iron Age people to the north were developing an inventory of traditional ecological knowledge different from that of the Mediterranean, for it was keyed to living in their own environments. Much is now known about the traditional ecological knowledge of historic Mediterranean peasants because literate Greeks and Roman agronomists wrote it down. Very little is known about the traditional ecological knowledge of barbarian agriculturalists, be they Celt, German, or Slav, because no one in those non-literate societies wrote any of it down. That they had such knowledge is evident from the material remains of what they did, but no surviving words articulate what they thought about it. Even incidental hints of that sort must wait until deep into the Middle Ages, when some such information will start to be written down for quite different purposes. It is important to recognize, however, that although Greeks and Romans stereotyped these people as ignorant barbarians, their cultures were well adapted to the world in which they lived. In some respects, however, their adaptations, which were more recent, were still evolving in ways that the Mediterranean adaptations had already accomplished by the time of classical Greece.

Then the Mediterranean world erupted into the north. After a century and more of increasing contacts, between the first century BCE and the early second century CE, the Romans conquered all of the Celts except those furthest off in the foggy and uninviting north-western islands, and simultaneously fended off, conquered, and settled as federates the nearest or invading German groups. So, besides most Celts, some Germans in eastern Gaul and the angle between the Rhine and the upper Danube were pulled into the Roman Empire.

This Mediterranean conquest of a large part of especially western, maritime, Europe produced a Roman frontier across the narrow waist of Great Britain and running on the mainland along the Rhine delta and halfway up that river, before turning southeast over to the upper Danube and following it eastwards to its delta on the Black Sea. The frontier (Latin *limes*) was pushed back and forth locally for some generations during the first and the early second century CE, but then stabilized (see Map 2.1). The *limes* was garrisoned and protected; it was meant to be that way. It was permeable and meant to be that way, too. People, goods, and influences crossed the frontier in both directions; so long as the travellers behaved themselves, Roman frontier forces served only a police function.

Inside the frontier Romanization proceeded apace. The Latin language spread to become the dominant language in the area. Agricultural expansion introduced new crops of Mediterranean origin. This helped supply the new markets provided by the Roman military establishment along the frontier. Romans were building roads. The provinces were being integrated into the Roman world; small communities were turning into municipalities on the Mediterranean model. The whole complex that was Romanization took its course.

Outside the frontier, northern Europe may be understood as a periphery now to the Mediterranean core civilization, an area set apart but integrated in certain ways that were useful to the core, and also integrated because local peoples responded to the proximity of this core culture. From the second century BCE all across the barbarian world people built what the Romans called *oppida*, mounds of fairly large dimensions or natural hills with walls around the upper crest.

Oppida provided fortified sites for regional defence, where a tribal group protected its families and its livestock. Over time artisans settled within some *oppida*, which evolved into proto-towns. Julius Caesar described many *oppida* because he attacked and destroyed them in the process of conquering Gaul. Similar structures lay across the rivers that the Romans turned into frontiers. Some Gallic ones were abandoned, others became the centres of Roman cities. *Oppida* on the other side of the frontier continued to evolve, becoming places where barbarian elites stayed for a time and thus traders could find willing customers. Chiefs and warriors found Mediterranean tastes seductive, projecting high fashion, technical superiority, and high status. They liked Mediterranean wine; they liked consumer durables such as pottery and metalware. They were prepared to pay to obtain these goods. (They would obtain them by plunder, too, but Roman frontier forces were meant to dissuade them from that method.) Barbarian elites also found that they could provide in return raw materials, in particular the metals, furs, amber, and other natural products the Mediterranean world desired. They provided as well the one commodity the classical Mediterranean world almost always wanted, slaves. So a lively transfrontier trade moved certain kinds of luxury goods north and east and people and raw materials south into the Roman world. Some who entered the Roman world were not slaves but barbarian warriors who recognized a demand for their services there. Roman forces employed whole barbarian units as auxiliaries and took individuals as recruits. Veterans who survived to the end of their enlistment and did not wish to remain as Romans went back and visited their kinsfolk, showing off how well they had done in civilization. Through the demand, the taste, the trade, and the service there arose in communities even far outside Roman walls very serious competition for wealth and for status: people showing off their importance wanted to acquire the exotic and prestigious. On both sides of the *limes* a dynamic process of acculturation and its environmental impacts grew steadily right up to the point of imperial collapse.

As the Roman Climatic Optimum, so propitious for extension of cultural and biotic ranges north from the Mediterranean, slowly waned during the second and third centuries CE, neither the natural nor the cultural sphere in Europe rested in a stable equilibrium. Classical culture exerted pressures on soils, woodlands, and animal populations, driving unintended changes and calling up human efforts to contain and protect colonized agroecosystems. Barbarian peoples still learning how best to make their surroundings serve their wants saw those wants shifting towards new cultural models. The large regional landscapes of Europe, created and evolved by post-glacial climates and ecological succession, still, as from time immemorial, responded to the effects of human exploitation and colonization. Roman soldiers or their camp followers knowingly carried grape vines to Britain in their baggage and unknowingly the malaria parasite to the Rhine delta in their bloodstream. A complex natural world, yes, but long no wilderness.

INTERSECTING INSTABILITIES: CULTURE AND NATURE AT MEDIEVAL BEGINNINGS, c.400–900

—— • ——

Europeans' relations with their natural surroundings were recalibrated during a long, slow breakdown of one dominant culture, the classical Mediterranean, and piecemeal emergence of another, more distinctly European one. The half-millennium from around 400 to 900 CE can be labelled 'late antiquity' or called the 'early Middle Ages'; the names of historical periods depend on where the observer stands and what she looks at. Grasping the processes of early medieval environmental change starts from the breakdown of Roman hegemony in the west. A synergy between cultural and natural variables so affected Mediterranean and northern Europe alike, that notably the archaeological and material evidence marks sharp breaks in relations between people and the land on both sides of the Alps. A simultaneous loss of literate interest in material life effaces historical view of how contemporaries understood this. Then just as some new patterns seem to emerge, historians become able to see more clearly, thanks to a cultural revival, the so-called 'Carolingian renaissance', that had little directly to do with environmental relations. The late eighth and ninth century reopened literate access to this world. Even with self-conscious reference to what some thought classical models, powerful and ordinary people were together organizing agroecosystems and landscapes unlike those of the now-vanished classical Mediterranean or its barbarian neighbours.

ENVIRONMENTAL RELATIONS IN THE DECLINE
OF CLASSICAL CIVILIZATION

Of course the proverbial 'decline and fall' of the Roman Empire in the west was an extremely long, slow, complex process not to be foolishly determined from any single perspective and notably not with any crude environmental determinism. Consideration of the place of environmental issues must start by acknowledging that fundamental aspects of Roman political, social, economic, and cultural life broke down between the third and the fifth or sixth century. (Henceforth all dates not otherwise specified are to be read as CE.) Transformation of political authority began with a century (192–284) of conflict over succession to the imperial office, which was resolved by the military victor, Diocletian (ruled 284–305), and his successors turning the former loosely ruled civilian Empire into a centralized fiscal-military state. Often a pair of imperial colleagues divided territorial responsibility of the revived Empire along roughly the eastern Adriatic. Nearly a century thereafter the Empire began to suffer repeated invasions of barbarians along its Danube and Rhine frontiers, leading to the piecemeal loss of Roman authority over the western provinces and culminating in 476, when Roman officials in Italy closed down the western imperial office. The whole evolution was associated with regional political violence (civil war, invasions) and the gradual militarization of social power. At the same time a long series of epidemics and other losses to regional populations caused inhabitants of the western provinces to decline steadily in numbers from the 15–20 million range of the second century to 8–10 million by about 600. The economy lost its urban focus with, especially in the west, mutual atrophy of towns and the long-distance trade that fed them. Most economic activity became rural. Considered socially and spatially the compass of Mediterranean culture contracted. Its long-dominant high-status literate and philosophical world view was supplanted by salvationist Christianity, a populist movement of eastern Mediterranean origin, which gained toleration from Diocletian's successor, Constantine, in 313 and a monopoly over official religious practice from Emperor Theodosius by 391. Environmental forces of both natural and anthropogenic origin had some significance in this evolution, while even more can be attributed to environmental effects of the cultural changes themselves.

While none would seriously propose natural causes for the political conflicts that initiated Rome's long decline or the ideological transformation which punctuated it, autonomous natural instability certainly altered the context for such events. Century-scale variation in European climate did not cease with the relatively warm and dry Roman Optimum. Yet approaches to this history should observe two critical caveats: differences of scale in space and time distinguish local weather effects such as storm floods from long-term changes in temperature and precipitation patterns; and the several climatic zones over which the Roman Empire had spread could respond differently to hemispheric or global shifts. The west is most relevant here, but northern and southern conditions were not necessarily identical. While the Optimum brought wind erosion in semi-arid Sicily, for example, its stable precipitation patterns had enabled soil formation in the Po basin. As the second century waned, a different, stormier and wetter, trend materialized in climate indicators of various sorts – sea-level changes, erosion/deposition rates, ice cores, tree rings (all further discussed in chapter 9 below) – and in the written record especially from Italy and Gaul. By the third century, falling general sea levels reveal, and traces of volcanic activity in ice cores help explain, a general cooling that continued into the fourth century, though some regions then became drier. In the Alps glaciers were advancing and the tree line creeping downwards. In winter 406, the lower Rhine surprisingly froze solid, giving Germanic invaders easy passage to plunder in Gaul. The ensuing fifth century, in Europe at least, was cooler still, and in the north up to c.450 wetter, but aridity in the southern Mediterranean is blamed for abandoned North African farmland. If, as some writers now estimate, mean annual temperatures declined by 1–1.5 °C from the second century to the sixth, Europe outside the Mediterranean basin was becoming less amenable to the favoured crops of Mediterranean agroecosystems.

In contrast to climate, the late antique disease environment, where humans interacted with pathogenic micro-organisms, is known mainly from the written record, which also refers to epidemics and endemic diseases in earlier ancient history. But after a long time without large-scale effects in the Mediterranean world, severe pandemics ravaged the Empire during the late second century and again in the mid-third, killing as much as a third of its inhabitants. Some may rather have succumbed to ensuing food shortages and famines. Reported symptoms and epidemiology support no convincing retrospective diagnosis, but most modern authorities now think these were smallpox, measles, or influenza rather than plague. Regional epidemics of unknown cause continued on and off through the fourth and fifth centuries. (There is a more thorough treatment of medieval disease environments in chapter 8 below.)

Most famous among the epidemics of late antiquity is the 'Justinianic plague', named retrospectively for East Roman (Byzantine) Emperor Justinian (527–65). This swept across the Mediterranean and further west between 541 and 545 and, in the view of some modern writers, returned a dozen or more times up to 750 (or 767). Most late twentieth-century scholars accepted this as the first pandemic of bubonic plague (*Yersinia pestis*), a rodent disease spread to humans by fleas. Another less common but less tendentious label for the entire episode is 'Early Medieval Pandemic'. Whatever the pathogenic agent, it was new or long unfamiliar in the region, entered from Africa, probably by way of Egypt, and caused many deaths.

To the widespread epidemics of Mediterranean late antiquity should be added some rising number of deaths from regular regional epidemics and a possibly new endemic presence of malaria, a multifarious protozoan disease of African origin whose several varieties had colonized the Mediterranean since at latest the sixth and fifth centuries BCE. Ancients associated its typical intermittent fevers with swamps, but remained innocent of their mosquito-borne quality. The form most common in the western Mediterranean debilitated rather than immediately killed, leaving victims with weakened immune systems and life spans shortened by other diseases, and persuading survivors to abandon marshy areas. No single pattern captures the role of malaria along the northern shores of the Mediterranean, for its several possible vectors are differentially adapted to fresh or brackish waters and seasonal flooding. Once it is in a region, local variabilities are key. It is plain, however, that coastal and interior wetlands expanded during those crucial centuries and that infected humans – not the mosquitos with their limited feeding range – then carried this parasite from Italy to the Rhine delta, triggering possibly large mortalities on both sides of the *limes* there.

If climatic change and many deaths from new or newly active disease contributed to demographic collapse and economic difficulties in the late Roman west, what of clearly anthropogenic environmental conditions? Potentially most germane are the arguments for overshoot, with Roman clearances and overgrazing blamed for soil erosion, then subsequent deposition for valley and coastal marsh formation, all compounded by soil exhaustion. But as already indicated, the classical Roman period saw less, rather than more, erosion. Subsequent failures of stewardship then appear to follow, rather than precede, population losses and socio-political breakdowns. Abandoned farmland became a recognized problem from the late second century, first as a result of epidemics, next from third-century civil wars and invasions, and eventually from fiscal pressures of a new land tax to support the militarized state. Small Roman farmers were pushed to a subsistence threshold by normal weather risks, to say nothing of the greater natural instability then setting in. Survivors were less able to continue caring for the soil; many gave up, departed as refugees, or sought protection as subjects on large estates. In this view the loss of human control began in the cultural sphere with a failure of the socio-political hierarchy and spread into a natural sphere of destabilized climatic and disease conditions. A telling case comes from the same lower Rhône valley where Romanization had driven first-century development. Archaeologists there find deserted rural habitations from the late second and the third century in all natural settings, but always at small, late-settled, peripheral places, those with the poorest infrastructure of drains, terracing, and other tools of stewardship. Careful stratigraphy finds erosion occurring after, not before, abandonment and, while some such sites were resettled in the fourth century, the same sequence recurred at larger scale in the fifth and sixth.

A more likely story, then, finds late classical agricultural practices successful, even in the face of natural changes, only so long as the social fabric remained intact and secure farmers could enjoy the results of investment in maintaining their own lands. But cultural failures increased the vulnerability of agrarian society, pushing it to a tipping point where a synergy of damage and decline threatened ecological foundations of classical culture and thus the nature it had colonized. At some point cultural confidence in human action was itself broken and fatalist attitudes towards nature gained importance. Around 500 the Christian Eugippius wrote a *Life* of his religious hero, St Severinus, who had died in 482 in the still Roman society of Noricum, the province between the Alps and Danube approximating present-day Bavaria and Austria. The community's dire experience of cold winters, famines, epidemics, and destructive wars was, said the hagiographer, God's punishment for human sin. A consistent, though not uniform strand in early Christian thought despaired of the material world and welcomed the soon-anticipated Apocalypse. Christian praise for ascetic aversion to sexual activity and childbearing likely contributed to falling birth rates and consequent failure adequately to replace the victims of higher mortalities.

The destabilized Empire weakened or contracted its frontiers. During Rome's third-century internal crisis, generals withdrew border units to fight other generals over the imperial succession. That level of disorder lasted for about a century while bold barbarian raiders crossed the frontier for plunder. Among the cleanup tasks of restorative rulers like Diocletian and Constantine was to defeat, destroy, expel, or settle the invaders. Once pacified, most were settled down inside the Empire as a remedy for its population losses. But when the frontiers gradually did crumble again during the late fourth and the fifth century, forces were removed and not replaced. A breakdown of trading relations ensued and the flow of wealth out of the Roman and into the barbarian world halted. This reverberated all the way to the Baltic. Quite suddenly a distant chief could no longer show off his position with Roman wine and tableware, for such southern deliveries had ceased. There is clear evidence of impoverishment of elites deep in barbarian country as the frontier system broke down. But at the same time, with the frontier removed, those outsiders more strongly felt the pull of Mediterranean civilization, of that distant place where a strong arm might gain all the wine, servitors, or other luxuries desired. So far-away elites lost sources of income and large areas of barbarian central Europe were depopulated in the course of the fifth and sixth centuries, the land left deserted. Pollen profiles from this region show, first, some presence of cultivated plants (that was the barbarian adaptation) and then their disappearance as agricultural clearings reverted to secondary woodland all across central and east-central Europe. Indeed even before 400, German-manned federate units of the Roman army had been settled south of the Danube in Noricum and Pannonia, so that Eugippius and Severinus knew a linguistic division between towns that were still talking Latin and a countryside where people spoke Germanic tongues ancestral to Austro-Bavarian and other medieval and modern south German dialects.

As Roman ways of living disintegrated and Roman frontiers collapsed, a separation from the past becomes plain. Since long before the Roman hegemony, certain kinds of patterns had been evolving in both the Mediterranean and the northern worlds, with each culture adapted to its regional environment, its particular conditions, and its own typical impacts on the natural sphere. Then the world changed.

THE DISCONTINUITIES OF LATE ANTIQUITY,
*c.*350–750

Between roughly 350 and 750 Europeans underwent a deep break in the fundamental structures of their cultures. Although key aspects of the cultural transformation itself also obscure the process, it included basic redirection of relations between whole human communities and their natural world. What environmental aspects did this discontinuity have? Movements of whole peoples, the so-called age of migrations, *c.*375–568, placed many culture groups in new surroundings. Yet even where ethnic identities changed little, the manner in which people connected to and used their landscapes shifted in important ways. Those shifts seem to work in synergy with distinctive features of European climatic conditions at this time. Case studies of two groups, Frisians and ancestral Venetians, who adapted well to extreme aspects of climatic and other changes, will highlight the unusual situation which stymied others.

As earlier noted, whenever Roman control of the frontiers weakened, barbarian raiding occurred. Undistracted Roman authorities knew how to minimize this chronic risk. But clearly different was the movement of whole peoples observed between 375 and 568. By the latter date no Roman frontiers remained in the west to be violated or defended. Some particulars of the process are needed to grasp the relocation of identifiable populations and cultures. This brief review does not pretend to address the issues which vex specialists on early medieval ethnogenesis, but rather aims to indicate patterns of cultural change potentially relevant to environmental relations.

The large-scale movements, as opposed to plundering raids, were set off far from Europe in an aggressive expansion of nomadic Huns, a central Asian tribal confederacy, in the late third and early fourth century. Some scholars now think severe drought and loss of pasturage was the trigger. By the mid-300s the Hunnish advance had swallowed up many steppe-based groups and driven others westwards as refugees. One large Germanic confederacy long at home on the Black Sea steppe, the Visigoths, fled as a refugee community into the Roman Balkans in 375. Their violently mixed reception kept them moving for two generations, provoked their culturally shocking sack of Rome in 410, and eventually let them establish rule over southern Gaul and the Iberian peninsula.

Breakdown of security in the Balkans made the Romans draw reinforcements from their western frontiers, and barbarian groups along the Rhine soon took the occasion to cross it westwards and southwards. Bands of Franks and others, for instance, went over the river into Gaul in 406. At the same time northwestern coastal peoples were crossing the narrow seas into Britain, where they soon named the island's southern and eastern parts after themselves, *Englelond*. Franks spread into northern Gaul, settling as far south as the Seine and Loire, and in the seventh century drove Visigothic authority across the Pyrenees. Meanwhile Burgundians and *Allemani* (Swabians) infiltrated the *limes* between the Rhine and Danube into southwestern Germany and continued over the Rhine into eastern Gaul. After the Hunnish hegemony flew apart in successful late fifth-century revolts of former subjects, a re-emergent polity of Ostrogoths took control of Italy itself for two generations until destroyed by a resurgent eastern Roman Empire under Justinian. That Byzantine reconquest, however, so devastated Italy that in 568 a last major continental Germanic group, the Lombards, who had been living in Pannonia since the exit of the Huns, entered the peninsula. That year, 568, marks well the end of the age of migrations as the Lombards took control over northern Italy and some areas further to the south.

Meanwhile behind the Germanic peoples, who had vacated large tracts in central and eastern Europe, Slavic-speaking settlers less dramatically filled in as far west as the middle Elbe and along and across the lower and middle Danube. More to the east, steppe peoples took over the zone north of the Black Sea and also inside the arc of the Carpathians, the Pannonian basin, westernmost area of steppe. Though wetter and more wooded than open grassland, this was the furthest west nomads could settle with their herds and retain for a time the pastoral way of life. After a gradual move westward since the early sixth century, one such group, Turkic-speaking Avars, entered Pannonia during the 550s–560s, one reason the Lombards left. While occasionally plundering their western neighbours, the Avars would remain until the end of the eighth century as overlords of a mixed agricultural population. Barely a century after Frankish ruler Charlemagne then destroyed the Avars, Magyars would follow in the tracks of their herds.

Besides the spread of human and animal pathogens which accompanies all such movements of refugees and communities, and however their mass or minority aspects are now debated, the migrations altered

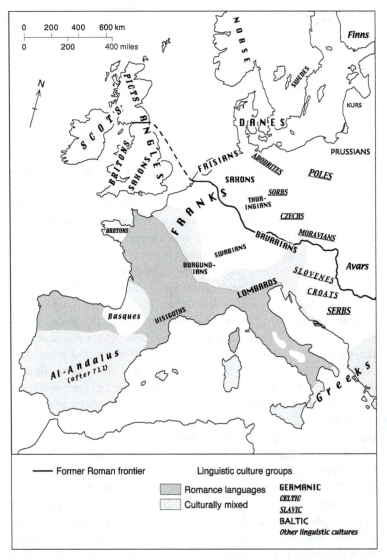

Map 2.1 Europe after Rome: linguistic cultures and peoples in the seventh century

the linguistic and hence cultural map of Europe (see Map 2.1). The primary languages of Europeans changed from being Latin-based to Germanic-based across most of what had once been Roman Britain, all the Roman Rhine provinces, and in northern Gaul nearly as far south as the Seine. Germanic tongues replaced Latin along the upper Rhine, in the Vosges mountains, and high into the Alps. Outliers of Germanic speakers, especially warrior elites, extended south to the Loire, for a time into Iberia (where Visigoths soon acculturated), and with the Lombards across the Po basin and even in pockets further south than Rome. At the same time Latin-speaking remnants remained in the Alps and others survived in the Carpathians to resurface much later as Romance-speaking Romanians. If spoken languages serve as cultural indicators, people with past experiences elsewhere had then entered into different parts of Europe. Groups bearing traditional ecological knowledge were going to encounter new kinds of places. Some found themselves in situations where their familiar practices might fit poorly. There was a general southwards shift of the northern cultures. Adaptations formed in the north before and during the Roman Iron Age now extended in greater or lesser densities across large parts of formerly Roman Europe.

In step with the linguistic change, new monarchies of barbarian origin fragmented and replaced Roman rule everywhere except at Rome, Ravenna, and a few other Italian pockets where the Byzantines hung on. This meant different rules of the game, different ways of talking about who has power, how power was allocated, what kinds of decisions the powerful could make and what they could not. Yet in some critical respects the new elites more mutated than erased the Roman imprint. Germanic kings and their resurgent Celtic counterparts in the farthest west retained a deep respect for things Roman, seeking not to destroy but to gain the benefits for themselves. Some proudly ruled over large sub-Roman populations, accepted Roman/Byzantine titles, and emulated aspects of Roman behaviour. In Italy, Gaul, and Iberia Roman fiscal regimes long survived, still run by native officials who could also teach their new masters other ways to display civilized, i.e. 'Roman', rulership. Imperial precedent suggested compiling legal codes for both their Roman subjects and their Germanic followers. Around 470 Leo, a Roman lawyer from Toulouse, assembled the oldest of these now known for Visigothic King Euric (*Codex Euricianus*) to apply in his ethnically mixed kingdom in southern Gaul. The Merovingian Clovis, first to unite all the Franks, had four commissioners put together his 'Salic Code' in 507/11. While gathering together older unwritten vernacular custom, these and later such texts were written in Latin and emulate, even take over, Roman legal principles. Not incidentally, they now provide unparalleled, if partial, insights into the ways these societies handled land, animals, and other natural resources.

But the principal collaborators and beneficiaries of the new rulers' attraction for things Roman were the leaders of the only 'Roman' institution clearly to survive the Empire's political demise, the Christian church. During late imperial centuries Christianity had established a monopoly over authorized public religion, obtained strong endowments in landed and other resources, and come to enjoy both popular support and local leadership from surviving elite families. Although most barbarians followed pagan or heterodox Christian practices as they entered the Empire, they commonly acknowledged the de facto pre-eminence of bishops in local Roman communities. After more or less brief periods of conflict, barbarian kings, like Constantine before them, saw the advantages of alliance with men who held the spiritual allegiance of many subjects, controlled a wealthy and usefully literate institution, and claimed privileged access to supernatural power. Between the late fifth and early eighth century the rulers of new kingdoms on once-Roman terrain (and beyond, in Ireland and Scotland) became orthodox 'Roman' but 'Catholic' Christians and brought bishops, abbots, and chaplains into influential court circles. They also demanded public conversion of their subjects.

On both sides of the former *limes* the break with the past was much larger than a changed cast of human characters. Between the fifth century and the ninth several fundamental changes occurred in physical and socio-cultural relations between people and their material environments. Relationships between the people and the land on which they lived shifted between 400 and 800 in at least five major ways: historic forms and sites of settlement were abandoned; new settlements appeared in different kinds of locations; old ways of organizing and demarcating the landscape vanished; grain farming lost much of its previous dominance; and finally, at least in part as a result of the other four changes in human–land relationships, there was a renaturing of western European landscapes. In terms of the interactive model this might be called decolonization of large portions of European nature. Of course some pristine state unaffected by human actions could not return, but for several centuries natural forces again increasingly shaped environmental conditions. Now to delineate these synergies more fully.

At the end of antiquity or the start of the Middle Ages, Europeans left their historically dispersed rural settlements. In the Roman world most settlement was in *villae* scattered about the countryside. The regime was not characterized by the rural nucleations today labelled villages. Typical barbarian settlements likewise had been dispersed hamlets with still some degree of generational relocation. Now people gave up on both those patterns of scattered settlement, abandoning the traditional sites. Examples are myriad. Barely sixty or seventy kilometres from Rome in the district called the *Ager Faliscus*, present-day archaeological surveys have identified 116 settlement sites dating to the classical period on a terrain of some dozens of square kilometres. In the second century, 82 per cent of those sites were still being lived in. But by the end of the next century only 58 per cent remained occupied and in the fourth century only 19 per cent. Put another way, under Marcus Aurelius (d.180) people inhabited some eighty sites in this countryside but only about twenty by the time of Constantine (d.337). The other places lay abandoned. Far from the Roman heartland, on the Rhine plain of northeastern Gaul, a comparable field survey also found that 80 per cent of classical settlement sites fell vacant between *c.*200 and *c.*400. So, too, across at least the northern half of the Iberian peninsula a general collapse of Roman settlement patterns occurred in the fifth and sixth centuries. Remarked above were the pollen profiles from the other side of the frontier that revealed large areas in central and east-central Europe emptied of their human populations during this same period.

Romanization had peppered most of the Empire with urban centres, while barbarian counterparts, the *oppida*, were found outside the *limes*. Both kinds of central places survived more often than did rural ones. All shrank, however, some by 80 and 90 per cent, and many in out of the way or simply unfortunate locations were wholly abandoned. De-urbanization brought land inside former city walls into agricultural use, even within Rome itself. People just stopped living in the places where they had been.

Human settlement shifted to a different kind of place. Settlements first established during the fifth to eighth centuries differed in quality from those whence people then departed. Sometimes, mainly but not only in the Mediterranean zone, people moved from valley bottoms to higher slopes and ridges. This is clearly visible in the Lombard plain, where settlements established in the course of the seventh and eighth centuries lay not along the rivers but up on the edge of the hills.

Outside the Mediterranean, comparable shifts are visible around Salzburg in the old Roman province of Noricum, rising south from the Danube into the Alpine foothills. The Roman period had seen elite *villae* built all over the plain. Now those habitations were abandoned and not resettled, as newer sites were founded further up the hillsides, and places like Salzburg, originally a salt production site, gained importance. The new sites were often nucleated, so the change was also from scattered small to fewer larger settlements. The same new spatial pattern also appeared on the Spanish plateau around Toledo and Madrid.

In northern Gaul new settlements established in the fourth to sixth centuries, sometimes by reoccupying former Roman sites, sometimes on new locations, consistently used new methods of construction. They were no longer built with Roman-style masonry, but rather were timber-framed structures modelled on those wooden buildings long used by the barbarians. The sites inhabited in that region in the seventh and eighth centuries, whether old or new, numbered fewer than before, but each now held more dwellings. The shift in northern Gaul took place even where there is no sign of new population growth or new population groups. In some areas with good signs of continuity, the same people with the same culture in the same general neighbourhood nevertheless had moved to different kinds of places and built differently, too. So, too, around Narbonne and on the plain of Roussillon, where more than half of Gallo-Roman sites were deserted by 500, during the following two centuries people redeployed to higher locations and built more in wood. For whatever mixed motives of cultural fashion or material need, relations to land and resources were altered.

Transformation of settlements in Britain went on long after the Anglo-Saxon establishment. Three well-excavated sites illustrate some typical phases. At West Stowe in Suffolk, Anglian settlers arrived at a long-abandoned Roman pottery by the fifth century and stayed for about 250 years. Throughout that time the place held three farmsteads in reasonable but loose and shapeless proximity, but its inhabitants shifted the positions of their farms by several hundred metres before leaving altogether in the seventh century. A generation or two after the start of West Stowe, some six to eight households of Saxon farmers established residence at Catholme in Staffordshire, west-central England, where they remained until around 1000, when the place was destroyed. Farmsteads in this later and larger settlement held

to their initial and vaguely ordered locations. Finally, the later Saxon
village established in the sixth or seventh century at Wicken Bonhunt
in Essex survives to the present. The original houses were aligned in
one regular row and a subsequent expansion in a second. In progression from Stowe to Catholme to Wicken Bonhunt, settlement
became more durable and the number of farms doubled at each
stage. The oldest dispersed sites were left behind and more orderly
new ones commonly established at different kinds of locations.

   Nor was the process just described peculiar to England. In Picardy
three separate sixth-to seventh-century nuclei have been found on
terrain of later Goudelancourt-les-Pierrepont. Near Orleans on the
site called Saran, the five farmsteads established c.650/750 some distance from long-forgotten Gallo-Roman structures were themselves
abandoned in the late 800s only to be replaced a century later with
more elaborate places 200–300 metres away. Swabian settlements to
the west of modern Stuttgart followed a similar fluid and step-wise
evolution during Merovingian and Carolingian times, and some
Danish vills moved about within their landscapes even into the
twelfth century.

   The ways farmers shaped their land into fields and access routes
disappeared in the process. Ancient patterns of parcels vanished as
their boundaries became invisible; Roman and native roadways and
ditches ceased being maintained and were then ignored. That earlier
features were once present is now known only in special cases where
landscape historians and archaeologists can detect their traces beneath
the different medieval field patterns that lasted into modern times.
Figure 2.1 shows an example from the Vale of the White Horse
in historic Berkshire, to the south of Oxford in southern England.
Differences in crops distinguish the big blocks of medieval fields, but
close study of especially the lower portion of the aerial photograph
traces underlying boundaries of an older arrangement, in this case
probably of Roman date but Celtic British origin. The ancient fields
were squarish in shape and differently oriented from their medieval
successors. The one feature that seems to continue is the line of an old
road, which provided a base line for laying out part of the later set.

   Arable land itself was not necessarily abandoned in the process of
settlement transformation, for in some places pollen analysis suggests
continued cereal cultivation even as local settlement sites and boundaries changed. But new patterns and new layouts replaced the old
and were based on different paradigms. It is not now possible to say

Figure 2.1 Change in field systems, Vale of the White Horse, Berkshire

what thinking shaped the new models, for no one then wrote down what they meant to accomplish.

Changes to settlements and field systems together transformed the whole look of European agricultural landscapes, even where production systems may have persisted.

Most evidence indicates that grain farming lost some of its primacy in the subsistence strategies followed over large areas of western Europe. Arable land was abandoned in northern England, as, for instance, in places where farmers had once supplied Roman frontier forces. Arable ceased at higher elevations in Scotland, too, which had never been under Roman rule. In the Eifel hills west of the Rhine not far from Cologne, areas known to medieval and modern sources as Hambach forest and Kotten forest had been densely populated in

Roman times. The sixth century saw those farms vacant, trees grew on what had been fields, and the terrain was not again cleared until modern development of coal mines there. But the same retreat from cereals took place far from the frontiers. In one of the richest parts of Gaul, near Laval just to the west of Paris, pollen from the Glatinié bog reflects an open first-century landscape with fields of cereal grains, orchards, gardens, and much pasture. Profiles dating to the subsequent period of 400–700 sharply differ: evidence of domestic plants and those pioneer species that grow in broken soil is absent; pollen from woodland trees dominates. What had been farmland and pasture had become woods. In many other areas pastoral uses continued, with arable turning only to grazing land and not all the way to woodland. It was cereal farming that was being reduced. Remaining Gallic fields further grew more rye and an especially hardy variety of wheat called spelt, which had originated to the east along the Danube. Wine and olive growing also retreated from their northernmost outliers where Romans had once actively promoted them; elsewhere these, too, shrank. In central Spain once-specialized agricultural production yielded to a diversified polyculture which archaeologists now interpret as a peasant strategy to reduce risk.

At the same time domestic animals diminished in size. Skeletal remains show Roman cattle stood on average about a head taller than later Frankish cattle. While Romans had typically practised stall feeding, the new agrarian regime used rough pasture, where a smaller animal is more likely to succeed. Perhaps because husbandry of sheep and swine changed less, those beasts shrank less – though the latter did so even in northern Spain – while dogs and horses remained unaffected.

But the numbers of animals and their role in early medieval human diets grew. People kept more livestock and ate more meat. Codes of Germanic customary law compiled from the sixth to the ninth century by kings determined to emulate Roman cultural norms are full of references to livestock, yet assume the domestic animals frequented the same settings as wildlife. Discussions of swine and cattle are mixed together with treatments of deer and the occasional relict aurochs, suggesting the varieties shared common habitats.

Emergent arrangements may be called sedentary agropastoralism. Rural Europeans did not give up on arable agriculture at the start of the Middle Ages, nor did appreciable numbers move around with their herds or practise more transhumance. They rather adjusted the balance between livestock and cereal grains in ways reminiscent of Bronze Age and Iron Age farming in the wooded country of northern Europe. All of the changes in rural settlement and agricultural systems left Europe's natural world less under human control. From the fifth to the eighth century a renaturing, a decolonization, of western European landscapes occurred almost everywhere. The regrowth of woodlands already remarked in England, the Eifel, and the Île-de-France can be traced in many places. On the plain of Parma between the Apennines and the Po, unstable braided mountain tributaries, wetlands, and woods carved up, interrupted, and covered over tracts of Roman land surveys. Less easily assessed is any comparable resurgence in the fauna. Although wild animal remains are a relatively small proportion of the mammal bones found on early medieval human sites, it may be possible to assemble results from the growing number of excavations and test for any shift in what people were consuming as food. Did the species mix or the habitats there represent change over time?

What might have occurred on land is hinted at by research on an aquatic organism. While chapter 1 remarked Roman depletion of the sturgeon population of the Rhône estuary, by the eleventh and twelfth centuries very large specimens of this slow-growing fish are again abundant in remains from there. Archaeozoology thus suggests a reassertion of natural forces in the aquatic realm analogous to what is shown by pollen analysis for early medieval plant communities.

In sum, where Europeans lived on the land, the resources they took from the land, and the degree of freedom natural forces enjoyed on that land all changed between the fifth century and the eighth.

THE PRESSURE OF A DIFFERENT CLIMATE

Atmospheric phenomena helped shape the discontinuity. Following the regional irregularities which helped debilitate late Roman authority, present-day climatologists identify a 'climatic anomaly' from the late fifth century into the early eighth. The preferred term emphasizes a period with distinctive attributes on the weather–climate continuum but avoids generalizing those features or prejudging their causes. These times have also been labelled the 'Migration Pessimum', 'Late Roman Little Ice Age', 'Vandal Minimum', and 'Early Medieval Cold Period', all terms meant to contrast with the preceding 'Roman

Optimum'. While contemporaries lacked all awareness of these long-term and wide-ranging climatic variations, they surely felt the weather and its effects.

Taken as a whole, the evidence of mean annual temperatures during late antiquity is equivocal. Some writers would see c.400–c.600 as averaging as much as 1.5°C below Roman times and then the eighth and ninth centuries as marked by more continental conditions (colder winters, warmer summers) further to the west. The tree line in central Europe was 200 metres lower than before. The century scale looks rather like an alternation between relatively warmer and cooler conditions. More plainly typical of the whole multi-century period were general instability and wetness.

Wetness permeates the evidence as it must often have the lives of early medieval Europeans. Among the best now known comes from systematic fieldwork done all along the route of France's new high-speed rail line down the Rhône valley. Results from full palaeoscientific analysis show that between the fourth and seventh centuries the entire region repeatedly experienced heavy rains that destroyed infrastructures, eroded old soils, and deposited new sediments on top of what had been fields. The water table was also rising, so ground water rose up and soaked out the arable, a clear sign of more water than earlier farmers had experienced. In the upper valley between Lake Geneva (Lac Leman) and Lyon a small lake, Lac le Bourget, lies beside the river, receiving water from it only at times of flood. Cores from the bottom sediment show what was running into that lake over about 3,000 years, until nineteenth-century dykes contained the Rhône. In the well-dated eighteenth and nineteenth centuries, each spike of silicates (sand) in the sediments coincided with well-documented heavy local erosion and a large flood of the Rhône. Much earlier a huge spike of sediment set in between 450 and 500 and continued to accumulate until around 700. Even though arable land in the watershed was then being abandoned and revegetated, fierce and repeated runoff events poured sand into the lake. Soil and erosion studies likewise reveal extensive sixth- to seventh-century flooding in the central Apennines, especially along rivers draining to the Po. At high elevations in the humid British Isles, cooler and wetter conditions caused peat bogs to expand over upper slopes; farmers abandoned hillside fields for better-drained valley sites. All these observations are from palaeoscientific data securely placed in time. They demonstrate trends, not events.

Then in the middle of this larger pattern is the record of one remarkable event, the well-attested 'dry fog' of 536. Its many good eye-witnesses included the most learned westerner of the day, Cassiodorus (d.575), the Roman chief minister for Italy's Ostrogoth monarch. Cassiodorus wrote from Rome that the sun was failing to shine as normal, not as in the sudden darkness of an eclipse but rather for some months as if behind a fog, though the air felt dry. At high noon in summer the light failed to cast shadows. In his official capacity, Cassiodorus worried about future crop failure, a concern validated by subsequent signs of food shortages in the west (less so in the eastern Mediterranean). While traditional historians ascribed little meaning to this obscure report, late twentieth-century palaeoscientists independently discovered a simultaneous halt to tree growth all over Europe. Just before 540 annual growth rings abruptly became extremely thin and remained so for ten to twenty years, depending on region and tree species. A more sparsely collected tree ring record from the southern hemisphere may show similar effects.

Research conducted in the early twenty-first century provides a most probable explanation, even if specialists continue to dispute some details. Newly refined dating of annual layers in ice cores from both the Greenland and Antarctic ice caps establishes the presence of high sulphate levels in the atmosphere from $533/34\pm2$ years. These deposits most likely resulted from an explosive volcanic eruption near the equator which blasted dust and aerosol chemicals into the stratosphere where they screened solar radiation. While early medieval writers knew nothing of the volcanic events, atmospheric processes, or tree rings, well-documented medieval and modern cases do establish a close relationship between a high concentration of volcanic particulates, a reduced flow of solar energy, and several years of regional declines in mean annual temperatures and plant productivity. The latest review of tree ring data makes the decade or so after 536 the northern hemisphere's most severe short-term cold episode during the past two millennia.

More easily observed and at a longer multi-century scale was a readvance of glaciers in the Alps. Glaciers characteristically expand at times of cold summers and wet winters, so an advance that set in around the mid-sixth century and continued into the eighth fits the other climatic evidence. It coincided, too, with a fall in sea level. As this world-wide phenomenon commonly occurs when more of the globe's water is locked up in ice, it argues for more general growth of glaciers.

Summer warming seems to have set in after 700, but as Europeans went through the late eighth century and early ninth, a movement of revival in high literate culture provided more scribes and documents than before. Now written records identify specific short periods of severe winters, cold wet summers, crop losses, and famines – in that sequence a coherent and plausible chain of events for a deeply localized agrarian society. Carolingian chroniclers recorded this pattern in 763/4, 821–4, 855/6, 859/60, 873/4, 913 and 939/40, totalling nine such annual events. Eight of the nine coincided with known volcanic layers in the Greenland ice cap, clearly marking short-term events that reduced solar radiation to the earth's surface in the northern hemisphere. So short-term events certainly occurred and had historic impact, though probably not enough themselves to trigger longer (century-scale) coldness and wetness. Absent any grounds to suspect a human cause, explaining these natural processes is the business of atmospheric scientists, not historians. Not so their consequences.

Beyond intrinsic interest, the climatic anomaly has dual significance for European environmental history. Across much of Europe wet conditions damage arable land by raising the risk of hydraulic soil erosion. Excessive rain, snow, and fog diminish arable crops by inhibiting germination, beating down the stalks of ripening grain, and encouraging growth of fungi and moulds. Even after a successful harvest, damp cereals spoil in storage, leaving the food supply insecure. In semi-arid Sicily, however, more precipitation reduced wind erosion, and on steppe in Pannonia or further east, more forage for livestock grew. The second pattern of the climatic anomaly was instability. Greater storminess and erratic weather always heighten insecurity for the farmer. In an unstable environment even an experienced grower could poorly predict future variability, so he could not assess what risks he was taking, or manage those risks competently. For some periods of the fifth to seventh centuries, moreover, significant regions of northern and parts of southern Europe were inhabited by households whose familiarity with local conditions was limited by their arrival only a generation or two earlier. Extreme caution was called for.

The late antique and earliest medieval centuries were a chilly, often wet, and unstable time in Europe. In most situations wet conditions threatened especially the cereal growers. Many abandoned long-worked settlements and fields; survivors moved to new kinds of sites. But humans adapt. A culture well adjusted to wet conditions can flourish in them. Consider as case studies two anomalous communities in extremely anomalous early medieval settings: early medieval Frisians lived quite successfully in a wetland; the forebears of Venetians learned to do so as well.

ANOMALOUS ADAPTATIONS FOR ANOMALOUS TIMES AND ECOSYSTEMS: FRISIA AND THE ORIGINS OF VENICE

Long at home in the coastal zone between the mouths of the Rhine and the Elbe, where mainland Europe gently slopes into the North Sea, early medieval Frisians were the forebears of many people now known as Hollanders or Dutch. (Map 2.2.)

The aquatic habitat and habits of these speakers of a Germanic dialect not unlike that of Angles and Saxons long bewildered, even disgusted, their neighbours and would-be masters. The civilized eye of Roman naturalist Pliny, who served in a first-century naval expedition to Frisia, saw the crudest of barbarians, for they lived in a marsh and ate mainly fish. Centuries later another outside witness, the Frankish bishop of Utrecht, who had religious responsibility for much of Frisia, concurred. In composing around 810 a religious *Life*

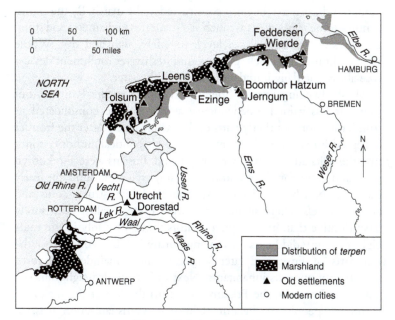

Map 2.2 Early medieval Frisia

of his predecessor, Boniface, whom disgruntled Frisians had martyred a half-century earlier, the bishop stereotyped his flock as *brutos ac barbaros*, essentially 'stupid savages'. After all, said he, they live in water like fish, travel only by boat, and because they dwell in a swamp, rarely interact with their neighbours.

Frisians did live in a treeless salt marsh, albeit with a firm clay bottom. Towards the sea a row of barrier dunes protected their settlements from storm waves on one side and landwards their salt marsh graded off into freshwater bogs that bound off their territory. These distinct bands of habitat zones were all drained by tidal creeks where relatively salty and relatively fresh water alternated twice a day. Some plants tolerate this environment, others do not. At one time of day a man or a cow could stand on damp but firm ground, and six or so hours later be belly-deep or more in water. No surprise, then that land-based cereal eaters from Pliny to the bishop simply could not comprehend people whose cultural adaptation and relation to the world about them so differed from that of proper civilized landlubbers.

Early medieval Frisians and probably those of Pliny's time, too, dwelt on artificial mounds called *terpen* (in German also *Wurten* or in compounds, *-wierde*) they had constructed in the marsh. By the eighth century some *terpen* were as much as 150 metres in diametre and stood 2 metres above normal sea level, so safely high and dry. Whole villages, houses, livestock, gardens, and freshwater catchment devices rose above the daily inundations of brackish water.

Marsh-dwelling Frisians briefly paid tribute to the Romans, but more or less gained independence as the Empire consolidated its frontier in more southerly parts of the Rhine delta. After the frontier collapsed Frisian tribal kings extended their political authority south into the delta and north to western Jutland. Frisians were also known then and now for their commercial importance around the early medieval North Sea. Hoards with both Frisian-struck coins and coins from elsewhere suggest they were quite wealthy (and surely less primitive than imperceptive visitors thought). Only in the mid-eighth century did Franks advancing northwards first conquer southern parts of Frisia and later subjugate the remainder and force Christianity upon its inhabitants. Next only to their neighbours the continental Saxons, the Frisians were thus the last of the mainland Germanic peoples to become Christian. Christianization was, of course, a centrepiece of Frankish frontier policy.

Frankish conquest itself damaged neither the economic nor the ecological relations of the Frisians. Population densities at the very period of Frankish victory (*c*.750–800) were probably as high as those in the best Frankish areas around Paris, when Flanders held up to twenty persons per square kilometre. But unlike the Franks around Paris or in Flanders, Frisians were not grain eaters. Archaeological sites show Frisian consumption of oats and rye as the principal cereals, significant eating of vegetables, and of much meat, dairy, and fish. It has been estimated that 50–75 per cent of Frisian calories came from animal products, while on contemporary Frankish sites 60–75 per cent of calories came from grain. The diets mirror each group's distinctive relations to the productive biosphere.

The Frisian diet rested upon a subsistence base of adaptations to the salt marsh soils and diurnal flooding which their ancestors had developed since the early Iron Age. Their particular ecological niche used their whole environment as it had been modified by generations of human activity. The soils on the *terpen* were well fertilized, for each housed humans, animals, and cultural processes that accumulated and deposited organic materials, even when not so intended. Nutrient-rich slopes of the *terpen* could grow salt-tolerant barley and oats, vegetables, and fibre plants like flax. Down on the marsh, however, the daily dose of salt water killed cereal grains. Yet many native grasses grew well on the marsh soils, and when the water was low, cattle could graze in the firm-bottomed marsh. People could also harvest the salt grass, dry it, and store it on the *terpen* to feed cattle when winter kept the beasts from pasture. House-barn dwellings on the terpen had room for a family and twenty or more head of cattle. Sheep were far fewer and other livestock insignificant. Frisian cattle produced meat, hides (the form in which Frisians paid tribute to Rome), and dairy products, which could also be exported. There was little risk of overgrazing the salt marsh because the cattle had to be moved off it at certain seasons and times of day. More fodder could also be harvested from freshwater inland peat bogs, where treacherously soggy ground kept cattle out. Both peat and tidal waters held rich stocks of certain fishes, which Frisians also consumed. Small boats were thus a common necessity and tool of these people, useful also when they caught the myriad resident and migratory waterfowl.

Pastoral emphasis in an economy reduces labour demands for human subsistence purposes. Frisian labour was available for such broader economic opportunities as trade. The peculiar way Frisians could use the alternately submerged and dry marsh also meant that most of the land belonged to no one in particular. People used spaces for specific purposes and then left them open. This is probably the main reason large private lordships failed to develop among the Frisians. This society was not feudalized. Nor prior to the Frankish hegemony was it manorialized, being without large estates and/or use of forced labour for agricultural or other economic purposes. Hence even in the eighth century, Frisia was quite distinct in a variety of ways from the Frankish situation.

Change to the economic and ecological niche of the Frisians did not arise directly from the Frankish conquest, because the wetland areas remained unsuited to the Frankish way of life. But grounds for change began, in part with the imposition of Christianity. Christian teachings and practices offered new cultural norms more attuned to the Mediterranean tradition: use of bread, use of wine, authoritative written texts, literate religious professionals. Further, as Christianity had developed in the western Empire and then in the Frankish state, churches acquired landed estates for their economic support. Formal conversion of Frisia thus established ecclesiastical lordships there. Secondly, the Frankish political system imposed structures that leaned towards change. Frankish governance assumed, in line with Roman precedents, regalian rights to unoccupied land, something unknown in independent Frisia. Land not farmed, and so not visibly owned by anyone, belonged to the king. The king could then put this 'unowned' land out to people whom he wished to favour. More materially, the Franks brought with them a framework of legal and political administration. The territorial representatives of the king were the counts, the counts ran courts of justice, and the courts needed some kind of legal reference. Around 800 Charlemagne had the customary law of the Frisians (*Lex Frisionum*) codified and written down. These patterns of change operated largely on the cultural side, affecting mental constructs and programmes.

The commercial aspect of the Frisian niche was destroyed in the ninth century first by Viking raids and then by Norse commercial competition around the North Sea. But far more fundamental change to the Frisian way of life began in the years around 1000 with the start of embanking and draining, at which point they began evolving towards a grain-growing, grain-eating 'normalcy'. That story will belong to a later chapter. Here rather the Frisians provide a telling example of an unusual human adaptation gaining marked success under unusual conditions which stymied or hurt most other Europeans. The climatic anomaly made everything wet. People whose traditional culture was anomalous for its very adaptation to the wet situation had the advantage

Others who worked out ways to handle wetness and insecurity could also find early medieval conditions useful. At the other side of western Christendom from the Frisians arose some analogues to their relation with watery nature. After much fear of floods and worry over drainage along the Po in the sixth century, by the eighth people in northern Italy seem to have become a good deal less upset. Historian Paolo Squatriti suggests some of this equanimity simply followed from the reduced population, which lessened competition for safer sites out of the flood plain. As, moreover, the Po's flood plain renaturalized, its capacity to absorb floodwaters with less damage to human interests increased. The landscape may still have been inundated but people were at less risk. Additionally, through the seventh and eighth centuries people in Lombardy were learning to recognize and make use of flood plain resources. They exploited the wildlife, both animals and birds; they exploited the fisheries; they used the natural meadows for hay and for pasture in seasons when the water was low.

A remarkable counterpart to the Frisians evolved in and beyond the delta of the Po, where early medieval refugees on barrier islands, mud banks, and sand bars literally set the foundations of Venice, city in the lagoon. Inhabitants of Roman Venetia, the province between the Alps, Adriatic, and Po (see Map 2.3), had probed the edges of the coastal marshes and embayments, but natural and political events of the fifth and sixth centuries halted or transformed these efforts. Flooding rivers covered Roman Torcello with silt and successive incursions by Visigoths and Huns chased country people to temporary safety on offshore islands. In the 530s Cassiodorus thought the region a thinly populated, semi-aquatic link between Ravenna and food supplies from further northeast in Istria. The maritime population he described as travelling by ubiquitous boats along channels through fields and marshes, dwelling 'like seabirds' on tidal bars and islands, and living, not from cultivation but from fishing, waterfowling, and the salt they extracted from seawater. Indeed, the shallow upper Adriatic holds the Mediterranean's most productive waters.

Still in Cassiodorus's lifetime the Lombard invasion of 568 again drove inland Roman (Byzantine) subjects, including whole urban communities under their governmental and religious leaders, to take

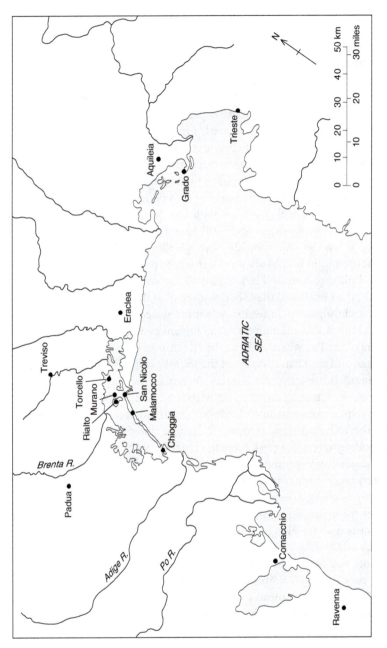

Map 2.3 Early medieval Venetia and environs

what proved to be permanent refuge on the islands of the lagoon. The newcomers, too, had to make settlements and a necessarily amphibious living from what little this environment could be made to provide. Early colonization leaves traces in documents which consecrated new churches, like a cathedral at Torcello in 639, to serve places long otherwise unrecorded, and so, too, in the late sixth- and seventh-century radiocarbon dates of the oldest wooden piles found beneath the future sites of churches on Rialto, heart of the later Venice. Neither agriculture nor pastoralism fit this landscape, so controlling land meant little compared with products which could be traded for food. Salt and some exotic goods available through the long-lasting Byzantine connection were what commercially precocious Comacchio, located where sea, Po, and lagoon came together, was shipping upriver in the early eighth century. Torcello had a glass-works, probably then just supplying local churches, by around 700. Real economic takeoff came only a hundred years later and under the leadership of Rialto at the lagoon's safer centre, which became the seat of government in 810, fighting off attempted Frankish conquest and gaining a sort of protective balance between Byzantine suzerainty and Frankish power on land. Still centuries from future greatness, Venice and its lagoon evolved together: the waters and their devious channels provided physical security even by unknown means when fevers felled Frankish troops and their commander, Charlemagne's son Pepin; from mud, sand, and shallows could be wrested tradable salt, glass, fish, shellfish, and birds; simple but laborious constructions of logs, wicker, and imported stone shaped sites for human habitation and routes between them. The anomalous adaptation of Venice to a wet environment deeply rooted in the instabilities of late antiquity still amazed early eleventh-century clerks at the Italian royal palace in Pavia, who marvelled at a people 'that does not plough, sow, nor gather vintage' but supplied their needs from ports on the Po.

So at different scales and with or without distinctive social institutions, peoples in northern Italy found cultural adaptations that fitted the anomalous wet situation in ways not unlike those that Frisians had long evolved. People found themselves in a world that was different; people who could adjust to that world used the new opportunities and avoided the new risks. Their outcomes look better than those of people who tried to stick to the old ways of doing things, particularly in terms of cereal agriculture. What can be learned about the Frisians and what was happening along the Po and lagoons fits this notion of anomaly. Some such adjustments match as well the characteristic 'barbarian' patterns of resource use, an emphasis on animals, wild or domestic, a reduction in importance of cereal farming, shifting relations to boundaries, and more. The successful, if unusual, adaptations themselves drive home the general effects of the wet and unstable early medieval European environment and mark its general discontinuity with ancient patterns of relations between humans and the natural world.

THE CAROLINGIAN AGE: WINDOW ON A WORK IN PROGRESS

In normal historiographic tradition, Frankish conquests in eighth-century Frisia and decades later in central Europe and Italy under Charlemagne (768–814) mark the end of the early Middle Ages. For the first time since the Roman age, a large political entity encompassed most of the Christian west (see Map 2.4), while larger polities

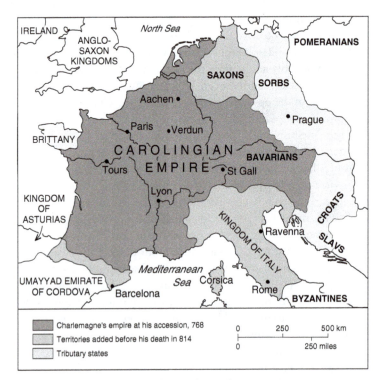

Map 2.4 The Carolingian hegemony

also emerged in Britain. More significantly, the Carolingian age (broadly *c*.700–900) became one of self-conscious cultural revival carried out by an alliance of the church and the monarchy. This brings historians a new wealth of documentation that reveals new representations and new programmes associated with economic growth and environmental change. From the perspective of environmental history Carolingian texts suddenly open a window not on something completed but on very much a work in progress: many developments had been emerging out of the discontinuity and people were responding to a different kind of world. The period has special importance for environmental history because suddenly this activity becomes visible and sometimes plainly also intentional in path-breaking new syntheses for organizing human use of European nature, notably the land.

An environmental perspective thus dwells not on the conquests, church, and broad institutional and cultural programmes of Charles 'the Great' (Charlemagne), but on five features of the age which illuminate how people were adjusting and attempting new ways to situate their culture in their nature. These include a revival of central authority with hegemonic cultural norms, the expansion and uses of private lordship, the predominance of family farms, creation and proliferation of the bipartite manor, and all this in a setting of renewed local population growth and agricultural intensification. For all its self-conscious return to ancient modes, the Carolingian age confirmed the intervening discontinuity by taking a new and, in retrospect, pregnant course.

The revival of central authority under Charlemagne's grandfather and father, culminating in his own efforts and a slow deterioration in following generations, is a commonplace of medieval history. It is also well known that this was carried out together with a cultural revival, propagated, it should be emphasized, very much in terms of hegemonic cultural norms. Just as all were to behave themselves lest the king bring them to heel, all were supposed to follow the right way of doing things. None were to eat meat on Friday or fleshy foods for a month or two before Easter. Value was placed on the consumption of bread. Great stress was laid on the codification of law, not just as oral custom but to fix it in writing. These were construed as Roman ways. They were how one behaves if one is civilized. Such efforts with environmental implications were of a piece with Carolingian reform of handwriting, as they rejected forms used by Merovingian scribes and tried to figure out how a proper Roman wrote (resulting in present-day lower-case letters shaped after what Carolingians found on Roman inscriptions). They sent emissaries to Rome to learn the right way to perform liturgical chant. The way things were done in Rome was the right way. Those were the civilized models and the Franks would learn to be civilized.

The approved ways all opposed northern barbarian practice. Even as Charles himself clung to ancestral habits of dress, conjugal relations, and recreational hunting, Carolingian authority pushed certain kinds of cultural norms that ran against what had been long-standing century-scale trends. All such models had been actively promoted by clerical culture, which grew out of the late Roman world, and were now adopted as a programme by Carolingian and also by Anglo-Saxon monarchs, especially Alfred of Wessex (871–99). Those norms would continue as ideological preferences even after favourable temporary political unities broke down in the course of the later ninth and the tenth century. All of these programmes nudged at and shaped how people could make use of the natural world.

And who would apply those programmes? Among Romans and barbarians alike there had been for centuries of late antiquity a gradual evolution towards the privatization of power. The term 'lordship' can refer to this private holding of power, to personal authoritative superiority over specific other people. The Carolingians, willingly or not, forged a fundamental compromise between their centralizing proclivities and Roman precedents on the one side, and that long socio-political trend towards privatized power, towards a world of lordship, on the other. In such a world, a strong ruler, a Charles the Great, could use lordship to enhance his official position, but only if he accepted its social reality. A weaker ruler, however, had simply to acquiesce to the private power of great men. The records of the Carolingian age bear witness both in the ways the dynasty constructed its own power and in those which later eroded it away. This evolution affected the locus and scope of effective decision-making for large programmes and projects in the material world. To take a limited example, Charles determined to dig a canal through the low divide between tributaries of the Rhine and of the Danube for better movement of men and supplies to his southeastern frontier. After thousands of men had excavated some kilometres (30 metres wide and 10 deep) of the still-visible *Karlsgraben* (*Fossa Carolina*, 'Charles's Ditch'), the project was quietly abandoned. Recent researchers dispute a contemporary chronicler's assertion that rains and other commitments left it unfinished, arguing instead that the costs of using the canal just made it fatally inefficient. Later medieval works of comparable magnitude would be attempted by lay and clerical lords (see chapter 4).

At the other end of the social spectrum, where Charles drafted his workers and soldiers, Carolingian documents reveal the predominance of peasant family farms. These units had not been organized in the same way as either Roman rural life or that of Germanic barbarians. Peasant family farms emerged during the period of discontinuity from the breakup of both the Germanic kin or extended family socio-economic organization and the Roman slave estates. With the Carolingian age they were explicitly acknowledged as the norm of agrarian society and hence as its operational cells, the fundamental units, in micro-economic terms the smallest 'firms', of resource use. Henceforth to the end of pre-industrial western history, the operative cultural assumption and social reality was that agricultural people (80–95 per cent of the population) lived in a nuclear family unit with some resources assigned to them and operated that resource base as an enterprise. These people did not work as a gang of slaves, nor did they function together in a single economic unit with members of several different interrelated families.

The practice of lordship and the predominance of the peasant family farm came together in the Carolingian age in an institutional structure now called the 'bipartite manor'. Carolingian scribes writing in Latin used *villa* (the same word as the Roman *villa* but not the same thing). The bipartite manor was a form of small-scale resource management for landed estates. It organized land of all types – arable, pasture, woodland, farmsteads – simultaneously in the legal possession of a lord and the practical use of an agrarian community, peasant farmers. Self-supporting peasant families there gained their subsistence by farming small holdings called *mansi* (singular *mansus*) and provided the labour for production on the lord's own farm, called in Carolingian documents the *mansus indominicatus* (otherwise 'domain', 'demesne', etc.).

The idea of the *mansus* as a unit of exploitation comes from a late Latin word for 'house' (*mansus*) with a root idea of physical stability, of being fixed in place (Latin *maneo*, 'stay', 'remain'). The *mansus* somehow belonged to its occupant. Treating households as fiscal units came in with reforming emperors Diocletian and Constantine who used them to allocate the taxes due to local Roman military units. As a label connected to the household, *mansus* first appears in the early

documents associated with the bipartite manor, where it was assimilated to the old Germanic concept earlier encountered as *huba*, *Hufe* or
'hide', as an assessment of usable arable resources. So the term *mansus*
in the Carolingian texts meant a body of arable land and associated
resources that was about the right size to support a typical farming
household. These were not likely surveyed as identical measures
of area, but rather understood by contemporaries to conceptualize
the agrarian world, both as identifiable individual *mansi* and as
enumerations of those, perhaps of differing legal status, in a named
villa. Around 850, for instance, Aguilcourt, a manor of the church of
Reims some sixteen kilometres distant near the river Aisne, contained
some ninety-two and a half 'free' *mansi* and thirty-five 'servile' *mansi*,
each held by a named head of household and with different obligations to the lord.

Aguilcourt was the site of a *mansus indominicatus*, too. This did not
support family households but was rather the economic unit where
the lord took labour from those households and used it to produce on
his own account what he wanted.

The concept of *mansus* was the key, joining together Roman ideas
from the fiscal realm of taxation for identifying a household as a unit
for discourse and Germanic ideas referring to a body of land. This
resulted in a Latin term and a German term becoming virtual syno-
nyms as a quantity of resources roughly suitable for the operation of an
agrarian household, the social unit where work was applied to the
land. Relatively well-documented Frankish assimilation of households and resources into a unit of assessment may not have been
peculiar to that socio-political community. At about the same time
leaders in the Pictish monarchy of northern Britain introduced the
term *davoch* for a 'bundle' of resources supporting a taxable farm.

The bipartite manor was therefore apt for restructuring the management of existing rural settlements and for organizing new ones to
open up uncultivated land. It provided lords with a way of controlling
both land and labour for productive purposes. Put another way, it
provided infrastructures for colonizing with human labour a piece of
nature to produce the sorts of things those with the power to decide
thought they wanted. Athough some sparse and cryptic earlier documents may suggest earlier precedents for the terms, concepts, and
institutions, the bipartite manor, *mansus*, *mansus indominicatus*, all
clearly emerged and came together in the Carolingian heartlands
between the Seine and the Rhine, especially the area of northern

Neustria, in the course of the early to mid-eighth century. The programme was then actively encouraged, propagated, and installed under royal auspices in peripheral and conquered areas such as Provence and Bavaria. This is well known now because royal and allied church patronage saw to the keeping of written records, notably property inventories from large church estates and instructions to the king's officers (often in the multi-titled form called capitularies) on how to manage the king's estates and solve local problems. In these situations central elements of the ruling elite advanced this form of estate organization as yet another hegemonic cultural norm, now for determining local land use and human work.

A final and overarching feature of the Carolingian age is its evidence of local population growth and agricultural intensification. An emphasis on mixed farming reflected on one side pressures from the rich, who wanted wheat and meat and would take them as tributes from peasant farms or use peasant labour to produce them from the lord's own land. On the other side, poor farming families needed to raise subsistence foods, those crops promising the most calories for the least labour, to overcome well-documented shortages, not all of which could be blamed on bad weather. After three to five centuries of generally contracting arable and shrinking human numbers, the early eighth century reveals at least locally rising numbers of people and some new expansion of arable. Carolingian texts now indicate increases in what German scholars call 'cerealization' (*Vergetreidung*), a trend towards a greater role for cereal grains in both production and consumption. People were attempting to put more grain on to the land and get more out of the land, to get more grain into their diets, and to eat more of that grain as bread. More bread in the diets of elites showed they were civilized, for civilized folk consumed bread and wine, not gruel and beer. More grain for the poor was a way to feed a larger family from household labour because cereal-growing on arable land promised more calories than running livestock on the same land resource. A renewed emphasis on cereal growing, and hence on arable agriculture, will be among the most important trends to follow into the central Middle Ages (roughly *c.*900–1100). So, after a long period of arable loss, the Carolingian age provided at least a model and local impetus for reversing the process.

Quite apart from the especially visible Carolingian programme, Frankish lords and the princes simultaneously consolidating power in eighth- to ninth-century England and Denmark saw the same value in these agrarian changes. Larger villages, larger main buildings, a more planned layout, and more cereal growing can be detected across the region. That a broader setting of natural and human threats to productive security long kept all such rising material output precarious is, however, suggested by the regional food shortages which recurred throughout this period and the likelihood that the Frankish realm maintained no net population increase between 750 and 950.

Tracing the path whereby agriculture shaped the landscapes of medieval Europe under institutional arrangements introduced by the Carolingians and some of their contemporaries will occupy a coming chapter. But first the Christian and other ideologies of nature held in the Middle Ages call for closer examination, followed by consideration of their possible roles in shaping representations and affecting programmes for the work of colonization. How did medieval European culture make sense of the natural world?

3

HUMANKIND AND GOD'S CREATION
IN MEDIEVAL MINDS

The immediate material discontinuities late antiquity brought to Europe's environmental relations were matched by cultural transformation. In diverse ways, including some that have no connection to what this book explores, classical Mediterranean civilization broke up and vanished, leaving behind only cultural relics to influence its successors in Byzantium, Islam, and medieval western Christendom. Indeed, while by the eighth century this last was defining itself as Christian and 'Roman', what members of this culture meant thereby referred as much to use of the Latin language and Latin letters by the literate elite as it did to the general respect, but not authority, they acknowledged to the bishop of Rome, the Pope, as successor of Peter and Vicar of Christ. Westerners shared certain seminal assumptions about the nature of culture, the place of humankind, and the quality of human connections to other things. Some of their assumptions were of Christian origin, others were much older and deeper but now most commonly expressed in Christian terms. Matters metaphysical have little relevance here; ontology and philosophical essentialism are not to be conflated with examining how medieval cultures interacted with the world of natural causality. This chapter seeks to establish how medieval people thought about their relationship to God's Creation as they understood it, and notably how their evident thinking meshed with their experience and activities in the material sphere. In terms already introduced, a primarily emic probe into medieval minds is thus glossed with etic views of medieval behaviour.

It is important to recognize that the European Middle Ages lacked self-conscious or even coherent tacit discourse on relations of humans to nature or on nature as an entity, to say nothing of such concepts as environment or ecology, both of which are modern, not medieval, ideas. As in classical antiquity, to look for them as such in medieval Europe is to risk wishful self-deception.

Historic assumptions in medieval culture do bear upon the natural sphere, but they must be teased out. This chapter argues that the closer an investigation manages to come to actual things of nature – an animal, a plant, a planet, a rock, a human body – and their explicit medieval representations and programmes, the greater the diversity that appears in medieval minds. Likely operative ideas varied across time and relative to context, social rank, gender, and more. On the other hand, the more basic and all-encompassing the ideological elements examined, the more tenuous the connections and the greater the gap between these ideas and the experience and work of human beings in the material sphere. Much of this distance between recorded ideas of nature and human activities in nature is due importantly, but perhaps not primarily, to the peculiar place of literacy in medieval society and culture. Because literacy was a tool used by a particular set of people and not by most others through much of the Middle Ages, few who had deep experiential familiarity with the natural sphere could write about it. Furthermore, few of those who were literate thought that literacy well employed for the purpose of writing about the natural sphere. As professional churchmen, most medieval writers were far more interested in the supernatural than in the natural.

Medieval western Europeans were aware of non-Christian groups in their midst or at their frontiers. The internal presence of Jews and external presence of first pagan, later mainly Muslim, neighbours became at various times essential reference points for self-identification as a Christian society. In self-conscious distinction, the vast majority of medieval Europeans claimed collectively to approach the world around them in terms of what their leading voices declared to be Christian truths.

Historic Christianization in late antique and medieval Europe (as earlier around the Mediterranean) produced, however, no single transcendent reality. A believer can, as a matter of faith, understand Christianity as one single unified body of orthodox doctrine, but such essentialism cannot usefully encompass Christianity as a historical phenomenon in medieval Europe or anywhere else. Historians rather recognize that Christianity was delivered, accepted, and used as a large and diverse package of sacred texts, beliefs, doctrines, and cult prac-tices. These were layered and changing understandings; there was debate, dissent, and difference of opinion. Different sorts of people, clerical and lay, variously grasped and differently defended their Christianity across a millennium and more between the laying of medieval western ideological foundations in the age of Augustine of Hippo (d.430) and acknowledgement of sectarian division at the Council of Trent (1545–63). Persisting across these variations, how-ever, is a profound separation, a recurring gap, between known ideas of nature in medieval minds and the actions carried out in nature on the part of medieval Europeans.

This chapter explores the minds and contemplates the diversity and the gap. It takes off from the still-influential, if much criticized, assertion by historian Lynn White Jr that fundamental Christian doctrines made medieval Europeans approach nature in a new and eventually destructive way. White's claim that medieval Christian thought drove exploitation of nature is then tested against the evidence of missionary teachings and long-term medieval discussions about the actual beliefs of ordinary people. Three less abstract, more firmly demonstrable, if not mutually compatible, threads in medieval thinking about nature – its hostility to humans, its value as a sign, the possibilities of human collaboration with a friendly personified *Natura* – are then examined. The last part of the chapter looks at selected areas of applied thought which by later medieval centuries manifest increasing signs of experience influencing cultural processes and programmes tailored to material conditions.

THE WHITE THESIS, ITS CRITICS AND ADHERENTS

In the first flush of a self-conscious North American environmentalism during the 1960s, Lynn White Jr argued that medieval thought about nature and action in nature were in fact joined at a most vital point. An innovative historian of technology, White had trained as a traditional humanist research scholar, served as president of a church-related liberal arts college, and helped establish one of North America's first major centres for the interdisciplinary study of the Middle Ages. His 1966 address to the American Association for the Advancement of Science, published in the following year as 'The Historical Roots of our Ecologic Crisis' (*sic*), remains perhaps the single most widely read piece of writing connecting medieval thought and the natural world.

White argued that Christianity in general and medieval western Christianity in particular was responsible for the present-day environmental crisis. Medieval ideas about nature and action in nature came together eventually to produce a late twentieth-century breakdown of human relations with the natural world. His argument worked through several very simple stages. First, said White, be aware that humans change their environment. The greatest and surely first industrial-scale transformation of global environments was carried out by bearers of western culture. These transformations were pioneered by western technology and guided by western science, both of which trace their essential origins to the European Middle Ages. White asserted that already by the end of the Middle Ages, Europeans held a technological lead over all other civilizations, and this gave them an ability to transform and exploit nature beyond any other culture. Over the half-century since White wrote, most scholars would still concur regarding how Europeans acquired technical superiority over Islamic, Indian, and Amerindian civilizations, but they now doubt that Europe held any clear advantage over Chinese technologies as early as 1500. None would reasonably deny, however, that the hugely potent modern world traces its technological might to any but European culture or that the western trajectory had begun by the end of the Middle Ages.

White next pointed out that the ability to exploit nature has to be coupled with ideas, a cultural programme, that encouraged or permitted a society to do so. This, he asserted, came to Europe from fundamental Christian ideas that allowed humans to exploit and dominate nature. Three key cultural developments grew from the Christian creation myth and understanding of the presence of God in the world that Christians gained from their Scripture. In the first place, the Judeo-Christian myth of creation of the universe by a single god presented in the stories of Genesis and particularly in the passage of Genesis 1:28 meant that humans received from God 'Dominion' over nature to use it for their ends: 'And God blessed them and said to them, "Be fruitful and multiply and fill the earth and subdue it and have dominion over the fish of the sea and over the birds of the heavens and over every living thing that moves on the earth."' This doctrine of Dominion, asserted White, let Christians treat the natural world in whatever exploitative way they desired.

Secondly, White argued, by vesting all spiritual power in the Creator God, the Christian creation myth destroyed the spiritual content of material nature, obliterating the animism that pervaded Greco-Roman and other pagan ways of thinking about the natural world. It pushed spirituality out of nature and granted the universe to humans to run without any fear of contrary powers.

Third and more indirectly, the Christian understanding of nature, particularly as it evolved in the Latin west, worked towards a notion that not only did God inspire holy books, his mind and his will also created everything in nature. Nature thus necessarily reflected the mind and purpose of God. Medieval western Christians determined that they could attempt to understand the mind of God (in fact felt obliged to do so) and one important route to that end would be through investigating nature. This notion of 'natural theology', White argued (and he was not wrong), constitutes one key root of western science. It was the science that emerged and grew out of (not in) the Middle Ages that magnified western power to destroy nature. And much later that power was taken up by other modernizing civilizations as well. Hence, in White's terms, Christianity, notably medieval western Christianity, 'bears a burden of guilt' for the destruction of nature then and in the modern age.

White's essay is curiously devoid of evidence. About its only major substantive reference is to Genesis 1:28. That was perhaps partly due to White first presenting it orally to an audience of scientists and then in the journal *Science*, where a subcultural aversion to notes militated against the elaborate examples and citations of texts beloved of historians. Also, much of what White said there about the development of western technology he had and would elaborate in print elsewhere. Nor are his technological claims subject to great dispute.

White concluded with the suggestion that an alternative view of Christianity was present or emergent in the Middle Ages, one humbler towards nature and approaching pantheism in its recognition of nature as filled with divine spirit. White associated that view with Francis of Assisi and further proposed Francis as the patron saint of ecology. Pope John Paul II did issue a bull to that effect in 1980 and later preached on Francis as an example of human love for fellow creatures.

White's essay provoked immediate, wide-ranging, and long-running dissent. Some of that dissent is historically credible; some is irrelevant. The first articulated opposition came from those like geographer Li-fu Tuan (1968), who pointed out that cultures other than Christianity also damaged nature. That true statement is, however, historically irrelevant: engaging an argument that says the culture which greatly magnified human power to destroy nature was western culture requires examination of western intellectual roots. Just because others did similar things with different ideologies does not disprove this role of Christian ideology in the west. The second body of dissent comes largely from theologians who, again probably quite correctly, pointed out that Christian Scriptures hold more elements than just Dominion and that they can be read in various ways, including to show humans bearing stewardship responsibility for nature. This, too, is probably accurate exegesis but not history. History demands more than ideas embodied in a book at one time that was read by people at a later time, and asks whether and how the people whose actions need to be explained perceived and used the ideas in question. A third set of dissenters hold that western Christian theology is not itself a cause but rather the effect: theological positions themselves resulted from developing material economic interests, and notably European ideas about nature evolved from changing material experience. It may, however, be as difficult to demonstrate, particularly in the general case, how experience produced an abstract idea as it is to prove that such an idea motivated action. White and his critics easily lapse into simple determinisms, and both the materialist and the idealist position raise genuine problems, even within the limits of the history of ideas.

Few scholars so far have really traced what White saw as core Christian ideas about nature into medieval texts and then into medieval actions in the natural world. Clarence Glacken's still indispensable history of western ideas about nature, *Traces on the Rhodian Shore*, does pick up on some earlier work of White, by then a colleague at UCLA, but its composition effectively antedated 'The Historical Roots' and Glacken's attention remains fixed on specific texts, not specific actions. In one strong enquiry Jeremy Cohen examined exegesis of Genesis 1:28 by medieval Jewish and Christian scholars and established that neither paid much attention to the issue of Dominion. When either group found the verse worthy of comment, they focused on the injunction to 'go forth and multiply' and debated whether or not the world had so changed as to leave this command moot. Ascetics held sexual congress and reproduction as either unholy or undesirable in their own time, while other commentators reiterated the duty to propagate their own people and their race. Other scholars have drawn attention to early Christian hermit saints deeply imbued with a sense of the divine who lived happily in nature and performed miracles there. Thus the two areas wherein scholars have examined precisely which medieval people did read the scriptural passages White thought seminal, and how those same people at least talked about consequent actions in nature, both fail to support White's overarching claim.

White's interpretive hypothesis has to be listed as certainly not proved for the Middle Ages; many would argue that it is inherently not provable. The leap is simply too great from reading Genesis to making gunpowder or from ploughing a furrow in the tenth century to inventing a better world through chemistry in the twentieth. Nevertheless the White thesis necessarily claims the attention of medievalists because it is still thoughtlessly repeated, particularly by environmental writers, not historians, and/or serves them as a touchstone for other comparisons.

THE LIMITS TO BASIC MEDIEVAL CHRISTIANIZATION

The way in which White's thesis was presented and debated forces consideration of what Christianization meant in the Middle Ages, particularly in the early centuries when Europe went from a multiplicity of pagan beliefs to a religion only recently spread out of the eastern Mediterranean and become official in the Roman world just as it was collapsing. By the fourteenth century, however, no acknowledged social groups in western Europe other than Jews and some relict Muslim communities in Spain were other than ostensibly Christian. What was basic to the process of medieval Christianization? What understandings of humans' place in the world did medieval Christian teachers and preachers laboriously convey to elites and general populations alike?

Texts composed by missionaries and parish priests or by bishops who advised and supervised them lay out what they wanted people to grasp. Initial emphasis in early medieval missionaries' handbooks is on the *power* of the Christian God. This God created the earth and everything on it; he created humankind, even the unbelievers. Because humans disobeyed his commands, he cast them out of paradise into a world of pain, work, and death. God continues to control all of nature, which works according to his will. He provided Christ to lead the disobedient humans back to true worship, which requires that they reject and drive out other gods, who are but false spirits. God further demands that his believers, his followers, behave rightly so that they will be saved. Such was the fundamental message of the Christian heroes who went off to preach particularly to Germanic and Slavic unbelievers around the frontiers of the Carolingian world, and before them those who confronted Germanic and other pagan communities settled inside the nominally Christian Roman Empire.

At the same time, at the highest intellectual level, essential features of western Christian doctrine were being assembled from Scripture and works of early Christian leaders and crystallized particularly in the writings of Augustine of Hippo. Augustine wrote in his *City of God* how all history revolves around Christ, and the believer must, as a fundamental condition of true belief, love God above all else. If so, if one truly loved God above all else, the home for the immortal soul is heaven, the other world, the hereafter. This material world, though divinely made to be useful for good Christians and thus full of signs about what God wants, is only a temporary place. Now and here is not the place for real allegiance. That lies in the near future and forever elsewhere in heaven. The teachings of Augustine became theological foundations for all western thought deep into the twelfth century and influenced religious thinkers well into modern times, including important sixteenth-century Protestant and Catholic reformers. Augustine and other late antique/early medieval writers also contrasted the immaterial immortal soul with the sinful material body in which that soul was lodged. While carefully holding short of the dualism of the rival Manichaeans, who equated material with evil, spiritual with good, and understood the universe as created by two divine powers, the Christian teachings that spread across early medieval Europe had a strong ascetic strain that devalued and feared materiality. The best Christians, all agreed, were those monks and nuns who sought to withdraw from the material world, to control their material bodies, and to propel their souls towards union with the spiritual nature of God.

Such were the fundamentals of Christian beliefs propagated to Europeans from the closing centuries of the Roman Empire right on up to the last conversions in Europe during the twelfth, thirteenth, and early fourteenth century. More elaborate and nuanced doctrinal ideas entered the consciousness of ordinary believers only very slowly.

But simultaneously in this self-consciously Christian society and culture, there persisted a pre- and non-Christian understanding of a natural world pervaded by spirit and negotiated by magic. In other words, Lynn White and medieval clerics alike erred in thinking

Christianization purged animism from medieval minds and environments. Early Irish literature, though written down by Christian scribes, displays an almost seamless transition from an immanence of spirit in pagan views of nature and that of a later Christian divinity. Impressive evidence is also to be found in the penitentials, handbooks composed in central medieval centuries to help clerics spot the sins in people's talk and actions and, after taking their confessions, impose suitable penance. Burchard, eleventh-century bishop of Worms in the Rhineland, wrote one authoritative such manual. This shepherd knew well his peasant flock, by then nominally Christian for 500 years, yet found them managing the natural world through magical acts and rituals of non-Christian origin. Ending a drought, for instance, through a procession to the river by naked village girls bearing branches of specially harvested herbs and mutual splashing with river water rested on a different system of explanation, different assumptions about how nature works. Burchard's penitential is but one record of such behaviour. When the right kind of documentation survives – which is very rare – the same tacit understanding among the large mass of Europeans is for a millennium confirmed by the complaints of clerical writers. They begin as early as the fifth and sixth centuries with witnesses like Bishop Martin of Braga and run right up into the seventeenth century, a hundred years and more after the Council of Trent, and well after the Protestant Reformation had removed many Europeans from a formally unified church. Yet Protestant pastors and Catholic reformers alike carped that their peasants were all superstitious, thinking the world full of fearsome spirits and trying to figure out ways to manipulate those powers.

Fundamental to medieval thinking about nature were differences between representations, understandings, and programmes that were commonly written down by and for a literate elite and those held in popular cultures, which were written down very little. This identifies a fatal flaw in the arguments of White and indeed many of his critics, who want simply to equate medieval understandings with Christian Scripture and with official dogma, in other words with a hegemonic Christianity that claimed to monopolize truth and identified dissent with error. Prelates and princes may have thought popular superstitions wrong, as does modern science, but the Christian authorities were nowhere near as much in charge as they wanted (others) to believe. This historical awareness must ground any approach to the issue of what was in medieval heads and what cultural processes may have connected medieval experience in nature through representation to programmes for medieval Europeans to work in the material world. One productive route is to identify how medieval people referred to their own surroundings.

A HOSTILE MATERIAL WORLD

During late antiquity and the early Middle Ages, clerical and popular thinking quite frequently intersected in two then-common sets of attitudes towards the natural world. In 1980 historian David Herlihy usefully labelled these as eschatological and adversarial. Both negative responses to nature were plainly on the minds of some late antique and early medieval people.

The eschatological attitude views nature in the context of the impending last days, which Christian teachings derived from the biblical book of Revelation, the Apocalypse. The mind set is inherently pessimistic about the entire material world, from the microcosm of individual human bodies to the macrocosm of all Creation. Christian writers from the fourth to the eighth century keyed in on God's curse upon humankind as Adam and Eve were driven from paradise. As Augustine put it: 'The accursed earth shall bring forth thorns and thistles for thee. Are you not ordained for sorrow and not for delights?' This earth is a place for humans not to enjoy but to suffer. Men were doomed to hard labour and women to the pains of childbirth. Some of the same writers opposed human procreation on grounds that the earth was full, replete with all the human souls God had ever wanted. There was awareness of moral corruption, of physical decline, and of this world's limits, material and temporal. As prophesied, all is proceeding inexorably towards the necessary last days, the end, an outcome already determined by the divine will and its imminence visible in every disastrous flood, fire, earthquake, or famine. Writing in 726, Pope Gregory II told the Anglo-Saxon missionary Boniface (Wilfrid), who then worked among the Frisians, not to flee deadly pestilence, for all was the will of God. God determines whether you will die or not; you cannot run away from your mission just because of an epidemic. All is God's will. Human beings are not responsible to or for this world. A better world is to come, also as set by divine will. At bottom, an eschatological attitude relegates human relations with the natural sphere to a matter of indifference, but attention to material things could dangerously distract the soul from what was more important.

Likewise late antique and early medieval writers often articulated an adversarial understanding of nature, a belief that it was not only worthless and unpleasant, but actively hostile to God and humankind. The first Christian ascetics, notably those associated with the first reputed Christian monk, Anthony of Egypt (c.250–350), fled civilization for the Egyptian desert because there, like Christ in his desert, the soul had to struggle with the demons that sought to capture it. One must do battle with powers that lurk out beyond human habitations. In the sixth century Martin of Braga, working with semi-Christianized Ibero-Romans and Swabians in what is now Portugal, reported peasants sacrificing to trees, rivers, and springs in order to placate the powers that resided there. When seventh-century wandering Irish ascetic Gall went into the Alpine foothills south of the Bodensee, he had to drive demonic otters from the pool beneath a waterfall. Turning to the vernacular, the originally pagan Anglo-Saxon myth in the epic *Beowulf* seems to derive from the sixth century, but survives only in a baptized version from the tenth, even possibly early eleventh century. There a monster from the desolate rocky hills looming over human landscapes, Grendel, a scion of Cain, the first human murderer, revenges himself on revelling humans, who had disturbed his subterranean slumber, by tearing them apart. The hero must kill Grendel and then his mother, an even more ferocious monster at home beneath the ominous surface of a cold lake. These creatures are things of nature. And at the end of his life Beowulf must again fight to the death with another great thing of nature, a dragon that attacked his people because one of them had violated its sanctuary. Plainly, powers dwell out there and those powers do not like humans. They dislike places where humans enjoy life; they want to destroy them and burn up those who dare to transgress. Thus, reports a contemporary, did demons in the air always torment the eighth-century monk Guthlac, who had established his hermitage on an islet in the depths of the (mosquito-ridden) Lincolnshire fens.

At a level less dramatic than *Beowulf*, the same fear of natural powers comes through an elementary textbook that a later Anglo-Saxon monk, Aelfric of Eynsham, composed around 1000 to teach small boys to read Latin. Its exercises provided social vignettes for translation into Anglo-Saxon. In one of these a fisherman is happy to fish in a river, but refuses to venture into the sea where there are monsters, whales that would swallow him and his little boat. A generation or so later still, Adam of Bremen emphasized the dangers of the sea endured by Rimbert, second archbishop of Hamburg-Bremen. Nature as a fearsome and hostile place is a theme strongly articulated in early medieval texts. Indeed a friendly or helpful nature was in this view nothing less than a miracle, as when St Cuthbert persuaded birds not to damage crops and otters warned him of coming danger.

Common among early writers, such negative views of the material world endured as strands within later medieval thought and teachings. A well-known literary motif, *contemptus mundi* ('contempt for this world'), which urged believers to fear and avoid the corrupt and evil world, could make a school exercise or little play. One thoroughly conventional example was composed at Paris in the 1180s by a student from southern Italy, Lothario de Segni, barely more than a decade before his background and training helped bring about his election as Pope Innocent III (1198–1216), a powerful and aggressive pontiff. A fatalist strain remained central to the ascetic tradition where the monk always withdraws from the world to what, picking up from the myth of St Anthony, is referred to as *deserta*, the desert, the wilderness, where the very harshness of nature enabled a strong soul to purify itself from human and social temptation. So when Burgundian abbot Robert of Molesmes decided in 1098 that his erstwhile monastery was insufficiently pure, he and three monks who accepted his leadership went out into a swamp called Cîteaux. From their settlement in the wetland waste grew the key monastic reform movement of the twelfth century, the white-robed Cistercians, whose putative ecological consciousness will call for further mention below. Not long before, St Bruno of Cologne (1030–1101) had likewise gone up into high and desolate mountains to establish Grand Chartreux, mother house of Carthusian hermits. But even at the far end of the Middle Ages the struggle between humans and nature still drives a vision poem by a Saxon humanist, Paul Schneevogel (Paulus Niavis, 1460/65–after 1514), who contemplated his native Erzgebirge, the 'ore mountains' today between Germany and the Czech Republic. That mining district appears as an arena of mutual wars of attrition between aggressive men who burrowed into the earth, destroyed woodlands, and befouled streams, and an earth that fought back, caving in the tunnels, poisoning the waters, and blighting harvests. This struggle against nature is, the poem concludes, the inescapable fate of humankind.

Adversarial relations between humans and nature are a continuing strand in medieval thought, very clear in the documentary record at certain points of time but also present in other times and other kinds of writings. But even as people considered going out into the wilderness to challenge their souls or to dig into the earth to wrest out needed materials, there is already more than a hint of instrumentality, a trace of the conception that nature has meaning because it serves human goals. Even hostile nature is there, to be understood for human purposes.

NATURE AS SIGN

A thoroughgoing instrumentality lies behind what is probably the best-documented view of the natural world in medieval and much of early modern European culture, the understanding of nature as sign. Even clearer upon reflection are the implications of so apprehending nature and things of nature – animals, plants, the planets, etc. – as counterparts, counterpoints, symbols, and signs *for* humankind. They are present to inform humans about God's will, to mark human identity, and/or to play off against humanness. So understood, however, nature and things of nature lack any intrinsic value of their own. They exist and matter only because humans can use these symbols or messages to make sense of divine and human affairs. At the level of literate culture, this paradigm of nature as sign began as theology. It spread during the course of the early and central Middle Ages into artistic, literary, and all other forms of cultural expression. It is a wide-ranging, perhaps distinctive, cultural feature of medieval civilization to treat things of the material world as signs of something else. Nature matters because it *means* something else.

In formal terms, Augustine of Hippo validated a Christian theory of signs in his 426 essay 'On Christian Doctrine', which he wrote to confront the problem of Christians reading the Old Testament, the Jewish Scriptures so full of perplexing, violent, and erotic tales. How were Christians to understand these as God's word? Augustine stepped back and asked what happens when one reads. The reader, he says, looks at words but those words stand for something else. Indeed, continues Augustine, words and all other material things always really stand for something else, something deeper, something more real. The symbol is not reality. For Augustine even history and nature are but markers of God's will and thus tools to help believers understand those other signs of God's will that are in Scripture.

A discourse in which what is said or seen is not what is meant is called allegory. A basic medieval cultural method uses allegory as the tool to learn what is meant in the words of Scripture, in other texts, and in the world of physical nature. So if roses are shown, the Virgin is meant; if Scriptures say the ancient Israelites fleeing captivity in Egypt followed divine command to seize the goods of the Egyptians, that means Christians may read classical secular literature, the learning of the pagans, and pluck the good from it without inevitably contaminating their Christian beliefs. And in all other matters, that which is seen or said is not what is meant; what is meant lies deeper but has greater reality. (Plato's influence on Augustine was strong.) This theory of signs underlay all subsequent medieval and Reformation biblical interpretation. It provided a method for theological understanding of secular literature and for understanding of the natural world. And it offered a schema for representing the natural world itself.

The consequence is that, in the words of twentieth-century cultural historian Ernst R. Curtius, 'medieval descriptions of nature are not meant to represent reality'. Not empirical information but meaning is there to be conveyed. Should such descriptions also portray some material aspect of nature, it is by accident. A prime example is the text called the 'Bestiary'. This compilation of stories presents the supposed characteristics of animals, plants, and stones as Christian allegories for moral and religious instruction. Its prototype, the Greek *Proslogion* from early Christian times, was translated into Latin between the fourth century and the sixth, possibly more than once. The Carolingian cultural revival inspired many manuscript copies and ensuing centuries yielded translations into all the European vernaculars. By the 1100s everyone who was the least bit literate or had been exposed to literate culture probably knew stories from the Bestiary. It achieved print as early as the 1480s.

Consider, then, one story from the Bestiary, that about the beaver, in Latin, *castor*. The animal's name, says the Bestiary, here following encyclopedist Isidore of Seville (d.636), comes from *castrando*, 'castrated', because the beaver is hunted for the musk contained in his testicles (actually in different internal glands). When, says the Bestiary, a beaver is hard pressed by a hunter, that beaver bites off his testicles, throws them at the hunter and, self-castrated, he escapes. When next pursued by a hunter this beaver lies on his back and points out that, lacking testicles, he lacks interest for the hunter. This means, says the Bestiary, that the beaver stands for prudence, taking measures in advance to avoid bad things in the future; it further represents the need to cut off inclinations to sin so that still more evil things do not happen. That is why the beaver is there. That is what the beaver is for. The fact of the matter is that the beaver's testicles do not descend outside the body and so when observed superficially it seems to have none. This 'fact', surely obvious to any who did hunt beaver for their musk, is not, however, what matters. Its 'factness' is now but a modern view to try to 'explain' the story. What the medieval beaver is for, however, is to convey a moral lesson, a meaning.

The Bestiary tale of the beaver illustrates not only the allegorical treatment of this natural object and the allegorical method of this widely disseminated text, but a whole broad medieval theory. The 'Book of Nature' (Latin *liber naturae, scientia creaturarum*, 'the knowledge of things created') is itself a metaphor. Everything is to be read in parallel with Scripture, so that just as Scripture is the book of God's word, so, too, is nature. Rightly read, nature teaches how to understand God's word and God's word teaches how to understand nature. The understanding is what matters; the meaning is what matters and thus is carried forward.

Orderic Vitalis (1075–c.1143), a Norman monk and historian, reported a great storm on 24 December 1117, which destroyed churches and towers and felled unnumbered oak trees. In a line of reasoning closely parallel to that of the Bestiary, Orderic saw this event as connected to an imminent human disaster, the contested papal election of 1118. He likewise reported the appearance of the Devil to a woman in childbirth as an example of the interconnectedness of the human and the cosmic. Indeed medieval writers betray some tension between seeing all nature as signs and only such deviations from the norm as Orderic observed and interpreted.

Medieval descriptions of nature can serve a further semiotic function by conveying the meaning that their composer was in command of traditional cultural knowledge. Among other techniques this could be accomplished through use of rhetorical figures called *topoi* (from the original Greek), little tropes that served to demonstrate the author's cultural skill. For instance, the ninth-century Irish scholar-poet Sedulius Scottus, who had left Ireland to spend most of his career in Liège (a solidly cool and clammy inland location later noted largely for coal mining), wrote a poem on spring. Spring has come, says Sedulius: the olive, vine, palm, and cedar are in bud. There are, however, no olive trees in Liège and never were. The most wishful

Roman colonist could not persuade an olive tree to grow outdoors in Liège. There are no palm trees either. There may have been some unhappy vines unprepared to bud at the start of a north European spring. Cedars, again, are unlikely. None of that mattered to Sedulius. His words instead show off his knowledge of how Virgil and other antique poets talked about spring and his own ability to do so too. That was what mattered. This is also why reading twelfth- and thirteenth-century romance literature in French, German, or English often soon reveals lions popping up in the middle of what is said to be northern France or Britain, for those writers, too, needed to tell a certain kind of story about wilderness and other things. It was not meant to represent reality as understood today.

Besides allegory serving as a means of understanding nature or showing off cultural knowledge, it also served as a way to send a message. In an article on the garden of Francis of Assisi, literary scholar Lisa Kiser explained how the author of Francis's *Life*, Thomas of Celano, described the garden and thereby conveyed the message that Francis fitted normal monastic expectations (see below). But at the same time, Kiser points out, Francis's garden was neither utilitarian nor privately enclosed: wide open and useless, it subtly critiqued the protocapitalist world of early thirteenth-century Italy in which Francis had grown up and against which he was, at least as portrayed in Thomas's work, reacting. Here, too, nature stands for something else; what is happening is a sign.

Beyond the world of pure allegory, of the recognizably coded programme, the same instrumental cultural attitude is manifest when people understand nature as the non-human, as the 'other', with the intent to contrast, critique, or justify human society. This reading of medieval texts is well known among present-day scholars, who so interpret the beast epics of Reynard the Fox and other characters, who are effectively humans in animal guise, and the judicial trials of actual beasts as both serving to demonstrate human dominance. Joyce Salisbury's *The Beast Within: Animals in the Middle Ages* takes a similar course, seeing in medieval portrayals of apes and other beasts a characteristic use of animals as foils to define or decentre humanity. Famous literary creations like the 'dawn songs' (*alba, aubade, Tagelied*) of love poets, Geoffery Chaucer's *The Parliament of Fowles* (1381), and both the wintry weather and hunted quarry (deer, boar, fox) in *Sir Gawain and the Green Knight*, plainly fit this mode. Worth speculation and investigation is the extent to which such cultural representations of the natural world depended on audience familiarity with the organisms in question or relied on such fictions as the self-castrating beaver.

With the exception of the trials of animals, which prosecuted domesticates and vermin, some significant proportion of the things of nature that appear in medieval literary and artistic representations were not animals or plants of everyday European experience. They are exotic: lions, acanthus leaves, pelicans, apes. They are imaginary: the basilisk, the griffin, the unicorn. They did not engage people's normal experience, for such was not the intent. Of course, even a well-educated, well-travelled medieval European was rarely in a position to draw the distinction just made between imaginary and exotic beasts. Consulting a present-day bird guide establishes the small likelihood that anyone west of Hungary ever saw a pelican, for in Europe they live only around the Black Sea and eastern Mediterranean. Nor did Europeans ever see a unicorn, though their princes and prelates held in their treasuries many examples of unicorn horn (now identified as narwhal tusks). The evidence was equivalent and so the boundary between the imaginary and the exotic thoroughly obscured. In a related and more important sense, if nature is a sign, that distinction matters not at all. What matters is the meaning being conveyed.

Medieval nature understood as sign confronts present-day environmental historians with a problem: at what point, if any, do these meaningful notions of the natural world actually intersect with materiality? When and how, if at all, do they arise from experience that is becoming representation? How, why, if at all, do these ideas serve to inform programmes for work? Or are the beaver, Sedulius's olive, and the basilisk objects that float about in the realm of cultural process without bearing on how medieval Europeans engaged with their surroundings? If so, this very large gap between medieval ideas and materiality must itself become a central and hitherto unexplored question for both environmental history and medieval studies.

PARTNERS: BENEFICENT *NATURA* AND HUMAN COLLABORATION

Without fully abandoning either the allegorical or the instrumental mode, a medieval attitude in some ways opposed to the ideas already examined held forth a collaborative and protective relationship between humans and a figurative *Natura*, conceived herself as the creation of a beneficent God and/or as a subordinated, allegorized expression of the Creator's powers. This way of thinking emerged in a highly teleological context, namely an understanding that the earth, nature, and whole of Creation were meant for humankind.

The concept of a benevolent nature with which humans cooperate was most explicitly articulated in cosmological speculation amongst some twelfth-century northern French clerics. These men worked in a time and region of active and successful social, economic, and institutional development. They are themselves associated with the revival of formal schools and learning with a strongly Platonic cultural flavour. They famously include William of Conches, Alan of Lille, Gilbert of La Porée, and Bernard Silvester. The last, writing in his mythico-scientific *Cosmographia*, had an allegorical *Natura* give form to all on earth. God created, but *Natura* formed it for the sake of humankind. Man (*homo*) is made, asserts *Natura* herself in the *Cosmographia*, 'high priest of Creation that he may subordinate all to himself, rule on earth, and govern the universe'.[1] That is a clearer medieval statement of Dominion than any Lynn White provided. Tracing its resonance in material action would much strengthen White's theory.

Bernard's friend Gilbert of La Porée similarly distinguished between God's initial Creation *ex nihilo* – for example, the cow – and the continued production of like from like – the cow that stands before you today and her milk – which arise from nature. But nature, too, says Gilbert, provides only the raw material for a third level of Creation, where humans take the things of nature and create from them distinct and useful objects. To continue the example, humans make leather shoes and cheese. The idea of cow was created by God from nothing, today's physical cow and milk created by nature, and the shoes and cheese created by humans. Thus the order of nature is autonomous; it is self-perpetuating. Humans participate in it, working in tandem with nature to continue God's original act of Creation.

Collaborative relations could take several forms. In Alan of Lille's 'The Complaint of Nature' allegorized *Natura* herself encourages men and women to use the 'hammers and anvils that I have given you' to

---

[1] *Cosmographia, Microcosmos*, chapter 10: *The Cosmographia of Bernardus Silvestris*, tr. W. Wetherbee, Records of Western Civilization (New York: Columbia University Press, 1973, 1990), 114.

multiply their kind. That programme was later reiterated in the thirteenth-century French literary allegory, the 'Romance of the Rose', where a king (also allegorical, of course) exhorts 'plough, for God's sakes, my barons, plough and restore your lineages'.[2] Going forth and multiplying was one way humans worked together with nature in support of God's plan. Then a century later, in similar, if no longer allegorical, vein, Burgundian soldier and diplomat Philippe de Mézières described the vast schools of herring in the Danish straits as 'the bounty of God towards Christian men', who caught from them the food for their Lenten fast.[3] For all the allegorical quality of these thought processes, representation of experience and programmes for work do begin to emerge in these writings.

This idea of a nature where humans cooperated to advance Creation could work in other directions, notably that of taming the wilderness. Traditional hermit saints had been shown living in harmony with wild beasts, but this relationship was always presented as a miracle. The spiritual power of the saint is evidenced by the bear coming to lie gently beside him. But the prototype for western communal monasticism, the *Rule* of Benedict of Nursia (*c.*480–*c.*540), obliged ascetics to work. That work was to be carried out in nature as a means of constructing the monastic environment itself, the cloister, the 'enclosed garden' (*hortus inclusus*). In theory, at least, the monks' labour made the walls within which they lived into a garden, and in making that garden they created a *paradisos*, not merely reminiscent of but replicating the enclosure of Genesis (though the word's root is Iranian). Now the ascetic in the desert not only struggled with the world and the flesh, but that effort created an enclosed and sacred space. This understanding, already present in the Benedictine rule, was made more explicit in its twelfth-century revival by Cistercians. A century thereafter still it recurred in the report of Francis's garden discussed above. Whether material or spiritual, however, these enclosed gardens were a cultivated 'second nature', not nature wild but nature changed, transformed, indeed 'colonized' (in terms of the

[2] Alan of Lille, *De planctu Naturae,* Prosa IV: *The Plaint of Nature,* tr. J.J. Sheridan. (Toronto: Pontifical Institute of Mediaeval Studies, 1980), 146, further on 155–6; Guillaume de Lorris and Jean de Meun, *Roman de la Rose, The Romance of the Rose,* tr. H.W. Robbins, ed. C.W. Dunn (New York: Dutton, 1962), chapter 91, line 160.
[3] Philippe de Mézières, *Le Songe d'un vieil pèlerin,* ed. G.W. Coopland, 2 vols. (Cambridge University Press, 1969), I: 129–30.

interaction model). The monastic approach does not involve a love of
the wild. It rather asserts that nature on its own is all *dis*order, so the
task of the humans is to bring it into order, bring it into conformity
with God's will, which is a will towards order presented as an anthropogenic landscape. Romance literature commonly plays off the same
distinction between the disorder of the forest, where strange events
and characters occur, and the ordered gardens of (conventionally)
King Arthur's court.

The resultant discourse bears simultaneously instrumental and allegorical qualities. Both the abbeys established under the Benedictine
rule in the Carolingian age and the new twelfth-century Cistercian
houses very quickly produced their requisite foundation legends.
Many such foundation myths related how monks went out into the
deserta, a 'wilderness' not necessarily of sand and rocks but possibly
dark and fearsome trees or oozing wetlands, to build their garden. But
in a surprisingly large number of specific instances, modern historians
and archaeologists have found that the site on which a monastery was
built had held prior human settlement. At Lubiąż in Poland, late
twelfth-century charters have the white monks settling beside villages
where they took on a religious role, but those monks' successors at the
start of the fourteenth century composed verses portraying the desolate wilderness into which the founders had come. Indeed in certain
cases (not Lubiąż) Cistercians removed peasants and destroyed villages
so that they could establish their monastery in a *deserta*, a place without
human society. The foundation of Rufford in Nottinghamshire in
1146 brought about the disappearance of four local peasant communities; similar removals took place in Wales and in the medieval
Empire. But also back in 744 Boniface and his disciple Sturm erected
Fulda on the site of a large hunting estate, not the glowering woods of
the legend. The desert is a myth, a myth essential to understand and
background the founding of a monastery. That is what it takes: ascetics
must seek out the desert. So critical historians must be very careful
with readers who take foundation legends as proof that medieval
monks did go off into howling wilderness because they held it to be
their mission to cultivate it, bring it to order, and care for it. The
mythic element is deeply present whenever literate cultured medieval
people wrote about their relationships with nature.

For all the great contrast between traditional monasticism and the
stance of Francis of Assisi (*c.*1182–1226), the latter's expressed love for
all Creation and what might best be called his borderline pantheism fit

him better within an authentic medieval representation of humans in a benevolent nature than they do to an anachronistic setting of present-day ecology and environmentalism. Having experienced a deep religious conversion, this son of an Italian cloth merchant inspired a movement of reform based on personal imitation of Christ's life, notably identified with poverty, preaching, and humility in a social, not a desert, setting. With regard to the natural world, tales passed on soon after Francis's death report his preaching to the birds and bringing a ravenous wolf into harmony with the people of Gubbio, a small town in the Apennines (although questions remain as to what fellow creatures the townspeople agreed to feed to the wolf to keep him a good neighbour). His 'Canticle of Brother Sun' (commonly mistranslated as 'Canticle of the Creatures', *Cantico della creature, Laudes creaturarum*) praises God for and in the names of the sun, moon, stars, wind, water, fire, earth (i.e. the four recognized physical elements), and finally 'our sister, carnal death'. All were for Francis 'God's created', meaning objects of God's Creation, and thus brothers, sisters, even mother (earth) to humans, whom Francis separated from nature less than did any of his contemporaries. In part this comprised an attack on the rival Cathars, whose dualist teachings denied all spiritual value in material Creation. Yet even the miracles attributed to Francis display a supernatural authority over animals not out of line with that of the early medieval hermits already mentioned.

Francis's call for spiritual and social transformation of the church and Christian society resonated strongly with his contemporaries, inspiring great changes in how religious institutions responded to the needs of newly urbanized communities. His sympathetic understanding of the natural world, however, has garnered far greater attention in much more recent times than it did in his own. Pending corrective research findings, it seems fair to say that no medievalist has discussed any medieval disciple of Francis who followed him down the path of an equality of all creatures, including humans, in the divine Creation.

In another perhaps surprising juxtaposition, expectations of human engagement with nature as hopeful as, but very different to, those of Francis underlay the development of Christian Aristotelianism and the rise of natural theology already mentioned in relation to the White thesis. Rediscovery of Aristotle's works by twelfth-century European intellectuals led to a gradual awareness that the 'book of nature' was not simply allegorical but offered a parallel way to understand God's will from his works. Rather than only reading nature as signifying mystical truths, the believer acknowledged that nature runs in definite ways because God had set it up to do so. As it was possible for humans to learn those natural routines, they came closer to fathoming the mind of God. These ideas were developed particularly by the two great Dominican Christian Aristotelians, Albert the Great (1193–1280) and his student Thomas of Aquino, called Aquinas (1225–74). Albert, Thomas, and their disciples sought a new Christian philosophy which would integrate Aristotelian methods and observations to reinforce traditional principles of Christian revelation and dogma. So doing, they argued, would recapture and reproduce the harmony and order of the divine plan. The divine plan is present in Scripture and in the world of Creation. Because the natural world and natural values have been created by God, there can be no inherent conflict between what humans experience in the natural world and what God wishes for humans to understand. For Thomas, humans and the rest of Creation are joined in a kind of intellectualized version of the great Chain of Being, the idea of a linkage from humans to animals, plants, and ultimately the most inert of material, stones. This entire created realm followed a natural order, a set of 'natural laws' laid down by the Creator. Thomas popularized a dichotomy of the natural and the supernatural, in part to distinguish between magic, which he saw as an illicit manipulation of nature's rules, and miracle, a work of God. More generally nature did follow some kind of predictable order while the supernatural was not so constrained. But humans are also set apart within the natural order because they alone possess souls and because God created them as such to complete and cap his Creation. Though the world of material Creation has its own legitimate value, the soul ascending towards God will leave it behind. In Dante's *Commedia* ('The Divine Comedy', 1320) this vision of the universe gained its poetic apotheosis.

The philosophical justification for this programme for examination of nature was importantly formulated by Thomas; Albert was more engaged in the scientific observations and compilations. Odd and interesting juxtapositions of the empirical and the culturally symbolic arise as Albert tries to make sense of what he thinks he knows about the natural world. Writing of the beaver in his *Historia animalium* ('[Natural] History of Animals'), for instance, he debunks the myth of self-castration, but further reports its habit of felling trees to build its den as well as the hazards of using beaver musk in medicine. When bad, it can kill the patient, but when good it helps a woman in childbirth. In his 'Book of Minerals' (*De mineralibus*) likewise Albert distinguishes his own observation ('I have seen . . .') of a sapphire with power to cure abscesses or help remove dirt from the eye, but qualifies: 'They say, too, that this stone makes a man chaste and cools internal heat, checks sweating, and cures headache and pain in the tongue . . . They say that it invigorates the body and brings about peaceful agreements and makes one pious and devoted to God, and confirms the mind in goodness.'[4] Elsewhere Albert refers to the belief that large flocks of vultures, eagles, or ravens predict human death and depopulation, and reports that credible witnesses observed many ravens around Rothenburg in Swabia just before the sudden demise of the local count. He continues, however, with the caveat: 'But to dispute over the wisdom and the conjectures of augurs is the business of another investigation.'[5]

In a slightly younger scholarly generation, the English-born Franciscan Roger Bacon (fl.1240s–1290s) sought in his *Opus maius* of 1267 to account for the observed diversity of natural phenomena in terms of universal physical principles. Once learned, he asserted, these explanatory principles would allow men to manipulate nature in their interest. Bacon envisaged superior Christian weaponry driving Muslims from Jerusalem, recently lost by crusaders. The friar was, however, well aware of the diversity and complexity of the natural world and admitted ultimate limits to human knowledge of it.

Also related to the concept of a nature with which humans can work, learn, and improve is the empirical bent of the Emperor Frederick II (1194–1250), called by contemporaries *Stupor mundi*, 'wonder of the world', for his boldness and curiosity. Frederick's deep interest and expertise in falconry is manifest in his book *De arte venandi cum avibus* ('On the Art of Hunting with Birds'). He there saw observation of falcons as informing about nature in general, as well as the birds in particular. Frederick apprehended nature also as a source or site of recreation and in that sense his book reflects another newly visible way of thinking about it relative to civilized humans.

---

[4] Albertus Magnus, *De mineralibus*, lib. II:ii, cap. 17, in his *Book of Minerals*, tr. D. Wickhoff (Oxford: Clarendon Press, 1967), 115–16.
[5] Albertus Magnus, *De animalibus*, lib. VIII, cap. 111, tr. by K. F. Kitchell jr and I. M. Resnick as *Albertus Magnus 'On Animals': A Medieval 'Summa Zoologica'*, 2 vols. Foundations of Natural History (Baltimore: Johns Hopkins University Press, 1999), I:717.

In sum, central medieval centuries did manifest examples of what social psychologists now call an 'individualist' attitude towards a benign, predictable, equilibrating nature with which humans can successfully cooperate. Some representations even seem to reflect experience in the natural realm. This approach on the part of professional clerical intellectuals was, however, hampered, if not entirely blighted, when ecclesiastical authorities at Paris formally condemned certain philosophical novelties in 1278. Among other positions declared erroneous was the separation between a realm of natural causes and a realm of supernatural causes. Further diversity in European ideas regarding nature could better develop at levels below such overarching theories.

VOICES OF EXPERIENCE

A wider range of empirical representations and programmes for the medieval natural world, at least as articulated in verbal sources, is especially associated with the more secular literate cultures that emerged among noble elites (where Frederick II also belongs) and urban merchants and professionals during the course of the twelfth and thirteenth centuries. Some of these used Latin, some the vernacular. Three exemplary areas of activity suggest how a more pragmatic attitude towards nature took shape.

First there is law, evolving in legislation and codifications but also works of legal theory and jurisprudence. Legal scholars were working on the revived Roman and codified canon law from 1100 onwards, and subsequently gave attention to the secular laws that were being compiled widely from the late twelfth century. Many situations of interest forced jurisprudence to confront problems which arose in the context of human interactions with the material world. Whatever the ultimate meaning of the natural sphere, lawyers and judges had to deal with its evident presence and its resistance to cultural dismissal. Such issues appear in the *Sachsenspiegel*, a codification of customary north German law completed in 1225. This treated how one determined and demonstrated a division of landed property, how to establish one parcel as this man's and a second as another's. It connected a person's taking possession of a natural object to human alteration of the natural condition. What served to distinguish one precise piece of nature from another? The answers could not be merely theoretical, but had to work in practice. One family of manuscripts even provided schematic illustrations of the trees, animals, and tools upon which legal claims bore.

Other ideas emerged on the legal side in case books by the important Roman law commentator Bartolus of Sassoferrato (1314–57), a law professor and jurist in Italy, who wrote treatises on, for instance, how to distinguish the boundary between day and night. Sometimes the law made it matter greatly if a given crime had taken place at night rather than during the daytime. How, similarly, is the division set when a contract requires certain work – the maintenance of a sharecropper's fields – to be completed within a particular season? In another treatise Bartolus considered how a wild animal becomes the property of its captor. But then what if he loses it again and someone else catches it? Had this animal become wild between times and therefore do the same rules apply or are some others now appropriate? How are property lines and jurisdictions to be established along a watercourse which changes from year to year? Who can claim priority rights to the water between the miller needing power, the boatman needing passage, the person who wants to drain his land, another who wants to irrigate his, and the man who wants to use the water to brew beer? These are all real problems of people engaging with natural phenomena and demanding cultural solutions. Chapter 7 will investigate more fully the interplay of lordship, possession, rights of use, and authority to limit uses as legal parameters for medieval decisions about natural resources.

A parallel trend emerged in the medical sphere. Medieval medicine inherited the classical theory of humours, the concept of interplay among four elements of air, fire, earth, and water, and their application as qualities to human beings. Medical writers produced treatises on human nutrition, dietary advice, food handling, human health, and the treatment of human health problems. With self-conscious care medieval physicians observed natural phenomena and then attempted to explain what they had seen. Such a course of action is now called science. That medieval efforts at explanations use a theory now thought silly misses the point, which is rather that they were seeking to make systematic sense of the world of nature. At scales from the personal to the planetary, humoural theory sustained programmes for the treatment of sick people, design of diets, and official responses to epidemics. Clear perceptual models structure action in the natural sphere.

A final array of exemplary empirical approaches is to be found in a whole genre of written texts: practical manuals on gardening, estate management, surveying, hunting, and other such everyday activities. For instance, Pietro de'Crescenzi, a Bolognese jurist, professional city manager, and landowner, in 1307/9 wrote for the king of Naples a

work called *Ruralia commoda*. There Pietro compiled information
from the Roman agronomists and from his own contemporary experience, treating such topics as soil testing, management of nut trees,
land drainage, apiculture, curing sick sheep, and so on. The issues
were mundane and the methods combined book learning and practical knowledge.

At the end of the fourteenth century there is the *Livre de la Chasse*
('Book of the Hunt') by Gaston Phoebus (1331–91), count of Foix, a
principality in the Pyrenees. Gaston offers specific practical instructions on how to hunt thirteen varieties of animals in various different
ways (*not* including the self-castrating beaver). He treats their biology,
their habits, and their behaviour, then goes into an elaborate discussion of how to rear, train, and care for different kinds of hunting dogs.
Himself a hunter of great renown, Gaston was also a fiercely powerful
noble lord with interesting feuds, family conflicts, and other political
issues. He wrote about what he knew and turned his experience into
instructions for others. Information on medieval resource use from
writers like de'Crescenzi and the count of Foix will be of use in the
following chapters.

Ideas of the natural world in these and other kinds of pragmatic late
medieval writings operate at a more restricted, more goal-oriented
scale than do the overarching philosophical and theological concepts
explored earlier in this chapter. In these contexts human separation
from nature and dominion over things of nature are perhaps implicit,
capable of being inferred but not held essential to the purposes being
pursued. While more empirical than the earlier norm, they remained
instrumental. Knowledge about nature permitted humans to use
things of nature more effectively for human purposes. These works
also, however, reflect an autonomous nature, a realm that followed its
own principles. Humans are here capable of knowing and predicting
the natural processes, and therefore humans are capable of turning
their knowledge into programmes and action in the natural world.
Unclear in them is how much, if any, sense of the fragility of nature
might be included.

SUMMATION: HEGEMONIES, DIVERSITIES, AND THE GAP BETWEEN MEDIEVAL IDEAS AND ACTION

To be sure, medieval western Christendom possessed a hegemonic
culture rooted in the literate elite's understanding of Christian

doctrine, of a created universe, and of a human obligation to learn and follow divine will. That likely encompasses the most important aspects of fundamental Christian thinking that are to be detected in or behind almost any medieval text. But the theoretical truths and precepts of a hegemonic Christianity are not necessarily the specific context for particular human understandings and actions in the material world. A critical student of history cannot leap from reading Scripture or a theological *Summa* to explaining how medieval Europeans behaved in their dealings with nature. This is especially the case in view of the evident diversity of ideas that lay beneath the surface of a hegemonic Christian orthodoxy.

This diversity is here suggested to have arisen in the first place from a bifurcation between elite literate culture and illiterate popular cultures. For the literate group, Christianity was a religion of the book; its Scripture and traditions held ultimate truth and the means of establishing it. Elite literate culture also lent huge prestige to antique learning, to the use of the Latin language and all its accoutrements. All of this is to be contrasted with the patterns of illiterate popular cultures that were rooted in people's immediate experiences of the world around them and traditional understandings of spirits and the other non-human entities that surrounded them. Such entities and understandings were sometimes susceptible to being Christianized, but they were certainly not Christian in origin and people using them likely thought more about power than about belief. The diversity beneath the surface of hegemonic medieval Christendom further arose from purely cultural evolutions over the millennium of medieval experience. The world of Augustine and his contemporaries living through socio-political collapse, for instance, was a very different place for thought and experience from that of twelfth-century Platonists and their contemporaries who composed courtly lyrics and romance. Many similarities joined the Platonists and the romance writers, but they also had quite significant differences, even though both operated in elite culture at the same time. Move forward in time to Francis of Assisi and the Christian Aristotelians and it is clear how even the dominant cultural elements concealed diverse strains and strands linking people differently to the world around them. The halting Christianization of orally transmitted popular representations remains to be mapped out.

So to what extent was the medieval gap between, on the one hand, evident human experience and work in the realm of natural causality and, on the other hand, recorded thought about nature and the natural world wider than occurs in other cultures? Reading canonical medieval texts lends that impression. Most explicit writing about nature in the Middle Ages, both then and now, bears no relation to actions. Few scholars who in the most recent two centuries have sought intently to study ideas of nature in the Middle Ages have looked beyond the literary and theological sources, texts which already rest some cultural distance from where people actually experience the natural sphere. What has not been undertaken is serious expert investigation of those genres and substantive themes like medicine, law, or the instructional manuals that did confront and manipulate nature in a hands-on setting. Three alternative explanations thus remain. The apparent gap could be real; medieval behaviour and medieval thinking with respect to nature were to a large extent two different, disconnected things. The gap could itself be a cultural artefact of medieval origin, an illusion arising from medieval writers failing to treat subjects in which their literate culture lacked interest, which does not mean these matters were absent from society. Or, thirdly, the visible gap may be a modern artefact, a consequence of the fact that present-day medievalists, though interdisciplinary in their work, focus on certain kinds of topics and pay little attention to others. In any case, a research agenda for medieval studies should be clear.

As succeeding chapters examine land use, agroecosystems, woodlands, aquatic resources, animals, energy, and urbanism in medieval Europe, the puzzle will recur. What intentions, what assumptions, may have informed the easily demonstrated problems and efforts of medieval people active in the natural world? They certainly did things there; they certainly experienced things there; their experiences and actions in nature affected their lives and subsequent histories. The question that keeps resurfacing is how historians can get at the ideas that medieval Europeans used to make sense of what was happening around them and to support the actions they undertook.

MEDIEVAL LAND USE AND THE
FORMATION OF TRADITIONAL
EUROPEAN LANDSCAPES

•

When medieval Europeans chose how to use land they set physical parameters for their own interactions with the natural world and created the recognizably traditional landscapes of Europe. Landscapes of medieval Europe differed from those of classical or barbarian times, but established the foundation or model for much of what may still be seen across most of the subcontinent. From the late antique discontinuity examined in chapter 2 came seminal shifts in how people lived on and made use of the land.

Most, not all, modern landscapes in Europe derived from medieval ones. The countrysides now visible in Tuscany, on the north German plain, or in Ireland were largely formed during the Middle Ages as a result of how people on the land, *in Natura*, made use of their surroundings. On top of natural 'endowments', landscapes were in the Middle Ages shaped (as are their present-day counterparts) by the productive practices and physical structures of human beings' cultural heritage. In consequence, over time most landscapes become layered. The term 'palimpsest' likens the land to those valued pieces of medieval parchment on which someone wrote one text, another scribe erased it, and then wrote a second, while leaving the first still detectable by a careful observer. Over large areas of Europe a trained eye sees what came before, even though exactly how those surviving traces once fitted into a larger pattern may be grasped only from often rare local texts or fieldwork.

As used in environmental history the term 'landscape' drifts ambiguously across three semantic fields. It refers in geographical terms to an area or tract of land with its distinguishing visual characteristics: Tuscany with its hill towns and vineyards or low and flat Holland where clouds race across a huge sky. Ecologists, however, think of a landscape as an assemblage of ecosystems in mutual interaction, less densely than occurs within each individual ecosystem but more than with more distant ones. A grain field, woodland, and pond, for instance, though each containing intense exchanges among living and non-living things, also have flows of energy and materials between them (as when a frog eats a mosquito and is itself eaten by a heron, which nests in a tree, whence the bird's wastes run off into the field . . .). Thirdly, landscape is conceived in cultural terms, referring to people's experience of their physical world, how they define and assess their surroundings. Medieval apprehensions of landscape are, of course, commonly now obscured by the cultural conditions just discussed in chapter 3, notably the problem of reaching attitudes and feelings through barriers of selective literacy and cultural purposes. Whichever meaning best applies in any given historical situation, historically formative landscapes did result from medieval Europeans exploiting their land. And land use in this agrarian society most importantly derived from basic understandings of how land could produce food and other culturally defined necessities.

Hence this chapter starts with how the food needs and preferences of medieval Europeans strongly shaped their land use. It proceeds from growing, even extreme, demand for cereal grains to a massive medieval transformation of landscapes through general woodland clearances, arable intensification, and the construction of new drained or irrigated landscapes in certain parts of Europe. More directly cultural grounds for changing land use also had regional, local, or other defined effects. Following this extended discussion of Europe as a place where anthropogenic landscapes were formed in the Middle Ages, the chapter identifies immediate environmental consequences of these human actions. While colonizing European landscapes to meet culturally defined wants, medieval people both created distinctive new ecosystems and semi-consciously destabilized relationships between large natural systems.

BREAD AND MEAT, POWER AND NUMBERS

What people eat determines very importantly how they use land, but what people eat itself derives as much from cultural expectations as from physiological needs. In an agricultural society diet is the main driver of land use, but the intermediary between diet and land use is power, whether that power comes from a legal or coercive authority or from the sheer force of numbers of individuals who may be relatively powerless taken one at a time. People exercising either the power of numbers or that of legitimate or illegitimate coercion determined land use and thus constructed their landscapes. In medieval Mediterranean and northern Europe, elites and peasants ate differently. They imposed different demands on food production systems, resulting in large changes, important commonalities, and great diversity in European landscapes.

A good first approach considers whether people eat bread and meat or not. Northern living called for more energy than living along the Mediterranean, and northern cultures were distinctly more carnivorous than were Mediterranean cultures. But from the early to the central Middle Ages, the choice of bread and meat was more a matter of wealth and status than simply where a person lived, what they could afford, and what was needed for nutritional purposes. Elites wanted meat and elites wanted white bread. Hence the French word *blé* (Latin *bladum*) means 'bread grain', not cereals in general, just grain for bread, specifically 'wheat'. (Although in fact it commonly included rye, which also produces a dough that rises.)

Bread not porridge: bread was what civilized Romans ate. To early medieval elites bread was an essential sign of being civilized. Wheat or rye bread had been established in late antique Italy as the only suitable element for the Eucharist and thus essential for Christian life. So, too, was bread generally acknowledged the best vegetable food for humans. Late antique physicians, Arab physicians, and subsequently medieval Christian medical authorities affirmed this ranking. The prevailing theory of humours defined bread grain as the only cereal both warm and moist. (Other grains were either cool and moist or warm and dry.) Humoral theory also held the human body to be warm and moist, so a person who consumed a warm and moist cereal properly nourished the body. If one would build up a human body and its vital blood, one ate bread if one could. It was superior food. On these mixed cultural grounds, often unvoiced, bread and bread grains were actively promoted and explicitly demanded by Carolingian authorities already in the eighth century, long before any manifest subsistence needs called for large numbers of people to live on the relatively cheap calories that can be produced by growing and eating cereals.

Peasants ate cereals, too, and collectively in vast quantities, but not so much bread. Peasants ate porridge (gruel) and peasants drank ale (beer). Peasant cereals went into these more fluid forms. Their cereals were more commonly barley, oats, millet, spelt, and other such grains. *Blé* they raised, particularly in western Europe, to provide what their lords wanted and demanded from them. But cereals still provided the cheapest calories; raising cereals supported more consumers at the subsistence level. Hence there was an elite cultural thrust towards cereal production and there was a growing mass cultural, actually nutritional, thrust for cereal production to meet the needs of lesser folk.

By around 1200 inhabitants of central Europe were obtaining from grain twice the portion of their calories as had their early medieval ancestors. The trend of late antiquity reversed as consumption and production had already moved away from meat, livestock, and pastoralism by the late eighth century, continuing into the thirteenth and fourteenth. The cereal-based diets of 1200 supported more than twice as many people, too. Between 800 and 1300 the population of Europe almost tripled, from about 25 million to something more than 70 million (Figure 4.1). The overall population increase, which was underway in certain areas by 800, becomes generally visible to historians by around 1000, and continued into the 1300s. This is a fundamental condition for understanding the relationships between humans and their natural surroundings that can be encountered during the Middle Ages.

Culture and nutrition together propelled what is generally acknowledged among historians all across western and central Europe as a trend of 'cerealization', with cereal grains gaining a larger role in the diet and in the agrarian regime. As earlier noted, this had set in by the Carolingian age and continued into the fourteenth century, so Europeans eventually consumed more than five times the grain they had five centuries before. The move towards grain eating called for greater emphasis on arable in the agricultural sector. More land was put to the plough. The large scale of this trend can be seen, for instance, in pollen profiles from southern France, which show four hundred years of ever-rising proportions of cereal pollens and those of weeds from grain fields. Similar trends are found on English Anglo-Saxon sites and almost anywhere pollen material can be recovered from regions with relatively flat or rolling land.

Peasant farmers tended nevertheless to retain large pastures because they were obliged to provide so much grain to their lords that they lacked further surplus to feed livestock. As livestock energies and

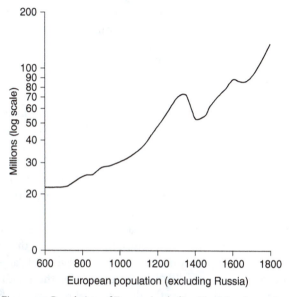
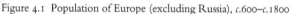

Figure 4.1 Population of Europe (excluding Russia), *c*.600–*c*.1800

excrements provided essential inputs to the peasant production system, peasant communities were desperate to keep land for their animals to graze. What kind of pasture that was and how it was used is an issue to explore below. So not absolutely everything was turned into grain fields. People may have wished to do so but there were limits.

Elites who kept their carnivorous habits provided another force countervailing cerealization. They notably retained a gourmand's delight in flesh from the tastiest, fattiest, juiciest young animals. Distinctive elite eating habits are sharply displayed at what is now Olargues-le-vieux in Dep. Herault, where around the year 1000 a peasant community lived among the barely visible remains of a one-time Roman villa, while not 200 metres away a group of warrior knights lorded over them from atop the local hill. Animal remains recovered from village middens came largely from old goats and sheep, that is beasts kept for their milk and wool until the end of their productive lives. In so far as peasants consumed meat at all, they had stringy mutton. Up on the hill, however, the knights tossed on their rubbish heap bones of pig and lamb, having eaten the flesh of small, tender sheep that never lived to become old and tough and the good juicy meat from hogs with no use except for food.

That distinction between elites eating fatty young animals and peasants occasionally chewing bits from tough old ones is replicated in evidence from southern and northern France, Flanders, England, and Lombardy. It is so generally typical that one Flemish archaeologist, Anton Ervynck, has referred to the noble elite of the central Middle Ages as 'top predators', for they ate only the very best animals and lots of them. That consumption pattern meant men of power were interested in continued production of certain kinds of animals, which also thus shaped management of land and configured the landscape.

Assertion of elite interests in specific foods can also be recognized as driving changes in land use and peasant agricultural operations. The Vallès Oriental north of Barcelona was in the tenth century domi-nated by free independent peasant farmers, who practised a variety of agropastoral activities and consumed a diverse diet of plant and animal products, cereal grains and other foods. In the course of the eleventh and twelfth centuries warriors achieved power over Catalan society. Some historians call this a 'feudal revolution', for the knights, pro-fessional fighters, took over to the detriment of the farmers. Peasants lost lands to the new lords. A new elite-centred spatial structure pulled peasants, willingly or not, to the forts where the militarily dominant group lived. Peasants now paid rents for the lands they worked and dues for certain activities. By the twelfth century the elite diet in this valley featured heavy consumption of protein and fat, mainly meat (especially pork) and white bread made out of wheat. It was a way to display status: the man who mattered showed off on his table a tender pork joint and white bread to sop up the juices. Requirements to produce that diet were then imposed upon the peasants, forcing them to focus on cereal culture so as to provide the *bladum*. Farmers were pressed towards reduced diversity in their own production and hence in their own diets. Their agricultural system became more susceptible to crop failure and their diets simultaneously degraded.

The historic connection is established: what people decide they want to eat, the power they have to obtain what they want, and the effect on land use of the enforced decisions shape the encounter of humans and nature in an agrarian society. Bread and meat, power and numbers, together drove medieval transformation of European land-scapes. As a result of demand pressure, that is humans expending resources to meet their wants and needs, landscapes were reconfigured all across medieval Europe. The largest single form of such trans-formation, arguably the biggest single human force on the medieval environment, was a large-scale process of clearance and intensification in agriculture that was primarily oriented towards the production of cereals. With deep and prescient insight an Anglo-Saxon riddler named the ploughman 'the grey foe of the wood' (*har holtes feond*).[1]

Most of what follows examines the process: first the great clearance of the woodlands of northern Europe, then the parallel intensification of cereal production on Mediterranean landscapes earlier and differently transformed in ancient times and under distinctive physical conditions. Additionally, drainage of wetlands in both north and south served to create more land to plough for cereals. All these material developments corresponded with normative cultural disparagement of people who did not focus on cereal production and thus know proper civilized behaviour. All such cultural and material construction of landscapes involved an interplay of lords' power and peasants' work while creating micro-ecologies all across Europe. Worth further recognition are two smaller and distinct but parallel innovations: creation of irrigated landscapes in Mediterranean Europe under the impetus of an 'Arab green revolution' less preoccupied with cereals; and the reworking of certain local landscapes less for immediate material ends than for public display of personal or institutional power. Expectations of religious practice played an independent role, too. The chapter concludes by considering all forms of medieval landscape change from a more explicitly ecological standpoint.

MEDIEVAL LANDSCAPES TRANSFORMED: THE GREAT
CLEARANCES

Landscapes of northern Europe were transformed during the course of the central and high Middle Ages. What had been mostly covered with multi-use woodland (Map 4.1), including parcels that were for short periods of time used as farmland and then left to go back to woods, then became permanent arable. Simultaneously human settlement patterns shifted from the small and transitory hamlets typical of the early Middle Ages to large and stable villages. Most of those medieval villages survive in or under modern-day settlements across northern Europe.

---

[1] The Exeter Book, Riddle 21: *The Exeter Book*, edited by G. P. Krapp and E. V. K. Dobbie, *The Anglo Saxon Poetic Records, a Collective Edition*, vol. III (New York: Columbia University Press, 1936), 191.

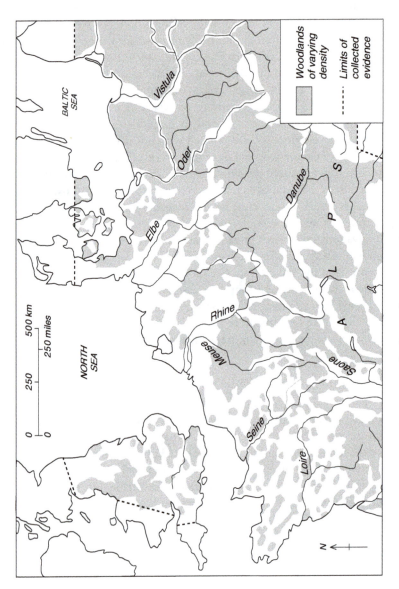

Map 4.1 Woodland in tenth-century northwestern Europe

The process of clearance was no simple matter of cutting trees. Taking down trees to use the wood had been, as already remarked, normal practice since the Neolithic. Medieval clearances were not attacks on pristine wilderness in the North American mythic sense. They rather involved what the English, borrowing from the French, called 'assarting', meaning people grubbed trees and shrubs out of the soil, pulled them up by the roots, ripped them from the ground so they could put a plough into that ground. One cannot plough where one has just cut down trees. Roots and stumps will break the plough and then grow back into a woodland. Even with the help of fire, medieval people had to tear the trees out one at a time by muscle power, open the soil surface for plough agriculture, and convert the land from woodland to arable fields.

Examples from across the North European plain and central uplands illustrate what happened. Clearances were well under way in Anglo-Saxon England long before the Norman conquest of 1066. King William's Domesday survey conducted in 1086 found England only 15 per cent wooded, a figure some modern writers argue indicates prior loss of a half to two-thirds of the country's early medieval tree cover. The Domesday record for the county of Middlesex surrounding London shows little woodland in the southern part of the county, where the oldest Anglo-Saxon place names were concentrated on light gravelly soils which had been the first to be farmed. But the north of the county had been opened up in a second phase. Places with names derived from 'wood', 'tree' or similar elements occur there on heavy clay soils that were cleared later and more slowly. Much late eleventh-century woodland still provided seasonal pasture for pigs. Continued clearance took England to barely 6 per cent wooded by 1348, a decline of 60 per cent since Domesday. During those two and a half high medieval centuries English men, women, and draught animals removed the tree cover from nearly twelve thousand square kilometres.

The record elsewhere is more impressionistic. The 55 million hectare territory of modern France (not, of course, its medieval boundaries) around the time of Charlemagne included something in the range of 30 million hectares of woodland, but by the time of King Philip IV (1285–1314) only around 13 million. Over those five centuries, the wooded cover shrank by more than half (56 per cent). Further east, where the Fulda and Werra rivers join to form the Weser (at the medieval town now called Hannoversche Münden), the historic boundary between Franks and Saxons ran along the northern edge of the uplands. Around 500 the surrounding area was almost entirely wooded, much relatively light after long and extensive use by barbarian peoples but with denser woods covering higher ground. By *c.*1290, however, most of the woodland had given way to arable and human use had thinned out all that remained. A final estimate comes from Poland: the roughly 16 per cent of the terrain now in that country under the plough in 1000 had risen to 30 per cent by 1540, approximately a doubling of the agricultural land use.

Arable increased and woodland shrank all across the north European plain, all around its margins, and up the valleys into the uplands, Alps, and Pyrenees. In a half-millennium wave of assarting, Europeans tore out the trees and set in their place permanent farmland around permanent village settlements.

Medieval transformation of northern landscapes was accomplished in important part through the diffusion of improved agricultural equipment and techniques oriented to the production of cereals on heavy damp soils. Unlike the Mediterranean, northern Europe and especially its more westerly maritime regions enjoyed year-round moisture and relatively heavy soils, which needed care for successful agricultural use. Three technical innovations helped medieval farmers lay bare the heavy soils and put them to the culture of cereals.

The tool here called the heavy mouldboard plough had been known in the north probably for some time before the central Middle Ages, but had been used only in very local circumstances. It now spread through most of the area. Figure 4.2 illustrates common and some variant attributes of this technology. Essential operational features include handles for steering and a beam on which are mounted a vertical knife (coulter) and horizontal wedge-shaped 'share'. These commonly metal blades together cut a slice from the soil. An angled or curved mouldboard (literally 'soil board') follows to turn that slice over. The Alsatian picture (Fig. 4.2a) almost buries the working parts in the soil being tilled; the Saxon plough (Fig. 4.2b) is depicted as on display in a judicial hearing, but also with the furrows it turns. A wheeled forecarriage eases handling in certain circumstances and was a common regional adaptation, but is not the defining element of the tool's function.

The heavy mouldboard plough does not just crumble the soil surface as does the light Mediterranean plough (ard), but digs into the ground, picks up the soil, and turns it over. This action helps drain wet soils and

(a) Fol.112ᵛ

(b)

andren mannes lant vn
eme en ander ghe dan her
ume ghe schudeghet de w
arebeyt uerluset he dar e
ne le halt. weit eme au l

Figure 4.2 A heavy mouldboard plough and draught team as represented in: (a) Abbess Herrad of Landsberg (Alsace), *Hortus deliciarum* (1176/96) (nineteenth-century tracing of destroyed original); (b) an early fourteenth-century illuminated manuscript of the north German *Sachsenspiegel* law code

further lifts the soluble plant nutrients that humid northern conditions leach downwards, returning them to the surface where they can be reached by the relatively shallow roots of annual grasses (i.e. cereal grains). At the same time, by turning a furrow the ploughman was able to control drainage in the field, guiding surface water in a preferred direction or off the field entirely. Especially on heavy soils all of this is much more easily achieved with the heavy mouldboard plough.

The heavy plough had, however, technical, hence economic and environmental, implications. As compared with a lighter tool it called for a stronger draught team: the ploughman had to put more oxen into pulling it and therefore had to have a larger herd or to pool his oxen with those of another. The twelfth-century drawing from Alsace (Fig. 4.2a) shows a single pair of oxen yoked by the horns, a regional variant seemingly as effective as the more familiar neck yoke. Yet limited space may have constrained this artist, for while one pair was sometimes strong enough, more pairs would pull better. However keeping more animals required more fodder to maintain them. There was always tension: more land to plough meant more animals to pull and feed.

Another way to obtain more draught power was to use a more powerful animal, the horse, as appears in the Saxon manuscript. In using horses for heavy draught, however, the yoke suited to oxen did not serve. The horse's different anatomy required a device called a horse collar and a special harness to allow the animal to exert its strength. (The iconography of *Sachsenspiegel* omits the former and shows the latter but roughly.) Still the stronger and faster beast had a countervailing disadvantage, expensive fuel. Oxen will work on a diet of grass; horses will not. Hard-working horses need specialized fodder and that means cereal grains. Horses eat the same things as humans; the medieval farmer who employed them had to produce more grains for their feed as well as for his family and his lord. As an additional drawback, the horse was a special-purpose animal. Just as the pig provided only food, a medieval European horse provided only draught and riding. Europeans did not eat horses, or at least ate very little horse meat after the eighth century, when Christian authorities moved against behaviour they associated with the cult of Wotan (Oðin), chief of the Germanic pagan gods and a favourite of warriors and princes. From the point of view of agriculturalists, then, horses were good only for pulling things, and a farmer would need much interest in draught power before giving up on oxen which, when incapable of pulling, could become a meal.

Soil types and drainage influenced the value to be placed on strength and speed in tillage and the availability of pasture and hay meadows determined the ease of obtaining fodder. In consequence the choice between horse and ox was rarely as simple as some later historians have portrayed, the history of animal draught no unilinear development, and the long-term result a fluid regional patchwork of agricultural power sources which lasted into the modern age.

The need for additional fodder could be met through a third technical innovation with great power to shape the landscape. This was the practice of arable management best labelled the 'three-course rotation' (employable on any number of fields). Mediterranean agriculture typically adapted to the region's perennial shortage of water by farming a parcel one year and then resting it the next, using the fallow to gather two years of water for the next crop of winter grain. The north had a wetter climate and heavier soils; water shortage was not the critical factor. Northern soils can grow grain two years out of three, carrying winter grain for a year, harvesting in early summer, leaving the stubble on the land until the following spring, then ploughing and planting spring grains which will be harvested later in summer or early autumn, and then resting the land for a year while ploughing the fallow to deal with weeds and leached nutrients. Hence northern practice could move from the two-course alternation between winter grain and fallow to a three-course rotation of winter grain–spring grain–fallow on any given piece of land. It meant the land produced two years in three rather than one in two, raising overall output by a sixth (17 per cent) by cultivating annually two-thirds rather than half of the arable.

The spring grains were particularly oats and barley. Barley was the main ingredient for porridge and for beer, in the Middle Ages essentially a somewhat more liquid porridge with fairly low alcohol content fermented in it. While calories were lost in fermentation, brewing made good use of stored grain. Barley, and oats, too, can feed horses as well as humans, though neither made genuine bread. But making a three-course rotation work requires year-round moisture; it cannot operate under normal Mediterranean conditions where the summer drought kills spring-sown crops.

The innovations improved adaptation to northern production conditions. People were adjusting more knowledgeably to the world in which they lived, gaining more grain while retaining pasture, too. Both during the fourteen months or so of the fallow year and the seven or eight between harvest of the winter grain and the next spring's sowing, animals could go on the field to eat weeds and stubble and to drop their manure. The system incorporated pasture into the permanent arable. This, too, seems to be advantageous on heavy soils where moisture is available year round.

Hence under the right conditions of climate, topography, and soil, the whole arrangement produced more crops per hectare per year than did the two-course rotation or had the older infield–outfield regimen mainly used on light soils. But the new regime was a great deal more *work*. It required more work from the draught animals and more work from the humans. People would have to work more months of the year, more weeks of the month, and more days of the week to make this system produce. Why would a peasant want to do that? What motivated the agricultural clearances and transformation of European landscapes?

The answer is that medieval peasants came under pressure. Pressure came from subsistence needs: growing families that embodied the rising European population had to have more calories to feed everyone. Pressure came because lords could coerce peasants, could demand crops or labour of them, and enforce those demands through the threat and exercise of violence. But peasants could also determine to work harder on positive grounds, the wish to operate more land and produce more crops, particularly if some local markets might be accessible. If a larger output generated a surplus of cereals in particular, they could exchange the surplus for other desired goods that were not easily produced on a subsistence farm. So the innovations were more work for peasants and they undertook that work, possibly under subsistence pressure, possibly for positive motivation, but surely in many instances also and perhaps mainly under pressure from their lords.

The pressure that lords might exert itself varied with what the lord sought to gain. A lord wishing to increase his own cereal production by putting more labour on his demesne pushed peasants in one direction. If the lord wanted rather to obtain more cereals without providing more supervision, the push was for peasants to produce grain rents, preferably wheat and not barley. In other circumstances a lord with much land that was not being used very much might have been more interested in getting somebody to work it and provide him with some kind of income. A lord's decision to extract more labour, or more bread, or just any additional income strongly influenced the kinds of pressures lords put on peasants and thus how the process of clearance and intensification took place and relevant institutional structures took shape. The result was different landscape adaptations depending on local soils, on what local lords were demanding, and on regional social, political, and economic conditions, all across the vast area where over four to five centuries medieval Europeans cleared woodland and created grain fields in its place.

Two extended examples from opposite ends of northern Europe will help highlight commonalities, diversities, and driving forces in the great medieval clearances. The first comes from Anglo-Saxon England, the second from central Silesia, westernmost of the historic and present-day Polish lands.

Tom Williamson has recently summarized and transcended generations of debate over the agricultural landscapes of southeastern England. The clearance process there got underway during the eighth century and was winding down by the time of Domesday in the late eleventh century. Further north and west in England woodland was still being actively converted to arable in the early to mid-1200s, but this story is more of the central Middle Ages than of the high Middle Ages. Partly because of the rich documentation available and partly from long and attentive fieldwork, scholars see the process as resulting in two generic landscape types. Comparable large-scale clearance and intensification of peasant labour under lords' pressure there formed local variants on what are now called 'champion' and 'woodland' or 'ancient countryside'.

'Champion' (from the French *champagne*, open country) is a big open landscape with great expanses of fields and few groves or even individual trees, still visible at large scale as illustrated in Figure 4.3. The fields now seen resulted from eighteenth-and nineteenth-century enclosure. Medieval field blocks were rather subdivided into multiple strips, each belonging to a village farm, but the overall aspect of openness is very much the same. Champion country emphasized open-field agriculture in the medieval and early modern period. The predominantly large settlement nuclei (i.e. big villages) possessed large field systems, relatively little woodland or pasture, but a good supply of hay meadows. The need to feed draught animals made reciprocity between rough pasture and hay meadows an essential, even controlling parameter. Either places too damp to plough could grow good grass to preserve as hay, or some land had to be set aside for grazing. Champion was a landscape meant to facilitate gang work by peasants for the lord, but also where peasants together engaged communally in the ploughing, the harvesting, and the pasturing of livestock on the arable, though each strip belonged to an individual farmer. Heavy clay soils called for large and powerful plough teams able to seize brief moments when soil moisture would neither bog the

Figure 4.3 A 'champion' landscape in southeastern England

team down nor form dry impenetrable clods. Champion arable was not possessed in common nor did its yield of cereals go to the peasant community in common, but the farmers pooled their resources and worked the land collectively through plough teams, harvest teams, and putting their animals under the common supervision of a village herder to graze on parcels not currently bearing crops.

Champion regions were full of what look like planned features: big fields, standard farm units (different areas of English champion named these differently as 'virgates', 'bovates', etc.), and a sense of something like a standard farm (in comparable continental areas certainly derived from the notion of *mansus*). The arable land itself was subdivided into units that are relatively uniform in any given place. Arable strips were oftentimes allocated in the same sequence across a field as the peasant farms on the village street. The regular aspect of the landscape resulted from a regular and supervised process of medieval clearance, reorganization, and intensification.

Not far away the same generic process produced a very different rural scene that some call 'woodland' and others 'ancient countryside'. (For a non-specialist, the term 'ancient countryside' (coined by Oliver Rackham) has the benefit of reserving 'woodland' to refer to actual patches of tree cover in England and elsewhere.) This was, however,

Figure 4.4 'Ancient countryside' in southeastern England

as visible among other features in Figure 4.4, a landscape distinctly more wooded than was and is champion. It is also distinctly irregular in layout, even when ordered into a modern, post-enclosure state. Ancient countryside curves and twists, it is carved up by fence rows and dotted with small settlements. Where champion had one big village, here are three or four smaller ones, each with its own cluster of farms and fields. The arable is more dispersed, the meadow less but the pasture more. Greater diversity in soil types and greater opportunity to carry out tasks at human rather than natural schedules meant less constraint on the time for ploughing and other agricultural operations.

Ancient countryside is a less communal landscape in terms of both nucleations and institutions; it is also less planned, more just 'grown'. Its proliferating microecologies are variations on this theme. In the English setting it can even be traced quite clearly back to the loose arrangement of scattered farms and hamlets from early Anglo-Saxon times described in chapter 2. It is argued that greater diversity at smaller scale then minimized lords' interest in gang work and in exercising close control over large groups of peasants, while encouraging retention of more dispersed nuclei. Although much pasture was common, fields were less often so. Little was to be gained from assembling men and animals from a wider area into collective work teams or herds. Certainly Anglo-Saxon lords and peasants were following different priorities when, in what became ancient country-side or champion, they differently adjusted their relations to the natural world.

The notion of microecologies as variations on a theme applies all across the European plain. Pioneering agrarian historian Marc Bloch and others distinguished in certain areas of central and northern France between what they called *bocage* ('woodland') and *champagne*. The distinction occurs at the regional scale in parts of Bavaria and the northern Saxon plains. Much the same can also be viewed, though on very different landscape and following different historical develop-ment and documentation, another thousand kilometres to the east in central Silesia, specifically the area around the province's principal city then and now, Wrocław (German Breslau).

In western Polish lands large-scale cerealization, demographic increase, and woodland clearance probably started only in the course of the eleventh century, then continued strongly through the thir-teenth century and deep into the fourteenth. In the central basin of the Odra (German Oder) river, what would in the later Middle Ages be the principality of Wrocław extended some ten to fifty kilometres around the only large urban site in the vicinity, a ducal and ecclesias-tical centre of maybe five thousand in the 1100s and a busy trading city of more than twenty thousand by 1350 (ecological contexts and the consequences of medieval urbanization are treated in chapter 6 below). With a climate tending to more continental extremes than plainly maritime England, some fairly light and fertile black earth soils or periglacial loess there were well suited for quite simple agricultural use; these knew long prehistoric settlement and since the early Middle Ages a relatively dense farming population. Over a larger area, in the twelfth century trees still covered heavy but quite fertile loams and small areas of gravelly moraines. Map 4.2a locates settlements documented between about 1150 and 1250 in the first good written records from the region. The loess and some of the black earth was then densely occupied, much in small hamlets, some still in multiple or transitory sites within a single named area. These were undergoing a process of consolidation whereby over time only one such site came to be dominant. Also in generations before 1200 a section of black earth that had for some reason not earlier been inhabited was cleared and settled. New villages established there stayed small, holding anywhere from a dozen to twenty farmsteads. But as late as the early 1200s there remained zones with almost no settlement, some on loess but more on loam and in the moraine north of the river.

In the course of the thirteenth century, especially after the devastating but brief Mongol invasion of 1240, the formerly empty area was opened up and settled (Map 4.2b). That this had been wooded is explicit in charters meant to encourage and organize the clearance. Pioneers on tree-covered land could have three and more rent-free years until their fields were ready to produce. The emerging landscape took the form of big open-field villages, none with fewer than twenty-five projected farms and the largest with twice that number when fully occupied a generation or two later. Demesne farms were

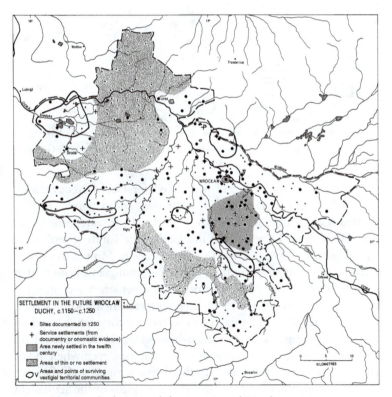

Map 4.2a Settlement and clearances around Wrocław: *c*.1150–1250

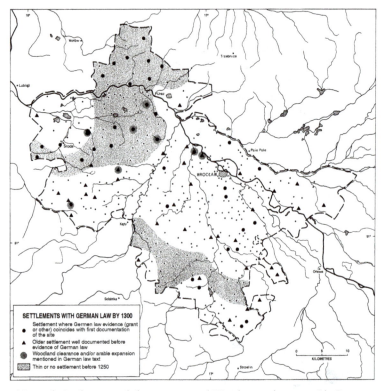

Map 4.2b Settlement and clearances around Wroclaw: settlements with German
law by 1300

small or absent, so lords had little need for forced labour. What
landholding dukes, churches, monasteries, and knightly families
wanted was to attract some farmers to settle and provide some return
from their lands. They put out this land in the hands of settlement
entrepreneurs, whose task was to recruit peasants. Most of those who
were initially willing to try their luck were immigrants from further
west in German-speaking territories. The settlers were attracted
because they were offered legally free rental tenancies, so they were
personally free and paid a fixed annual rent for their farms based on
their arable acreage. A set of German-based village customs provided a
template by which to organize new communities, even when indigenous peasants quickly picked up the desirable rights and practices.
Communal institutions set up under the auspices of the settlement
entrepreneur allowed internal self-governance under his successor as
village head man. As the movement continued through the thirteenth

and into the middle of the fourteenth century, the whole formerly unsettled area, once woodland, became arable. Agriculture operated on a three-course rotation, though more cold-tolerant rye commonly replaced wheat as the principal bread grain and the principal rental payment, too, if dues were not paid in cash. Big expanses of fallow fields allowed villagers to pasture numbers of sheep, and rough grazing probably remained, although away from the river meadows were scarce. Despite nuances of local differences and different institutional particulars, this area developed along the same lines as had the champion landscapes of southeastern England several hundred years before.

Not far away, however, on the black earth and loess, detailed nineteenth-century maps of central Silesia show the twisting roads and many small settlements reminiscent of French *bocage* or English 'ancient countryside'. Medieval inhabitants grew wheat, rye, barley, and oats on rich and well-drained soils, but where annually flooded river bottoms provided natural meadows and pasture, they reared more cattle, horses, and pigs, animals more tolerant of wet conditions than were sheep. Comparable pressures and distinct resource endowments nuanced social adaptations to microecologies.

Regional variation and local diversity come to light best where especially good documentation allows close study to probe behind the general pattern of anthropogenic change in northern Europe, namely the removal of most multi-use woodlands and their replacement by cereal farms, by whole systems meant to maximize the production of cereals. Chapter 5 will more closely examine the long-term operation of these innovative medieval agroecosystems.

INTENSIFIED CEREAL LANDSCAPES
IN MEDITERRANEAN EUROPE

Mediterranean Europe followed a distinctive, if parallel, course relative to the north. As earlier observed, Mediterranean societies did not typically clear woodland and replace it with entirely different land use. The evolution was more cyclic, with a territory cleared for a time, then returned to woods, then the sequence repeated. This historically deeper and more flexible pattern was due in large part to the whole Mediterranean physical landscape being in much smaller units, which fragmented the large-scale transformations found across the Alps. So what happened in Mediterranean Christendom during the central Middle Ages commonly involved newly intensified arable use on land that had during late antiquity been turned to pasture, wood pasture, or that open parkland called savannah. In the long run land use oscillated along a gradient of inherited practices and therefore of landscape formation and re-formation, but from the ninth century at the latest, the prevailing direction was towards more arable and more cereal production.

While the north provided large regional examples, Mediterranean ones take more local form. Along, for instance, the French Mediterranean coast, so many Christian refugees flooded in after the Arab conquest of the Visigothic kingdom in 711 that writers dubbed particularly the littoral between the Rhône and the Pyrenees as 'Gothia'. Carolingian authorities encouraged agricultural clearances along that southern frontier zone. Beginning in the ninth century and carrying on into the thirteenth, pollen diagrams there show continual increase in both cereal pollen and that of typical arable weeds. Later, moreover, Christians who remained in Spain followed a similar trajectory: Basques at *Gasteiz*, later called Vitoria, in Alava lived from the seventh to the tenth century as herders with supplemental cereal farming; from about 950 and into the second millennium, however, they changed their production strategies to keep less live-stock, grow less barley and millet, and increase output of wheat.

Further east in the Alpine foothills of Savoy, the basin of the Petit Lac Annecy had been farmed by Gallo-Romans, but after the fifth century it reverted to bush. Following foundation of a Benedictine monastery beside the lake at Tallaires in 879, the monks sponsored assarting on the valley floor but did not clear the upland, preferring to pasture livestock there. This itself, of course, affected the nature of the woods. In 1132, a Cistercian house, Tamie, was established in the same little basin around the lake. Given unoccupied uplands, the Cistercians proceeded to clear their estate, converting some of the slopes into arable farms. By the thirteenth century they even tried farming above the tree line. The timing of expanded cereal cultivation coincided with that further west, but here it moved upwards from (unknowingly) restored ancient arable to an altitudinal margin.

Landholders in coeval eleventh- to thirteenth-century Italy likewise undertook re-elaboration of organized agricultural landscapes, some of them enclosed and not unlike the English 'ancient countryside', and some in very open forms. In parts of Lombardy city-states sponsored new settlements on rough and marginal terrain near the outer bounds of their territories. For instance, in 1185–6 the Veronese, worried that

VILLAFRANCA DI VERONA

Map 4.3 Planned landscape of twelfth-century settlement around Villafranca
de Verona

their neighbours in Mantua might appropriate unoccupied land, constructed a new agricultural settlement in that direction, calling it
Villafranca Veronese ('the free town of the Veronese'). They invited
33 farmers to settle there, granting to each of them a free *manso* within
the designated 65 Veronese 'fields' (a measurement of land) and collectively another 656 'fields' to serve as communal woods and pasture.
Thus the arable settlement also received the necessary non-arable
resources. The newly occupied terrain followed a planned rectilinear
layout still visible on modern maps (see Map 4.3) – straight roads,
straight farm boundaries, rectangular fields – all set out as a whole
landscape under the authority of the municipality but with the work,
of course, to be done by the 33 farm families.

Mediterranean Christendom thus also knew the same distinction
between places with a planned aspect, pushed by authority, and those
a little looser, more the result of local adaptive choices. But in all
instances, the ever greater enlargement of cereal production remained
a driving purpose. In the Mediterranean this was often on former

arable land redeployed into cereal production after some centuries' hiatus, while northerners rather converted temporary fields and open woodland into permanent cereal farms.

Coastal wetlands along the Mediterranean and especially in northern Europe were drained between the ninth and fourteenth centuries in order to use the land to grow cereals. An extended illustration can return to the familiar Frisians, only now into the interior southern reaches of their country, the Dutch Rijnland, the area around the old mouth of the river Rhine, which silted fully shut in the eleventh century (see Map 4.4). Inland from the coast, barrier dunes and salt marsh gave way to a wide zone of raised freshwater bog.

Peat bogs are wetlands formed by water-loving, acid-tolerant plants that absorb surface water and, when they die, sink down into water made so acid by organic matter that the dead material does not exactly rot but becomes substrate for new growth on top. Capillary action causes the growing bog to pull the water table up with it, creating a raised or domed cross-section wet to the top. Though thoroughly wet and by Alpine standards very low, the bogs stood several metres above sea level. Humans equipped with special footwear could walk the surface in places or go with small boats up the creeks that drain down from the bog. The terrain could serve for fowling or as a source of plant materials, but was too soft to graze livestock on. Inhabitants of this interior freshwater area dwelt on drier terraces deposited beside the rivers and practised the Frisian way of life described in chapter 2. Prior to the mid-tenth century the peat bogs of central Holland were by and large unsettled.

Sometime before 1040 people in the area started doing a very simple thing: cutting ditches up into the bog behind their dwellings and letting the water drain down the ditches into the river. Close to each ditch it took but a year or two for the peat to dry enough to put animals on it to graze. After a few more years or more ditches, the animals could pull a plough and the rich peat soil would produce cereal crops. Settlers moved successively further up small creeks, dug drainage ditches, let gravity remove the water, and after a few years set up farms and established villages, all to raise grain on the dried peat. The whole area, once without human settlement, was fully inhabited by 1370.

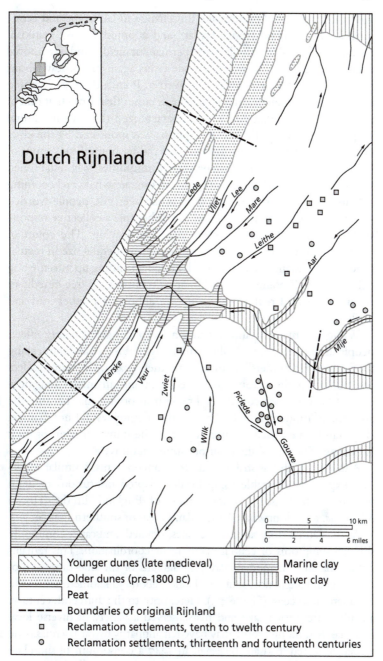

Dutch Rijnland

Lede
Vliet
Lee
Mare
Leithe
Aar
Mije
Karske
Veur
Zwiet
Wilk
piclede
Gouwe

0   5   10 km
0   2   4   6 miles

	Younger dunes (late medieval)		Marine clay
	Older dunes (pre-1800 BC)		River clay
	Peat		

– – – Boundaries of original Rijnland
□ Reclamation settlements, tenth to twelth century
○ Reclamation settlements, thirteenth and fourteenth centuries

Map 4.4 Medieval drainage and settlement in the Dutch Rijnland

Local people could undertake this change in landscape and economy if they stopped being 'Frisian' and adopted a new 'Frankish' mode of life: stable populations, permanent fields, and a manorial economy, though few large demesne farms again meant few labour services. By 1300 the people who lived in Rijnland were obtaining half or more of their calories from cereals rather than from that mix of pastoral resources that had earlier characterized the Frisian cultural adaptation. Much of the metamorphosis was sponsored by the chief noble in the vicinity, who had taken to calling himself the 'count of Holland'. He encouraged free peasant communities, who established self-government and worked together to operate what was becoming a drainage system. After several ditches had been cut, people worried about where the water would run out. It became a collective responsibility to keep the ditches clean and free-flowing. The count of Holland's settlements typically arranged farms of equal size in regular order along a main ditch with smaller ditches running up into the bog behind them. Peasants operated their own farms with free hereditary tenure and owed rent to the count, an abbot, or another lord and landowner.

While the material and institutional changes were taking effect, people in the area stopped calling themselves 'Frisians' and start calling themselves 'Hollanders'. They gave up their coastal Germanic dialect resembling Anglo-Saxon and started speaking an inland one now called Old Low Franconian, so Frankish in origin, that became the ancestor of modern Dutch. The people themselves did not change; they transformed their culture as part of the transformation of their landscape. The two shifts went on simultaneously.

Although with less striking cultural concomitants, a similar medieval expansion of arable using locally adapted institutions to drain wetlands can be seen in some parts of England, in the Tuscan *Maremma*, and along coastal and inland areas of southern France.

As the Dutch story already indicates, drained landscapes commonly showed symptoms of central planning or coordination. This remains boldly manifest in modern-day photographs of the one-time lake of Montady in Languedoc, southern France, about 30 kilometres from the Mediterranean coast (Figure 4.5). Here, prior to the thirteenth century, an inland freshwater lake and marsh served a variety of diverse local resource uses, though some may have felt antipathy towards a miasmatic source of feared 'bad air' (*malaria*). In 1247 a consortium of shoreline landowners and nearby townsmen undertook to drain the lake. Among

Figure 4.5 Montady, a thirteenth-century drainage project in Languedoc

other features this called for tunnelling 1.4 kilometres beneath a hill several metres high, capped by a Celtic *oppidum*, to carry the water to the nearest river. Once dry, the lake bed was surveyed in a radial format and sectors of three circular degrees leased out for peasant grain farming. The modern aerial image contrasts the planned quality of the one-time lake with a surrounding landscape of less regular pattern resembling English 'ancient countryside' that is, in fact, also typical of southern France.

Also on more distant cultural, even missionary, frontiers civilized high medieval cereal eaters exhibited clear cultural bias against less sedentary, less farming-focused, still more agropastoral peoples. Anglo-Norman churchman Gerald of Wales expressed this attitude clearly in his *Topography of Ireland*, composed in 1185. Having joined some kinsmen to watch and participate in their efforts to conquer Ireland and impose Anglo-Norman rule, Gerald wrote of the natives:

They are a wild and inhospitable people . . . They have not progressed at all from the primitive habits of pastoral living.

While mankind usually progresses from the woods to the fields, and from the fields to settlements and communities of citizens, this people despises work on the land . . . and desires neither to abandon, nor lose respect for, the life which it has been accustomed to lead in the woods and countryside.

They use the fields generally as pasture, but pasture in poor condition. Little is cultivated, and even less sown . . . The nature of the soil is not to be blamed, but rather the want of industry on the part of the cultivator . . .[2]

The Irish were, in the eyes of this Anglo-Norman, not civilized. The Irish and their Highland Scots cousins, also more herdsmen than cereal growers, were 'wild', in Norman French *sauvage*, in Latin *silvestris*. Although skilfully attuned to a well-populated pastoral landscape, the natives were matched to the literary stereotype of the wild man, the deviant epitome of *dis*order. And so in self-justified response, Anglo-Normans 'planted' English settlers in open-field villages in the eastern areas of conquered Ireland.

At about the same time as Anglo-Normans sought to civilize wilder reaches of the British Isles, German and indigenous lords did likewise in acculturating parts of twelfth- and thirteenth-century Mecklenburg, Brandenburg, and Saxony. The Teutonic Knights, a military religious order, attempted the same increase in ordered cereal farming in the portions of Prussia that they conquered and forcibly Christianized during the thirteenth and the early fourteenth century. An ideological association between cultural and agricultural deviance that contrasted with civilized Christian grain farming worked in parallel with change derived from economic need for certain incomes and/or cheap calories.

Wherever examined, the process of landscape change for cereal grains entailed an interplay of power and work, the historically essential but distinctive roles of lords and peasants. Lords took the initiative, but they did so between 800 and the years around 1300 from diverse starting points. If, as in the Carolingian age, many lords' desire was for their own household bread consumption and the production to support it, their concerns for control over soil and labour differed from those with access to even local markets in agricultural products. The latter situation encouraged transferring the risks of production to peasants, who would have to sell their cereals on the market to earn money to pay

---

[2] Gerald of Wales, *The History and Topography of Ireland*, book 3, chapter 93; tr. John J. O'Meara, rev. edn (Harmondsworth: Penguin, 1982), 101–2.

rent to their lords, who, in turn, could use this cash to acquire on the market what they wanted, whether locally produced or not. When peasant numbers grew and population pressure and land hunger could be recognized, lords had opportunities for gain from new clearances, from encouraging the introduction of new and productive techniques and community organizations, or from simply imposing higher rents on old tenures. The response arose from cultural tastes, a subsistence demand for land, or the market demand that was being expressed from the twelfth century onwards in rising prices for cereals. Lords provided the authoritative role, engaged in some level of planning, associated with standardization, lying behind an ordered structure imposed upon a formerly less disciplined countryside.

Lords provided the initiative and authority; peasants did the work. But medieval peasants needed some reason to do it. They could be motivated by coercion; they could be motivated by family subsistence needs; they could imagine greater freedom or income. The prospect of fixed annual rents could encourage technical improvements in productivity because the returns would come to the peasant, not to the lord. Still, peasants were poor and dependent cultivators, directly subject to natural and political insecurities that threatened their livelihood and at times their very survival. Under many circumstances peasants thus favoured communal organization, whereby they could pool and manage collectively some key resources: draught teams (if it took more than an ox or two to plough the new heavy land); access to pasture to feed those larger herds; pooling of harvest labour (which might have to be used first on the lord's land and then as quickly as possible in the window while the grain was good to gather it from their own); on drained landscapes, collaborative efforts kept the drains clear and the water running down and away. The implications and effects of such communal resource management are explored in chapter 7 below.

The greater share of this organization and effort was, however, directed to the end of ever greater production of cereals, of *blé*, of 'daily bread', the dietary staple of medieval European culture. The massive expansion of cereal production had, moreover, to be carried out with minimal reduction in the meat that was so beloved of elites and of the livestock that was necessary for peasants to grow their cereals. So the creation of new landscapes across Europe during the period of the eighth to the fourteenth century resulted in countrysides dominated by mixed farming. The pressures, thrusts, and structures were reasonably coterminous across Europe, but each district had its local environmental and situational variables. Hence outcomes established regional and local heterogeneity in the rural regimes of both northern and Mediterranean Europe. Even the large view of Map 4.5 reveals a patchwork of diverse regional agricultural systems across northern Europe around 1300. Local variations on regional adaptations within a shared civilizational paradigm had by then supplanted older and looser arrangements across most of the best potential cereal land all over Europe.

NOT BY BREAD ALONE

While cereals and cereal growing drove thoroughgoing landscape change in most of medieval Latin Christendom, other cultural programmes and work also transformed regional and local relations between Europeans and the land.

Striking new irrigated landscapes were created and much expanded in medieval al-Andalus and southern Italy. While Romans had irrigated in some of these areas, the medieval Arab 'green revolution' brought to Europe a novel polyculture distinct from the cereal emphasis of western Christendom. During the centuries of early Muslim conquest in southwest Asia new crops were developed in Iraq and Iran. These then spread westward under the aegis of the newly expanded Arab Muslim world across North Africa and into Spain and Sicily by the twelfth century (by Christian reckoning), indeed in most instances by the eleventh.

Cereals – rice, sorghum, hard durum wheat – were certainly a component in the new Arab agriculture, but as and more important were non-cereal crops of Indian and African provenance. Sugar cane, cotton, various fruits and vegetables, and several varieties of citrus entered Europe under this system; so, too, did watermelons and egg plant (aubergine). Medieval Arab innovations spread cultivation into semi-arid areas around the Mediterranean that had not previously supported sedentary agriculture. They employed complex intensive rotations that raised the productivity of what now had to be well-watered and was commonly heavily irrigated land. The productivity and the rotations were sometimes so large and so complex that the same parcel provided two or more crops in a single calendar year.

In such heavily colonized agroecosystems human forces pressed against natural causality to create deeply anthropogenic landscapes. Irrigated landscapes, Spanish *huertas* or *vegas* (meadows, wetlands), do

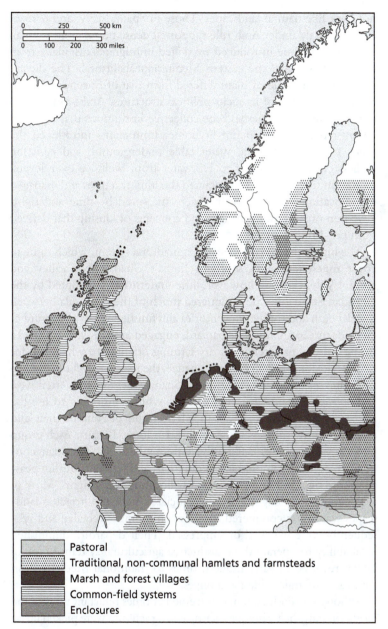

Map 4.5 Agricultural systems in northwestern Europe, *c.*1300

not look like natural landscapes. Those in Spain, Sicily, and parts of mainland Italy under Arab rule supported dense populations with an agriculture regime introduced by skilled immigrants originally from southwest Asia and the eastern Mediterranean littoral. The dietary culture of the world of Islam differed from that of Europeans and so did central aspects of its socio-political structures. Arabs carried into the west the techniques and the collective institutions that they had discovered and worked out at home. Immigrants introduced the *qanat*, tunnels to tap the water table underground, and *noria*, an endless chain for buckets to lift water from wells or over levees. Communities, not lords, maintained the infrastructures and managed the allocation of water. Shares were measured by time and rights keyed on organizations of clans and concepts of kinship that derived from pre-Muslim Arabia.

The highly productive irrigated agricultural system, which came to cover much terrain in southern Iberia's Guadalquivir valley and around Valencia, was, however, little understood or adopted by the Christian Spaniards who conquered much of the peninsula between the eleventh and thirteenth centuries and finished with the capture of Granada in 1492. Christian Spaniards engaged in the *Reconquista* had a strong cultural preference for dry farming oriented to wheat and for large-scale, long-distance transhumance, the seasonal cycling of sheep from one set of pastures to another. Spaniards either converted *vegas* and *huertas* to grain farms and pastures while continuing to use the irrigation that was there, or else they left Muslim peasants on their land as tenants, now subjects of new Christian lords. Because each group understood resources differently, tensions between Christian conquerors, especially immigrants and settlers, and resident Muslim peasants arose over, for instance, ways of allocating water rights. More of the special knowledge and skills associated with the irrigated landscapes was lost as conquered Muslim communities rebelled and subsequently were expelled or suppressed. Their departure diminished local ability to operate these distinctive agricultural systems, some of which reverted in early modern times to traditional Mediterranean landscapes of grain, vines, and olives.

Although Spanish conquerors seemed at times reluctant users of the *huertas*, in Italy the techniques of irrigated agriculture were picked up by Christian imitators who by the later Middle Ages had spread technology probably acquired in Sicily to the Po basin in Lombardy. There it supported production of newly introduced rice. In the course of late medieval and early modern centuries rice became a dominant cereal crop in large newly irrigated parts of the Po basin. Otherwise, however, irrigation in medieval Latin Christendom remained primarily a small-scale enterprise used to encourage the growth of meadows and to support multiple crops from heavily manured small-scale market gardens close to some cities. Large-scale irrigated landscapes were not to be found elsewhere in the medieval west.

Not dietary cultures but those of power and religious practice formed other programmatic settings for medieval Europeans to create new landscapes. Then and now some of the latter have commanded literate attention beyond their quantitative extent. Historically well documented and sometimes still visible are landscapes that men of power had manipulated in significant ways to show off their ability to do so. Power is manifest in its control over nature.

Early medieval monarchs displayed this behaviour, thereby in part emulating Roman models. A good example is the earthwork (a mound and ditch of 2–5 metres in height and depth) stretching for more than 100 kilometres parallel to the Welsh border in western England. Although its dimensions and siting preclude any medieval military role or even permanent frontier function, 'Offa's Dyke', built under the aegis of the eighth-century king of Anglo-Saxon Mercia whose name it bears, still testifies to his ability to bring together men, land, and resources to leave his mark on the ground. A comparable statement is incised into the land in north-central Bavaria, where, as earlier mentioned, 'Charles's ditch' is still several kilometres long, several metres deep and some thirty metres wide. While Charlemagne eventually gave up on his wish to link the Rhine and the Danube, the imprint of his workers' labour remained on the land, eventually helping inspire the late twentieth-century Main–Donau canal not far away. Elsewhere such exercise of princely authority can be seen in a series of large ditches and mounded earthworks in central Schleswig, in the seventh to tenth century the southernmost portion of the Danish monarchy. Later collectively called *Danevirke*, these were constructed under successive rulers of an emergent Danish kingdom to signify their frontiers and their political stature.

None of the famous earth-moving projects could serve military, frontier, commercial, or other material functions commensurate with their construction cost in men, material, and time. All rather demonstrated, in the physical labour of hundreds of conscripts and enduring physical marks on the ground, the power and durable reputation of early medieval rulers.

At less monumental scale, but with more widespread and sometimes still impressive visual effect, later princes and lords likewise set
castles where they held sway over the landscape in symbolic as much
as tactical terms. Though never really defensible, the hillside site of
Bolton Castle in Yorkshire displayed after its construction in 1378–99
the influence of the Scrope family over upper Wensleydale. Between
the 1130s and early sixteenth century, Landgrafs of Thuringia from
successive dynasties built up the Wartburg as the powerful anchor and
expression of their dominion over the western Thuringerwald and
routes to the rich agricultural basin and mining districts to its east.
A later chapter will also point out how landscapes modified to serve
aristocratic fascination with the hunt further advertised power over
nature and men alike. All these programmes may be equated with the
wild beasts put on show in Roman arenas and with heavily designed
baroque palace parks.

Monastic communities undertook and even proudly proclaimed in
writing their own demonstrative transformation of local landscapes.
Medieval texts, and often still material traces on the ground, show
monks manipulating especially water courses which they then offered
as proof of the mastery held by their saintly patrons over their physical
surroundings. For example, this can be seen from the early medieval
period, particularly Carolingian times, on the part of Benedictine
foundations in the Ardennes. Monks at Stavelot-Malmedy and
Andages/Saint Hubert so understood and publicized captured springs,
tamed channels, and engineered fountains to assert the ability of their
sainted patrons to control these natural phenomena. The same idea
echoes in the *Life* of Odo, second abbot of Cluny (927–42), who
reputedly brought about the miraculous creation of certain ponds to
meet the needs of his monastery. The programme and the cultural
representation endured and were even magnified in the practical
but also mythologized efforts of twelfth- and thirteenth-century
Cistercians to manage the water courses that flowed by their monasteries and turn those waters to monastic purposes. In all of these cases
landscapes became objects of permanent transformation, not solely for
economic ends, nor for cereal production at all, but as demonstrations
of power over humans, land, and nature.

Conceivably the most pervasive landscape change between the early
and high Middle Ages, however, found its primary motivations and
manifestations in the cultural sphere, and only indirectly, even uninten-
tionally, in the natural. From the work of late Roman bishops to that

of high medieval preachers in the east Baltic, the process of Christianization transformed the social perceptions and meanings of objects and places. New stories altered the manner in which people experienced and represented their landscapes. Holy men and missionaries converted older sacred space by destroying pagan shrines and erecting monasteries and churches in their place. Sixth-century Benedict of Nursia replaced a temple on Monte Cassino and tales told of his Welsh-born contemporary Samson of Dol who gave Christian identity to hostile sites (springs, gorges, etc.) in Cornwall and Brittany. When Anglo-Saxon missionary bishop Boniface felled Wotan's holy oak at Fritzlar in 723 and used its timber for a church, he was uniting Roman and Celtic Christian practice to cleanse pagan meaning from northern reaches of Frankish territory. Twelfth-century crusaders among the pagan Slavs of Mecklenburg did likewise. Other Christian leaders created their own geography by sanctifying new sites: legend has wandering seventh-century Irish ascetic Gall following the river Steinach up from the Bodensee to find his hermitage, which later grew into the prestigious and powerful abbey of St Gallen. In the tenth century Cluny, in the eleventh Cîteaux, and in the twelfth Clairvaux were similarly transformed from 'no place' to sacred centres where spiritual heroes drew wide attention and the memory of their deeds was preserved. Eventually pilgrim routes linked sites of special veneration at Compostela in far western Galicia, at Canterbury, at shrines of St Olaf in Trondheim and St Giles in Provence, and many more of local or regional significance. In this geography Rome had become the holiest western centre of a Christian culture deeply rooted in Europe's landscape.

Christian practice reoriented everyday spatial routines in ordinary places, too. In the Rennigen basin west of Stuttgart, as settlement shifted in Carolingian times from multiple hamlets to fewer nuclei, what became core villages were originally sites of a lord's private chapel (*Eigenkirche*) which became a parish church and thus the focal point for local Christian identity and such culturally essential events as baptisms, funerals, and regular religious observances. So, too, in Cornwall and neighbouring southwestern Wessex, future parish communities consolidated around centrally located churches, while more peripheral localities were associated with disorder, danger, and even demons. A contrast is here observed between once-Roman areas where early Christianity continued into medieval times, marked especially by local place names derived from Gallo- and Italo-Roman saints identified with the vicinity, and most parts of England or Germany where parish organization was fitted into prior, non-Christian, conceptual forms, as marked by the relative paucity of villages named for saints at all. Still, holy wells, wayside crosses, chapels, and the like everywhere set Christian meaning on medieval landscapes.

In al-Andalus an analogous pattern arose from a different ideological starting point. Redefinition of the Iberian landscape evolved as new stories of Muslim heroes and noteworthy places were told in the two or three centuries following the Arab conquest of 711. Like Christians to the north, Muslims took cultural possession of the lands they were changing.

ENVIRONMENTAL CONSEQUENCES OF NEW
ANTHROPOGENIC ECOSYSTEMS

Medieval Europeans set out to transform their landscapes largely as sites for producing cereals, but also for non-cereal agricultures, and even on grounds that had little at all to do with material outputs. Yet in all instances they colonized nature to create new anthropogenic ecosystems. The interventions had deep environmental effects. Human actors meant to bring about environmental change and accomplished their purpose, but building the new medieval agroecosystems also had unintended consequences.

The intent in the clearance of woodlands, drainage of marshes, and irrigation of dry land was human colonization of natural systems. In modern ecological terms, the purpose was to create new niches where humans would capture a larger share of primary biological production. In the course of the central Middle Ages, in order to obtain what they defined as food, medieval Europeans replaced old natural ecosystems with low annual productivity relative to the standing biomass of long-lived organisms (mainly trees) with new artificial ecosystems containing a lower biomass of short-lived pioneer plants (mainly grasses). With the transformation from the relatively natural to the more anthropogenic, a high diversity of producing and consuming organisms gave way to a low diversity, ideally a monoculture, of annual cereal grains. A once diverse and complicated food web was replaced with a short food chain comprising a few domestic herbivores and many, mainly plant-eating because mainly peasant, humans. Such ecosystems with low diversity of short-lived organisms and truncated food webs are characteristically unstable. They require continued inputs of energy to keep them at the pioneer stage. Annual grasses grow on bare dirt. They live for a year or two, they cover the soil, and then in nature they are succeeded by other kinds of plants. Those who would keep on growing cereal grasses have to keep taking the land back to the bare dirt. Intensive cereal growing demanded more human labour and more natural plant nutrients throughout the annual production cycle than had earlier more loosely manipulated mixed agropastoralism.

Very large unintended consequences accompanied the creation of the new medieval agroecosystems. The very process of cutting and uprooting trees and converting open woods to permanent fields destabilized relations between soil, plants, and water. In the late thirteenth century a Dominican in the town of Colmar on the Rhine wrote tellingly about what had changed in the area between the Vosges mountains and the river during his own lifetime. He said the trees had been removed that once grew along the mountain slopes and the loss of woody cover had resulted in more rapid and erratic runoff. Alsatian streams now alternated seasonally between springtime floods and dry beds in summer droughts. This he attributed to the clearances.

An erratic runoff regime was simply the first element in a causal chain connected to transformation of the landscape. Human colonization on new lands and intensification of production on old ones initiated and accelerated large-scale soil erosion and deposition. The unintended results affected new landscapes even at some distance from the sites of direct human intervention. Broken vegetative cover coupled with soil and nutrient loss exposed large expanses of soil surface for seasonal removal. This most often occurred by water which then deposited the sediment further downstream. A three-course rotation leaves approximately seven months between the time a winter grain is harvested and a new spring course planted. It is about fourteen months from the harvest of a spring grain, through the year of fallow, until sowing of winter grain on that field. Were that fallow left bare and open, and especially were it ploughed, the soil surface would become vulnerable to being washed away by precipitation and the ensuing flow of water.

Pioneer farms are especially susceptible to environmental degradation because newcomers lack familiarity with local factors of risk. Settlers undertake to transform their environment and necessarily undergo an adaptation process while learning the limits of their new home, its climate, soils, plants, animals, and even micro-organisms of which they may be totally unaware. Commonly one well-attested result is major erosion in recently cleared regions.

Precisely this pattern of soil loss is visible at representative sites in those European areas where and when medieval clearances and intensification were actively creating new permanent arable land. A pair of lakes in the French Alps make a telling case. At Lac Paladru to the north of Grenoble a falling water level enabled free 'peasant-knights' to settle on the shelving shoreline in about 1003 and clear the land for arable and pasture. At this point well-dated sediment cores taken from the lake bottom abruptly contain particles of loam and organic matter eroded from the broken soil. By 1035, however, the lake level was again rising, possibly because clearance increased the rate of runoff, and a few years later the settlers gave up, letting the slopes revert to woodland succession. Further north in Savoy, bottom cores taken from the larger Lac d'Annecy show a similar jump in sedimentation, here later because coincident with the thirteenth-century decision of local monasteries to convert their lakeside lands from woodland to arable exploitation. With trees removed, soil flowed from the bare ground surface into the lake and settled to its bottom.

A more general view around the western Mediterranean basin shows the cumulative effect of such small-scale clearances, drainage, and irrigation which transformed local hydrologies. From the twelfth century onwards there is well-demonstrated coastal deposition and marsh formation along the shores of Sicily and parts of southern peninsular Italy where this had not previously been the case. Along the Gulf of Lions on the French Mediterranean shore embayments that had been stable since Roman times were now quite suddenly filled in or turned into lagoons as a consequence of deposition of soil eroded from newly cleared lands.

Northern European alluvial zones and estuaries reveal unintended medieval changes that were abrupt, dramatic, and followed closely on regional clearances. Rates of alluviation in the upper Thames valley peaked during late Anglo-Saxon and early Anglo-Norman times, the eleventh to thirteenth century exceeding all other post-glacial periods. Consequent shifts in British river channels followed. Similarily in the Rhine basin the rate of alluvial deposition hit a maximum in the 1100s, coinciding with new agricultural disturbances there. More generally in Germany, geomorphologists find that soil erosion had for several prior millennia averaged less than 5 mm per year. But after the woodland cover was reduced to a mere 10 per cent of surface area by the end of the thirteenth century, extreme precipitation during 1313–19 thrust this alluviation rate up to five times the annual mean, in other words, 25 mm per year or a hand's span of soil loss in less than a decade. Still further east on Europe's northern plain, the large-scale clearances carried out at the upper end of the Vistula basin in southern Poland during the 1200s changed the hydrographic balance of the entire watershed. At its lower end the silt and nutrients that had washed off new inland fields came in the course of a century to fill the historic bay between Gdańsk and Elbląg, create a chain of offshore barrier islands, and then build those islands into a solid barrier spit with a lagoon behind. The physical changes to the shoreline and likely accompanying changes in water chemistry which resulted from this pulse of erosion and deposition contributed to the commercial failure around 1300 of the herring schools which had for several previous centuries spawned and been harvested along coastal Pomerania. Those schools now vanished.

The fate of south Baltic herring suggests how transformations in the physical landscape also provoked changes to biodiversity. A switch from woodland to permanent fields altered the runoff regime, which affected soil erosion and deposition, and all this affected the habitat for animals. Loss of woody vegetation transformed terrestrial habitats and altered carrying capacity for wild and domestic beasts. Of course no biological field surveys were undertaken at the time, so relevant indicators can only be pieced together from tiny scraps of both material and written evidence. It is, for instance, telling that modern studies of bird life around England's last surviving open-field village, Laxton in Nottinghamshire, found fewer bird species and only half the density of birds on what were still open fields of medieval type as compared with nearby areas with the mixed plant communities more character-istic of ancient countryside or what had existed before that. Likewise remains of woodland birds dominate in archaeological sites around Madrid dating to the fifth to twelfth century, but lost importance in the later Middle Ages after the re-Christianization of central Spain with its emphasis on dry farming of cereals and long-distance transhumance of sheep. Animals preferring other habitats could, however, gain. Evidence of great bustard, a ground bird of open grasslands, increased at this time in both England and Pannonia. Likewise, among domestic livestock, sheep and goats, creatures well adapted for living in the interstices and around the edges of mixed arable landscapes, came increasingly to supplant the woodland-dependent pig. Pigs would have to find a new kind of habitat. Changes to wildlife subject to purposeful hunting will be explored in the next chapter.

The overview of medieval landscape formation finds a process driven by the wants and needs of the few powerful and of the many poor. The process – call it colonization – transformed medieval Europe into a mosaic of artificial ecosystems, most of them designed to maximize cereal production. Grain fields interspersed with meadow, pasture, and large permanent villages replaced earlier mixed-density multi-use woodland where scattered islands of arable had supported small, dispersed, and generationally transient human settlements. Present-day analytical perspectives can also reconstruct the large-scale motives for this colonizing intervention: both cultural and economic considerations evidently applied. Within the larger process, particular cultural and natural conditions resulted in local and regional diversity of great historical longevity.

The outsider observer's etic perspective provides less access to how participants themselves experienced and represented the change. A search for the emic comes up with disappointing hints and some promising proposals. Occasional *exordia* of charters or chroniclers' references reflect elite awareness of purpose. Polish texts use the concept of *melioratio terrae*, 'improvement of the land', to encompass clearance, settlement, and agricultural development; monastic ideology lauded the *deserta* made into *hortus*. Comparable intent is but latent in privileges offered to new settlers by the archbishop of Bremen in 1106, in twelfth-century Castilian charters of *población*, and in the 1184 customal for Beaumont in the Ardennes, which became a regional prototype.

Many Anglo-Saxon charters contemporary with active clearances in England use the vernacular in their boundary clauses, making the landmarks named in perambulations fully accessible when read aloud in the language of local people. Similar clauses elsewhere, even when composed in Latin, are rich repositories of local vernacular place names reflecting thorough awareness of the interpenetrated natural and human in the landscape. Trees and brooks, ditches and roadways, as well as purpose-set stones or crosses, delimited physical and social space around twelfth-century Scottish Melrose and early thirteenth-century Silesian Kozanów, village of the duke's grooms. Cartularies assembled by corporate lords from central France to central Silesia organized literate thoughts about the past of their landed possessions. From such references in record and narrative texts Nicholas Howe, a specialist in Anglo-Saxon literature and culture, inferred a deep and concrete awareness of place and change among the English, who saw their community identified through its providential migration to Britain, which they had subsequently made into their 'homeland' (*eþel*). Although rooted in land(scape?), the literate concept paid little regard to contemporary human constructions and uses, which it either tacitly assumed or dismissed as ephemeral.

Like the boundary clauses, illuminated labours of the months seem to connect to people working in a humanized nature, depicting their agricultural routines and occasionally even tasks of assarting. The sequences and seasonality even of art crafted in northern workshops, however, remained stereotypical representations of Mediterranean practice and even pagan classical tradition long after northern land use had been thoroughly adapted to its different environment.

The investigator of the drained lakes in Languedoc, Jean-Loup Abbé, argues that each development project manifested a newly ordered and rationalized world, one of surveyed fields oriented towards cereal production in a systematic and orderly way. Open to question is the degree to which Abbé's own (and convincing) understanding of the new landscapes reflects what may have been in the minds of the people who worked to make them. Likewise Massimo Montanari, writing about Italian landscapes of the central Middle Ages, has drawn a clear contrast between the ordered world of the emergent city with its city-centred countryside and the disordered world of nature. But in a certain paradox, that disordered world of nature also provided to contemporaries a new restful perspective different from the stressful city. Was this in the minds of men and women who broke the stony ground at Villafranca Veronese in the 1180s? A generation later Icelandic politician-poet Snorri Sturluson looked back in his *Egil's Saga* with nostalgia for a mythic idyll of tenth-century resource abundance in contrast to the more densely populated and managed landscape Icelanders had made by the early thirteenth.

The need is plain to explore contemporary environmental perceptions and programmes behind the medieval transformation of European landscapes. Wide space beckons scholarly investigation of how medieval Europeans understood what they were creating through their work in nature. That the effort is rife with methodological pitfalls has already been amply lamented.

The next two chapters shift the focus from acts of landscape formation to the longer-term problem of sustainability, the implications of medieval Europeans operating their evolved systems. How for generations were they capable of maintaining productivity in the agricultural sector with its inherent pastoral adaptations, in their use of those woodlands which had survived the great clearances, and in their exploitation of wild resources? Thereafter attention turns to relations between humans and nature in the use of energy and in the manufacturing and urban sectors which engaged a rising, though always small, share of medieval populations, activities, and environmental impacts.

MEDIEVAL USE, MANAGEMENT, AND SUSTAINABILITY OF LOCAL ECOSYSTEMS, 1: PRIMARY BIOLOGICAL PRODUCTION SECTORS

.

This chapter and the next examine how medieval Europeans made use of their local ecosystems and historic consequences of those uses. The first of the pair has to do with biomass, hence with living things, and attempts an ecological understanding of primary biological production sectors in the Middle Ages. To start, agriculture and related activities are considered as anthropogenic ecosystems; sections thereafter treat medieval colonization and exploitation of natural wild ecosystems through wood cutting, hunting, and fishing. In each instance the aim is to gain a sense of operational features – how things worked – and to assess their sustainability. The following chapter will turn to non-living aspects of the environment. While chapter 4 was about change and its impact, chapters 5 and 6 treat structures, how they worked, and the extent to which they were sustainable.

SUSTAINABILITY IN SYSTEMS BASED ON INDIRECT SOLAR ENERGY

All pre-industrial societies live off solar energy from biomass production, the living materials that green plants create by photosynthesis. Agrarian societies since the Neolithic had domesticated biomass production, but their regular use of the wild world also fits the same parameters. Medieval Europeans in particular organized themselves and their colonization of nature for this purpose. Grasp of the long-run operation of medieval agroecosystems must start from thinking in metabolic terms about the whole society and its component units of production and

consumption – farming households. Parts and whole alike needed
sufficient and stable energy and other inputs to ensure regular outputs
at sufficient rates of return without in the process generating more waste
than the surrounding natural system could safely absorb.

The ecological concept of sustainability, alluded to in the
Introduction, is a dynamic equilibrium between human activities in
nature and the ability of the natural system to respond to those
activities. Humans need to be able to extract resources from the
natural world, to emit wastes that the natural world can neutralize,
and to colonize natural productivity and turn it to their own purposes.
In at least the medium run the three kinds of activities must balance.
Should humans define and demand certain aspects of nature as resources fitting their needs and available technology, but the natural sphere
lack sufficient of those resources to cover the needs, the system is
unsustainable. If the non-human environment cannot make harmless
the wastes from human activities, the system is unsustainable. For
humans successfully to divert natural productivity to produce the
specific things their culture demands, nature must be productive
enough to do so, even though most colonized systems yield *less* total
biomass than the natural system they replaced. So the limits of the
productive and absorbent capacities of the natural systems with which
a society works set some kind of balance. Where pressures overshoot
the balance, something pushes back. Recognizing that natural conditions and cultural demands both change over time, Figure 5.1
represents such a *dynamic* balance. A sustainable system, then, denotes
an equilibrated relationship between human demands against the
natural sphere and the continued ability of that natural system to
respond to those demands. Applied to a past society such as medieval
Europe, the concept of sustainability helps identify areas of human

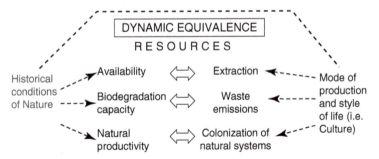

Figure 5.1 Sustainability as a dynamic equilibrium of society and nature

environmental impact and stress, and also those cultural adaptations which could mitigate the damage. Did anyone reveal awareness of limits? History here alerts present-day students to both the hazards and the potential in past experience.

In historic agrarian societies soil erosion, nutrient loss, management of animals, and limited energy have posed the principal risks to sustainability. Erosion causes the soil to disappear. Nutrient loss deprives the soil of substances plants need to grow. Most pre-industrial societies must negotiate fitting animals other than humans into their social metabolism. All pre-industrial societies had to work from only that fraction of current solar energy output that daily radiates through space and the atmosphere to the earth's surface where it can be captured by green plants. Their situation differed from present-day fossil fuel systems which draw on the much larger but fixed stock of energy accumulated through many millions of years of photosynthesis and preserved in the earth's crust. The next chapter will begin with limits to energy supply in medieval Europe. But while every material can be expressed in terms of energy, for practical purposes energy is not all that counts. Hence, to consider agroecosystems and other medieval uses of the living environment this chapter needs to focus more on soil erosion, nutrient loss, and handling animals.

Historical study of any human society exploiting its local ecosystem must recognize the agroecosystem as belonging to a larger *inter*relationship and thus as a special case of the general interaction model. The processes of colonization that transform the interaction of natural and cultural spheres are driven by fundamental cultural values. These bring people to formulate programmes, go to work in nature, and exploit nature in certain ways. Figure 5.2 puts this view of an agroecosystem in graphic form. It entails relationships between plants, soils, water, animals, etc., all managed for the sake of certain kinds of production. This effort involves technology and social organization, so includes such elements as draught power and the product flowing from the colonized system into the production system while seed and human labour cycle back in. But the production system itself is intimately connected with the farm household that runs it, and that 'ecosystem manager' is simultaneously also a human population with culturally shaped demographic structures and behavioural norms. Hence human demography and productive economy are coupled and that whole system is further linked with the ecology of certain plants, animals, soils, and water. Yet even this entire agricultural

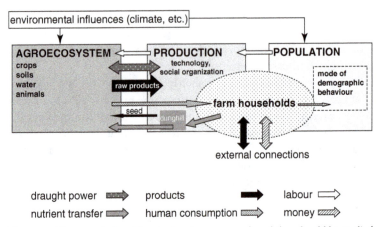

draught power ⇨   products ⬛➤   labour ⇨
nutrient transfer ⇨   human consumption ⇨   money ⇨

Figure 5.2 How pre-industrial agricultural systems work and thus should be studied

system is not independent. External connections entail flows of product and money, while the whole operates under the influence of such environmental factors as climate, which must be taken into account.

So agriculture is to be studied as coupled systems, interactive not deterministic. Metabolic flows of energy and materials join the ecosystem, economic production, and the humans who sit atop the food chain but also endeavour to shape the flows. The very people who live from this output are those who manipulate it, making the role of humans in an agroecosystem a clear example of the hybridity of society between culture and nature. Applying this heuristic more directly to the Middle Ages would add to the material externalities a further cultural one, coercive power. Medieval European agriculturalists were mainly peasants, people who lacked power but were subject to coercion from those who had it. Medieval farm households made decisions under often strong socio-political constraints.

All of these considerations form the backdrop to examining certain historical particulars of medieval agrarian regimes in both their arable and their pastoral components and in the latter parts of this chapter the *non*-agricultural colonization of the European biosphere.

TRADITIONAL EUROPEAN AGROECOSYSTEMS: THE NORTH

Agriculturalists in Mediterranean and northern Europe adapted their practices to their different physical, especially climatic, conditions.

They faced different problems, bore different risks, and provoked different environmental consequences. As already discussed, to the north of the Alps much of maritime and continental Europe became dependent on short fallow cereal farming. Medieval transformation of native woodlands into a vast grain field coincided with the three-fold increase in the population of those regions between 800 and 1300. Those human numbers were mostly peasant farming families, but also included non-productive lords, lay and clerical, and others, notably from 1100 burgeoning urban dwellers, who added little to agricultural outputs. This dominant characteristic lasted into the fourteenth century. Despite crises and changes during the later Middle Ages, to some lesser degree short fallow cereal farming remained the economic foundation of society into the eighteenth and nineteenth centuries. Only then did Europeans start living off other than their own cereal harvests and an economy based on them.

A useful first approximation of how what had become a traditional way of life operated as an agroecosystem can be obtained by considering the stereotype of 'open field' or 'common field' agriculture, often called in its most extreme English form the 'Midlands system', and until recently taught to school children as 'the medieval manor' (Figure 5.3).

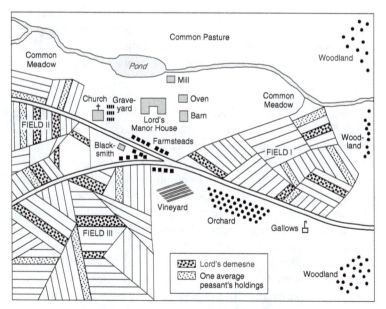

Figure 5.3 A stereotypical 'medieval manor'

Though a cliché ignoring the regional and other diverse agrarian regimes just discussed, it serves to highlight arrangements and practices that did prevail across much of the great European plain for most of the period. These are quintessentially the champion landscapes whose formation was discussed in chapter 4, now considered in their operational aspects. This cereal-centred production system raised grains on permanent large fields of intermingled strips, each held by a different individual farmer who also had similar strips in other fields. Had the lord any arable, this might be separate or itself also integrated into the strip set-up. The fields were the managerial and rotational units. Management decisions pertained to the community collectively, not the individual holder of any particular strip. They characteristically operated a three-course crop rotation, with each field following a triennial cycle of winter grain (wheat, rye), spring grain (barley, oats), and a fallow year when the land rested. Horse- or ox-drawn heavy mouldboard ploughs tilled the soil and neighbours worked side by side to reap the harvest from their parcels. Members of the village community, or at least the male heads of leading village households, also shared rights to pastures, which graded off into woodland, and to such grazing as the fallow field and the post-harvest stubble of grain fields provided. Grain from each strip belonged to the individual landholder, but once that grain was removed, the land became common pasture. Village hay meadows, however, were more rarely used in common. Though often owned collectively, they were used individually. (More about meadows and communal controls, too, appears below.)

Besides structuring medieval landscapes, this stereotypical open-field regime subsequently became the object of now classic debates in English politics and historical study. To start, by the eighteenth century these agricultural practices were said to inhibit agricultural capitalism and hence economic and technological progress. By some time in the nineteenth century, the common-field village drew political and cultural concern because some contemporaries believed it embodied social stability 'since time immemorial'. (Chapter 4 shows that historians no longer concur.) Eventually the Midlands system further drew scholarly controversy for its alleged technological flaws and rigidity under population pressure in the late thirteenth and early fourteenth century (*c.*1280–1340). These deficiencies, it was argued, brought overexploitation of marginal soils, nutrient loss, production failures, and ultimately a Malthusian collapse of medieval populations.

This last argument was notably articulated in the mid-twentieth century by economic historian Michael M. Postan. No ecologist, Postan did not refer to 'overshoot', but set forth exactly that diagnosis: the most common form of medieval agrarian society transgressed its limits. Indeed while this latter debate might have been conducted in environmental history, the contestants remained innocent of this approach and persisted in a somewhat misleading traditional discourse about 'field systems' when discussing what now would be recognized as entire agroecosystems. Despite these two centuries and more of lively debates, however, the first self-consciously *ecological* treatment of traditional open-field agriculture was undertaken in the 1970s by William Cooter. His interpretations echo in those of H. S. A. Fox, Jules Pretty, Tom Williamson, and others.

Two cautionary ironies deserve mention. Scholarly debates about medieval northern European agroecosystems intensely centre in the English language and about England. This is because financial accounts from English manors of the thirteenth and fourteenth centuries offer amazingly rich data about their operation. Yet easy access to such documents encourages students to confuse profusely recorded demesne farming with often ill-recorded peasant farming practice under very different patterns of constraint and relationships. What demesne lords had done on the land cannot be taken for what peasants may have been doing. The very plethora (by medieval standards) of documentation from the manorial side makes demesnes the focus of debates and so lends them a deceptive substantive centrality.

Also worth notice is the sparse attention scholars elsewhere have traditionally paid to the English discussion. One German historian, Wilhelm Abel, did take up Postan's diagnosis of overuse of marginal land and a subsequent Malthusian crisis to explain the late medieval abandonment of many villages and much arable in Germany. Also, in even more general terms, influential French medievalist Georges Duby blamed what he saw as food shortages and death rates increasing from the 1290s, if not earlier, on rural overpopulation and consequent cultivation of infertile, soon-exhausted, soils. More commonly historians on the continent, perhaps overwhelmed by the mass of English sources and unsure how different sources might still engage similar issues, simply ignored them. (To be sure, English writers reciprocated regarding the continent.) Nevertheless, on both sides of the Channel, across the whole of the European plain parallel agroecosystems prevailed. In the fourteenth century almost all of western Europe suffered a common demographic collapse and economic contraction. Yet plainly all of Europe cannot be explained on the basis of conditions peculiar to England, nor English experiences as if they were entirely alien to their continental neighbours. While most of the explicit scholarship and findings available for close study arose in a debate about the English Midlands system, what will advance understanding is the answering of similar questions from different kinds of sources across at least a zone stretching from the Loire to the Vistula and northwards into southern Scandinavia.

The basic agroecosystem is straightforward. The plants that capture solar energy as biomass by synthesizing sugars from air and water need soil minerals – nitrogen (N), phosphorus (P), and potassium (K) – in order to assemble their vegetative bodies and eventually to feed all humans and other consuming organisms. Natural processes continually cycle N, P, and K between chemical compounds in various physical states and locations, only some of which are accessible to plants. Lacking adequate supply of any one of these elements, plants grow poorly if at all (nineteenth-century chemist Justus von Liebig's 'Law of the Minimum'). Also essential to plant life are calcium, magnesium, sulphur, and carbon. The soil nutrients are available to plants through interaction between the plants' roots and humus, decaying organic matter in the soil. Humus needs to be broken down by soil biota, first macro-organisms such as insects, other arthropods, and worms, then mainly fungi and bacteria. Other bacteria oxidize the decay product, ammonia (NH_4), into nitrous oxide (NO_2), the form in which plants can take up nitrogen. A physical process makes the soluble minerals accessible to feeder roots of plants. Some plants are aided in this process by certain soil bacteria that have the ability to take nitrogen out of the air and 'fix' it into soluble compounds. Nitrogen-fixing bacteria naturally present in the soil or those living in a symbiotic relationship with leguminous plants (peas, beans, clover, and their relatives) are thus essential to sustained operation of an agroecosystem because the cycling of nitrogen is needed so that plants can actually grow. Phosphorus and potassium are naturally replenished in part through weathering of rock materials, as are calcium and magnesium. Old soils have lost their weathering products and become barren.

Problems inhere in colonizing a natural process tied to sunlight, water, and essential minerals. Hours of sunlight and supplies of water vary seasonally and with changing atmospheric conditions. Other plants, 'weeds', take up nutrients in competition with the favoured crop. Every soil contains pathogenic organisms (moulds and other fungi, bacteria) that threaten the soil biota or the plants themselves. Finally abundant water in the northern European setting leaches soluble minerals from the soil surface downward beyond the reach of shallow-rooted cereal grains. But tillage (ploughing) counteracts weeds, soil pathogens, and leaching. Ploughing of the fallow and again before sowing keeps down the weeds, opens the soil to air and sunlight which kill the pathogens, and when a furrow is turned, restores soluble minerals to the soil surface. But tillage poses new risks. It opens up the soil surface, exposing it to erosion by wind or water. To some degree tillage inhibits also the beneficial soil biota, many of which are also sensitive to air and sunlight. Tillage further tends to oxidize the humus, shrinking the matrix where mineral exchanges take place. Hence long-used arable soils, those that have been ploughed year after year after year, tend to become acidic as a result of the oxidation and removal of certain soil chemicals. Such soils also form 'plough horizons', discontinuities between a surface soil repeatedly stirred by the plough and an undisturbed layer below. This, too, interrupts movement of water and minerals in the soil. In effect, to sustain successful agricultural colonization requires management of a whole soil ecosystem which pre-industrial peoples could neither see nor imagine, but had rather to learn and negotiate by local trial, error, and oral transmission of results.

Further, agroecosystems necessarily export biomass, including nutrients, out of the arable fields. This, too, is both simple and critical: the crop once grown is in whole or part removed from the field and consumed elsewhere, so its biomass and nutrients are not automatically recycled into the ecosystem that produced them. The export may be to village consumers, both humans and livestock, or further away, whether to a normally non-resident lord or to an urban community. So an agroecosystem characteristically loses nutrients – up to 10 per cent per year in typical temperate climates – and tends in the direction of soil depletion. The very operation of any agroecosystem – and here in particular those of northern Europe – removes nutrients, and the techniques used to counteract that problem oxidize the humus, form the soil horizons, and export biomass. All open the land to erosion, as well as nutrient loss.

The traditional northern European agroecosystems which emerged early in the Middle Ages have remedies for nutrient loss and erosion.

Of course contemporaries did not then understand this in modern biochemical terms and may or may not have applied the techniques self-consciously. Some people in medieval society did see certain methods as solving identifiable problems; others may merely have accepted 'the way we do things' lest something worse happen. One piece of the remedy was the mixed production system itself, an arrangement employing both arable farming and livestock. In northern Europe the latter typically included both draught animals and sheep, the latter reared more for their fibre than the welcome byproducts of meat and dairy. Both kinds of domestic animals pastured on the stubble of the grain fields and weeds of the fallow, and in the process restored some nutrients to the fields. Contemporaries were sufficiently aware of that function for lords often to require that the village herd on the stubble or fallow be folded (put in a mobile corral) first on their own land. Another countermeasure brought in manure, animal or human waste, either from the village (also a return of nutrients) or imported from elsewhere, in order to raise the humus content and, seen from a present-day etic perspective, recycle nutrients back into the soil. In temperate climates the return of crop organic matter by such means is estimated to maintain soil humus at 75–80 per cent of pre-cropping levels, or at least much slow decade-scale decline. Ten years without recycling takes it down to half, which is not zero. The famous Rothamsted experiments run for more than a century in nineteenth- and twentieth-century England showed, however, a long-term plateau of grain yields at barely twice the amount seeded.

Further subsidies could be introduced from outside the agroecosystem proper. It is not unusual to find medieval reports of people removing branches, leaves, or leaf mould soil from woodlands and putting them on the arable land. Turves could be dug from pastures and transferred to the fields. Bottom sediment was scraped from ponds or small watercourses and spread for the same purpose. If the immediate problem was a 'sour' soil, excess acidity, medieval farmers knew they could dig out a limey mineral called marl, which is available in various regions, and put that on their fields. Marl contains calcium and counterbalances acidity. By the late seventeenth and the eighteenth century very detailed agricultural manuals that treat traditional northern agriculture just as Roman manuals had that of the Mediterranean encourage importing all sorts of off-farm organic matter and spreading it on fields to maintain the health of the soil. At least some of these practices receive occasional passing mention in medieval texts.

A more radical step was to deviate from cereal monoculture by introducing as field crops the plants now called legumes (e.g. clover, alfalfa, lucerne, vetch, peas, beans). These plants have evolved a symbiosis with certain nitrogen-fixing bacteria that colonize their roots. Growing legumes and then ploughing them under boosts the nitrogen content of the soil. This chemical or biochemical feature was certainly known to no one prior to the late 1800s, but some medieval agriculturalists (and before them some Romans) had established that growing clover and ploughing it under kept their soil productive.

The historic issue is the extent to which such soil amendments, all of them extremely expensive in terms of time, labour, or food crops temporarily foregone, were accessible to and used by common-field peasant farmers as opposed to lordly demesne. We now know, notably from research by B. M. S Campbell on manorial accounts, that demesne farms in much of England around 1330 were tightly attuned to the market, able to invest in future yields, and aware that this was worth doing in anticipation of prices that specific crops might achieve upon sale in London. Campbell's long-term data and those independently obtained by others indicate rising land productivity on English demesnes during the thirteenth and even the fourteenth century. Peasants shared this awareness. They were, however, always poor and that entered deeply into all their decision-making. Peasants were further not entirely free economic actors, but subject to social control both by power elites and in the social consensus of collective management of those big fields. In terms of modern economics, that situation meant peasants show 'a high discount of future benefits', which is a sophisticated way of saying that a large output some years hence could not offset inadequate supplies in the present. Those close to bare subsistence and lacking other sources of income had to have grain 'now' to feed their families even if yields remained constrained. Some agricultural ecologists do question how much under northern European conditions and medieval technology the capping of yields was a consequence of limited nitrogen rather than potassium or phosphorus. Quite probably the latter would show significant variations depending on specific soils, while nitrates might be a more general problem. And it is therefore argued that from the peasants' perspective obtaining enough 'now' was the best to be hoped for and the Midlands system persisted in lieu of other options. After all, as chapter 4 observed, lack of adequate pasture in that very region kept farmers from increasing the quantity of livestock and hence using more manure. In the absence of land that was not worth making into arable, animals there had to compete against humans for the grain harvest.

A larger historical issue lies beyond the precise questions about agricultural biochemistry, however much those may matter. Was the thirteenth-century peasant system in fact capable of operating within ecological limits? Was this indeed a sustainable system up to the historic point in the 1290s when a major upsurge of war and taxation, which was largely peculiar to England, proceeded to disrupt markets and damage the agrarian economy and ecosystem at the very time population growth spiked and a series of extreme weather events placed northwestern Europe under still greater pressure, resulting in a collapse from a convergence of causes? Any consideration of the sustainability of medieval northern agroecosystems must acknowledge that something went quite wrong during the first part of the fourteenth century. The issue is whether what went wrong may be attributed to an unsustainable agrarian regime. One argument says collapse came from failure to balance the productive biochemistry, from 'overshoot'. Another asserts that all went well until politics increased pressure on the peasants at the very time when the population rose beyond earlier levels and then was struck by extreme weather (to be examined more closely in chapter 9 below). Ecologists would respond that these 'external' factors were themselves part of a long-term pattern of changes: the cultural and natural spheres are not to be thought of as in static balance but rather as oscillating equilibria. While a destabilized system topples when something else hits it, stable systems have the resilience to deal with increased stress and shock. Again, of course, threshold conditions are at issue. Chapter 10 will revisit the intersection of these perspectives.

To the problem of agrarian sustainability Jules Pretty and others have taken a variant approach, arguing that despite limits and risks the traditional medieval agroecosystem persisted because it met values and priorities other than high productivity. The strips and communal control of tillage offered a stability of production that could not come from more individualized decision-making. The location and organization of fields right around the village provided easy access to labour and allocation of labour inputs. Scattered strips lowered risks to total production from unusual climate or weather: crops on high, light soils might do better under wet conditions when low, heavy soils suffered and the reverse occurred in times of drought. So the system was well adapted to deal with the reality of normal meteorological variability. Pretty goes on to point out that peasants simultaneously followed diversified strategies with multiple sources of income, gardens to supplement field crops, and many enjoying by-employment in crafts (if less in the thirteenth century than later). They did not just rely on eating cereal. As is more fully explored in chapter 7, many medieval peasants possessed common rights and through them access to wild resources such as edible plants and small animals present in pasture land that graded into woodland.

Pretty almost attributes present-day misunderstandings to over-dependence on manorial sources that fixate on arable output because lords did. Cereal production mattered to lords but less so to a peasant girl gathering mushrooms for a family meal. So many aspects of the larger peasant ecosystem are ignored in typical manorial sources as to leave a partial view of how the agroecosystem functioned. Historical assessment must play off the balance of advantages between lords and peasants and further try to compensate for the one-sided records on which scholarship has hitherto relied.

The sustainability of agroecosystems always rests on known stabilities in nature. Unintended, even unperceived, responses to colonization can have unexpected effects. A good example from grain-centred medieval northern Europe shows how unexpected results come from natural conditions changing in ways that people could at first only barely recognize. Nature 'struck back' in the drained and successful cereal-growing medieval Netherlands. Chapter 4 describes Dutch use of simple ditches and gravity to drain water from naturally raised peat bogs there. The water ran down to a nearby river, cattle were put in to graze and compact the surface, and after further drying, grain grew very well on the humus-rich soil. But problems emerged because drained peat loses volume; as it oxidizes like other humus, it subsides. Burning and trampling by animals have the same effect, helping to cause the level of land to sink by about a centimetre a year, a metre a century. Where the natural bog had stood scant metres above the river or sea, after a century or two the land first drained became vulnerable to high water and storm floods. No longer well suited for cereal farming or habitation, the lowest acreage reverted to pasture, while arable fields and houses were shifted inland. Gradually the heirs of the drainage pioneers were pushed up hill to the last-drained centre of the original bog. In those parts of Holland and Zealand drained around 1000, people were already moving up hill by 1200. On through the thirteenth century this continued at province-wide scale.

Subsidence worked in synergy with forces outside human control, notably a relative rise in local sea levels due to regional isostatic effects and probably global warming. In the course of the 1200s, strong storms and flood tides caused the North Sea to break through the northern dune line and flood the Dutch interior, forming first a freshwater lake, then a large body of salt water called the 'South Sea' (*Zuiderzee*). Further marine incursions followed from 1350. Those in the south of the Netherlands coincided with active mining of the peat as an energy source (discussed in chapter 6). Flooding, mining, and erosion together resulted in a whole group of lakes there. By 1544 these covered all the middle of Holland. Big new water surfaces resulted from settling of the peat as a consequence of the agricultural use of this humus-rich soil.

People had to respond to such changes. The Dutch took new measures for flood control and drainage, building infrastructures they had neither needed nor built when they were busy draining peat bogs. Dykes, dams, and sluices spread from the twelfth century onwards, employing new construction techniques, for now the problem was to keep the water out of land that was sinking. The new enclosed, dyke-guarded fields called polders required sluices to run the water out. Continued subsidence meant they had to start to pump, lifting water out of the arable land which had gone below the level of rivers which themselves were barely above the level of the sea. The first wind-driven pumps were successfully tested in 1408, probably near Alkmaar, and working in series near Rotterdam by the mid-1430s. As Holland sank below sea level, all the water had to be pumped out. Early fifteenth-century regional communities started collective coordinated institutions to manage what soon became an interlocking system of pumps, drains, canals, and flowages.

So the former land-use system had been sustainable except for the natural tendency of farmed peat to shrink. Once the peat had shrunk far enough, medieval Dutch cereal agriculture ceased to be a sustainable system unless the society created an elaborate set of structures to keep and take the water out. The Dutch case may be unusual in its particulars, but well illustrates a general pattern that agricultural use changes soils. Societies that keep using soils in the same way must adapt to the changes or find themselves confronting ecosystem, in particular agroecosystem, collapse.

TRADITIONAL EUROPEAN AGROECOSYSTEMS:
THE MEDITERRANEAN

Agrarian issues in medieval Mediterranean Europe resemble those of the Romans mentioned in chapter 2, though with significant structural differences. The same two basic models endured: dry farming to grow the Mediterranean triad of grain, vines, and olives, and various more intensive horticultural options. Few of the medieval agricultural innovations covered in chapter 4 applied south of the Alps, Massif Central, and Pyrenees, for they were adaptations to northern conditions. But the wide range of intensified cultures available to Mediterranean farmers was covered in considerable detail in, for instance, *Ruralia commoda*, the handbook on agriculture written by Pietro de'Crescenzi (Petrus de Crescentiis) in 1307/9. The author's landholding experience had been in the area of Bologna and the Po plain, but he wrote for the king of Naples and provided good references for the south as well. Visible in Italy, southern France, and Christian Spain is a historic pattern of ebb and flow in agricultural land use, sometimes more intensive, sometimes less, as distinct from the directional process of cerealization typical of the north. From the eleventh to the thirteenth century that oscillating rhythm tended to increase agricultural activity significantly, for it supported a large regional growth of population and the greatest rate of urbanization anywhere in medieval Christendom. Those masses were fed from Mediterranean agroecosystems.

Medieval rural settlement in Mediterranean Europe was more densely concentrated than had been the case in Roman times. In Italy this major change in the relationship between people and the land resulted from a process now called *incastellamento* that took place between the late tenth and the twelfth century. Farming households moved out of scattered rural locations and into larger, often fortified, sites around castles. The relocation occurred under coercive seigneurial pressure as Italian lords firmed up their control over the populace. But that forced trend developed in simultaneous counterpoint with the formation of rural communes, so at just the time when people were being pushed together by their lords, they were also creating institutions in which they were a little more self-governing as communities than had ever been the case in Roman or early medieval times. So a certain balance emerged between communal power and the power of the seigneurs, with the lords exercising power in certain ways and communities in others. In Spain a similar spatial pattern appeared because the Christian *Reconquista* and resettlement of the central peninsula during the eleventh through to the thirteenth century was carried out by means of large agricultural communities ('agrotowns') of basically peasant militia fighters.

Large and densely packed habitations resulted in a pattern that can be called 'farming at a distance' becoming typical of Mediterranean Europe. Arable fields did not cluster closely together around the settlement as in the stereotype of the open-field village. Farmers had to go out to their fields and return to their homes, sometimes distances of several kilometres, to work a single parcel. Arguably this occurred because Italy, southern France, and Spain contained few significant demesne farms, and those ran using full-time servants, not forced peasant labour. Lords who did not need to muster a gang to work their own fields cared little if other people had to live far from theirs.

Medieval Mediterranean agriculture was also characterized by more market access earlier than was the case in the north, freeing lords and peasants from having themselves to produce all the goods subsistence might require. The greater local diversity already remarked around the Mediterranean made crop failures less dramatic crises for any given set of people, who could find other sorts of ways to survive, by exchange or by using other resources. In the mountains people relied significantly on chestnuts, which can be ground into flour. Chestnut bread was not acceptable for the Eucharist but people could live on it. In bad years in the mountains of Tuscany many peasants did just that.

Notably in communal (i.e. city-state) northern Italy, the central medieval period is one of very systematic extension of cereal cultivation across the plains and up into the hills. Mechanisms differed from those beyond the Alps, but the trend throughout medieval centuries was towards more arable use of land and more cereal production. In the course of the twelfth and thirteenth centuries these arable uses began to push against the limits of soil types, altitude, and the margins of the sea. Most of this farming was undertaken in enclosed parcels, for Mediterranean arable was not managed collectively as in a common-field village. Sometimes individual parcels were long associated with a particular farm so that generations of people lived in the same house in the same village and farmed the same scattering of fields thereabouts. In other instances lords maintained tighter control over the operation of their fields and leased them out for fairly short terms to the highest bidder. A given individual might every few years actually obtain differ-ent pieces of land to work for his farm.

Bare fallow everywhere continued to be a standard arrangement, as Mediterranean agriculture operated in synergy with transhumance. During summertime animals were characteristically grazed not on the fallow but up in the hills. This risked a vicious circle of nutrient loss, for the livestock did not eat and leave their droppings on the field. This problem for Mediterranean agriculture differs slightly from that of the north but also was *not* addressed by the agroecosystem itself. The fact that animals were kept out of significant areas made fodder shortage frequent in this region. People counteracted it by taking fodder from the remaining woodlands, where branches and new growth were cut and carried to the livestock, thus transferring biomass and nutrients from woodland areas to wherever the animals might be – upland pastures in the summer and, if woods were available, after harvest in the lowlands during the winter. Hence livestock was less integrated with arable farming in the Mediterranean than it was in northern mixed farming.

As occurred in the north, the early fourteenth-century Mediterranean experienced food shortages, particularly in Italy, although more docu-mentation for Spain is becoming known. At Florence food shortages or high food prices are recorded in 1329, 1339, 1342, and 1346–47, to mention only the period before the Black Death. The question arises as to whether these indicate failures of supply – did something happen in those years to cut production of foodstuffs or shrink the amount offered on the market? – or a systemic excess of demand – had the population as a whole so pushed beyond the supportive capacity of Mediterranean agriculture that any minor problem meant a shortage of food? One contemporary Florentine alleged in the late 1330s that Florence could obtain only five months of its yearly grain needs from its Tuscan territory. Seven months of demand would have to come from elsewhere, mostly, in the event, from Campania in southern Italy or from Sicily. If this observer was right – and there is no reason to think him wildly mistaken – why was it that early fourteenth-century Florence knew so chronic a shortfall between what local agriculture could produce and what local society needed? From one perspective the considerable rural–urban migration which occurred in thirteenth-century Tuscany simply left a fairly stable farming population supporting a newly larger number of town dwellers. Another point of view, advanced by J. Donald Hughes and others, sees the situation as 'overshoot', where people have pushed the agroecosystem so hard that it caused soil degradation and loss of productivity. The crises were, in that view, a consequence of the possible output falling below human demand.

A competing interpretation would deny overshoot on grounds that local and regional diversity and a tradition of alternative foods encouraged early commercialization of Mediterranean agriculture. Hence normal local crop failures and food shortages were met by trade, which generalized instability but avoided collapse. This position sees the continuation of political debate over 'hunger' even after the population crash of the Black Death as proof that the problem lay with food distribution, not agricultural production, making it a matter of economics, not ecology.

Because agricultural productivity has hitherto received little serious attention from historians of medieval southern Europe, the best evidence relevant to the overshoot thesis is the history of erosion and deposition in that region. Phenomena that had been seen there earlier as characteristic of late antiquity, when soils just disappeared from the fields, seem to have ceased during most of the central and high Middle Ages. They again recur in the Christian Mediterranean probably in the course of the thirteenth and fourteenth centuries. Note that these erosion episodes are interpreted as resulting from long and constant agricultural practice, and not the sudden removal of natural vegetation seen in the north. Several examples can be offered. In the south of Portugal, the Algarve, a fairly well-dated episode of significant soil erosion occurred around 1250, apparently coinciding with completion of the Christian conquest and subsequent Muslim emigration. The situation may resemble some in late antiquity, when people who had been managing land very carefully in a highly anthropogenic setting departed for reasons little related to the landscape itself, which then deteriorated as the infrastructure simply fell apart. In that same area of Portugal 150 years later, a significant late fourteenth- and early fifteenth-century episode of erosion and deposition seems rather a part of an agrarian crisis well documented in the written sources. Indeed failures of agricultural output in the late fourteenth and early fifteenth century are offered as one reason why the Portuguese turned their attention overseas. What they sought as they sailed south along the African coast were cereal supplies or commodities they could there acquire and use in exchange for cereals elsewhere. Basic agricultural productivity does seem to emerge as a significant problem in fourteenth-century Portugal.

Moving from the far west into more central areas of the Christian Mediterranean, the Montagne Sainte Victoire, a hill massif just east of Aix en Provence, experienced serious and well-recorded erosion just after 1300. Across the Maritime Alps in Piedmont's upper Po basin around Montecalieri, erosion episodes occurred after the mid-1100s and again after the mid-1200s. These events are plain but so far dated only from the human structures they buried, which can establish only *termini post quem*. Likewise in the Ombrone valley of southern Tuscany a period of soil loss and deposition seems possibly to have taken place after the late eleventh and the twelfth century. Around Rome, however, little major erosion is suggested until well into the fifteenth century. Hence the sort of evidence that should mark over-exploitation of grain lands in particular, and so tie in with the over-shoot hypothesis, remains ambiguous. The peripheral Portuguese case looks among the clearest, but this may simply reflect those areas that have been most carefully studied, if studied at all.

How much of this evidence of deterioration in fundamental relations between soils and societies resulted from overexploitation, as the overshoot hypothesis would have it, and how much is it a consequence of abandoned land and stressful weather conditions? As chapter 9 will make plain, by the end of the thirteenth century and start of the fourteenth climatic instability became a very important part of the story in the Mediterranean world as elsewhere in Europe.

Seekers after an up-to-date specialist assessment of what occurred in Mediterranean agriculture through the high Middle Ages might turn to a collection of essays on medieval agrarian societies edited by Isabel Alfonso Anton. Here surveys of the past twenty-five years of agrarian research on Italy and Spain simply lament the failure of scholars to explore long-term issues of agrarian stability, while the chapter treating southern France reports researchers more concerned with the origins of the medieval agroecosystem than with its actual operation or any crisis in that regime. Many still unknown aspects of agro-ecosystems in the late medieval Mediterranean call for study before the whole – or its diverse parts – can be discussed coherently. Only with a more thorough idea of material relationships in the countryside can historians start comparing Mediterranean situations and outcomes with the sorts of arguments debated in such detail for England and a few other northern areas.

Research on pre-industrial agricultural systems acknowledges a coupling of the ecological side – animals, plants, soil, water, minerals – with an economic side that cared about allocations of labour, handling of seed, etc. and further with the larger socio-political systems that influenced how people could make certain kinds of decisions. No one of those aspects can be assessed on its own. This interconnection between the ecological, the economic, and the larger socio-cultural system applies not solely to arable agriculture, but equally to other forms of human colonization of the natural sphere.

PASTORAL CONNECTIONS

Livestock – cattle, hogs, sheep, goats, horses, donkeys, and poultry, too – were essential and ubiquitous elements in all European agro-ecosystems. But medieval pastoral arrangements also existed independently of the strong arable orientation, constituting a different kind of adaptation to resources and nature but also to links with other societies. Pastoral groups and livestock-based enterprises likely succeed only when they can operate in exchange with more agricultural societies, especially cereal producers. The mixed farming just discussed entailed metabolic flows within the system between animals and the fields, crops, and people. For those who were livestock-centred, comparable flows were less internal and more between them and other societies. The animals that were reared and the products of those animals moved elsewhere, and notably food in the form of grain came reciprocally to the pastoralists. So animal keepers whom contemporaries and some modern viewers might represent as primitive and simple were in fact commonly engaged in exchanges between societies as complex as those elsewhere internal to mixed farming systems. Examination of livestock and pastoral activities in medieval Europe can begin with recognition of three relations of herds to space: local herds, i.e. animals that did not move very far in the course of their lifetime; patterns of transhumance in which animals may move dozens and up to hundreds of kilometres repeatedly during their lives; and situations involving open-range livestock that in some respects fitted between the former groupings and in others responded to quite different variables.

Local herds contained domestic animals that lived and died within a space of perhaps a day's journey, a dozen or so kilometres, always under the control of more or less the same people. This applies in the first place to the livestock of those mixed farming peasants just examined from the arable side. These were the beasts, draught stock, perhaps sheep, that would be put on the common pasture and would make common use of stubble and fallow. They were sedentary. In some places they fed largely on rough pasture, stubble, and weeds. In others, depending on resource endowments and uses, much of their fodder came in the form of hay. Hay is produced from meadows, places where grasses grow sufficiently that they can be cut, dried, and so kept for future use in that location or to feed animals elsewhere. Meadows in the Middle Ages were natural growth, not sown crops. They are characteristically associated with wetlands, small river floodplains, and some upland sites. English landscape historians distinguish, for example, between the Midlands, where there was significant meadow but little rough pasture, and some 'ancient countryside' with large resources of rough pasture but relatively few meadows. Communities had to organize different institutional structures to make effective use of their various sources of fodder.

Grazing on common pasture, which ranged from the stubble field through wild herbaceous growth, small bushes, even to woodlands (as will appear below), the animals of a given village community were typically under the care of a common herdsman (or, more rarely, -woman). Households did not send out someone to look after their own few head of animals. Rather the community organized itself so that one individual gathered up the beasts from where they had spent the night, put them on the pasture, and watched over them during the course of the day. These were mixed herds of sheep, cattle, and draught horses when they were not working; pigs might or might not be included. The animals were taken to their forage, then often 'folded' on the fallow overnight. A temporary enclosure on the fallow caused the entire herd to leave its droppings there and thus return nutrients to the arable. Excrement left on pasture escaped the arable cycle; that from animals kept in stables or barns was the responsibility and resource of the owner.

The livestock of mixed farming peasants was one kind of local herd important for animal production and use in medieval Europe, but whole agropastoral societies also focused on local uses of live-stock. Good examples during the high Middle Ages are the *shieling* systems of Scotland and Ireland. Gaelic communities there long continued to live using agropastoral adaptations that elsewhere were generally thought characteristic of earlier times when animals had a greater role in the resource mix than did arable farming. Native Irish and Highland Scots cultivated the better land in protected and well-drained valleys, while keeping numerous cattle and sheep to provide dairy foods of great cultural and dietary importance, as well as meat, fibres, and leather. The last two products constituted valued exports. The animals were wintered at the farmstead and in summer moved short distances to pasture at *shieling* sites in open upland woods. Literary sources suggest that both household and more collective herding were employed. Documented since the eleventh century in such Highland valleys as Glen Affric, traces of the long-abandoned practice survive as special vegetation communities where centuries of seasonal use enriched naturally thin and acidic soils.

A third kind of local herd was more specialized. These were the property of big seigneurial sheep owners, particularly in northern England, southern Scotland and Ireland, where by the end of the thirteenth century Cistercian monasteries held thousands, perhaps in some instances tens of thousands, of head. Those sheep grazed on moors and salt marshes, natural grasslands possessed by these monasteries through seigneurial rights and not ploughed up. The herds were managed to produce for export markets. Late thirteenth-century Cistercian houses ran auctions at which Italian merchants bid for the clip from all their sheep. Full-time professional herdsmen cared for these animals, using at least some aspects of selective breeding. They were moved systematically between large pastures in an effort both to grow the finest wool and not to overgraze any particular parcel. All was coordinated as a single multi-site enterprise under the control of a monastic economic manager, but specialized herders under him could be lay brothers or actual laymen. Plainly a good deal of expertise was called for to tend and profit from these animals. But none of the livestock so far mentioned was being moved very far, if at all, while alive. Hence all the local forms of pastoral connection need to be contrasted with transhumance.

Transhumance (from Spanish *trashumancia*, movement of animals) is the seasonal movement of livestock and their herders from one pasture zone (biome, ecotone) to another without movement of the settlement to which the herders and animals belong. It is not nomadism. A further distinction between vertical and horizontal transhumance relates to whether the animals changed altitude or travelled

across the landscape. Both were important to certain regional economies and regional ecosystems in medieval Europe.

Vertical transhumance between lowland and mountain pastures
had typified much of the Mediterranean since pre-Roman times. As
earlier mentioned, arid summers make forage sparse in Mediterranean
lowlands, so in the springtime the animals are taken up into the hills,
be they a few dozen or a hundred kilometres distant. Then in the
autumn the animals return. That was an essential element in the
traditional Mediterranean agroecosystem.

Alpine areas developed during the Middle Ages (and probably not
earlier) a more specialized vertical transhumance to use high-altitude
heath and grasslands for dairy production. A surviving fragment of an
early eleventh-century account book kept by the economic manager
at Tegernsee abbey on the edge of the Bavarian Alps carefully inventories everything that belonged to the dairy. Besides a hundred head
of cattle and more than fifty goats on six farms, they possessed a full set
of equipment to make cheeses. By the 1200s that same monastery was
requiring from its subject peasant communities up in the valleys payment of rent in cheeses, not grain, of which these people grew little or
none. Here large disc-like hard cheeses were later delivered by being
rolled or slid down the mountain slopes from Alpine meadows where
the cows spent the summer, were milked, and the milk made into a
long-lasting food. Down below some cheeses were stored for family
use and others went to the abbey. Tegernsee performed an interesting
exchange role between complementary regional ecosystems, giving
its servants annual salaries in grain that had been grown further north
on the Bavarian plain where the monks received rents from cereal
farmers.

The first really clear documentation for the use of Alpine meadows
above the tree line comes from a little further west in Vorarlberg
above Lake Constance (Bodensee). Both goats and cattle were driven
up there and back each summer. Origins of the Scandinavian counterpart, especially important in Norway, are of unknown date. But
already in the thirteenth century that country was exporting butter,
another durable product from livestock using terrain unsuited to
arable.

Horizontal transhumance is traditionally and famously associated
with medieval and early modern Spain. With the Christian
Reconquista and in the course of the thirteenth century, migratory
herds of sheep were evidently moved each year hundreds of

kilometres from winter pastures in southern river valleys (especially Guadalquivir and Guadiana) to summer pastures in the northern mountains and then back again. The animals belonged to individual large sheep owners – monasteries, military religious orders, and secular nobles – who formed a cartel that managed the entire system in Castile. The cartel, called the *Mesta* (a word like 'guild'), seems to have taken shape in the 1220s–1230s. It must therefore have formed in the immediate aftermath of the Christian triumph at Las Navas de Tolosa in 1212, while Castilians were asserting military control of the southern third of the peninsula and working out how to profit from the spoils of victory. The migratory sheep become well documented in an agreement between the *Mesta* and the Crown of Castile in 1273. The sheep owners conceded that every sheep using certain official river crossings (most large Iberian rivers run conveniently east to west across the central plateau) would pay a toll to the king. In return for this guaranteed annual income, the crown authorized the cartel to use designated migration routes called *cañadas* without interference from local peasants or landlords. Disputes over damages blamed on the sheep or shepherds went to special courts run by the *Mesta* itself.

Only seven years later in 1280 appears the first firm evidence of the Merino breed, special sheep that give wool of the highest quality. Merino soon came to dominate the whole transhumant herd in Spain. By 1300 migratory sheep numbered 1.5 million in Castile where the human population was 4–5 million. In 1467 Castile had 2.7 million migratory sheep. Wool exports generated the largest foreign exchange for the entire Castilian economy. Long-distance transhumance keyed in to very particular institutional structures and economic relationships. Similar arrangements later appeared in parts of peninsular Italy.

Medieval Spain also provides one of the best medieval examples of large-scale cattle-rearing on an open range. While the *Mesta*'s sheep walked back and forth across the central part of the Iberian peninsula, in the southwestern corner taken by Castile in the later course of the thirteenth century Christian settlers remained too few to replace or augment the Muslim population. This thinly inhabited area with significant seasonal wetlands came under the control of large lordships owned by military religious orders and great magnates (including those who would later finance the Columbus voyages). On the savannah landscape, some dry, some damp, with scattered trees and lower vegetation, large herds of cattle could prosper with little human care. The large estates reared tens of thousands of head in an open-range environment to produce hides for both local and export production of leather. This pastoral system was clearly in place by some time in the early 1300s. Open-range cattle herds also appeared at the other periphery of western Christendom on the steppes of Hungary and Podolia (then part of the Polish-Lithuanian state), but they are less certainly dated as early as the high Middle Ages. Their importance in beef exports at the close of the Middle Ages is discussed in chapter 10.

Open-range pastoralism is a different adaptation from driving organized herds of sheep long distances or a village herder minding perhaps a few dozen cows and a hundred sheep. Herdsmen in both southwestern Spain and Pannonia were cowboys: they rode horses, used ropes to manage the animals, and had dogs to help out. In fact historians of the North American cattle industry argue that the Iberian *vaquero* was the direct antecedent of the American cowboy. English and Gaelic speakers did not handle their herds that way. In England, Scotland, and Ireland herders did not ride but walked, and carried not ropes but a staff. Some of them worked in company with dogs, some did not. These are interesting ethnographic and hence both economic and ecological diversities in people's relation to their livestock and forage resources. Further regional differences involved whether the animals were brought under cover in certain seasons, how they were provided with or taken to their fodder, and other managerial customs. Just as the agricultural side of the ecosystem has complexities which must be probed to grasp diverse local historical situations, so has the pastoral.

Of course resource management issues arose. Inescapable conflicts pitted peasant communities that needed access to common pasture against lords who claimed a certain prerogative. As pressures increased different users competed for limited resources. Very characteristically operation of common pasture entailed some efforts to regulate use. Access was notably rationed, most often by criteria meant to favour full-scale farms (*virgaters, Vollbauer, laboreur,* 'ploughmen') over small holders or day labourers (cottars, *Gertner, manouvrier*). Widely shared features of medieval common property regimes are more fully addressed in chapter 7 below.

Pastoralism, though normally practised on land always or seasonally unsuited or unneeded for arable farming, still entailed potentially large environmental impacts. The pasturing of large herbivores changes a plant community. Some forage plants react to grazing by dying and others by sprouting and producing ever more biomass. Effects also differ with the variety of livestock, for cattle, sheep, goats, and horses prefer to eat different plants and plant parts. Again, the plant varieties respond differently to this pressure. Additional consequences arise when large numbers of animals are imposed on the landscape, for their hooves will compact certain soils, further affecting which plants will continue to grow there and the amount or speed of runoff. Hooves may alternatively churn up the soil surface and so open it up for erosion. Introducing meaningful numbers of animals into a landscape thus triggers a whole array of potential ecological consequences. Almost no scholar who has worked on medieval pastoral societies has paid any attention to this reality, making it a promising topic for original research.

What is best known about specialized livestock management and its environmental interactions comes from the early Middle Ages, sometimes also later, and concerns swine. Pigs are by nature woodland or woodland edge animals, not inhabitants of open country. Pigs eat what they find at and in the soil surface. In the early and later Middle Ages when Europe held significant oak and beech woods, those trees each autumn produced nuts that are collectively called mast. Mast is a very rich source of vegetable protein found lying on the ground or easily knocked down from the trees. People had privileges to bring pigs into these woods to fatten. The pigs ate heavily during September and October and were slaughtered some time in November or December. Pork hung in a smoky chimney kept through the winter. Many pages of scholarship and original documents treat early medieval assessments of woodlands in terms of mast production or the numbers of hogs that could be grazed in them. It is important to remember, however, that oak and beech naturally produce mast in great quantities only every second or third year and this rich fodder was then available only for about two or three autumn months. Swine cannot subsist entirely on acorns and beech nuts, for the nuts are absent most of the year. If an owner was running large numbers of pigs in the mast woods, those animals had also to be in woodlands or pastures during other seasons, rooting around to eat whatever they could find of sprouting plants, invertebrates, small mammals, bird eggs, or anything a pig a could catch and get its mouth around. Hogs need to be seen as part of an interactive and rather complex ecosystem. But the pasturing of pigs, and in particular feeding pigs on beech and oak mast, though strictly seasonal, was a highly valued use of woodland.

Meat consumption was linked intimately with the interplay of social and ecological conditions for rearing domestic livestock. Cattle, pigs, and sheep fairly consistently make up between two-thirds and almost all the tens of thousands of mammal bones recovered from hundreds of archaeological sites across medieval Christendom, leaving other families quantitatively insignificant (different survival and recovery rates for bird and fish bones prevent comparison across vertebrate orders). While on average Europeans ate approximately 60 per cent beef, 33 per cent pork, and 10 per cent mutton by weight, variations in time, space, and social rank are telling. Pork in particular was popular in early medieval centuries, averaging 40 per cent in remains dating before 1000CE, but declined to only 20 per cent by the thirteenth century. Pork eating revived briefly in the fourteenth century – a sign of regrowth of woodlands? – but by the 1500s had fallen to only 17 per cent of meat consumed. As remarked in earlier chapters, military elites especially enjoyed pork, which averaged 35 per cent by weight in seigneurial sites of all dates, while urban households ate only 20 per cent. Most peasant sites were dominated by beef. Across a wide band from northern France, the Low Countries, and Sweden east to Hungary, beef provided a third to half of meat consumed, followed by pork, which even rose to equal beef in the uplands of France and central Europe. In the British Isles and the coastal lowlands of Flanders and Holland, however, while beef remained supreme, mutton replaced pork, probably a consequence of the early and extreme clearances already discussed. Mediterranean consumers had a different carnivorous culture, eating mutton (and goat?) more frequently than even beef everywhere except in the Po valley. Even before the establishment of the *Mesta*, Christian Spaniards ate more mutton than any other Europeans.

Medieval livestock were ecological connectors. The animals linked humans and the cereal culture on one side and woodland or open pasture on the other. They helped form the ecological relationships wherein agriculturalists and consumers made use of the medieval biosphere.

WOODMANSHIP

William the Conqueror's 1086 Domesday survey of English resources found trees on only about 15 per cent of the realm; by 1340 that ratio had dropped to 6 per cent. England ranked among the least wooded countries in medieval and early modern Europe. The Midlands especially had very sparse wooded cover, which helps explain those special constraints of the Midlands agricultural system already described. Nevertheless even in England the great medieval clearances left woodland because it was recognized as useful, as an important piece of nature to be colonized by humans. In most areas of western Europe by 1200 woodland was rising in value and increasingly being protected by people who thought they had some power over it. Woodland became an object of widespread competition, conflict, and regulation. In the 1160s Malcolm IV, king of Scots, granted to the abbeys of Melrose and Coupar-Angus easements only for their use of his woodlands along the rivers Tweed and Tay respectively. A century later Cistercian monks from Tennenbach accused four neighbouring Black Forest villages of usurping their abbey's woods. Early fourteenth-century Florentine legislation limited commerce in building timber, chestnuts, and fuel wood, and later protected specific varieties of trees as sources of fuel, fodder, and raw materials as well. Lesser Tuscan municipalities were by 1337 restricting licences to use their woods and trying to zone wooded parcels for specific uses.

A 'parable' used by an early fourteenth-century cleric, perhaps a Rhinelander, to encourage selective use of his guide for preachers (*Speculum humanae salvationis*), reveals the variety of uses to which knowledgeable medieval Europeans put trees and woodland.

A certain monastery had a huge oak standing in its grounds, which had to be felled and grubbed out on account of the smallness of the site. When it had been felled, servants of the monastery gathered there and each chose the pieces appropriate to his office. The master smith cut off the lower trunk which he realized was suitable [for an anvil-base] in his smithy. The master of the leather-workers chose the bark for himself, which he crushed into powder for tanning his hides. The master of hogs took the acorns, with which he intended to fatten his piglets. The master builder chose the tall trunk, from which to cut beams and roofs. The master fisher chose the curved parts, to make the ribs of ships from them. The master of the mills grubbed out the roots, which he realized would be suitable for the mill on account of their strength. The master baker gathered together the branches with which he afterwards heated his oven. The sacristan carried away green leafy boughs and with them decorated his church for a feast. The scribe picked about a hundred galls or oak-apples with which he made up ink. The master cellarer took various pieces from which he wanted to make amphoras and other vessels. Last of all, the master cook collected the fragments and took them away for the kitchen fire.[1]

---

[1] A. Henry, ed. *The Mirour of Mans Saluacion[e]. A Middle English Translation of Speculum Humanae Salvationis. A Critical Edition of the Fifteenth-Century Manuscript*

Writing at about the same time in a different literary genre, Pietro de'Crescenzi devoted a whole book of his *Ruralia commoda* to the particular attributes and uses of nearly forty tree species.

The availability of four general kinds of resources, namely forage, fuel, raw materials, and timber, influenced how medieval Europeans colonized and managed woodlands. In the first place, woodland provided forage for animals: 'wood pasture' was open to grazing animals which ate new growth, low branches, and as far up as they could reach. Goats will climb trees to reach their browse; cattle and sheep do not. A wood grazed by cattle is visually distinctive for its absence of ground cover and any still succulent branches less than about two meters from the ground. Wood pasture is also exploited by humans going out and cutting 'leafy hay', green branches that were then dried and used like hay for feed and bedding.

Secondly, woodland was critically importantly to pre-industrial European societies for providing fuel as wood or as charcoal (carbonized wood from which water and other volatile substances had been cooked off in a kiln). Wood and charcoal were the primary sources of heat energy for all of medieval society and so will be treated in much greater detail in chapter 6. Relevant now is that neither fuel wood nor charcoal typically came from full-grown trees. Big trees were too cumbersome to handle; they had to be labouriously cut up or hauled in great weight and bulk out of the woods for use elsewhere. Fuel wood and charcoal were made from branches cut from trees or out of smaller woody plants, stems of a finger's to an arm's thickness. Conveniently portable bundles of fuel wood called faggots provided good heat or burnt nicely to charcoal, still easier to transport.

Woodland provided raw materials. From what grew in woodlands medieval people made baskets, wicker, woven fences, wattle to hold plaster in a wall, and carved or carpentered useful objects of various sizes and scales. Also from the woodland people gathered plants that met dietary needs, yielded dyestuffs and medicines, and served a wide array of other purposes. Because, unlike the hard parts of animals, uncarbonized woody material quickly decays in damp European soils, this aspect of medieval material life is less easily verified in the archaeological record.

Illustrated from Der Spiegel der menschen Behaltnis Speyer: Drach, c. 1475 (Aldershot: Scolar Press, 1986), 227. Translated by R. Hoffmann.

Finally, woodlands were the source of timber, meaning large beams, whole massive parts of big trees, the sort of material used to frame large human structures such as houses, castles, cathedrals, catapults, city gates, mills, or ships. Even regions that built largely in stone or brick had great need for construction timber and went to considerable effort to obtain it. Timber had to be hauled: the oak post for a windmill, approximately 0.6 metres square and 13 metres long (2 × 2 × 40 feet) weighed in the range of four tons (and 20 per cent more when first cut); a ship's mast or ridge pole 0.3 metres in diameter and 15 metres long weighed some 500 kilograms if spruce, more than 750 if oak, after drying for a year. It took heavy animal draught power to move such an object overland from a place in the woods where it had grown to another place where it was to be put to use. A nearby body of water flowing in the desired direction was most welcome. Rafting of timber is well recorded along the larger rivers of northern Europe, certainly from the twelfth and thirteenth centuries onwards. The Arno carried timber to medieval Florence, too. Elaborate rules were eventually developed for floating timber because the log drives endangered riverside facilities and transient drive crews posed social and legal problems. Log drives were an important part of the way medieval Europeans organized their use of woodland.

To accomplish these valued uses of woodland required know-how. Someone had to be familiar with the habits of trees and apply skill to their growth and harvest. That body of traditional ecological knowledge is called woodmanship — the knowledge and techniques for managing trees, whether by cutting them or by otherwise using them and still keeping the woodland going. Most traditional woodmanship was very much directed towards what is now called sustainable use. Woodmanship was always applied for specific purposes and oriented to particular tree varieties. Managers and workers in medieval woodlands handled different kinds of woods differently and for different results. The schematic illustrations in Figure 5.4 present several of their techniques at the time a tree is to be harvested, right after the harvest, and then a year or so later.

Most unfamiliar to moderns, especially North Americans, is the woodman's technique called coppice. It takes advantage of the fact that most broadleaf species will sprout from a stump. You can cut the tree and have it, too, for it sprouts again. From those shoots (called 'spring' in England) will come a continual crop of rods, poles, or logs depending on the interval of years the manager will wait until they are

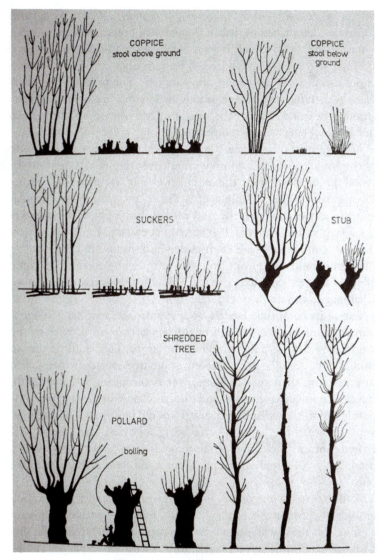

Figure 5.4 Ways of managing wood-producing trees

cut again. An English wood so managed is a 'copse' (also 'underwood' or 'smallwood'), and the technique had its equivalent specialized terminologies in Latin (*silva minuta, silva caedua,* in Hungary *silva permissionalis*), German (*Niederwald, Unterholz*), Dutch (*hakhout*), Danish (*lavskov* or *stævningsskov*), Polish (*zagajnik*), Croatian (*šikara*), Hungarian (*eresztvény*, later *sarjendó*), Italian (*bosco ceduo*), French (*taillis, brousaille*), Catalan (*bosc baix*), Castilian (*soto, sotobosque, bosquecillo, monte bajo*), Portuguese (*talhadia*), and indeed all western languages. Diverse indigenous names attest to ubiquity and antiquity. The practice itself likely went back to the Bronze Age, as indicated by material remains of large amounts of wood all about the same diameter and age, nicely uniform dimensions being a characteristic product of coppice.

Management of woods as coppice gained importance in the course of the Middle Ages as land under tree cover shrank and demand for wood proliferated with the population and its material culture. Coppice offers the possibility of sustained production of a regular annual yield of raw materials and of fuel, for coppice wood makes good faggots and charcoal. Rather than coppicing, some tree genera 'sucker': elms, aspens, and cherries need no stump but can be cut to the ground and will sprout from the surrounding roots to the same effect. Ten-year coppice cycles are documented in twelfth-century Champagne and northeastern Italy.

For all its sustainable aspects, coppice management has ecological impact. Long-term coppice brought regular human activity to the woodland, cutting and removing the crop. This traffic tends to compact the soil. Coppice weakens some tree species, which fail to survive more than two or three rounds of cutting and regrowth. Beech, for instance, gives up and dies, so changing the species composition of the woodland. A coppice wood typically contains no trees any older than the coppice cycle being followed; there is no old-growth ancient woodland. Everything is small and brushy. It is a thoroughly colonized landscape, though still indubitably a wooded one.

A further risk with coppice is the attraction of tender new woody growth to browsing animals. Animals must be excluded from a coppice or they will eat all the sprouts and the trees will die. Coppice cannot, therefore, be combined with wood pasture. Small wood and forage are incompatible outputs. The alternative is to pollard, a technique involving cutting the tree further up the trunk, just above the reach of a browsing animal. Pollarding involved more human work and danger, swinging an axe atop a ladder. But then the sprouts came from above and animals could still browse below. A 'shredded tree' offered a further variant, providing the same protection as the pollard and timber production as well. By climbing the tree to cut branches for leafy hay the tree is left to grow, albeit more slowly. It provides a way to produce fodder, fuel, timber, and other raw materials, while still allowing pasturing livestock below, if at much greater labour cost.

Not incidentally, this discussion of managing hardwood trees for continual harvest has only mentioned using an axe. Almost all cutting of standing trees in medieval Europe was carried out with an axe or comparable blade and not with a saw. Medieval carpenters, ship-wrights, and other woodworkers had saws, but as soon as people became worried about possible overexploitation of woodlands or illegal taking of wood, they banned saws from woodlands. Compared with an axe, the ringing blows of which resound a con-siderable distance in the woods, the silent saw let a poacher sneak about and purloin timber or firewood undetected.

Not common in medieval woodmanship was the planting of trees, whether as seed or seedlings. This contrasts with modern ideas of 'forestry'. In all likelihood early medieval Italian country people helped spread chestnuts as a semi-wild food source. Otherwise plan-tation forestry was little used during the Middle Ages, being first introduced for wood production in the late fourteenth century almost simultaneously in both France and Germany. Plantations are unneces-sary in order to work with broadleaf trees managed as coppice, pollard, or shredded trees or left to mature until harvested as selected 'standards' for timber. It is needful if managing conifers which, with the exception of yew and one species of European juniper, do not sprout again when cut. Conifers were relatively unimportant compo-nents of historic European vegetation communities and most medi-eval woodlands, especially those north of the Alps, were not managed for them. Only when timber production became the primary concern did conifers become central, for timber is what these trees most easily yield. Different purposes for woodlands called for different choices and different strategies

The long-term trend in medieval woodland management moved from multiple uses, that is to say extensive diverse woods with multi-ple uses of wooded parcels, towards management for an intensive but limited use – one wood to produce fuel, another pasture, etc. The trend away from multiple uses and towards a single use generated conflict between uses and among users. A peasant community reliant on traditional wood pasture for their livestock opposed a lord for whom coppicing for fuel and raw material production promised greater returns. But disputes also arose within peasant society because households required fuel too. Other struggles set lords who sought income from their woodland against peasants who needed the whole mix of common resources to meet household requirements for fuel, building, and gathered resources. Agreements, contracts, or judicial decisions established the right of a possessor of a whole farm in the village to take a limited number of timber trees – as selected by the lord's forester – to repair a dwelling, but forbade such a householder from taking wood to sell. A whole array of intensified management arose when the resource became scarce. Remember, however, that complaints about wood shortage may really indicate that the complainant thought *his* wood was getting too costly, whether from competition among users or increasing distance of transport. Big trees remained but they grew ever further away, and so became ever more expensive. Mere grumbling about wood shortage does not mean there were no longer woods, only not enough flow of wood product to satisfy someone at a price s/he was prepared to pay. The woods remained, especially in and north of the Alps and Pyrenees. In northern Europe the characteristic medieval to early modern pattern was clearance and then sustained use of remaining woodlands. That contrasts with a Mediterranean pattern of cyclical overexploitation, abandonment, and regrowth detectable during both late antiquity and late medieval centuries. In both regions, however, possessors and users of woodland and its products adjusted to perceived limits on their resources.

USING WILDLIFE

One kind of medieval wood pasture fed not domestic cows, pigs, or sheep, but game animals, deer and boar. Some woodland habitats supported fur-bearers: squirrel, beaver, water rat, wild cats of several kinds, mustelids (the weasel family), fox, wolf, and bear. All these living things had their uses for medieval society, too. Terrestrial hunting was in medieval times relatively unimportant for subsistence purposes. Wildlife did not by and large serve human dietary needs. On twenty-six long-inhabited archaeological sites in northern France dating from the thirteenth century through to the seventeenth, for instance, game animals provided but 2 per cent of the food bones at secular elite locations (lord's houses, castles) and less than 0.5 per cent everywhere else (towns, monasteries, peasant villages). With the possible exception of wild birds taken en masse for urban commercial markets ('four and twenty blackbirds baked in a pie' is not just a children's song), most people rarely hunted for food. But hunting in medieval Europe had immense cultural importance. It was a key part of elite leisure and served to demonstrate superior social status. Hunting also had interesting significance as a luxury economic enterprise supplying fur garments for personal use and, again, visible claim to elevated social rank. Both the hunt and furs made animals signs of something else.

Western European woodlands were large enough that fur-bearers from them seem important into the twelfth century. In particular, early medieval records from self-sufficient estate economies – Carolingian rulers, some of the big ninth- and tenth-century monasteries – report huntsmen and local acquisition of furs. But inexorably, through central medieval centuries up to the twelfth, overhunting and habitat destruction in the form of the great clearances had damaging effects on wildlife populations. Western fur-bearers were depleted or extirpated. By the high and later Middle Ages a beaver was but vaguely known to most western European naturalists, as their confused descriptions signal. Wild cats disappeared, and so, too, did most animals larger than the smaller weasels from all but the most remote and rough uplands in the west.

The luxury fur trade shifted to the eastern Baltic, which became Europe's source for the largest quantity of furs, mostly squirrel skins, which Hanseatic merchants packed 40,000 to the standard cask and shipped west to be worked up in the Low Countries or Venice into garments for middling or lesser nobles. Northern Russia and Scandinavia supplied fashionably rich and dark furs from various members of the weasel family (sable, marten, etc.).

The west itself substituted domestic use of an introduced animal, the rabbit. Rabbits are native to North Africa and the Romans had introduced them to Iberia. By the 1100s rabbits were present in France and by the 1200s had been brought to the Low Countries and England. Around 1500 they were crossing the Vistula in Poland and had arrived on the plains of Hungary. The first medieval European rabbits were reared in protected 'warrens'. Fearing for these fragile little habitual burrowers, their keepers in the damp north put them on dry sandy soils or built them a light earthen mound for protection (see frontispiece). When needed, the rabbits were dug out, killed for the tender meat, and the skins used to line garments of lesser, but still well-off folk, especially townspeople. Rabbit provided an alternative to fur from feral domestic cats. Meanwhile the rabbits, having adapted ever more successfully to their new habitats, themselves went feral and spread all over the continent. At the same time the native member of the related family, the European hare, seems to have dwindled and in some areas disappeared. Good comparative zooarchaeological evidence from a wide sample of medieval sites shows hare remains diminishing in proportion to rising numbers of rabbits.

Elite infatuation with the hunt as recreation and display of status from Carolingian times motivated royal creation of special privileged jurisdictions called 'forests' (*forestis*). A medieval forest was no woodland, but a legally protected area managed for game. Forests – the first documentary mention comes from the seventh century – were established on Germanic precedents by late Merovingian and Carolingian monarchs, for whom hunting was a favoured pastime and a manifestation of their royal power. The term and concept were carried across the continent in Carolingian times and into Britain by Norman conquerors. Following on the model of the royal forests, later aristocrats created private parks for the same purpose. In forests and parks hunting held priority over other forms of land use. While other activities might be permitted, even frequent, they were always meant to defer to the needs of the hunt. Institutional features of the later medieval evolution from royal hunting preserves to state regulation of woodlands are discussed in chapter 7 below.

The prototypical medieval forest or park was a distinctive sort of managed landscape, not wilderness but more a pasture growing game rather than livestock. Its vegetation (*vert*) was meant to feed the game (*venison*), mainly deer and, on the continent, wild boar, and its landscape was shaped to facilitate the hunt. An illustration from the personal hunting book made in the 1380s for Gaston Phoebus, count of Foix, shows him riding to hunt the stag through a landscape of scattered trees and small groves, relatively sparse woodland now often designated 'parkland' (Figure 5.5). The mounted hunters could see and pursue the quarry and also be seen and admired by spectators.

The hunt was a ceremonial social act of display, initially by the prince, always by the great man. Surrounded by his huntsmen, his dogs, and his retinue of lesser nobles, the lord demonstrated through elaborate and bloody social ritual his identity, superiority, and prestige. Other hunts were undertaken by the prince's huntsmen and forest-keepers in obedience to his orders to harvest his deer for a great

Figure 5.5 The count of Foix hunts the stag in 'parkland', late fourteenth century

feast. Correspondence of the English royal court from the fourteenth century contains precisely such instructions to servitors at northern forests, where the king himself rarely appeared, to ship large quantities of venison for events planned at Windsor Castle. The forest was thus a managed game preserve used for the production and hunting of semi-wild animals.

The environmental effects of medieval forests and parks were, on the one hand, protective of the wild: certain habitats were retained and consumptive use of wildlife regulated by severe penalties against illegitimate taking. The effects were also destructive in several ways. Concentrations of game animals modified plant succession just as did herds of livestock. Management and pursuit of animals for trophy kills meant no concern for expending more energy than the quarry would yield. In this way the hunter did not behave as a natural predator must and pursue the most numerous accessible prey, but might rather select and chase rare animals to the point of extermination. Such prized game as bear, wolf, and wild pig were extirpated from the British Isles by the end of the Middle Ages. The last individual specimen of the great native European wild ox, the aurochs, was killed by a known noble hunter in Poland in 1637.

Medieval hunting also entailed purposeful environmental modification. Interest in the hunt motivated medieval elites to introduce exotic animals to Europe. Besides the rabbit, a small species of deer, the fallow deer (*Dama dama*), was also brought to Europe, probably under French noble auspices. These originated in China but European populations likely descended from an earlier transfer into Persia (also for hunting) that drew the attention of crusading aristocrats. In the thirteenth century the French crown owned several herds of fallow deer. Peasant neighbours were called out on *corvée* (forced labour) to dig ponds to water the deer, build fences to keep them protected, and plant crops for their fodder. Anglo-Norman lords brought fallow deer to Britain along with rabbits and pheasants, another animal exotic to Europe. Hunting parks, like that Count Robert of Artois famously had built at Hesdin in the 1290s, could entail wholesale environmental transformation with wooded and open sections, artificial watercourses, and other habitats tailored for native and exotic beasts.

The effects, of course, are simply the demonstrations of social power: the hunt showed off who one was. By the later Middle Ages in most parts of Europe commoners were barred from hunting and the activity reserved to nobles. Even if the social monopoly was never complete or well enforced, it still provoked conflicts on the land as, for instance, when peasants found their lord's protected deer coming out of the park to eat in their grain fields or meadows. This grievance, among others, helped trigger the German Peasants' War of 1525. English rebels in 1381 carried a dead rabbit on a pole as a standard.

Medieval Europeans used aquatic wildlife in a different cultural context from the terrestrial but the results were parallel. Water-dwelling animals, generically 'fish' in medieval classification, mattered for eating (and only marginally for recreation). This was because, from the eighth century, authorities in Christendom tried to observe and enforce a religious taboo against eating meat for about 35 per cent of the year, including the forty consecutive days of Lent before Easter and otherwise a day or two every week. But in western Christendom 'fish' were an acceptable substitute for the banned flesh of terrestrial beasts. Household accounts and food remains alike establish regular and seasonally intense fish eating by those people who could bear the cost. For the poor who could little afford meat, fish posed no problem; they rarely had either. But, regular eaters of much meat, medieval elites assuaged their resentful abstention by reluctantly taking fish rather than going wholly without. The result was the fairly heavy exploitation of local aquatic ecosystems everywhere, both freshwater and inshore saltwater, for immediate consumption or short-term preservation. Fast smoking or salting could keep freshly caught fish good enough to eat for a few weeks, but the poor selection and quality of fish available by the end of Lent was proverbial. Peasants seeking their own subsistence did some of the work of fishing, but probably a larger share was by full-time fishers who historically began serving their lords but soon were fishing for markets as well.

Rising European populations, the now-familiar pattern of clearance and soil erosion, and the rapid urbanization to be examined in chapter 6 all had the unintended consequence of driving depletion and destruction of limited natural inland fish populations. Almost as soon as references to fish prices appear in mid-twelfth-century documents, their upward movement reveals imbalance between supply and demand. Fishing pressure is shown, too, in the shrinking size of favourite varieties recovered from archaeological sites of long-term consumption. In kitchen middens along the southern shore of the Baltic, for example, early medieval sturgeon were of great size, those of the twelfth century much smaller, and the species nearly disappeared thereafter. Some local runs of salmon and sturgeon were extirpated from the twelfth century onwards.

Europeans responded to what they perceived as shortages of familiar foods. Fisheries which had once been more or less common or open were increasingly privatized, brought under the firm control of lords who then leased access at market rates to commercial fishers. The market sector expanded to distribute fish to those who had the wherewithal to buy. Rulers who claimed authority over large bodies of water (big rivers and western Europe's few large inland lakes) began to regulate those fisheries. A French royal fisheries ordinance issued in 1289 aimed to preserve fish populations, limit the catch, and allocate it among various users by restricting the size of fish taken and the types of gear employed. At the same time Europeans began to expand their fisheries on marine frontiers where the pressure had to this point been slight. The expansion targeted certain abundant species that available techniques of drying, salting, and brining could preserve in bulk for later consumption elsewhere. Such fish were herring and cod in the North Sea, Baltic, and nearby parts of the North Atlantic, sardine and hake south of the British Isles and in the western Mediterranean. A major commercial fishery developed from the thirteenth century along the north coast of Sicily to catch tuna for export. Just as dried cod and brined herring spread to markets across the north, the tuna flesh was cooked, barrelled in brine, and shipped to Florence, Rome, and other mainland cities.

The assault also targeted marine mammals, prized for their oil, tough hides, and flesh rated the best among the 'fish', as it most resembled terrestrial meats. Opportune finds or captures of beached whales and attacks on accessible seal colonies in Mediterranean, western, and sub-arctic waters became more purposeful after 1000, as Basques actively pursued whales in the Bay of Biscay and Norse and other sealers worked more systematically around the North Sea, Scandinavian coasts, and North Atlantic islands. By the end of the Middle Ages the southernmost breeding population of walrus on the Scottish North Sea coast had been extirpated and Basque and other whalers had so depleted some varieties from European waters as to move operations promptly to newly found coastal North America.

Finally the perceived shortage of fish also led to purposeful environmental modification. Twelfth-century France saw intentional construction of artificial pond structures to grow fish on landed estates and the next century their proliferation along with techniques to rear a species exotic to western Europe, the common carp. This native of the Black Sea drainages of the Balkans had recently spread from southeastern into central and western Europe. Now domesticated carp were reared especially in artificial aquaculture enterprises to provide fresh fish to inland elites, the well-off who were too far from the sea to obtain fresh marine fish. Whole headwater streams were dammed and diverted to fill ponds of eventually hundreds of hectares, creating stillwater habitats where few had previously existed and further blocking the runs of native migratory fishes. Like rabbits, carp established feral populations too.

An overview of medieval Europeans exploiting their living environment reveals common patterns of human need – which drove uses in general and each specific use, of potential destruction, of conflict over use – and of efforts to manage. At regional and local scale the diversity of Europe's natural ecosystems called for, indeed helped create, specific local knowledge and social adaptations, for all that each rested on similar principles both ecological and socio-cultural. The latter meant programmes and actions always served the interests of people with power more than they did others or the environment itself. Still the medieval colonizations of natural biological resources – from the cereal economy, through the sheep, to the coppice woods, to the rabbits, and the fish – often retained some sense of real natural limits, even when pushing against or beyond them.

The next chapter extends the analysis to mainly inanimate elements of the environment: energy systems, metals, water, and the creation and nature of medieval urban ecosystems. How and to what effect did medieval European societies make use of their non-living surroundings?

MEDIEVAL USE, MANAGEMENT, AND SUSTAINABILITY OF LOCAL ECOSYSTEMS, 2: INTERACTIONS WITH THE NON-LIVING ENVIRONMENT

·

From medieval colonization of primary biological production in agriculture, woodlands, and other biota, this chapter turns to human use and sustainability of mainly non-living parts of the environment. It begins with closer study of the energy basis for all medieval society. There follow issues related to inorganic material resources, particularly mining and metallurgy, and then the wholly anthropogenic artificial ecosystems that were medieval cities. Having observed metabolic flows throughout, the chapter closes with *provisional* consideration of how well such concepts as sustainability, ecological overshoot, and collapse capture medieval Europeans' experience of the world around them.

THE ENERGY BASIS FOR MEDIEVAL SOCIETY

By present-day standards medieval Europe, like all pre-industrial societies, was a low-energy civilization. Energy was costly and always in short supply. A pre-industrial society cannot do as twentieth-century industrial societies became accustomed to do and pour cheap and abundant energy on their intractable problems. Expending energy was not the first option and oftentimes not even the last. Energy was sparse; it had to be hoarded.

Nearly all the energy that medieval Europeans could command came from capturing a tiny fraction of the current flow of solar radiation streaming continually to and past the earth. That flow can be tapped, which is what non-industrial peoples did and do, quite without being aware of it. Medieval Europeans used almost none of the huge fossil stocks of energy that had accumulated on the earth through millions of years before their time. They had to live on the current solar flow, despite its acute limitations.

Only about 10 per cent of the solar radiation that hits the upper atmosphere reaches the earth's surface in a form that is useful for plants. Of the energy green plants pick up and absorb in the process of photosynthesis, only 0.2 per cent is converted into plant biomass, the living 'stuff' only plants can make. (The rest is used up carrying out the photosynthesis and keeping the plant itself alive.) So only a small part of what hits the surface of the atmosphere reaches the surface of the planet; only a small portion of that is used in photosynthesis; and only a tiny proportion of what is used for photosynthesis ends up in the continuing body of a plant. But that is where the solar energy has now been stored. Another fraction of the solar flow heats the earth's atmosphere, resulting in movement (kinetic energy) of air (wind) and driving the water cycle that raises water vapour to heights whence gravity will cause it to fall.

Neither stored energy nor that streaming past as solar radiation actually performs any work. Energy is stored and energy does work when it is converted from one type of energy to another. Work occurs when, for instance, the kinetic energy of flowing water is converted to mechanical energy in a water wheel or to electrical energy in a generator. Work occurs, too, when the chemical energy in a sugar molecule is burned by a galloping horse or that in a hydrocarbon to drive a bus, becoming kinetic energy. Energy is stored in mechanical form in a crossbow cocked by a soldier's muscles and in chemical form in a faggot of firewood, although in each instance it must then be released in some other way. Work occurs only when energy is converted.

Two kinds of conversion were essential to the indirect solar energy system of medieval Europe (and other pre-industrial societies). For one, people accessed the energy available after solar radiation had been converted by photosynthesis to chemical or biochemical energy; for another, they accessed the energy made available as radiation is converted to heat in the earth's atmosphere and oceans and then that heat, combined with gravity, becomes the physical and mechanical energy of moving air and water. Those are the two and only major sources of energy that non-industrial societies possess. (Direct use of the sun's heat to evaporate sea water for salt or to dry fish was quantitatively insignificant.) Both the (bio)chemical energy derived from photosynthesis and the physical mechanical energy associated with the natural movement of wind and water currents are inherently limited, either in their total availability or in the power that they can exert at any given moment. The medieval world was one in which energy resources were constrained both in kind and in the quantity of power they could generate.

Characteristic of humans as culture-bearing animals are both that acquiring knowledge of the environment allows them to identify sources of energy and that human technical innovation improves the effectiveness of use of those sources. Hence a given society has two ways to affect the amount of energy that is accessible to it. Both of these processes, finding new sources and extracting more from old ones, may be observed in the history of medieval Europe, serving to shape and alter relationships of people to their surroundings.

By far the greater energy resource available to medieval Europeans was biochemical, the biomass created through photosynthesis by green plants in areas under the control of European cultures. In practice the quantity of biomass and hence of accessible biochemical energy was bounded by the area and type of land available to plants and by the efficiency of the agricultural or woodland production systems that were the primary reservoirs of that kind of energy. Medieval people used this biochemical energy in two ways: to support muscle power and as a store of chemical energy in biomass.

The muscle power of humans and animals comes from their consuming as food the energy that plants had captured days, months, or at most years earlier. Almost nothing that people or domestic animals ate in the Middle Ages had existed for more than a few months, at most a couple of years. Food was not stored so very long. Even a sausage made from the flesh of a very old plough ox, which still may have retained some energy from year-old hay it had eaten as a calf, offered a store of energy that had but ten years earlier been solar radiation. That is the kind of short window through which the energy providing the muscle power of humans and animals came.

Humans consume between 2,000 and 2,700 kilocalories of energy on a more or less daily basis; that works out at 8–11 megajoules (MJ), the unit of energy in the metric system here useful for comparative purposes. We distinguish between energy and power, which is energy doing work in time, i.e. energy flow in time. That human consumption of 8–11 MJ corresponds to a little more than 90 watts (W) (the unit of power, 1 joule per second) per day. Mammals, whether humans, oxen, horses, donkeys, or any other of those organisms that did draught work in medieval society, convert into their own power approximately 13 per cent of the energy they digest. The rest of it serves to maintain the metabolic life cycle of the individual organism. Human work is powered by that 13 per cent of digested energy and so too, therefore, is all movement of material objects by humans or by draught animals.

A human can exert somewhere between 70 and 100 W, just enough for a low-friction bicycle generator to keep a light bulb glowing. A draught animal produces in the range of 500–800 W, with an ox nearer the lower and a well-fed horse the higher end. This is between five and ten times the power of a human. This biochemical energy that had come from the sun through plants and through animals, human or domesticates, provided almost all the mechanical force to move things in the medieval world. The mechanical energy dragged against friction, so part of the power being exerted became simply waste heat and dissipated into uselessness. The perpetual struggle against friction means that even hitching many people and/or draught animals to add up their power eventually reached limits that derived from the sheer weight of all the necessary harness. There are inherent constraints to the quantity and weight, the sheer mass, that can be moved using the muscle power that was the principal prime mover for medieval society.

Various mechanical devices, windlasses, capstans, treadmills, etc. were available to help, using mechanical advantage to multiply a small amount of power by reducing its speed and thus slowly moving greater weights. Wheels on vehicles will, if the situation makes rolling friction less than dragging friction, gain great efficiencies. But without a surface that has been flattened and made smooth and hard, wheels help little. Every cartload or pack sack, every plough, harrow, or weaver's shuttle, every load of spices, firewood, water, or manure used by medieval people was moved over the ground by human and animal muscle power. The food- and fodder-producing systems described in chapter 5 were essential energy producers for movement of bodies and materials.

The second way in which medieval Europeans used the biochemical energy provided by green plants was by converting into heat the energy that had been stored in biomass over a period of perhaps some decades. They burned wood fuel. Where muscle power worked using energy no more than five to ten years old, burning a fairly old tree released energy that it had captured maybe a hundred years earlier; coppice-grown fuel was, of course, much younger. By geological and comparative standards, the system remained in the very short-term flow of solar energy. Much of this was the burning of wood: recent estimates by Paolo Malanima and Paul Warde of needs for pre-industrial European heating and cooking converge in the range of 45–55 MJ per person per day or the energy equivalent of two to four kilograms of wood. A household of four or five people would thus average just less than 5 tonnes per year, with significant regional differences from about 1.5 tonnes in Italy to 10 or more tonnes in Scandinavia and areas of continental climate in the northeast. As in present-day non-industrialized countries, fuel costs for these subsistence purposes were genuinely high; this wood had to be obtained in one way or another. It was expensive in money, exchange value, or labour time. It meant that ordinary people tended to cook on very small fires and that most medieval buildings were chilly at best except in the Mediterranean summer.

Heating was accomplished with a small hearth made of stone, bricks, ceramics, or similar fire-resistant material. The small brazier was typical, a portable metal grill work where some fuel could be burned and moved around to heat the space being occupied at a given time. These served most Mediterranean buildings including very large Renaissance palaces. Hypocausts, the Roman central heating system with sub-floor ducts carrying warm air from a central fire, though known from early medieval episcopal palaces in Gaul and probably Italy, seem by Carolingian times no longer to have been installed in new buildings. Fireplaces, which enable a bigger fire and remove the smell and smoke from the room, were a development from the twelfth century onwards. They seem to be northern innovations, associated with elite structures, particularly castles that were slowly becoming more residences, less purely fortifications. While some fireplaces appeared in monasteries, by and large they were a lay development. Yet a fireplace loses most of its heat up the flue with the smoke. A more efficient medieval heating device was the brick or tile stove, what Germans call a *Kachelofen*. This technology originated in central and eastern Europe in the course of the later Middle Ages. Its combustion chamber was sealed away from the occupied space, both drawing air from and venting to the outside. The burning fuel heated the air and the ceramic cladding around the chamber and this radiated into the room. These highly efficient devices can produce significant quantities of heat. Distinctly a late medieval innovation from the central continent, tile stoves spread only gradually to the Netherlands and elsewhere in western Europe.

Otherwise if people felt chilly they had to cram more of them into a small space or live under the same roof, perhaps in the same room, as their livestock. Dwellings designed for the latter purpose developed in northern Germany and Scandinavia.

The perpetual need for fuel meant all kinds and sizes of wood could serve. Any combustible (straw, etc.) lacking other use and protection was potential fuel, especially if it were nearby and reasonably dry. Dry wood made a vastly superior fuel, for it provides 30–40 per cent more energy for a given weight than does green wood. Energy density is the quantity of energy per unit weight. That of the best dry European hardwood, beech or maple, is between 16 and 19 MJ per kilogram. Hence most wood was either collected dry by breaking off or picking up dead limbs or else harvested for fuel use but then stored for a year or more to dry it and gain more heat per weight and burning time. It is no surprise that both peasant and urban communities with access to woodlands jealously guarded their right to go in and acquire fuel by gathering dead branches or in some instances actually cutting trees, as potentially wasteful as the latter expedient might be. Wood provided the vitally important energy source necessary for space heating and for cooking.

Besides setting cut wood aside to dry, the other possible treatment was to convert it into pure carbon, an extremely good fuel. This was managed by heating the wood in an absence or limited supply of air, producing carbonized wood, now called 'charcoal' and prior to the nineteenth century simply 'coal' (as distinct from 'mineral coal'). A charcoal burner stacked wood and covered it with earth or turves so it burnt slowly, driving off all of the volatiles and most other components and leaving almost pure carbon. The resultant charcoal contains two-thirds more energy than an equivalent weight of wood: 28–30 MJ per kilogram compared with the 16–19 MJ of the dry hardwood from which it may have been made. It takes three or three and a half times the weight of wood to make a given weight of charcoal, a fuel that is much easier to transport, much lighter, and has a much greater energy density. Charcoal burns without smoke and emits no contaminants because everything else has been burned off. No pollutants affect a process or final product made with charcoal heat. In consequence charcoal was the fuel necessary for most work involved in firing ceramics and in smelting metals; other combustibles introduced contaminants that damaged the product. Lack of smoke and smell also made charcoal the preferred source of heat in elite dwellings. Not surprisingly, therefore, charcoal was significantly more expensive than wood, so was not typically used by ordinary people who had access to local wood supplies. Maple and beech were, at least in northern Europe, the preferred source of charcoal, and professional charcoal burners often selectively exploited woodlands of these species. However, in mountain mining districts, maple quickly disappears with altitude, while beech responds poorly to some kinds of coppicing and also thins out at higher elevation. The common European mountain conifers – pine, fir, spruce – were the woods those areas used heavily for charcoal production of admittedly inferior quality but it was close at hand and thus lower in cost.

Hauling fuel was a huge and difficult task, calling for expenditure of much muscle power for the sake of the heat energy that was to be gained by burning. An earlier chapter noted the insight of the Anglo-Saxon riddle which identified the plough man as 'the grey foe of the wood' to recollect that through the whole of the Middle Ages Europe was deforested mainly for the sake of arable agriculture. But as those arable clearances slowed in the course of the late twelfth and the thirteenth century until they stopped in the fourteenth, fuel demand came to exert the greater pressure on remaining woodlands. This is visible to historians in, for instance, decrees that the prince-archbishop of Salzburg issued in 1201 and 1237 as he tried to protect Alpine woods located near mines and salteries. Local fuel shortages in England lay behind royal restrictions placed early in the thirteenth century on forges in the Forest of Dean. By the late 1200s the concern emerged in the municipal statutes of most Tuscan city-states, in which clauses calling for general protection of woodland plainly echo much conflict. In central Germany wood management ordinances for the sake of fuel appeared in the thirteenth century, doubled in number by the fifteenth, and multiplied ten-fold in the sixteenth. A worry about wood fuel would become the really big issue as time passed. Whether as wood or charcoal, biomass fuels provided most of Europe's heat energy throughout the period here examined.

Some alternative fuels of sub-fossil and even fossil origin deserve mention. The same peat that Dutch farmers ditched, drained, and tilled made, when cut into blocks and dried, a rather nice fuel. Burning peat tapped energy that had been stored for the past few millennia: the great peat bogs of the Low Countries and areas of the British Isles were of mid-Holocene origin, so by the Middle Ages no more than 5,000–7,000 years old. Anaerobic acid conditions preserved the ancient vegetation while new grew on top, so peat is really a sub-fossil fuel. It provides good energy but with a low energy density, only 6–8 MJ per kilogram unless taken from high ground and thoroughly dried, but still below good hardwood at 16–19 and charcoal at 28–30. Peat, however, was regionally abundant, so for those who lived on top of great quantities, it was well worth using. Peat was being systematically mined in the Low Countries – which had soon destroyed the relatively little woodland with which they began – by the late twelfth century. The count of Flanders licensed some of his barons to mine peat in extensive areas. There followed continual expansion in the regional use of this fuel, to the point where it came to make a strong contribution to economic activity. Peat lay significantly behind Flemish and Brabantine growth in the later Middle Ages and the early sixteenth century, and then especially supported the phenomenal development of the Dutch economy in the late sixteenth and the seventeenth century. Deposits elsewhere around the North Sea and in the British Isles served local needs.

The Middle Ages also made real if limited use of fossil fuel, what on the continent would be called 'mineral coal' and in England typically 'sea coal', because it arrived in London, the main centre of medieval consumption in Britain, by sea from the mines of Newcastle in northern England. The British Isles were not, however, the earliest European area known to extract mineral coal for fuel purposes; coal mining at Liège in the French-speaking eastern Low Countries was recorded in a charter of 1113, though unlikely to have much pre-dated this. Within a century such extensive subterranean galleries underlay large parts of the episcopal city as to require regulations to ensure that one mine did not dig into another and that the whole industry did not undermine the cathedral itself. By the 1220s English sea coal was being shipped from Newcastle to London, where it served primarily to burn lime for plaster, an essential building material for a city then burgeoning from 40,000 to almost 100,000 people. Newcastle then also exported coal to coastal France and the Low Countries.

'Sea coal' was cheaply dug from shallow and rich surface deposits around Newcastle, but was expensive to ship due to its weight, for all its high energy density. The weight of coal meant it was rarely used away from the mines unless it could be moved by water. It was also disagreeable when burnt. As early as 1257 Queen Eleanor of England has the distinction of being the first known complainant against noxious fumes from coal, as the coal fires of Nottingham stank up her residence in the castle there. From the 1280s rising complaints about coal smoke in London eventually provoked a royal prohibition in 1315 against its use there – which evidently failed. Real decline in English use of sea coal occurred only after 1350 as the population collapsed and with it medieval demand for this relatively difficult and unpleasant fuel. Coal fires would not again multiply in England until the mid-sixteenth century, after the population had finally regained its early fourteenth-century numbers. In the medieval setting in England, then, coal use was very much associated with the high-pressure demographic conditions of the late thirteenth and early fourteenth century, not earlier. People really did not like the stench of coal smoke and accepted it only under duress when wood fuel was scant and costly.

The same chemicals that created a stink made coal unacceptable for both food preparation and metalworking. Although different coal sources vary in particulars, mineral coal characteristically contains significant sulphur and phosphorus compounds as well as traces of heavy metals (the latter probably unknown to medieval people). Food cooked directly over mineral coal tastes foul, so few willingly used it for that purpose. Smelting metal ores or working refined metals using a coal fire produced an alloy different to that desired. Resistance to coal for such uses persisted until new techniques were developed to obtain heat from coal without exposure to its fumes. Various methods separated the coal from the material being worked, so the heat could radiate from some kind of reverberatory oven or the like. Those new technologies for industrial use were developed piecemeal almost entirely after the mid-fifteenth century. The real breakthrough arrived only in the late sixteenth and early seventeenth century with the development of coke, a carbonized and decontaminated form of coal analogous to the charcoal made from wood.

Medieval Europeans did exploit these non-biomass fuels, peat and mineral coal, but only in very limited places for limited times or limited purposes. The greater supply of heat energy in this society came from biomass fuels, basically wood and wood derivatives like charcoal. Likewise the lion's share of energy for moving things came from the same biological processes.

Inherently limited available supplies of these sources of biomass energy need to be recognized as playing off against regionally different energy demands posed by the diversities in medieval cultures. In the north space heating had greater cultural importance than it had in the Mediterranean. Despite what are by global standards comparably chilly winter conditions in southern England and central Italy, palaces in Renaissance Florence were still being heated only with charcoal braziers, while London palaces had fireplaces two or three centuries before. People in maritime Europe just seem much more concerned to have warm spaces than did people in the Mediterranean region, which means the former were prepared both to develop the technology and to use more heat energy. On the one hand, the more abrupt relief and relatively few navigable rivers in Mediterranean lands likely raised per capita demand for draught power in transport; on the other hand, the lighter soils and simpler tillage techniques worked in reverse, calling less for big ox or horse plough teams to put traction energy into agriculture. Perhaps these differences balanced. With the issue defined in speculation, good research scholarship might model and test the difference. The point is to recognize that probing into energy needs calls up many potential connections. In a similar mode, beer-drinking cultures have different energy needs from those of wine-drinking cultures: the former require grain to make their beverage and fuel to prepare it, calling in total for much biomass; the latter use no heat to process their wine, but it is typically moved from production to consumption sites with the water already in it, and so entails more weight, packaging, and transport. Until the last medieval centuries beer was typically made in the locality where it was consumed and the water not moved any distance. So, quite apart from the different crop requirement, there are intriguing energy differences. Towards the end of this chapter discussion of urban metabolic footprints will make plain that per capita consumption of cereal and fuels in northern cities was significantly greater than rates in Florence, something probably to do not only with temperature differentials but with cultural distinctions involving how much people ate and how much energy they used in preparing their preferred dietary elements. The context for these decisions was as much cultural as it was based on strictly physical aspects arising from non-living elements of the natural world.

Medieval Europeans made indirect use of another important effect of the flow of energy from the sun: its working with gravity to drive natural movements of air and water. Winds and currents flow when air and water that have been heated by the sun become less dense and are displaced by cooler, denser, air or water, which slide 'downhill' towards lower altitude or pressure gradients. Moving air and moving water provided medieval Europeans (and all other pre-industrial societies) with the only available prime movers other than animate labour. Lacking muscle power, the only way to move anything in the medieval world was to exploit currents of water or air.

The movement of rafts and sailing vessels on the water was the only non-muscular form of transportation this society possessed. Running water was in fact essential for the transport of timber and fuel. Fuel wood floated more than a hundred kilometres down the Arno to Florence. Fifteenth-century log drives on the Rhine carried timber from the Black Forest downstream to eventual users in the Low Countries. Mountain legend even related that really tall trees were lacking because 'blond giants from the north' had come and taken them away. (The average Dutch person is a head taller than people from the Alpine area.) Little rowing and sailing skiffs, towed barges, and other small craft swarmed on waterways everywhere. Anything that could be set afloat, even with a boat barely four or five metres long, was so transported. Some of that movement did involve muscle power as people rowed, poled, and dragged vessels upstream or used draught animals to tow them, but they tried wherever possible to use the energy of running water.

Medieval sailing vessels were slowly adapted to make more efficient use of moving air. Around northern seas and the Mediterranean early medieval ships reflected different cultural traditions and designs with, in both instances, significant reliance on oarsmen. Iconic types are Mediterranean galleys and Viking longships. The regions subsequently shared parallel evolutions of clumsy but capacious wind-powered craft, called *navis* ('ship') in the Mediterranean by the twelfth century or so. Its northern counterpart, as in a fourteenth-century example recovered from the harbour of Bremen, was the *cog* (*Kogge*). These were not rowing vessels, being too short and tubby to set up for muscle power, but driven mainly by one or two sails. They were ungainly, needing the wind more or less astern to work. While not very fast, a *cog* or *navis* could handle bulky mercantile cargoes.

Only with later medieval innovations, which began to accumulate in the course of the fourteenth century and blossomed especially in the fifteenth, did Europeans achieve great improvements in ship technology, as Mediterranean and northern traditions merged, probably in the heads and hands of shipwrights along the Biscayan coast of Spain. The uppermost craft in Figure 6.1 dates to about 1430 and the lower depicts *Santa Maria*, lead vessel on the first known direct European transatlantic voyage in 1492. This was what we now call a

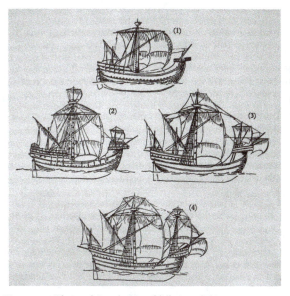

Figure 6.1 The evolving design of full-rigged ships, *c.*1430–1530

'full-rigged ship', with increased size, good sea-handling abilities, and a 'mixed rig' of a square and a triangular 'lateen' sail. The latter, known in the Roman Empire, offered greater manoeuvrability but delivered less power when the wind was in certain directions relative to the course of the vessel. The combination in the mixed rig seen by 1430 provided the ability to sail closer to a contrary wind and, if the wind became favourable, to use the big sail for greater power and speed. The subsequent trend visible in Figure 6.1 was to an ever more mixed rig, three masts, and more but smaller individual sails, which improved the ability to adjust to wind conditions and employed a smaller crew. The mixed rig thus used less biochemical and more wind energy. This late medieval chain of technological innovation created the means of connecting continents from the fifteenth century and into the nineteenth. It coincided with an innovation of knowledge and skill which Europeans developed in understanding the wind systems of first the Atlantic and later the global ocean, and harnessed so air currents drove their cargoes across the planet's seas.

Besides the weights of ship and crew, the greatest mass borne by medieval and early modern marine transport was itself energy supplies – foodstuffs and fuel. Really expensive goods, spices and precious metals in particular, came in tiny quantities and most of the weight carried on the earliest intercontinental voyages comprised the crew, their fresh water, and their rations. Then very quickly the ships were put to such work as hauling dried codfish from North America, wheat and rye from the Baltic, and similar commodities to and around Europe. Biomass sources remained key pieces of the energy system, even when sailors were better exploiting a non-biomass form of energy.

Moving air and water provided alternative ways of moving things, but likely the more important contribution they made was to drive the most complex and powerful fixed engines known to pre-industrial Europeans. These were mills. Watermills, that is grinding devices powered by water-wheels, were the older and more abundant. Romans had known and used the water wheel, even building some quite large ones, but the big spread of the water-powered mill in Europe was medieval. While nothing suggests the presence of water-wheels in Roman Britain, Domesday Book of 1086 records 5,624 watermills in southern and eastern England alone. That number has been estimated to represent one watermill to about every 350 people (70 households?) in the region.

Water-powered mills went through an important technical evolution during the Middle Ages. The machines began back in classical antiquity as simple small 'horizontal' mills, with a vertical shaft linking millstones at the top with a wheel suspended in the water below and oriented to rotate in the horizontal plane (Figure 6.2). Driven by the current, the spinning wheel rotated the upper millstone to provide the grinding. The design works on small, fast streams as found, for instance, in much of Mediterranean Europe and southwest Asia. Still puzzling to historians of technology is the precocious proliferation of horizontal wheels in early medieval Ireland, where more mill sites now known than anywhere else pre-date the tenth century and the technical vocabulary was of indigenous vernacular origin. Hypothesized is an increase in cereal production associated with Christianization and a well-substantiated cultural connection to the Iberian peninsula and thus Roman antecedents. There, too, horizontal mills lasted even into the nineteenth century in hilly areas where there was relatively little demand for flour and meal and small high-gradient streams could drive them.

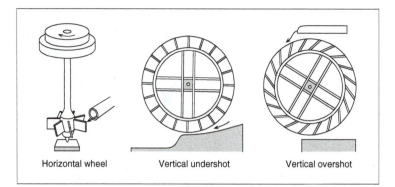

Figure 6.2 Forms of water-wheels

A larger vertical water-wheel geared to rotate horizontal stones became a great tool of economic development and source of power for medieval Europeans. A vertical mill-wheel still now probably fits most westerners' image of a traditional grist mill, but this device went through evolutionary transformations during the Middle Ages.

The earliest vertical wheels, sometimes called Vitruvian mills after the Roman writer who first described them, were undershot. This design dips the lower portion of the wheel into running water and derives its power from the speed of the current, the same as with the horizontal mill. It could also function where the flow was accelerated below a low, 0.5–3 metre impoundment. Figure 6.3 reproduces the schematic drawing that Abbess Herrad of Hohenbourg made of one that drove a mill at the mid-twelfth-century abbey at Landsberg in Alsace. Her drawing also seeks to represent the complex machinery all mills needed to convert vertical rotation to horizontal. Undershot wheels were common during the Middle Ages. By about 1300 there were sixty-eight mills along a 2 kilometre stretch of the Seine upstream of Île de la Cité at Paris, which was a reach without dams. All ran from undershot wheels, some of them mounted on abutments under bridges and others as ship mills, where the entire mill was mounted on a raft or ship hull anchored in a river where the current turned the wheel. This application was better adapted to fluctuating river levels than was a land-based installation, but when extensively used on the late medieval Rhine at Cologne could be shut down for weeks by winter ice.

Figure 6.3 Schematic drawing of an undershot water-wheel driving a grain mill as represented in Abbess Herrad of Landsberg (Alsace), *Hortus deliciarum* (1176/96) (nineteenth-century tracing of destroyed original)

An alternative design was the more potent breast wheel, where the water hit at about the midpoint of the circumference and provided power by a combination of the water's speed and weight. A breast wheel can work from a 2–5 metre head (difference in elevation), whether at a site with naturally falling water or where it might be backed up artificially.

Really successful energy capture came with the development and proliferation of the overshot wheel, also sketched in Figure 6.2. This design delivers the water from the top, so the wheel is driven primarily by the weight of the water as it falls from a height of 3 metres or more. Ideally the water hits at about the three-quarter point of the wheel. An overshot wheel works on a small high-gradient stream but, unlike the undershot or breast forms, also on a slow one. The latter situation called for a more elaborated weir or dam to back up a head pond, and then a mill race or leet to channel the water to and from the wheel. In 1177 at Toulouse on the Garonne, a fairly good-sized river fed by the snows of the Pyrenees, a consortium of townsmen and clerical landowners financed construction of a new dam called the Bazacle. This ran diagonally across the Garonne, so its length from bank to bank was 400 metres, and provided energy to drive twelve mills, some using breast wheels and some overshot. These more powerful devices replaced twenty-four ship mills formerly operating on the same reach of river. Bazacle was but one of three dams in the city of Toulouse, and its twelve mills were complemented by two other dams with eighteen and ten more mills of their own.

To judge from modern reconstructions, a typical Roman mill generated at best something in the range of 1800 W of power (compared with a draught animal's 500–800 W). Some large wheels known from around 1500, following a millennium and more of piecemeal technical development, little of it committed to written form, seem to have generated in the range of 6,500 W. The energy efficiency of water-wheels thus increased by a factor of three or four during the course of the Middle Ages.

Medieval proliferation of water-wheels was closely associated with the process of cerealization, for they were primarily designed and used to power the grinding of grain. They were also probably linked with seigneurial wealth and power in local society. Creating a watermill took considerable investment to obtain water rights, establish control over the flow of the watercourse, and then build the physical structure of the mill itself. Maintenance and repairs added to the cost. The great twentieth-century historian Marc Bloch argued that lords used coercion, building the mill and then compelling their subjects to use it as a means of exploiting them. That is to say, people of power built mills to extract compulsory milling dues and thereby seize a larger share of tenth- to thirteenth-century improvements in peasants' abilities to produce cereals. Bloch's theory was important for historians working out the history of the watermill. Recent English and Italian research, however, emphasizes that resistance to compulsory seigneurial mills was in fact quite rare and that they provided huge savings in peasant labour. The difference between grinding grain every day by hand in the household and doing so occasionally with the use of this power engine, even if for a fee, released from this level of food preparation significant quantities of household labour for employment elsewhere. One recent hypothesis suggests that the work of women in the household was now turned to much increased production of textiles. In any case, the labour-saving quality of the watermill was very real.

The person who ran the mill was a professional miller, a fellow who, with his own household, concentrated his time on it. He held the mill as a tenant or lessee and for his services collected a fee called *multur*, usually something like a tenth or fifteenth of the quantity of grain brought to the mill. The miller paid a portion of that to the lord and the other portion was his own livelihood.

Environmental historians observe with respect to the watermill, and especially the ever more dominant overshot design, that as soon as people erected impoundments, they interrupted the natural flow of the river and formed a barrier on it. The mill pond (power reservoir) flooded out riparian meadows or fields and might damage upstream properties. Others who wanted to use the river to move goods up- and downstream came into conflict with the miller or mill owner. Likewise animals such as salmon or sturgeon seeking to move upstream to spawn ran into problems, as did the eels which migrated downstream. Millers could often make a good side income by trapping fish as they concentrated along the barrier. The fishing rights for a mill, which resulted from human modification of the river's flow, are thus also among the features of this environmental intervention. So, too, were decrees and legislation from regional assemblies and territorial princes ordering mills to provide passage to both river shipping and migratory fish. Water-wheels might epitomize both medieval use of natural physical processes to extract energy and the social and environmental consequences of this colonization.

Windmills are not old European devices like water-wheels. They suddenly appeared in the continent in the twelfth century. Curiously, the first European windmills looked nothing like the simple prototype from southwest Asia, where people had been using wind energy for some time. In the course of the eleventh century European pilgrims or crusaders may have had occasion to encounter the windmills working in parts of Syria, Mesopotamia, and Persia. Those mills might best be envisaged as horizontal water-wheels turned upside down: a vertical pole mounting horizontal wind vanes at the top is supported by some kind of structure so it turns a millstone at the bottom (see Figure 6.2). Europeans never made windmills of that design. Instead someone with experience of European water-wheels that used gears to shift the plane of rotation from a vertical wheel to horizontal stones seems to have picked up the southwest Asian idea of wind power and applied it

Figure 6.4 A post windmill in a thirteenth-century English manuscript

to his own concept of a mill. Hence European windmills are as stereotypically imagined: vertical blades rotate on a horizontal axle with gears to a vertical axle for horizontal rotation of the stones.

The windmill is particularly well adapted for use on flat terrain like that of the Low Countries and eastern England, in regions with strong winds such as much of the Iberian plateau, Greece, and the Greek islands, and in dry areas. Windmills generate much less power than do large water-wheels, but they can be hitched up in tandem. The first form of windmill is called a post mill because, as seen in Figure 6.4, the entire mechanism and structure was mounted on a post and turned as one to align the vanes to catch the wind. Post mills continued to be used in many places. Further technical development evolved from the whole mill being movable to the tower or 'smock mill' design in which only the top part with the axle for the vanes was adjusted. This allowed the much larger structure of, for instance, traditional Dutch windmills. The technical evolution from the post mill to the smock mill permitted more effective operation. How development of Spanish and Greek windmills compared with that of those in north-western Europe needs further research.

Prior to the thirteenth century the overwhelming majority of mills now known to scholars served exclusively for grinding grain into meal or flour. As an aspect of cerealization, they aided the subsistence flow of energy from plants to food, from the agricultural sector into the kitchen, and thus the consumption sector.

Industrial mills proliferated especially from the late twelfth and thirteenth century, when such devices as sawmills and fulling mills were first described and depicted in illuminated manuscripts. The earliest known reference to a fulling mill in France dates to the 1080s, so its invention cannot be attributed to Cistercian monks. Houses of that order did, however, have water power fulling cloth and at forges on granges in Champagne and Burgundy by the 1130s. Paper mills, crushing mills, hammer mills, and the like followed in the later Middle Ages. Most of these devices call for a mechanism different from a grinding mill, which still employs rotary motion. The working action of a sawmill goes back and forth and a fulling or hammer mill up and down in reciprocating motion. Industrial mills are early applications of the camshaft, essentially an axle with humps or bumps that can trip something up and down and so convert rotation into linear motion. Use of windmills for pumping (also a reciprocating action) was worked out in the early fourteenth-century Low Countries at the very time that the peat soils there were sinking and causing worry about floods. The greater diffusion of pumping mills came only with and after the late fifteenth century. Water-powered pumps were probably the most powerful fixed engines that medieval or early modern Europeans could employ.

Just as energy needs could push medieval people to move economic activities closer to reliable sources of fuel, water power pulled various manufacturing enterprises to these energy sites. Paper-making and the fulling of woollen cloth, both activities carried out in twelfth-century towns, often relocated in the course of the late thirteenth and fourteenth century to rural sites where falling water could drive the mills. The Essone, a tributary which joins the Seine not far above Paris, drove a dozen flour mills in the thirteenth century, but by 1380 four power sites had been converted to mashing rags for paper. By about 1500, though, the paper business had partly relocated and ten flour mills clattered away, five fulling mills were at work, as well as others grinding tanbark and pressing oil. Access to water power was also essential to the growing number of processes engaged in extracting and working metals and sometimes used to drain mines. As early as 1284 a consortium of landowners and mine operators in the southern Black Forest contracted to build a fifteen-kilometre canal across the mountain ridge to power a wheel for a pump to keep a mine dry and a bellows at its smelter and forge. Moving water and air were not only themselves inorganic sources of energy for a culture overwhelmingly dependent on organic biomass, they became essential means of access to the inorganic mineral resources that medieval Europeans also came to employ in rising quantities.

INORGANIC RESOURCES: MINING, METALLURGY, AND OTHER MANUFACTURES

Life in medieval Europe rested upon biomaterials. Practically everything anybody handled came from something that had once been alive: leather, wood, wax, thatch, plant and animal fibres, oil, bone. Metals were nevertheless essential, always for edged tools and common wherever durability was a critical requirement. Most modern scholarship on mining and metals in medieval Europe, however, treats the monetary metals, specie, namely gold and silver, and says rather little about the metals then in everyday material use. The latter were certainly, by the high and later Middle Ages, a far greater mass than that consisting of silver, and, after the 1250s, gold, coins and other precious objects. One modern scholar estimated that an average late twelfth-century peasant household possessed only a few kilograms of iron and one or two kilograms of other metals, notably brass and bronze. But with a great expansion of the use of these materials, by the late fourteenth century the descendants of that same family would possess somewhere between twenty and a hundred kilograms of metal. This human colonization of inorganic nature had significant environmental and cultural linkages.

Medieval participants in both popular and high intellectual culture understood metal as something that came from the earth. Thinking in terms of four physical elements and the theory of humours, they conceived that in hollow places deep below the visible soil surface subterranean heat sublimated a mixture of earthy and watery materials into vapour whence, over time, the purer metal hardened out. Continuing slow metamorphosis ripened base metals into noble silver and gold. In *De mineralibus* Albert the Great likened this natural process to that used by skilled alchemists. He and contemporaries further remarked how smelters used heat to separate gold, silver, iron, copper, and other metals from the stone with which they were still mixed. After strenuous labour had dug from the earth some selected earth-stuff, in the space of a few days the smelter cooked it into metal. So, too, might one hope to take some base metal, carry out arcane procedures, and generate gold and silver. All was understood as emerging from the earth like plants or springs of water. But people did have to go to the earth to secure the metals.

Mining and metallurgical activities spread widely across medieval western and central Europe. Map 6.1 indicates mining areas scattered about wherever usable minerals might be reached, from the surface to, by 1200, hundreds of metres below ground. Many features of this industry were common irrespective of the metal sought. Once found, an ore body was exploited until it ran out or went out of reach into strata too deep or too filled with water for miners to work.

The weak understanding historians now have of medieval mining is because it was hardly ever described in writing and the rare exceptions were by authors who knew little about it. As for material evidence, early mines and sometimes also smelters were typically destroyed because subsequent miners dug and built a larger, newer mine on top of the previous site or else dumped tailings from new mines there. So finding genuine medieval mines in situ is very rare. Most now lie buried beneath sometimes hundreds of metres of modern mining waste in various areas of central and western Europe. What can on occasion be done is to analyse the chemical makeup of medieval metal objects and medieval slags and use the trace elements to identify the origins of the ore. Every mine site has not only whatever mineral was meant to be mined, but a distinctive mix of contaminants. Many trace elements, especially heavy metals, will survive smelting even into the refined metal. Copper in a brass candlestick from Notre Dame in Paris may, for instance, show traces identifying its ore as from the Harz mountains in Saxony. This method was an important, if still little exploited, breakthrough for the scientific archaeology of metals and mining.

Mining rights, the acknowledged claim to seek and extract that which is in the earth, were everywhere associated with the overlord. Mining was considered a regalian right, in Roman times held in fact and in theory by the emperor. In western monarchies medieval kings usurped this right, while in the Empire from the thirteenth

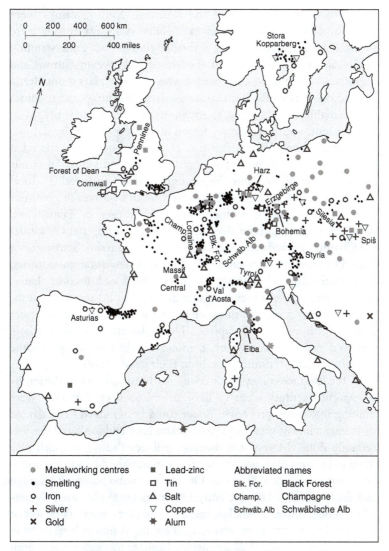

Map 6.1 Principal regions of medieval mining and metal-working

century onwards it was transferred to territorial princes. The holder of regalian right then granted access to free individual miners in return for their payment to him or her of a 'royalty' on what they took out of the ground. Miners typically started as individual entrepreneurs and formed self-governing communities under the authority of some officer of the overlord. Mining camps were boom-and-bust phenomena in the Middle Ages just as they were in modern times. This poses a further obstacle to understanding medieval mining, as many of those camps, however famous and important at one time, disappeared when the ore played out after a generation or two. Rather than single large workings, many mines long remained small, often seasonal, enterprises, commonly, as in parts of tenth-century France, found in clusters now to be defined by local geology. Where the size of an ore body allowed, what began with such family-scale shafts dug by individual labourers eventually developed into larger undertakings financed by local lords and nearby investors. In the twelfth and thirteenth centuries big Cistercian and Carthusian monastic houses in France and Germany were important developers of large mining areas in southern Champagne and some parts of the Harz mountains. Starting with a need to procure raw materials to construct new rural monasteries, these evolved into key sources of institutional cash income. Later, for example in the mineral-rich ranges around Bohemia, lay lords and urban entrepreneurs more often provided the necessarily quite large commitments of capital. Those investments particularly involved drainage, for water in mines would ultimately become the most common limiting factor in their productivity.

By the late 1200s many production sites that dated back to the tenth- or eleventh century seem to have delved so deep that they were running into water problems. Water could be removed from a mine by having a line of small boys pass buckets back and forth and this was certainly done. Miners dug drainage galleries ('adits') as much as a thousand metres diagonally through the mountain down to the valley floor so the water could run out. Of course, this did not work if a mine had already followed the ore body deeper than the valley itself. Water-wheels could power a windlass, pumps, or bucket chains of one sort or another. From 1277 there was erected for the Rammelsberg mine in the Harz a water-wheel of six metres diameter to extract water from one important shaft. Eventually this failed to keep up and after 1360 the Rammelsberg mines were abandoned for two centuries until more effective drainage techniques became available.

By the later Middle Ages mining and metalworking had become the largest single source of pressure on surviving woodlands in many localities. Mines need timber for pit props and other construction, while the whole growing metals sector required vast quantities of fuel.

Ores were initially, and in some places always, transported to the fuel: it was cheaper to move the rock to the fuel than vice versa. Prior to the thirteenth century both smelting and forging operated at relatively low temperatures and slowly consumed local fuel resources, then moved on to another fuel resource as each locality was depleted. By the early 1300s the copper-silver mines of the Herle district, along the southern fringe of the Massif Central in Languedoc, had used up economically accessible woodlands and went out of production. Development of high-temperature smelting in late medieval blast furnaces made it feasible to work larger ore bodies longer, though it demanded more fuel. In some mining areas extensive clear cuts, particularly of mountain conifers, were used to create fuel. Many mining areas developed an extensive trade in wood, floating fuel down mountain streams from higher altitudes to the smelters and forges. Some areas developed specialized coppice managed entirely for metallurgical purposes. A mine that controlled such a fuel farm was assured a regular but limited annual supply of energy. Some mines by the sixteenth century operated for only a portion of the year because that was as much production as they could handle with the fuel on which they could rely.

Mining had significant environmental impact beyond the issue of fuel. Mines cleared surface vegetation and broke the ground surface to reach the ore, opening up the ground particularly of mountainous areas to erosion. Miners, whose job underground remains the most dangerous industrial occupation in the modern world, faced gas, cave-ins, falling, and other hazards. Contemporaries were in fact aware of the risks of living as a hard rock miner. After extraction, the ore was washed and crushed: this polluted water with dirt and metallic toxins. Smelters emitted quantities of carbon dioxide, of which people were then unaware, and large amounts of sulphur dioxide, of which people would be entirely aware, as it produced highly corrosive sulphuric acid when mixed with water. Particulates and heavy metals from ores and smelters appeared in the soil, plants, animals, and human beings. A better understanding of these environmental impacts and the technological processes that drove the metal industry to consume so much fuel requires separate treatments of non-ferrous and iron metallurgies, as they worked quite differently.

The three most important bulk metals exploited by medieval Europeans were non-ferrous, namely silver, lead, and copper. Few places on the sub-continent then produced gold, which Europeans largely obtained from the African kingdom of Mali and elsewhere. On the other hand, Europe was most likely in the Middle Ages the world's principal producer of silver. But the then most-used silver ore in Europe contained in fact much more lead than silver. This mineral, galena, is an amalgam of lead and silver sulphides and still the richest lead ore employed in the world today. Because the lead-silver ores and also the copper minerals smelted during the Middle Ages were mainly sulphides, the ore had to be reduced, using some other chemical to pull the sulphur compounds away from the metal. The traditional reduction agent was carbon, which is why charcoal is such a critically important input for the metallurgical industry. About 98 per cent of the metal content in galena is lead and only a mere 2–4 per cent silver. Mining galena and purifying the metals from it yields a thousand kilograms of lead for each kilogram of silver. The medieval world was in some respects awash in lead. Europeans used lead for roofing large buildings such as cathedrals and for water pipes; lead served to hook together the pieces of stained-glass windows and as brackets and staples connecting some kinds of stone work. Lead was included in pewter, solder, and some other alloys that could be melted, cast, and easily worked. The impression is that the medieval world had more lead than people knew what to do with, at least until they developed firearms to hurl it at one another.

Lead-silver sulphide ores were smelted through a double roast–reduction process with an operating temperature of between 700 and 900 °C. At those temperatures the lead begins to melt and the silver dissolves in the molten lead, while other impurities mostly burn or float off as slag. The second step was to oxidize the lead, leaving behind the silver and great quantities of lead oxide, which can easily be taken back to lead if desired. This was how all silver was extracted from the Carolingian age, when Europe went over to a currency based on the silver penny, up to around 1200. At that time workers developed what is described as a high shaft furnace, which used an air blast to achieve temperatures in the range of 1,200 °C and liquefied the metals much more quickly. But to obtain a consistently successful air blast a water-powered bellows worked best. At that point the smelters, which had been located in the upper watersheds in order to be near their fuel supplies, moved several hundred vertical metres downstream to where a larger river could drive bigger wheels to generate the air blast.

A hundred thousand silver pennies, the normal coin used in normal medieval transactions up to and beyond the 1250s' reintroduction of gold coinage, were struck from a hundred kilograms of silver. That weight of silver was obtained by refining 200,000 kilograms (200 tonnes, roughly two modern railway carriages) of ore with the heat energy from 30,000 kilograms (30 tonnes) of wood. Were the lead also recovered, it came to 100,000 kilograms (10 tonnes). While medieval lead-silver smelters probably never kept production accounts, medieval monarchs did keep close track of the silver they received as royalties and the larger quantities their mints turned into coins. Where these records survive they provide a bottom-line proxy for how much silver was being produced and how much ore had been handled, thus providing some idea of the galena mined and the lead potentially produced as well. At peak output, probably the two most productive silver mines of the Middle Ages, Freiberg in Saxony during c.1175–1225, and Kutna Hora in Bohemia, c.1290–1360, each yielded about 20 tonnes of silver per year. The small but locally significant Tuscan centre, Montieri, produced 400 kg during its best years of the 1220s–1250s.

Copper is one of the few metals present in nature in its pure form; 'native copper' is simply lumps of copper produced by natural geological forces. This did exist in Europe but, having been used since the Bronze Age, was mostly depleted. Medieval copper production largely involved exploitation of copper sulphide ores, undertaken in a single-stage process whereby the ore was directly reduced by burning with charcoal. In the fifteenth century the so-called Saiger process came into use and allowed reduction of more difficult copper-silver ore. This opened up whole new ore bodies in the Harz mountains, Black Forest, and Bohemia. The new method first reduced the copper-silver mix, then introduced lead to dissolve the silver from the insoluble copper. After reducing the silver from the lead by traditional means, large quantities of copper also remained.

Copper was valued as the foundation for bronze and for brass, the latter being much the more important alloy for most of the Middle Ages. Brass, a blend of copper and zinc, was then made not by combining the two pure metals, but rather by roasting their two sulphide salts together and yielding the alloy directly. In a rare exception, a monk who called himself Theophilus had written down a clear description of that process already by 1100, but trace analysis of surviving medieval brass objects suggests that the technique was probably in use at least a century and maybe two earlier than Theophilus reports it.

Production of lead, silver, and copper through these smelting processes generated significant toxic contamination of the environment. They emit dust, fumes, and heavy metals, not only those being refined but traces of others as well. This medieval pollution can still be observed today. Even now vegetation anomalies occur in areas of the Harz mountains which are identified as smelter sites dating to around 1000 CE. Soils there hold so much toxic copper that certain plants will not grow, while the organisms that normally break down dead organic matter are at such risk that they do not appear at all. As a result early medieval organic objects are there found amazingly intact for lack of anything to decompose them. Pioneer toxicologists in the early nineteenth century diagnosed large-scale cattle deaths along certain rivers rising in the Harz as victims of zinc poisoning from medieval mines. When floods eroded waste dumps from long-abandoned zinc works in the mountains sixty kilometres away, suspended sediment flowed down the river and into the meadows. When cattle grazed on now dry grass, the metal content from what were 700–800-year-old zinc salts killed them all. Sediments along Black Forest streams below medieval lead workings still contain lead concentrations ten times the modern safety standard. Similar high lead values appear in riverside deposits dating from the ninth to the thirteenth century along the river Ouse in the city of York, England, and so, too, in those of post-thirteenth-century date along the nearby rivers Don and Tyne. All of these are consequences of mines and smelters which operated in the Pennines, the mountain backbone of central Britain, during the Middle Ages. While Romans had for a time worked the same lead deposits at smaller scale, no contaminated sediments are known from that period, but more substantial medieval use left great amounts. Were the right samples to be taken from human remains in the area, lead contamination would likely be found there as well. Human colonization of inanimate nature can leave long-lasting legacies.

Medieval iron-making produced comparatively little particulate, gaseous, or toxic effluent, but it imposed even greater energy demands than did the non-ferrous metals. Those demands multiplied greatly in the later Middle Ages. Iron was produced in ancient and earlier medieval times from what are called 'bog ores', accretions of iron oxide (rust) that form in acidic wetlands where iron is present in underlying soils and rocks. They are hydrous iron oxides, with a water molecule joined to the iron oxide molecule. Early iron-workers also made use of soft iron carbonate ore, and then developed the ability to work with red oxide ore, a harder mineral containing heavy concentration of iron oxides and silicates commonly associated with some other metals. From such materials medieval methods could extract a tonne of raw iron from ten tonnes of ore plus eight tonnes of charcoal. Producing that eight tonnes of charcoal will take thirty tonnes of wood, approximately the annual growth increment on a five hectare beech coppice wood. Fuel costs are 40–80 per cent of production costs for making iron in this way.

In the early and central Middle Ages, as since the early European Iron Age, iron production followed what is now called the 'direct process', going straight from the ore to nearly pure low-carbon wrought iron. This began with a hearth or low shaft furnace equipped with small air ducts and perhaps a bellows that fed air into the burning mixture of iron ore and charcoal (Figure 6.5). In this 'bloomery', temperatures in the range of 800–900 °C caused most of the ore's impurities to liquefy and run off as slag, while the resultant pasty lump or 'bloom' of iron, still retaining significant impurities, could be kept hot on a forge and the remaining slag beaten out physically with a hammer. The eventual product was a relatively soft and workable material, very tough but never molten. By the late eleventh century water-wheels appear in association with bloomery iron production, at

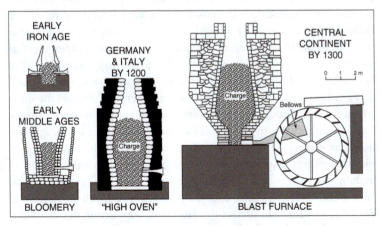

Figure 6.5 Changing medieval technologies for smelting iron

first more for grinding and polishing a final product, and later for driving hammer mills.

A second historical step exploited recognition that wrought iron could have carbon added to it: were it heated high enough, a small quantity of carbon made steel; but were the temperature higher still (1,500 °C) and larger amounts of carbon added, the iron melted and could be run into an ingot called a 'pig'. This 'cast iron' had been molten and now took the shape of a mould. Production of cast iron was achieved in a blast furnace, a late medieval European innovation or development. Iron made in a blast furnace can be identified because the high-temperature slags are chemically distinctive and the iron itself noteworthy for high carbon content. 'Pig iron' can be re-melted and cast into another mould. Cast iron is hard but brittle, good for certain kinds of applications and not for others. For some purposes cast iron must be re-melted and more of the carbon extracted to get it back to steel, which is a low-carbon alloy intermediate between wrought iron and cast. Hence, acknowledging that a second step was necessary to obtain wrought iron, the new process is called 'indirect'.

Late twentieth-century scholars made important progress in ascertaining the history and location of the development of the blast furnace. Experts now quite agree that the first blast furnaces appeared some centuries earlier and further east than had previously been thought. Some distinctive slags and metal remnants suggest that a prototype of a blast furnace was in use between the eleventh and thirteenth centuries in central Swabia, the fuel-rich Schwäbische Alb to the east of the Black Forest. It becomes quite clear that by the 1200s certain iron-producing locations were making heavy use of power bellows, equipment that would only be required where people needed an air blast strong enough to generate the temperatures at which iron melts. Development of this technology seems to have been completed somewhere in the zone between northwestern Italy and southern Scandinavia by the fourteenth century. At least the most advanced iron-production area, stretching from the western Alps of Italy, through western Swiss and German lands, and extending as far north as central Sweden, seems to have been deploying a mix of bloomeries and blast furnaces by that time. Spread of the advanced technology to France and England, however, took place only a little later. Scholarship had once focused on some quite well-documented French, then English, sites of this later date, supporting the view that the blast furnace emerged in that area. Then for a time it was argued that the innovation occurred in Lorraine. All were areas in which iron production had achieved importance at the end of the Middle Ages.

Big bloomeries could produce a few hundred kilograms of wrought iron; a blast furnace yielded between three and nine tonnes of cast iron from a single charge and operational cycle. It took some weeks to set the furnace up, to operate for several days, and then tidy up afterwards, but possible output of iron had suddenly increased by an order of magnitude. In places with long traditions of iron-making like the Forest of Othe on the border between Champagne and Burgundy, upland forges were abandoned from the late fourteenth century as new furnaces appeared along the river Vanne. But those iron masters had to compete for water power sites with operators of fulling and tanbark mills. By around 1500 it was not unusual to see water power operating a dual installation in which managers could switch back and forth between running the mechanized air blast into the furnace and running it into a refining forge.

In the early Middle Ages individual entrepreneurs with their own small bloomeries made Europe's iron. Iron-workers were often thought to possess almost magical skill, able to bring vitally important weapons and tools out of rock, coal, smoke, steam, and furious noise of hammering. Early Germanic legend made Wayland the Smith the master of arcane powers over metal. Such small-scale, often itinerant, workplaces were assembled into larger enterprises on the estates of twelfth- to thirteenth-century Cistercian and Carthusian houses in central France, England, Scandinavia, and Germany. But as some of the technical breakthroughs came to the fore, iron production became more associated with lay lords and investors, who recovered the initiative in central and east-central Europe. The same probably took place in Sweden, a major late medieval exporter of pig iron. Other production areas such as the mountains of northern Spain deserve much closer study.

Environmental aspects of other medieval manufacturing industries also need recognition. Some of them were very heavy consumers of fuel. Glassmaking heated to a viscous state a mixture of reasonably pure silica sand with a chemical substance called potash (potassium carbonate, K_2CO_3), which had been obtained by burning wood to ashes, running water through them, and then evaporating the water. Medieval glassmaking could create one kilogram of glass from somewhere between one and three cubic metres of wood, 97 per cent of which went to make the potash and only 3 per cent for the fuel to fuse the potash and sand together as glass. Very early on water power was brought to this industry to generate higher heat. Salteries were also major fuel users. Hot, dry places along Portuguese and Mediterranean coasts could produce salt by evaporating sea water in shallow artificial basins, but further north it was accomplished by boiling sea water or the output of natural brine springs in large metal vats. Around Friesland and further north salt was made from the ash of salt peat. Peat that had come to be impregnated with sea water was cut, dried, and used as fuel. Then the ashes were dissolved in water and this water boiled to extract the salt. The heat for each batch came from burning the peat for the next. In some areas along the North Sea peat mining was largely oriented towards the production of salt, using the peat as both raw material and energy source.

Another important extractive and manufacturing sector used essentially no fuel. The people supplying one of the main medieval building materials, stone, worked in quarrying. With picks, wedges, sledgehammers, and human and animal muscle aided by simple pulleys and derricks, they cut and moved tonnes of rock. The phenomenal multiplication of stone buildings, particularly in France and other areas of western Europe, after the turn of the millennium has inspired modern scholars to argue that churches and cathedrals, castles, palaces, and increasingly also private dwellings caused more stone to be excavated in France between the eleventh century and the thirteenth than had been quarried through the entire history of ancient Egypt. While it may not be feasible to test this assertion, it is true that modern Paris lies atop 300 kilometres of tunnels that served to extract the stone used to build the medieval city. Local sources saved great expenditure of energy to move heavy stone. Elsewhere and more generally large amounts of this essential and prestigious material were transported almost exclusively by water.

Manufactures other than metals and stone remained in the organic realm. Many small objects were cut from animal bone, the byproduct of the butcher's trade, as were the skins needed for leather. Besides animal hides, tanneries used a great deal of fuel and generated considerable noxious organic effluents as well. Both tanneries and woollen cloth production also used some mineral resources (fuller's earth, alum) as part of their processing. Fabrics made from flax or hemp used fibres extracted by a process of rotting out the rest of the plant (called 'retting'), which leaves an effluent lethal to living things that drink from or live in water contaminated by it. Most medieval manufacturing enterprises did produce certain toxic wastes and they absorbed some-times very significant quantities of materials. However, as all were typically localized and their scale far below modern outputs, large areas damaged by pollution are hard to find.

URBAN ECOLOGIES

Also localized but widespread and ever more central to the expanding socio-cultural system of medieval European Christendom were cities and an increasingly integrated urban network. Urban ecologies formed special relationships between the cultural and natural spheres of medieval Europe.

An earlier chapter briefly mentioned the effects of classical urbanism. Now the remainder of this chapter takes an environmental view of medieval urbanization, which established features of a urban sector that continued through the early modern period. After the late antique depopulation and disappearance of many urban sites, city living in the west reached a nadir during the seventh and eight centuries, when a realistic viewer has difficulty finding genuine urban communities outside Rome, a few other relicts, and, of course, al-Andalus. In Carolingian times the only large cities on European soil were Byzantine Constantinople (population 500,000–800,000) and Muslim Córdoba (roughly 500,000 in the tenth century), Seville, and Valencia. A western revival began in creeping form in ninth-century Italy and was strong there by the end of the tenth century. By the years around 1000 and thereafter, urbanization had again become a culture-wide socio-economic phenomenon, however small its prevalent scale. These little towns, both resuscitated and new, tended to acquire internal self-government after their original economic evolution during the course of the eleventh to the thirteenth century, while Europeans every-where undertook from the twelfth century into the early fourteenth a wave of new urban foundations. The result was that by around 1300 an urban network had become well established. Its basic shape would endure thereafter even into the industrial age and still underlies much of Europe's core urban network today. The medieval pattern featured intensive urbanization in northern Italy and a secondary dense zone in the Low Countries, with outliers extending to places like London, Paris, and Cologne, and elsewhere a sparser but widespread reticulation. In Spain the thirteenth-century Christian conquest shrank the big Andalusi centres as new inhabitants found places in a different European web.

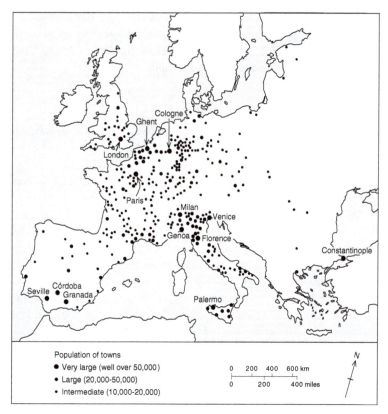

Map 6.2 Europe's larger medieval cities, *c. 1300*

Map 6.2 indicates the distribution of the larger towns of Europe around 1300. Urban historians now believe that certain places then much surpassed what was formerly thought a high range of 35,000–50,000 inhabitants. Paris is now agreed to have had a population of 200,000; Florence, Milan, Venice, and London all approached the 100,000 mark, and another dozen or so cities pushed 50,000. The pattern of urban life then extended out and down a gradient to literally hundreds of little towns with 2,000–5,000 people, spaced out all over the relatively developed parts of western Christendom.

Urbanization both created in medieval Europe a new kind of landscape with problems and possibilities for local environmental management and established metabolic patterns that affected environmental relations across much wider areas.

Medieval cities provided a new human environment (see frontis-piece). Juridical boundaries and physical walls cut the city off from its immediate surroundings. Within was very largely a built environment full of people. Cities crowded humans and commensal organisms – those creatures that have successfully adapted to living close to human beings rather then trying to get away from them – densely together. This they did in physical surroundings that had been purposely modi-fied for human social needs – late twelfth-century Braunschweig was erected on some two million tonnes of earthen fill put into low ground beside the river Oker – and at what was, in the perspective of Europe as a whole, an unprecedented scale. In the mid-thirteenth century, a recent estimate suggests, every human resident of Florence had some forty eight square metres as his or her share. Indeed so large a number is reached only by including the surface area of the Arno and its meadows, all the streets and piazzas, and everything else within the town walls. Florence at that time probably held about 80,000 inhabitants who were rapidly multiplying. Paris by 1300 housed more than twice as many in an area somewhat smaller than that of Florence, compressing the urban space of each to only sixteen square metres (a 4 × 4 metre unit). Seen another way, the population density of Florence was about 2,100 per square kilometre and of Paris about 6,200; the latter number is higher than present-day London, at 5,100 /per square kilometre the densest in western Europe. That few dwellings rose more than three storeys from the ground further constricted medieval urban living space.

Building practices and living habits replicated their vernacular rural origins. Wood, wattle-and-daub, and thatch construction, unpaved passageways, stored foods and raw materials of organic origin provided ample habitat for rats and mice, pigeons and sparrows, cockroaches, and certain exo- and endoparasites (liver fluke, tapeworms, lice, fleas), as well as the dogs, cats, chickens, pigs, and horses townsfolk intentionally kept nearby. The close proximity of people, households, and animals meant easy transfer of parasites between different households and hosts. The one mitigating factor was frequently recurring fire, which cleared things out for a time.

Further, the urban landscape was increasingly and then purposely impervious. Despite the sometimes significant intramural burial grounds, gardens, and even vineyards or meadows, towns were a terrain of beaten earth, of buildings, of increasingly paved squares, streets, and courtyards. Tenth-century Ulm was but a mercantile settlement beside a royal residence, but its two principal streets already boasted a hard surface. A chronicler reports that Philip II of France (1180–1223) ordered streets in Paris to be paved to make them easier to clean and to reduce the stench of accumulated waste, but this affected only a handful of principal routes. While residents were supposed to pave and maintain the street before their doors, as late as the 1390s royal officials were trying to enforce this obligation on major lay and religious lords. Florence instituted a paving programme for major streets in 1237. In so far as such policies succeeded, rain or melt water, as well as any spilt liquids, either ran rapidly off or pooled on the surface, flooded, and so offered more habitat for additional kinds of creatures willing to live beside humans. The city was environmentally very different from a rural village.

Urban authorities, be they officers of a traditional lord or officials of self-governing communes, were well aware of the hazards of medieval urban life. They promoted planning, sanitation measures, and the exile of offensive or dangerous trades to downstream or extramural locations. So, for example, the thirteenth-century statutes of Ferrara banned preparation of flax or hemp, cleaning of fish, and dumping of tannery waste in the river Po. At Bologna communal legislation forbade urinating in public and required butchers to take their waste to designated dump sites outside town. Municipal authorities in Coventry obliged each householder to clean the street in front of his or her place each Saturday under pain of a fine and, as in York and Norwich, provided city-run weekly rubbish removal services. Right-bank Paris, where the greater portion of the population lived, was ringed by a circumferential sewer canal that came off the Seine above town, went around the city, and returned below to the river with its load. This existed by some time in the 1200s, was covered over from the 1370s, and maintained by civic officials. Financial records of sewer maintenance operations remain in the Paris municipal archives starting from about the 1420s. On the left bank the little river Bièvre, named for long-extirpated beavers, was canalized in the thirteenth century and became an open sewer. Municipal funds designated to clean and restore it were diverted in 1390 to repair bridges and royal officials instructed to prosecute riparian residents for damage or neglect. But by the end of the Middle Ages its course was clogged with mills, tanneries, and dye-works. Buried not long thereafter, the Bièvre has lately become the object of campaigns to restore urban streams to the light of day, so undoing on modern cultural grounds medieval efforts to reduce risk.

The aim of this urban environmental management, as it would now be labelled, was improving the quality of life for citizens, not environmental protection. City governments were among the first in Europe to take on these problems. But still, the paved streets and the fire-resistant stone, brick, and tile construction came first to the prestigious commercial, administrative, and residential quarters in the city centre. The best part of town, as the centre was in all pre-industrial cities, remained remorselessly more salubrious than were labourers' dwellings crammed beneath the walls or clustered around the city gates.

Nevertheless, and not just from general cultural ignorance about how some diseases spread, medieval cities always suffered distinctly higher death rates than did the countryside. Infant and child mortality was always high in these societies, but in cities the rate was twice that of the countryside. Cities were death traps for little people. While established mercantile and craft families could last through generations, a very large floating population of impoverished newcomers – rural–urban migration is typical of pre-modern urbanism – turned over rapidly. Cities soaked up rural reproductive surplus because of their high mortality rates. This, too, was part of the environmental reality of medieval urban life.

Cities are unusual ecosystems because, unlike most others, urban ecosystems cannot maintain or replace themselves. City ecosystems are formed and maintained by cultural inputs, really in one sense by inputs of information. Much as rural decisions made woodlands into fields, urban cultural ferment generated programmes, which generated work, in this case the construction and maintenance of the city itself. Cities are not colonized ecosystems, either, but rather wholly artificial ones. Urbanization was not a transformation of nature, but creation of an entire second nature. Natural processes certainly go on in every city, but many of those processes were not in that place, did not exist, until the city was created.

Most city people were engaged in non-agricultural activities. Hence in metabolic terms they were not 'producers' and had continually to exchange materials and energy with a differentiated hinterland outside the city's boundaries (physical or conceptual). In 1287 Austrian monk Engelbert of Admont precociously estimated that four agricultural producers were needed to support one non-productive individual. Every city exists by exchange with what is outside the city. Cities cannot be without a more extensive ecological footprint because cities do not themselves produce what is required to maintain the life of the organisms within them. In consequence urban centres call for analysis in metabolic terms, examining the flows of energy and materials into a pre-industrial city, staying behind in the city as a sink, and flowing out of such a city, here, concretely, the cities of medieval Europe. From a spatial perspective this approach resembles the urban market supply regions famously conceived as concentric rings by nineteenth-century economist Johan Heinrich von Thünen (1783–1850), but augments that theory to recognize the non-contiguous quality of some inflows, the importance of urban effluents, and the environmental impact of all these movements.

Into every medieval European city flowed foodstuffs (cereals, meats), water, fuel, building supplies (wood, stone), raw materials (fibres, skins), and human beings with their all too material bodies. Cities do not engage in primary production, so they must import energy. The very nature of the urban ecology means cities are dominated by consumer organisms and consumer activities.

Londoners around 1300 consumed between 34,000 and 35,000 tonnes of grain each year. They used it for food, for drink (ale), and for animal feed. Those quantities of cereal took the output of 10–15 per cent of the arable land in a zone that extended some 250 kilometres along the Thames and its estuary, reaching from just short of Oxford down to places fronting on the North Sea, all accessible by water transport. The grain literally floated into the city. The supply zone reached barely 30 kilometres away from navigable waters.

Concentrated medieval urban demand for heat energy organized and sustained intense coppice wood management on thousands of hectares close to London and close to Paris. Wood fuel was produced as near to the city as people could devise or cheap water transport provide. For Paris, woodlands as much as 100 kilometres up and down the Seine were needed to feed wood into the city. The Danube bore fuel wood and timber for fifteenth-century Vienna from as far upstream as the Isar in Bavaria. Urban demand for energy also drove the first commercial application of fossil fuel, the coal coming down from Newcastle. So, too, were generations of Flemish and Brabantine townsfolk the principal consumers of the dried peat being mined from deposits anywhere between 20 and 100 kilometres distant in north Flanders, north Brabant, and Holland.

Water delivered grain, fuel, and building materials to towns and was itself a critical metabolic input. Water supply for urban sites is a matter of quantity and quality. In a world without the germ theory, culturally defined understandings of water quality had to do with smell, clarity, and the nature of the source. Most sites in the urban network of medieval Europe were located on rivers and streams, so townspeople began simply exploiting natural local supply, dipping surface water the same way as in a village. Urban growth outstripped or degraded natural local supplies. The response to that shortage depended on local conditions and the kinds of sources that could be acquired. Towns in some areas turned to a technology that had originated in monastic water systems, piping water in from springs or upstream diversions. Others used extensive rain-water cisterns, which had both monastic and castle forerunners. Medieval fortifications were sometimes built right on the water and others high up a waterless crag. Castle designers had to consider how deep a well could successfully be dug or else arrange runoff from every hard surface in the castle to flow into a storage tank.

Towns thus had models from which to adopt piping or cisterns. Paris brought its water down from the springs of Belleville, seven to eight kilometres northeast of the city, first through a stone conduit, then out through lead and ceramic pipes to domestic and institutional consumers. Italian towns repaired old aqueducts and built new ones. Spoleto was repairing its aqueduct in 1122; Salerno, Perugia, and Genoa all constructed new aqueducts from nearby mountains in the thirteenth century. The Sienese exploited the peculiar geology of their hill to excavate seepage tunnels beneath the city itself where the water gathered to flow to pools and fountains. More widely applicable was the innovative water-powered pumping system installed at Lübeck in the 1290s to bring water from the upper river Trave to the town's breweries. Such elaborate infrastructures were rare in England. It is next to impossible to find a serious urban water supply system there, even in London. Such systems were mainly private, which is to say they served the wealthy and powerful while most ordinary households obtained their water from wells tapping into ground water under the city or relied on water that professional water carriers brought in from the Seine, Thames, Rhine, Pegnitz, or a fair distance up the Tiber. (Even in classical times no one voluntarily swam in, much less drank from, the Tiber at Rome.) These arrangements for water supply help explain why medieval and early modern urban populations everywhere failed to reproduce themselves, so that rural–urban migration was a constant feature even though most new-comers soon died.

Some metabolic inflows came to rest in towns. Cities are a sink, a place where materials settle and energy is released into entropy. Medieval towns were sinks for wood and stone, as for cultural and biological wastes. Matter accumulates in cities. Medieval culture reused and recycled a wide variety of materials just as it did symbolic elements. Clothing was passed down from owner to owner until what once graced a prince had become mere rags wrapping a beggar. Bone was made into a wide variety of small utensils and tools, spoons, needles, and the like. Urine was recycled as a fixing agent for the dyeing of cloth: a bucket outside a dyer's shop invited passers-by to contribute. Built structures decayed, were refurbished, or pulled down and a new one erected on the rubble, often reusing the old materials. Bricks from a major Roman frontier post on the Danube, Ratispona, served to build elite family tower houses in twelfth-century Regensburg. Most undisturbed medieval urban sites have a richly organic black layer, as archaeologists call it, a gradually accumulated stratum of all the organic stuff and effluvia that blew, washed, or was kicked around the town until it settled between the stones or in a little-used corner. Carefully sieved, these now yield tiny but ecologically informative objects like seeds, small beads, beetles, or fragments of bird bones. As buildings were torn down, the ground surface rose. The place Vikings called Yorvik ended up to two to three metres below the surface of its successor, later medieval and modern-day York.

Medieval cities, unlike their Roman predecessors, were also sinks for human bodies. Romans had required that human corpses be removed from town. That is why all great early Christian sites lie outside the walls of classical Rome in places like the catacombs or St Peter's. Medieval cemeteries, however, were in town because early medieval Christians wanted to be buried as close as possible to the relics of saints, holy people whose remains were kept in or near an altar. As towns grew up around a cathedral church or another with many revered bodies, people tried to await eternity in that company. Space within the church was limited, so reserved for the most influential, but close beside the church up against the wall bodies were buried, reburied, and accumulated, and bones began to surface. To make room for newcomers, other skeletons were intentionally excavated, removed, and stored in charnel houses that lined the interior walls of the cemetery or the exterior walls of the church, or they were placed in a crypt below the building. This accumulation, too, raised the soil surface. The elevated level of old urban cemeteries is famous everywhere in Europe and in fact the rest of the ground of the city rose as well. Almost any old city is several metres higher than it once was. Part of the contribution is the insoluble remains of the human bodies gathered there.

Further materials stayed in latrines, cesspits, and middens. The average adult human produces roughly 150 g of faecal matter and 1.5 litres of urine daily. For a small but significant medieval town of 5,000 inhabitants that was 250 tonnes of solids and 2,500 tonnes of liquids annually. Florence generated twenty times that, 5,000 tonnes of solid human waste (omitting that of animals as too difficult to estimate), and this piled up. It is not surprising that a stranded side-channel of the river Seine at Troyes, key mercantile centre in Champagne, blocked by construction at both ends but still full of liquid, was in a formal charter of 1208 called *merderon* ('shit hole'). Then there were complaints of pollution in the thirteenth century onwards, with Londoners grumbling about coal smoke and fourteenth-century Paris colleges moaning that the offal dumped by butchers on the Rue Sainte-Geneviève befouled the street and the air. So in many ways a medieval city was a metabolic sink.

Outflows from medieval cities included re-exports and value-added manufactured goods, probably more biomaterials (woollen cloth, leather, wood) than metals. Equally out of medieval cities, as out of modern ones, flowed large quantities of waste. Widespread practice intentionally directed effluents out of the city into the surroundings, especially down any available watercourse. In Rouen latrines were typically placed directly over streams that flowed out of town. In Cologne, the biggest city in medieval Germany, cesspits had to be emptied into the Rhine through the lower gate after dark. Landlocked pits in Nuremberg were periodically dug out by members of a special guild, called the Pappenheimer or Nachtmeister, and the contents carted by night to the river Pegnitz. In one well-documented case a cesspit that had not been cleared in seventeen years took three and a half nights' work and filled 108 cartloads that were dumped into the river. The Milanese had perhaps a better idea when they occasionally diverted two Po tributaries that ran through town out into the city streets themselves and simply flushed everything away. London barged its solid waste down to tidal reaches of the Thames and let the churning currents slosh it out into the North Sea. Market gardeners and vineyard operators in the vicinity of Ghent, Paris, Florence, and Wrocław eagerly bought urban 'night soil' for use as fertilizer to keep up intensive horticultural production.

Written texts describe the export of urban waste and some fortuitous archaeological evidence confirms the practice. Excavations along the shore of the Bodensee (Lake Constance) beside the town of Konstanz have shown a slow change from the 1200s onwards in the vegetation of the shallows. Clear water organisms gave way to those adapted to eutrophic conditions which had resulted from nutrient-rich pollution. Study of sediments of late medieval date from the Pegnitz below the then walls of Nuremberg reveals all sorts of household and craft waste.

So at each medieval city, with particulars determined by local needs and opportunities, materials and energy flowed in, some stayed, and some flowed on out. Metabolic exchanges are visibly typical of medieval urban communities interacting with their natural surroundings.

As a result, each city's primarily market-oriented economy established its own extensive 'ecological footprint'. Some environmental effects of medieval urbanization recognizably anticipate those of present-day globalization, as well as echoing earlier Romanization. Medieval cities not only changed themselves, they imposed change on outside, sometimes even distant, natural and colonized ecosystems. Urban growth itself could provoke abandonment of nearby vills: forty-one of forty-two places immediately south of Paderborn were emptied in the fourteenth century and three of five beside Rottenburg am Neckar. The combination of transport costs and regionally different natural endowments meant that the material effects could occur in rings around the city or be discontinuous if the city drew from or sent its effluents to far-away places. Characteristically, bulk or perishable goods came from very close to the city as earlier remarked of the grain and wood consumed in London and Paris. Compared with London, the Flemish towns collectively consumed five times the amount of cereals, drawing most of this supply as surplus production from neighboring Artois, Picardy, and Hainault, where they competed with buyers for the Paris market. But with the 1200s they began also pulling grain by tens, then hundreds, of tonnes from the central Elbe. Land there had been cleared and ploughed up for arable in the course of the twelfth and early thirteenth century and its peasant tenants paid their rents in cereal grains. What the local lords thus accumulated was bought up by merchants, shipped down the Elbe to Hamburg, and then by sea to the Flemish consumers. When, however, Flemish urban populations fell after 1350, that trade ceased and much arable in western Brandenburg was simply abandoned. Loss of the distant market allowed cereal production to collapse and secondary woodland to grow.

Florence drew 10,000 tonnes of grain annually from Sicily and Apulia. In the view of some modern scholars, this market demand from Florence and other large northern Italian cities was the principal force driving, in Sicily especially, creation of large landed estates which used higher labour inputs from small sharecropping farms to produce large quantities of marketable grain that was then shipped to consumers in Rome, Florence, and elsewhere. The demand for food by Dante and his fellows in an urban aesthetic and political elite thus changed the colonized ecosystems of southern Italian peasants.

Flemish urban demand for peat likewise destroyed agricultural use of marshes and boggy landscapes fifty to a hundred kilometres away, turning them into sandy heaths or open-water lakes. Anthropogenic small lakes remain still as distinctive landscape features and ecosystems in the peat lands of north Flanders, north Brabant, and south Holland, all formed by the mining of peat to fuel the stoves of Ghentish weavers or merchants in Bruges. Medieval urbanization created significant pressure on the ecosystem in a set of widening rings or sometimes discontinuous sites of disturbance shaped by particular local metabolic relationships.

ASSESSING HISTORIC SUSTAINABILITY

In retrospect, does the evident environmental impact of medieval urban living, the inorganic economy, and energy extraction, speak of medieval failure to maintain sustainability? Did medieval society push beyond ecological limits and bring about its own collapse in a 'dismal fourteenth century'? Remember first that throughout the Middle Ages the urban sector (people, landscapes, material and energy flow) remained a small fraction of the material life of a predominantly rural society. The interactions that medieval people had with their inorganic and non-living environment were but a fraction of those they had with their living or once-living surroundings. Hence any assessment of the overall relationship of medieval civilization with its natural world must always acknowledge this as a predominantly agrarian society which had colonized the biosphere to tap the solar energy flow. This is the only standpoint from which to consider sustainability against overexploitation and endogenous anthropogenic collapse.

That medieval Europeans *changed* their natural world, even permanently, has been amply shown. The question now is whether their impacts brought about a breakdown of their own ecosystem. The difficulty is to assess or diagnose conditions, stresses, and trends in historical time where actual outcomes may remain ambiguous and caught up in other independent causal chains. Sustainability always applies within some bounding framework. The long-term continuity of a rate of coppice production becomes moot were a smelter's ore body flooded out or the wood itself cleared for arable. So, too, centuries-long maintenance of certain cereal yields to support a peasant household ceased to matter when the lord's or king's takings were abruptly increased. Some plausibly stable context is a likely precondition for helpful application of the sustainability concept.

On the side of primary production (the organic economy), medieval uses of local ecosystems were fundamental to the survival of individuals, families, and whole societies. Their adaptive colonizations of the natural world kept them alive, functioning, and reproducing for many human lifetimes while imposing demonstrable impacts on their environments. In that sense the initiation of certain uses and impacts plainly did allow future generations to continue living from those same ecosystems. At the opposite extreme, practices which visibly diminished productive resources are also clear: imagine mining soil nutrients, losing soil to erosion, and depleting, even extirpating, certain wildlife species. Yet historic situations were rarely so simple. What of subsidizing a 'home' ecosystem by extracting from another, such as fertilizing arable land with leaf mould from woodland or turves from pasture? Certainly some well-known medieval practices were intended to limit or mitigate rates of exploitation and to restore productivity for continued use. Carefully managed rotational cycles in arable, in coppice, or even in fish ponds demonstrably continued for centuries so long as the producing and supervising human unit remained in place. Who can show an inevitable loss of social viability for a western Europe lacking pine marten or sturgeon? Change, even change to be mourned from a biodiversity or conviviality standpoint, is not ecosystem collapse. A damaged ecosystem is no longer pristine but may not have lost its resilience.

The energy sector importantly linked primary organic (solar-based) production to medieval use of non-living and anthropogenic resource systems. Emergent local shortages of wood fuel are indisputable and so, too, are subsequent rationing or limits on its use, but also intensified production methods (coppice), efforts to reduce transport costs to draw on hitherto untouched reserves, and strong regional turns to mineral substitutes (peat, coal). But when human numbers and demand receded, medieval consumers largely abandoned the substitutes and wood fuel again sufficed. Increasing use of wind and water power drew on temporally limited but, as today recognized, fully renewable energy. Through and past the Middle Ages, future generations were again or still able to continue living from the same European ecosystem.

Inorganic materials had less quantitative significance for medieval society, although their use was always essential and gained importance owing to technological changes on both the production and demand sides. No use of stock resources such as minerals is ever infinitely sustainable; at issue is rather the depletion rate. Local exhaustion of stocks and wider environmental damage from destructive emissions have been shown for the Middle Ages. The formation, growth, and spread of the urban sector intensified many environmental pressures, but also efforts of urban authorities to manage these. Some of that management, however, simply transferred effluents to other, previously less stressed, ecosystems.

In sum, then, ought these relationships of medieval societies to their natural world be understood as unsustainable, as themselves leading to destructive overexploitation and collapse? Historians of a Malthusian bent have for some time argued for such an endogenous crisis of the European economy. As previously discussed, Michael Postan asserted that unsustainable rates of exploitation in the English agricultural sector brought declining yields by the late 1200s; Tom Williamson has labelled the Midlands system an 'environmental disaster' for being too rigid, too complex in its interlocking features, to adapt either to its own consequences or to broader social or natural changes. Donald Hughes has treated medieval Florence under the rubric of 'barriers to growth' and 'overshoot'. Sheep pastures for wool production and arable for cereals, both serving the urban economy, said he, reduced woodland to the point of general wood shortage and grassland to that of erosion. Long use of arable meant inevitable fertility decline. Commercial demand for silver outstripped medieval technical capacity to maintain output levels of mining. As overambitious princes defaulted on their debts to the city's bankers, a crash was inevitable. For those who see human material economies as embedded in larger ecosystems, it is an intellectually and ideologically inviting proposition that medieval Europeans pushed too far all of their relationships with the natural world, sent it over some kind of threshold, and left themselves suddenly vulnerable to ecosystem collapse.

As most historians know well and as will be rehearsed in detail below, the years around and following 1300 do offer clear signs of impoverishment, production failures, immiseration, and food and other resource shortages in many parts of Europe. At mid-century followed a great depopulation (from epidemic mortalities), abandonment of farmland, and regional episodes of soil erosion. Are these to be attributed to the failure of medieval European society to apply knowledge and develop appropriate technologies to sustain a stable relationship with the natural world? Did people make the wrong decisions? At the operational level, did they misunderstand their environment and their interaction with it?

There emerges a need to explore how medieval Europeans made decisions on their use of natural resources and responded to the effects of those uses. In terms of the heuristic interaction model, who and what established the programme, determined work, and eventually revised those efforts in view of new experiences? The next chapter sets out where medieval society vested the authority and power to make resource management decisions and the consequences of different actors doing so.

'THIS BELONGS TO ME . . .'

—————— • ——————

Medieval Europeans applied their ecological knowledge and technical know-how within socio-cultural rules which identified who could decide what of the natural world was to be used, when, and in what way. These were customary and legal determinations of relations among people rather than religious or philosophical understandings of relations between nature and humankind. As prototypical medieval canon lawyer Gratian acknowledged in his mid-twelfth-century *Decretum*, while divinely ordained natural law gave humankind all things in common, 'by the law of custom or statute, this belongs to me, that belongs to someone else'.[1] Property rights encompass the ownership, possession, usufruct, and acknowledged limits to uses of natural resources. They necessarily have social and environmental implications. Of course, the history of property rights and of the authority of the state contains much without direct bearing on human relations with the natural world, so this chapter will try to stay with those aspects which are or are said to be prime determinates of human decisions and impacts on natural resource use.

For present-day environmentalists, economists, and resource managers, the framing discourse linking property rights to problems of stewardship, overexploitation, depletion, and sustainability derives notably from a 1968 essay, 'The Tragedy of the Commons', which

---

[1] *Decretum Magistri Gratiani, Prima pars,* Dist.8, 1. pars, ante c1. *Concordantia discordantium canonici, vulgo Decretum,* in A. Friedberg, *Corpus iuris canonici,* 1, 2nd edn (Leipzig: Tauchnitz, 1879), column 12. Translated by R. Hoffmann.

American ecologist Garret Hardin published in the influential journal *Science*. Hardin there argued that individual users of a common resource will each necessarily pursue his or her economic self-interest to the point that, collectively, they would deplete and destroy the resource itself. His prime illustrative example was a stereotype of a medieval village common pasture, where, said Hardin, each farmer kept adding additional livestock at no cost to himself but increasing pressure against the whole until the forage was eaten up. Hardin's hypothetical case has subsequently justified especially the privatization of common resources – on grounds that individual private owners take more foresightful care of them – and occasionally the imposition of strict governmental controls over use of common goods. Both late twentieth-century creation of private ownership in regional water supply systems and in some ocean fisheries and growing government restrictions on pesticide use, waste disposal, and carbon emissions rested in part on this way of thinking. Its precursors rationalized eighteenth- and nineteenth-century destruction of European resource commons in the name of economic liberalism.

Critics of Hardin – and they have been many, mostly present-day social scientists and community activists – point out conceptual and substantive errors in his model, starting from his false equation of common property with open access. Property rights regimes are not, it is argued, a simple dichotomy between private and commons, but encompass at least four situations: no property right (Hardin's open access); communal property; state property; and private property. Hardin's assumption that resource users must compete and cannot cooperate ignores evidence both that users do act collectively and that communal institutions do delimit access to commons and regulate users' behaviour. The debate thus goes to the roots of sustainability. While assertions about medieval ideas and actions triggered the 'tragedy' debate, as with Lynn White's Christian 'Dominion' theory (not coincidentally published a year earlier in the same venue), conscious application of Hardin's ideas to medieval European thinking, behaviour, and environmental outcomes has been sparse at best. In fact, however, historians of medieval law and custom are familiar with many aspects of property rights regimes: the actual implications of these practices in diverse medieval settings are both varied and indicative of social insight into resource limits.

This chapter first sets out the grounds medieval western thinkers acknowledged for general and particular claims to possess and use things of nature, notably land and its fruits; it then examines historic arrangements and tensions between rights of lordship (ownership) and community use; and finally it traces through case studies the late medieval entry of a third party, the territorial state, into contemporary resource controversies. As medieval societies colonized and exploited the various natural processes examined especially in the three previous chapters, similarly configured human relationships were involved and similar conflicts erupted over uses and misuses of the environment. Stories so defined within medieval culture thus transcended – but could not overturn – the diverse technical and metabolic connections earlier here established. From the etic perspective, moreover, underlying all the discussion which follows is the extent to which any particular regime of rights and governance affected the sustainability or depletion of the resource in question. Was Hardin on the right track? How much did it matter?

HOW MEDIEVAL MEN (AND WOMEN) POSSESSED THE EARTH

Christian religious and classical natural law expositions of Creation shared a teleological view: whether conceived as an object of Dominion or stewardship, the earth had been made for humankind. Hence humans rightfully possessed it and all it contained. In the general medieval view, the natural prelapsarian condition had been one of equity and common possession of things of Creation; property rights, like social inequality, government, and human laws, arose from the Fall into sin. Only religious dreamers like Francis of Assisi and occasional social revolutionaries rejected private possession on moral and social grounds. Aspirants to religious perfection, from the earliest monks to twelfth-century Waldensians and fifteenth-century Taborites, held all their goods in common. Ordinary sinners did not.

As in other areas of social thought, in the mid-1200s Thomas Aquinas (see chapter 3) undergirded the prevalent social consensus with a religious and philosophical rationale. All law, if derived from right reason, reflected the divine will and thus necessarily served the common good, which had changed with the Fall into sin. Property rights were natural consequences of the postlapsarian world. Thomas then explained the drawbacks of common possession as opposed to private ownership of resources. Following Aristotle and partly anticipating Hardin, he thought the former encouraged shirking of mutual responsibilities, inefficient duplication of effort, and consequent social discord. His critique did not, however, include overexploitation.

While Thomas hinted that specific rights of ownership arose from human labour, only a generation later did the legally trained polemicist John of Paris (d.1306) clearly articulate such a fully secular idea of property: irrespective of sin, property rights were natural to humankind as a consequence of human work. Yet this position, too, had deeper roots outside the realm of theory. For instance, already in the 1220s *Sachsenspiegel*, a written codification of customary practice in Saxony, placed greater emphasis on possession of those trees, water, and land which a person had modified in making them his or her own. In contrast, naturally running water was open to all. Roman legist Bartolus of Sassoferrato (d.1357) later laid this out in an advisory opinion wherein he derived a falconer's ownership right from the man having caught and trained the bird. In a fully natural state, things of the earth belonged to no one, they were *res nullius* (also *ferae naturae*, 'naturally wild'). A human who took possession of an object made it into property, but not if it was already an object of common use or public ownership. The sea, for example, as Bartolus explained in another treatise, was by natural law open to all and the fish swimming there the property of no one until taken by an individual. Shores, ports, and rivers, however, were public with respect to their use, so that kings or other public authorities could make laws to manage them. Writing a century or so later in a different medieval legal tradition, English Common Law, John Fortescue concurred that, in biblical language, men did own what they 'gained by the sweat of their brow'. Several kinds of property rights and some link between them and human work in nature belonged, therefore, to the body of legal precepts shared among all families of late medieval European law, what jurists called the *ius commune*.

Medieval legal writers further agreed that property rights were subject to legislation, that is, definition, regulation, and control by the political community as found necessary for the common good (*utilitate commune, ad publicam utilitatem, bien publique, gemeine nutz, res publica*, etc.). The sinful origins of property and strong collectivist bent of medieval political thought left few theoretical barriers to the taking of private property for public purposes. Political authority further impinged on definitions of property as medieval writers made fully normative a distinction which classical Roman law had drawn only tentatively between rights legitimized by a sovereign's grant (*dominium*) and those based on possession or use (*ius*, 'custom'). Under a range of juridical or political conditions, therefore, a ruler's disposition might override proof of practice. Opposition of *dominium* and *ius* framed many of the resource conflicts treated below.

As distinct from stereotypical modern and Roman legal concepts, a 'layering' of property rights characterized the Middle Ages, with several parties potentially holding legitimate claims over the same piece of property. Allodial title, that to land 'owned', not granted by an overlord, the Normans abolished in post-1066 England by asserting that all land was held from the king by his right of conquest. Despite the adage 'no land without seigneur', allodial rights persisted in France and remained familiar elsewhere. 'Fiefs' (*feodum, Lehen*, etc.), in contrast, were conditional tenures, held of an overlord. A fief effectively conferred rights to use the 'fruits' of the land (*usufructus*), however specified, while superior right remained with another, who might restrict some uses or withhold permission for others.

While the distinctions of 'feudal tenure' arose within the realm of customary practice among powerful early medieval landholders, the widespread principle behind them was articulated among thirteenth-century students of revived Roman and recently systematized canon and customary legal systems. Jurists like Accursius of Bologna (*c.*1182–1261) adjusted the once absolute and unitary Roman concept of *dominium* to allow for its division: *dominium directum*, true 'private ownership' in the Roman sense, rested only with an unfettered suzerain or the possessor of an allod who recognized none but a political superior; all others could have only *dominium utile* ('useful ownership', a right of use), which could even be further shared among layered subholders, lessees, legal tenants, and so on. None denied, however, that both *dominium directum* and *dominium utile* constituted forms of property. From the point of view of Roman law and *ius commune*, the latter and other rights of use were varieties of 'servitudes' (*servitudines*), legitimate burdens on property which obliged the owner to allow others to use it and/or imposed limits on the owner's own use. Agrarian historian Bas van Bavel and others argue that this subdivision or multiplicity of rights had social and ecological benefits, deterring any one party from taking short-term gains at the expense of others or of long-term sustainability.

Long before these juridical niceties, however, analogous ways of thinking framed relations among private lords (landowners) and those individual tenants and whole communities who claimed customary rights to use 'commons'. These mental habits shaped contemporary discourse about the actual distribution of natural resources and conflicts over their use, though the ideas did not themselves create the material interests at stake.

Early medieval dependent peasants had tacitly to acknowledge that the land they used belonged to their lord and the lord in turn to recognize that peasants needed access to various resources to produce what he demanded of them. Contemporary free peasant proprietors disposed of their own *ager* (setting aside kinship constraints) and in many places enjoyed abundant nearby *saltus* (waste) and *silva* (woods) essentially uncontested and thus *res nullius*. Roman emperors and early medieval kings asserted public authority over such ownerless tracts, including the power, which they exercised, to grant the land and/or uses to favoured henchmen and churches. Over the centuries other lordships grew from princely allocation or sheer violent seizure of jurisdiction over people. The trend to privatization (creation of lordships) was nowhere total and need not immediately have affected farmers' disposition of resources. Some peasant communities retained unimpugned access to waste, woods, and waters. Most, at least in long-settled regions, had grudgingly to concede that they exploited fields, pastures, and other resources on sufferance and in accord with some kind of custom, known but unwritten and thus in all but its very existence now lost to historical knowledge.

In most countries the high Middle Ages gradually replaced customary practices with more formal legal regimes, perhaps more conducive to identifying points of conflict and certainly to recording disputes and their outcomes. During the same centuries as western legal theory itself emerged from the competing claims of kingship and religion to inspire concepts of canon and secular law, oral manorial custom – the way things were done on a lord's estate – likewise evolved into systems of manorial law, which defined peasants' obligations and conditional rights, especially to the land and communal resources from which they lived and served their lord. This evolution occurred in parallel all over western Christendom from the eleventh through to fifteenth century. Where free peasant allods survived or lords declined to exercise close supervision, farmers might enjoy very considerable freedom to divide, alienate, transfer, and determine the use of their resources. In all normal circumstances, then, there arose an expectation of communal self-regulation, long held in illiterate memory but eventually made material in 'bylaws', 'customs', 'ordinances',

'Weistümer', or 'statutes' and, mostly much later, in records of their enforcement and of their defence against reactivated or newly conceived lordly claims.

COMMONERS, COMMUNITIES, AND LORDS

In custom and law many medieval user communities shared decisions on resource management, whether they held common rights of use on what belonged to a lord – as in English common-field villages but also in French communal woodlands – or exercised collective rights of ownership – as over many Swiss Alpine pastures, Spanish irrigation systems, and Dutch drainage networks. For all the technological and institutional diversity of the exemplary regional cases here explored (and many more left unmentioned), they all visibly shared socially restricted entry, an awareness of limits, mechanisms to control and allocate uses, and efforts to fend off encroachment or wilful disposition by lords. Documentable instances of resource depletion rarely matched Hardin's 'tragedy' and sometimes, though not inevitably, turned it on its head.

Thanks to the remarkably rich early written record for common-field villages of the English Midlands, their subsequent political notoriety, and eventually massive scholarly interest (see chapter 5), they provide the most-cited general case of the importance of common rights in medieval Europe. For all the special features of the English case, it should be remembered that open-field arable communities with analogous institutional features also prevailed from the central Middle Ages far into early modern centuries across very large areas of northwestern and central Europe.

As from late Anglo-Saxon times to the thirteenth century a symbiosis of grain and stock-raising intensified on intermingled and unfenced strips, farming households in especially the champion country of the English Midlands shifted from relations of neighbourly cooperation to collective control over farming practice itself. The trend affected the rights of individuals within their communities and the relations of communities to their lords. Individual tillage of arable came to be paired with the common regulation of crops and seasonal routines on adjacent strip parcels which comprised a 'field' as rotational unit, and with common pastoral access to waste pasture, uncultivated spaces within the arable fields, and the stubble and fallow of the arable itself (recall Figure 5.3). Peasant ploughing of individually held parcels might be cooperative, but was not collective, while the sowing, harvesting, and possession of cereal yields pertained to each household separately. Community bylaws punished those who ploughed over the boundary or otherwise intruded on land of their neighbours, but also any who dared to sow in the field designated as fallow that year or to leave fallow a strip in a field under crop. This rule could compel reallocation of land among peasant tenures to ensure each had equal parts in each phase of the rotational cycle. Such closely regulated village-wide cropping systems were established in the twelfth century in southern Sweden and the Rhine Palatinate as well as the English Midlands.

Communal bylaws of harvest constrained even the use of individual arable holdings. Removal of the crop was commonly restricted to daylight hours. No one could put livestock to pasture on his or her parcel until the whole field had been harvested; and then other bylaws set dates or a process to determine when harvesting had to be finished. In another place seven days of gleaning (gathering fallen heads of grain) were allowed to landholders (only) before the stubble field was opened for pasture. Very frequently none were allowed to glean unless they had themselves laboured in the harvest and village land-holders required no more harvest workers.

English villages managed common meadows as they did arable, seasonally assigned to individuals to take the hay, and thereafter treated as common pasture. In 1327 the village jury at Holywell, Huntingdonshire, cited William Bondley for starting to cut in the common meadow before the plots had been temporarily allotted to the farmers. Many vills set 24 June as the day to mow the whole meadow, or, weather requiring, the day before or day after.

Other bylaws and institutional arrangements controlled use of common pasture which had, for instance, to be protected against conversion into arable. At Broughton, Hunts., in 1290 the manor court fined nine villagers for ploughing and sowing in common pasture. Pasture commons derived from long-term (immemorial) use by certain farmsteads and could only rarely be traced to specific grants by a lord. Legitimate access to these resources evolved over time from free use of unclaimed waste lands beyond the arable, through drawing boundaries between adjacent villages, to opening the arable for pasture after harvest and in fallow time. Making that intensified arrangement work required employment of a common herdsman and enforcing pasture rights as inalienable apart from tenure in the land itself. Long-standing residence, property holdings, and status in the community determined rights of limited (equal or pro-rated) access. Later under continued pressure of human and animal numbers, villagers began to ration (stint) pastoral uses according to similar criteria. Pasturing of sheep was legally delayed until less close-grazing cattle and horses were well fed.

As circumstances changed, communities adjusted their rules and stints. Intercommoning largely disappeared during the twelfth and thirteenth centuries as the human population doubled. Progressively smaller numbers of beasts, and those not sheep, were conceded to households of landless cottars. By the fourteenth century even good-sized peasant farms were increasingly limited to that number of head they could carry through the winter; and by the sixteenth none were to pasture cattle owned by others.

In strongly manorialized high medieval England the collective decisions embodied in village custom were established in the lord's manorial court, where his local reeve or an outside steward drew panels of jurors from the larger householders to state village practice, agree on adjustments to those bylaws, and identify and punish offenders. Many places appointed special 'wardens of autumn' to enforce the communal regulations. While the entire community attended the court to bear witness and accede to the decisions, violators' fines went to the lord. Village court books seem to suggest that offences against harvest bylaws predominated up to the mid-fourteenth century but violations of pasture rules thereafter.

Many places included the lord's demesne in the pattern of collective management simply because his strips intermingled with those of tenants. Though an unseparated demesne was thus held to the same cropping–harvesting–pasturing calendar as the peasants, lords often forced collective harvesting of their strips first (labour rent), forbade others hiring day labourers before the lord's crop was in, and reserved overnight folding of livestock (manure deposit) to their own strips. Besides exercising coercion within the common fields, the lord's superior ownership threatened their very existence, should he decide to consolidate his own arable and run it outside the collective regime, or to shut down peasant access to his pasture or woodland and then turn those resources to some other purpose. Bondsmen of Stoneleigh abbey in Warwickshire complained to the king in 1290 that their lord's assarts in manorial woods deprived them of fuel, pasture, and the right to collect nuts so that they were impoverished and unable to survive. Indeed, if true, essential components of their resource base had vanished. In the long term such landowner actions would bring an end to the common fields through enclosure, first for sheep pasture at the end of the Middle Ages, and more completely for capitalist agriculture from the seventeenth through to the nineteenth century. But this evidently did not occur from commoners overstocking and depleting their pasture. Indeed, as already discussed in chapters 4 and 5, the medieval English Midlands rather suffered from a shortage of livestock arising from a shortage of pasture, due in part to lords having permitted and encouraged its conversion into more grain-growing arable.

Nevertheless, an outstanding feature of common-field regimes is their historic resilience, providing the basic property rights framework for peasant agriculture over large expanses of the north European plain for more than five centuries. This amalgam of private and community rights evolved across transitions from sparse rural settlement to domestic and frontier expansion and great regional densities and then again to the depopulations and regrowth of the last medieval centuries. Begun in an age lacking real markets for consumables or labour, the common fields still prevailed in the thoroughly commercialized late medieval and early modern countryside. Is this better described as stagnation or sustainability?

The interplay of individual rights and collective constraints in medieval Swiss grazing commons closely parallels the English common fields. Iron Age Celtic peoples pioneered permanent habitation in the high Alps from about 500BCE, but it grew most actively after early medieval Germanic settlers erected scattered individual farmsteads and began to make use of surrounding areas bounded by natural landmarks. Germanic law held open to anyone land not worked by individual households. Alpine meadows, snow-covered for most of the year, offered good summer forage but are too diverse, variable, and difficult of access for this to be cut, dried, and transported as hay. Vertical transhumance is a better means of exploitation. As human settlement and cultivation of the limited suitable terrain intensified throughout the Middle Ages, communities of neighbours defended their mutual rights in what they called a *Mark* against both outside lords and other nearby communities. Local organizations of such fellow commoners (*Markgenossenschaft*) crystallized when population growth forced the exclusion of newcomers, while passing continued access to the high summer pastures (called *alp*) on to the recognized heirs of those with established rights. Some of these groupings coa-lesced as corporate entities for an entire *Mark*, others as villages with communal rights to a specific portion, and still others as collective recipients of grants by a lord asserting superior authority, who then also retained a share. Great monasteries in particular for a time claimed alps and allowed their use in return for rents rendered in cheeses, but by the end of the Middle Ages nearly all of these spaces had become communal. As early as the 1200s non-noble individuals and their corporate communities may be found in full ownership of lands and rights in high valleys of the Valais.

The most essential features evolved locality by locality between about 1100 and 1400, when people with access rights placed limits on their own shares. Many places allowed each farmer only as many beasts on the summer pasture as he could overwinter on his own crop of hay; others determined a total carrying capacity for their grazing and partitioned it among the holders of rights. Written records of these arrangements date to and after the fifteenth century, whence local archives still hold the very agreements named villagers then made to confirm and enforce their customs. Typically, no outsider who acquired land in the community received any right in the commons without the agreement of current possessors. They further set boun-daries on communal lands and roadways, regulated access to wood-lands for fuel, timber, hunting, and various gathered materials, prescribed the handling of diseased livestock, appointed overseers, and both set and imposed heavy fines on violators. Some places maintained village-level commons for draught and household animals kept year-round at the farmsteads; some included meadows and stubble pasture among the common resources, others did not.

Pastoral mountain communities did not lack pressures of rising demand but they responded by enlarging the communal resource base: one village in the Valais bought more land for pasture even up to seventy kilometres away. Their institutional arrangements for common use and management persisted because they proved well adapted to the Alpine environment and pastoral land use. Even in the late twentieth century, 95 per cent of alps in Canton Valais were communal. But the similarities between Swiss grazing commons and English common fields are the more striking for the contrast between the distinctly hierarchical, exploitative, and coercive social-political setting in medieval England, and the relatively weak influence of overlords or other outsiders in the mountain valleys. There are no signs that any superior either imposed or opposed these commons or their constitutive regulations.

From Sicily to Scandinavia and Castile to Kurland, while institutional arrangements varied, medieval country people claimed and sought to regulate a common right to use the local *saltus*. The provincial law of Scania, codified in the 1210s, declared that inhabitants of a village might hold 'common, wood, heath, or other waste together' and the later law of Sealand required a user to have consent of all the commoners. Slightly later, the *Sachsenspiegel* expected rural communes physically to expel illegitimate livestock from their pastures. Open access to the wide variety of vital soil, plant, and animal resources there available was far from the norm, indeed scarcely to be found across western Christendom. But as *saltus* graded into *silva*, while relations of superior lordship and common claims of usufruct remained fundamental, the interests and powers of lords came more sharply into play.

For some centuries after 1066 England offered the extreme example of a king's *private* lordship imposing a special law on great swaths of countryside, severely limiting common uses of his royal 'forest'. During the twelfth and thirteenth centuries about seventy royal forests covered up to 25 per cent of England, including non-wooded land, settlements, and nearly all the county of Essex. A special 'forest law' overlay common law and jurisdictions to run the terrain as a vast royal game preserve, managed primarily for the king's deer. Enforced by an army of foresters, forest law could impose ferocious corporal, even capital, punishment on offenders against the king's *venison* or *vert* (see chapter 5), but even in the twelfth century more often exacted fines, so gaining important incomes for the crown. Fear of overhunting reinforced financial incentives to regulate the hunt and limit, even ban, other woodland uses. Offenders paid a heavy price less often for poaching deer, or even keeping hunting dogs, than they did for assarting, cutting timber, extracting firewood, or pasturing livestock without royal licence. Such restraints on use of pasture and woodland pannage for pigs affected both private landowners and peasants. For instance, at Cannock forest in Staffordshire a 1286 enquiry found foresters denying villagers' common rights to wood and grazing, while some twenty years later Farewell priory was complaining about the same infringement on its own lands.

English royal forests were instituted by William the Conqueror – who famously expelled whole villages to create 'New Forest' – and his sons; they achieved their greatest extent under Henry II (1154–89), and evolved their most complex administration during the thirteenth century. Barons chafing under the rapacious rule of Henry II and his sons, Richard and John, resented the constraints suffered in their own lands that lay within royal forests, and made them a political issue. Limits on the extent and authority of the forests were imposed on King John in Magna Carta (1215), then incorporated in a separate Forest Charter in 1217 and repeatedly confirmed in following generations as an acknowledged curb on royal power. Large areas were removed from the forests ('disafforested') in the political crisis of 1327 and their administration progressively decayed. Although the last general judicial tour of enforcement occurred in 1368, local elements of forest administration remained active into the seventeenth century. Historians concur that the system fell out of strict use as kings' need for revenue from crown lordships and fees or fines came rather to be met through taxes on their subjects while the political price for the whole forest regime became unbearable.

As William created a feudal monarchy by exaggerating a French model, Norman England's royal forests pushed a continental import to its limit. Latin terms *foresta* or *forestis* and the related German *Forst* first appear in seventh-century Merovingian charters. While the etymology remains ambiguous (connoting 'outside' or 'bounded'), the core element was plain: a 'forest' was an area set aside by special restrictions on uses, notably hunting. The concept grew from Germanic custom allowing open hunting access on unclaimed land and the assertion by early Frankish rulers of control over its use. Their charters reveal Merovingian and early Carolingian monarchs establishing and circumscribing such royal preserves, setting servants to watch them, granting some to churches, and either restricting hunting or making it a royal monopoly. When Charlemagne granted woodland and the right to hunt to one archbishop, he refused to add forest rights on the grounds that a bishop could not so limit other people from hunting or trapping the wild game God had granted freely to all humankind. A king, however, could: Louis the Pious asserted in 818/19 the sole royal authority to establish forests. Unknown to Roman law and to Byzantine practice, this juridical institution was peculiar to the post-Roman west. It remained, however, an element of the Carolingian state, so subject to regular law and jurisdiction.

Expansion of the legal concept of forest beyond the royal domain rested on the king's *ban*, his power to command and punish, and on its attractiveness to great lords in areas like Normandy or Anjou, whose exercise of governmental authority so blurred the private and the public. As a result further evolution of special jurisdiction over game and its undeveloped habitats (German *Wildbann*) followed the divergent paths of royal authority in the Empire and in France. In the former, special legal distinctions long survived, as Saxon and Salian emperors kept and enforced their own *Wildbann*. Piety and politics, however, motivated donations of tracts with forests to church foundations and authorization of subordinate princes to create their own. As the German king's ban thus decoupled from royal landownership, during the tenth and eleventh centuries ecclesiastical lords, and in the twelfth and thirteenth lay territorial lords, assumed that authority over game and other uses of *saltus* or *silva*. Where these claims combined with landownership, they could provide building blocks for territorial principalities, offering the opportunity to form regional administrations and profit from allowing agricultural clearances or other more intensive uses by a growing population. Hohenstaufen dynasts in Swabia were among those who used forest jurisdiction in this way. Having succeeded to the imperial office, they applied similar methods in the imperial forests, but their mid-thirteenth-century extinction left special authority over game and other woodland uses in the essentially private hands of local and regional rulers. Only later, as treated below, did some emerging states in Italy and Germany assert forest governance as an element of 'common good'.

Late and post-Carolingian western Frankland experienced, like Italy and later the German lands, a merger of the royal *Wildbann* with landownership. Those tenth-century French princes who already claimed the king's high justice assimilated forest rights to its exercise. Many then further sub-infeudated this jurisdiction, so within short human generations the right to declare a forest was treated as seigneurial and its distinct royal quality vanished. The 987 election of Hugh Capet as king merged remaining royal forests with the royal domain as, essentially, the king's private estate, and the strongest regional rulers did likewise. (What the Normans installed in England merely gave a centralized twist to this model.) While most French woodlands thus fell under seigneurial control, continued peasant use of them meant that a new term, *warenna* or *garenne*, replaced *forêt* to denote strictly hunting preserves.

More widespread and influential, indeed ubiquitous at the local scale, was recognition by alert French seigneurs of the opportunities to be gained by asserting control over their woodlands and restricting their tenants' access and use. By the twelfth century recreational hunting had yielded priority to profit from growing population and material demand for wood products. Establishing new agricultural villages brought new income from peasant rents at the cost of the woodlands themselves (see chapter 4). Clearances further reduced, partitioned, or diluted the common resources of existing peasant communities. But ownership rights and common access were more deeply transformed in pursuit of the lucrative potential which remaining woodlands themselves offered as suppliers of fuel and raw materials to emergent urban, industrial, and elite markets. Private ownership of woodland (*ius proprietatis* or *dominium utile* under a territorial overlord) steered the return flow of money into the hands of seigneurs, but only by choking off much of the old multi-use silvo-pastoralism of peasant resource commons.

Research on Champagne, a demographically buoyant autonomous principality of northeastern France, provides ample illustration. Here the many twelfth-century charters wherein lords allowed village self-government (in return for higher dues) rarely limited peasant access to woods, but by around 1200 commoners' and other use rights were being constrained. In one instance, in 1197 Pierre of Saint-Phal and the convent of Notre-Dame-aux-Nonnains of Troyes together forbade men of Fays taking timber from Jeugny wood other than to fix their houses and that only after due notice to the lords' bailiff. The eventual outcome of many such disputes split formerly large wooded commons between a small share for communal ownership and a larger one, fully in the seigneur's hands, where peasant rights were extinguished. By this time commercial wood production held greater promise than did further clearance, and wood-cutting contracts proliferated. Town-based entrepreneurs ran the intensive coppice commonly so established, but did so under contractual conditions meant to ensure continued (i.e. 'sustainable'), but thoroughly anthropogenic, production.

Analogous trends developed in the Empire, where from the eleventh century peasant clearances under lordly leadership were reducing pasture and woodland. Institutional responses emerged with local perception of an imbalance between demand and a limited supply of wood, if not of other environmental consequences of clearances. Few conflicts over resource access occurred in the new settlement areas east of the Elbe because villages were there established with clearly chartered rights. In old Germany west of the Elbe, however, peasant use rested on custom (however locally named) with no clear law. Most evidence here comes from monastic cartularies, inherently biased towards cases resolved in the convent's favour. Neighbouring lords might themselves concur, as did the archbishop of Cologne and the Praemonstratensian house at Knechsteden in 1195, that a certain wooded parcel pertained to the 'commons of pasture and of wood' of a given village.[2] Or, on the contrary, church corporations holding once-royal woodland jurisdiction (*Holzgrafenamt*) could control or expel peasant users whose defence at best offered oral testimony to thirty, forty, or, as at Gindorf and Dudeldorf in the Eifel in 1226, even sixty years of wood cutting on a disputed site. In a longer-term response German peasants formed community institutions at the village level to defend their claims and manage woodland as commons. Perceived limits on those resources motivated local regulation of their use.

Actual handling of German woodlands differed little between private lords and resource commoners. As in an accusation by the Siegburg Benedictines against their local subjects in 1152 and one from the men of Gladbach against their local abbey in 1243, both could allege illegal and destructive overcutting. Subdivision was a frequent, if not always successful, solution. From the mid-twelfth century to and beyond the fifteenth, communities and private lords alike detailed in writing the rules meant to protect their wood supplies and pannage. A famous ordinance from Ostbeven in old Saxony (Westfalia) in 1339 confined access to possessors of farmsteads and arable in the community, but allowed them to pasture only pigs they had themselves raised or purchased before St Jacob's day (25 July). Farmers without their own pigs could sell the right to pasture six only, while residents without their own farms were permitted but one. Full rights included the cutting of oak and beech for household use only, not to be sold outside the community, while other tree species could be harvested for fuel during a delimited cutting season. Cut oaks were to be replaced. Gathering mast and making charcoal and ash (for

---

[2] As quoted from *Urkundenbuch für die Geschichte des Niederrheins*, ed. T. Lacomblet, vol. I (Düsseldorf, 1840), no. 550, in S. Epperlein, 'Waldnutzung und Waldschutz in Deutschland vom 13.–16. Jahrhundert (Besitzverhältnisse – Nutzungsformen – Herrschaftsausübung)', in S Cavaciocchi, ed., *L'uomo e la foresta secc. XIII–XVIII*, Istituto Internazionale di Storia Economica 'F. Datini', Prato, Serie II: Atti delle 'Settimane di Studi' e altri Convegni 27 (Prato: Istituto, 1995), 376. Translated by R. Hoffmann.

potash) were strictly prohibited and punished, the ash burner, for instance, by having the soles of his feet scorched in a fire. Private lords had comparable policies and their own foresters, forest masters, and guards to enforce careful exploitation and simultaneous conservation and expansion of woodland vegetation to serve fuel, pasture, and hunting purposes. Marmoutier (Maursmünster) abbey in the Vosges published elaborate regulations in 1144 and maintained them for centuries. Especially after the mid-fourteenth century German landowners further expanded their authority over woodlands of all types by enforcing social restrictions on hunting. As earlier noted, private landowners' protection of game and exclusive noble rights to hunt helped trigger the German Peasants' War of 1525.

Mediterranean woodlands display the same kaleidoscopic mix of private and communal claims to possess, manage, and exploit as found north of the Alps. Although vestiges of Roman public authority long persisted in early medieval Italy, the royal forest there remained an exotic Frankish import. On the Iberian peninsula from the tenth century resurgent Christian monarchs asserted and then dispensed authority over woods and waste by a right of conquest not unlike that of Normans in England.

By the later Middle Ages most woodlands in well-treed northern Spain belonged to rural communities who managed them collectively. Further inland similar arrangements prevailed, although annual exclusive leases to community members were not unusual and some villages held their woods only from a landed overlord in return for annual dues. Private woodland increased in frequency towards the south and east, especially in Andalusia where the Christian conquest had established more great private lordships than earlier occurred further north. Conflicts of familiar sorts over peasant access were thus well known. For Italy, however, analogous issues remain unexplored, as modern scholarship on the post-twelfth-century communal age has focused more on struggles between ruling urban and subordinated rural communities than on differences between collective and private resource management. Researchers need to ask and answer questions with comparative value.

As seen in the woodlands, throughout the Middle Ages resistance to privatization most commonly arose over non-arable resources. This certainly included the waters in both their aspects as elemental fluid and biological habitat. Late antique and early medieval times established a general trend of privatization of inland waters, attributing their ownership to the lord of adjoining or surrounding land. Lordly authority over inland and shoreline fisheries evolved in parallel with that over game, though, as remarked in chapter 5, exploitation of the former less served elite recreation than direct consumption or market sale. Along the French Atlantic coast the right of 'wreck' (*vorech*) gave landowners control over traps and weirs, as well as stranded whales, flotsam, and docks or landing places. By gift of Poitevin barons the far-away abbey of Cluny held the entire fishery of the Île d'Aix and half that of the Île de Ré. Vaccares salt pond in the Camargue could be fished only by licence of the seigneur. Yet, as articulated by twelfth-century clerical pundit John of Salisbury, ordinary people stubbornly held that 'the birds of the sky and the fishes of the deep are common property'. Norman rebels in 997 reportedly attacked private woods and waters, an episode which twelfth-century poet Wace narrated as including private fishponds. Four centuries later men of Mersey in Essex were challenging Sir Bartholomew Bouchier's claim to the fish and oysters of Tollesbury on grounds that 'all lieges of the lord king have common of fishery' in such tidal reaches connected to the sea.[3] German peasants in 1525 broke lords' ponds and tanks to feast cere-monially on the contents, while their counterparts in Tirol not only demanded but for some time actually gained legal recognition of a general right of free fishing.

In any case, as further described below, public waters did remain and collective institutions also came to engage in managerial decisions with regard to fisheries. The royal charter granted to Castilian Cuenca in the mid-1180s guaranteed local inhabitants the right to fish freely themselves and to arrest and hold for ransom any 'stranger' doing so. Private enclosures for fish and game were forbidden, as were certain capture techniques during low-water months of summer and autumn. Citizen-caught fish could be sold on the open market but only within the local district. Municipal guards enforced these rules. Similarly, in 1428, a majority of the fishers on the Swiss Greifensee agreed to set new seasonal restrictions on certain gear.

Nevertheless the interplay of private and collective rights is most emphatically to be seen in the management of fluid water on agrarian landscapes. Two well-studied regional examples, Spanish irrigation

[3] England, Public Records Office, Plea Rolls, King's Bench 27/588 (Pasche 9H4) m44 Essex. Translated by R. Hoffmann.

systems and Dutch drainage institutions, illustrate and confirm the shared and divergent features.

As Christian Spaniards ventured from their northern refuge and took possession of adjacent river basins between the late ninth and the twelfth century, they saw opportunities to augment dry farming of cereals by irrigating alluvial terrace soils with water from mountain-fed streams and rivers. Some free settlers took land and riparian water by squatter's rights (*presura*) and others possessed the same under royal charters to self-governing municipalities (*consejos*). Woodlands, pastures, and water, however, were considered under both old Roman and more recent Muslim (Andalusi) law to be public goods for collective management, which now fell to municipalities with their own local customs. In the upland valleys individual villages organized diversions from high-gradient streams to irrigate their local common pasture, while in the broader lower basins multi-village associations (*presas*) built and managed larger canal systems to deliver to their arable land water they had diverted from much farther up their low-gradient rivers. Even as the autonomy these communities enjoyed under their charters waned from the thirteenth century before the rising influence of Roman law and privatization of crown assets, *consejo* administration continued. The mid-century Castilian royal code *Las Siete Partidas* confirmed riparian water rights and permitted landowners, including the *consejos* themselves, to allocate their water to others. Even when villages and towns were appropriated by private lords, their collective use and operation persisted. Facilities on unstable large river systems as, for example, the Río Órbigo in León, required costly annual maintenance, which the *presas* could handle by pooling their resources and sharing expenses. Their corporate ownership let them create access rights for users, who could then be monitored for compliance with necessary rationing and other regulations. Water could be taken only as an appurtenance to land and under conditions set by the municipality, which included control over watermills. Irrigation rules allocating water in rhythm with collective cropping practices thus, like communal grazing regulations, attenuated private owner-ship of arable.

Irrigation systems in more southerly al-Andalus, however, were built on the initiative of clan-based peasant migrants from North Africa, whose knowledge of Roman precedents in Iberia was mini-mized by the multi-century hiatus since the latter had been opera-tional. Andalusi lineage-based social organization and rights to land resulted in stable small-scale collective and egalitarian distribution of irrigation water. Mills, whose intermittent water use might disrupt irrigation flows, were closely monitored. Andalusi customs allocated water, whether measured by time or volume of flow, in proportion to the land area being irrigated, following distinct local rules for turns, etc. as agreed among clans. The thirteenth-century Christian conquest reorganized these regimes within norms of private property favouring cereal production and thus milling. As in the north irrigation became a strictly weekly event. The large-scale long canal systems of Valencia, Murcia, and Alicante, themselves formed by agglomeration of local organizations, are generally acknowledged as long-term successful common pool resource regimes. On the steps of Valencia's cathedral, the 'Tribunal of Waters' has been meeting each Thursday since the Middle Ages to resolve conflicts over shared use of this critical resource.

Too much water is as hazardous and demanding of management as is too little. The interplay of private right and collective management in Dutch drainage law and institutions closely paralleled that among Spanish irrigators. Both initial drainage of Holland's bogs (chapter 4) and later medieval response to subsidence and flooding (chapter 5) early called for measures beyond the capacity of individual farms. Free tenants in the south and peasant landowners in northern Friesland and Groningen used their autonomous village communes for cooperative creation of drains and dykes under local rules for inspection and prorated the cost of maintenance by the area farmed. In long-settled areas such as along the Oude Rijn the local panels had already by the 1160s aggregated into regional networks of collective responsibilities and rights for secure control of water. Managerial boards of trustees (heemraden) based on common law traditions were operating well before the count of Holland formally acknowledged them in 1226. Even though the count's regional bailiff held the executive post of 'dyke-reeve' after 1286 and elite landowners gained more influence over time, the drainage boards retained their essential local participation and autonomy into modern times. Especially as new needs for dyking and pumping came to the fore in the fourteenth and fifteenth centuries, the boards coordinated local works; set performance standards for construction, inspection, and maintenance; allocated costs to landowners as labour or monetary dues; and arbitrated individual disputes. Around 1450 the Rijnland drainage board, for instance, used its authority to block Hoogeveen's sole outlet to force that delinquent village to meet obligatory maintenance fees; the board made this stick in court despite Hoogeveen's peculiar status as a peat-mining site owned by rich urban investors. Peasant initiative supported by lords for collective management of essential environmental services, even when this curbed rights of individual property holders, lay behind the ecological and cultural resilience of the medieval Netherlands.

This comparative survey of relations between private lordship and collective institutions (common rights) in arable agriculture, pastures, woodlands, and waters of diverse medieval landscapes has established that 'open access' regimes on the Hardin model were *not* the historic reality of medieval Europe. Indeed medieval handling of common resource pools shared several essential features. Membership in the commons was clearly defined and so, too, over time, was the pertinent resource itself. All well-documented commons had locally determined rules of operation and mechanisms whereby at least leading rights holders could and did change those rules, especially to limit or prorate each member's consumption or access. Compliance with the rules was monitored, whether formally or informally, and community sanctions imposed on violators. This necessarily entailed resolution of conflict between members and some recourse to political authority for enforcement. English villagers who broke bylaws were presented and fined in the lord's manorial court and public judicial panels ratified decisions of Spanish or Dutch water boards. Even when ill-managed commons did result in 'tragic' overexploitation, collective institutions had the ability to reform and restore. In the early 1300s a consortium of professional fishers paid the archbishop of Salzburg an annual fee of 27,000 smoked whitefish (*Coregonus* sp.) and 18 lake trout for a collective right to exploit a small Alpine lake, the Pinzgauer Zellersee. After one human generation the whitefish catch collapsed and replacement stocks of pike ate nearly all the trout. In response the fishing community decided to close the lake for three years and thereafter to establish a protected area within the lake, restrict the fishing season, and limit the number of nets each fisher could set. Collective self-regulation and consequent limitations on individual use of property rights, not unconstrained overexploitation, must be acknowledged a norm and typical practice of medieval resource commons.

Medieval resource conflicts did arise when lords motivated by prospects of revenue or recreation infringed common rights.

Well-documented 'tragedies' arose more from coercive interference than from collective depletion. Lucrative markets for agricultural products in urbanizing Flanders motivated breakup of commons there by the 1200s. All manner of thirteenth- to fifteenth-century Castilian elites were implicated in *usurpaciones*, expropriations of municipal commons for their own private purposes. English judicial records likewise document the mid-fourteenth-century demise of a common fishery in Lincolnshire's Spalding Fen, when to punish the four villages which shared access, the lord's bailiff simply seized their nets, boats, and catches, and privatized the resource in one quick move. Indeed the 1236 English Statute of Merton gave lords the right to appropriate commons when commoners were left with 'sufficient'. In 1306 Robert of Essington, asserting his right as lord to improve his manor, removed from the common 200 acres of wood and 200 acres of moor. Likewise in many provinces of central and southeast France, customary law codes acknowledged a *droit d'inonder*, allowing a landowner to erect a dam and flood the lands of others, then only retroactively offer to negotiate compensation for damages. In most of Christendom, moreover, recipients of mineral rights from the overlord could establish a mine without regard for affected commoners or other landowners.

Arbitrary exercise of private rights could entail ecological as well as social 'tragedies of the private'. It took only a lord's decision to initiate transforming the landscape from one biome to another. One instance of environmental destruction affected the Lago Bientina near Lucca, part of the lordship of the abbey of Sesto since a tenth-century grant by Emperor Otto III. In the thirteenth century the abbey still encouraged diverse use of the aquatic ecosystem, employing its own fishers on the lake, licensing consortia of market fishers from lakeside villages, and allowing extensive use of reeds, waterfowl, and other natural products. But the abbey also sponsored shoreline drainage and reclamation, which progressively by the 1600s eliminated the entire lake, wetland, and resource system. Lords and landowners at Montady in Languedoc (see chapter 4) turned a multi-use wetland into grain fields in less than a decade. Likewise the lack of detectable medieval relict woodlands in France may be traced to such actions as the late twelfth-century decisions by territorial lords in the forest of Briard to create *villeneuves* on land unoccupied, but surely not unused, in wooded interstices between older villages, and the choice by the chapter of Notre-Dame de Paris to grant to its knights clearance rights over a hundred *arpent* parcels with the proviso they not lease them out to peasants. The obverse of seigneurial initiative to whatever managerial purpose was often destruction of the natural resource as thorough as any arising from mere overexploitation.

Yet given stable environmental conditions private lordships could also provide long-term sustainability. In 1246 Pontigny abbey was managing its woods on a hundred-year timber cycle. The extensive lordship rights over woods and waters and close control over uses that Bavarian and Austrian abbeys exercised all along the northern Alpine front helped sustain timber and fisheries production up to their nineteenth-century secularization or disestablishment. Especially in medieval Europe care must be taken not to conflate environmental justice – equitable human access to things of nature – with the protection and sustainable use of natural systems and relationships. But conflicts over rights and uses of such systems provided one reason for a third force to intervene in late medieval times between private owners and common claimants.

HIGHER AUTHORITY: THE STATE, PUBLIC RIGHTS, AND THE 'COMMON GOOD'

During late medieval centuries struggles over the right to determine uses of natural resources were complicated but also made voluminously visible to historians by the entry of a third party, the overlord, prince, or territorial state. As observed at the start of this chapter, throughout the Middle Ages no one seriously denied the general notion that a higher public authority was rightly responsible and empowered to enforce the public good; its renewed practical application in fiscal and judicial realms by twelfth-century monarchs and their successors is familiar to medievalists. Progressive enlargement of the concept followed, more explicitly taking in religious practices, economic life, and environmental relations. Attention here is drawn only to the last, its applications, forms, and consequences for owners, users, and their resources.

Already in the twelfth but especially from the thirteenth century onwards, acknowledged public authorities intervened variously vis-à-vis both private lords (owners) and users (collective or individual) of especially non-arable resources. In halting steps and against continual resistance, what a later age would call resource management policy or even environmental legislation emerged and sought to constrain behaviours of both sorts of private interests. This late medieval inception of governmental interest in regulating resource use arose from mixed, even opposing, motives. In some circumstances these were at first fiscal or, later, driven simply by the increased ambitions of governments and their officials to curb the autonomy of great or lesser subjects. Equivalent pressures came from below, as disputants called upon their overlord to adjudicate between them and set regulations in the way of further conflict. With whatever mixed impetus, actual programmes and actions further required identification of resource issues as objects of governmental intervention. Princely and republican regulations came out in tandem with those of estate owners, villages, and urban communities, for this was an age congenial to legal enactments, but public authorities sought openly to ground their rules in a common good superior to private interests.

The particulars of constitutional forms, technologies, or the ecological place of the activities brought under public oversight affected how states actually sought to regulate resource use surprisingly little. Royal licence requirements served, as did those on commons and private concessions, to restrict access by private market contractors and subsistence commoners alike. Operational regulations singled out techniques, seasons, and particular resources: Italian city-states protected water quality by banning the processing of flax and hemp; an English parliamentary statute of 1388 promoted urban sanitation by prohibiting dung, filth, and other corruption from the lanes and waterways throughout the realm; French ordinances prohibited the (silent) saw in woodlands and reserved certain tree species for use as timber; from the 1330s Florence ordered weirs and other structures removed from the Arno to reduce damage from floods. Rationing of livestock on pasture, the quantity of trees cut, the amount of animals caught and sold, or even total consumption itself were meant to prevent overexploitation. Many territorial officials went from confirming and enforcing older local regulations to determining and enforcing similar ones of their own. While state control measures thus emulated the local rules they were meant to supersede, the enforcement mechanisms were more explicitly integrated into larger agencies of public order and justice.

A rhetorical shift commonly paralleled jurisdictional change. Despite different institutional particulars, state interventions to limit or constrain decisions by private owners and users increasingly appealed to a greater public interest, whether expressed in generic terms or more concretely.

The Constitutions of Melfi that Emperor Frederick II promulgated for Sicily in 1231 made community health and well-being the grounds for banning the soaking of hemp or flax within a mile of a *castrum* and requiring proper disposal of filth, dead animals, and human corpses. An appeal to England's parliament in 1377 against use of a beam trawl in coastal waters asserted its 'grant damage de tout la Commune de Roialme', and from the 1460s Venice regulated use of Lake Garda 'ad commune beneficium'.[4] Readers of such claims will want to remember that for resources with multiple uses and users one party's wasteful overconsumption might be a rival's careful way of life. Whose common good was served when mill dams were breached to ease river navigation? Not that of the miller or of people who needed grain turned into flour. Hydraulic energy had been reallocated from one use to another. Perhaps a critical historian should acknowledge the 'common good' as a cultural programme or marker (tag) rather than seeing therein any *prima facie* evidence of genuinely shared material benefits. Nevertheless, public suppliants and authorities alike were using language not earlier applied to human relations with the natural sphere, and that language devalued and potentially constrained individual rights to do as one pleased there.

The cases of late medieval state environmental regulation more fully sketched below were selected to illustrate shared patterns of rhetoric, approach, and social and ecological implications, while also indicating some variables and limits to governmental programmes. Taken collectively, the assertion of authority over woodlands by the French crown, south German princely states, and the Venetian republic, an effort at multi-basin flood control in the autonomous county of Roussillon, and the regulation of freshwater fisheries by the commune of Perugia, French kings, and Austrian dukes may suggest or help contextualize further topics wanting well-aimed local research on an aspect of medieval state-building hitherto oddly devoid of comparative scholarly attention. (In this context the much-studied Castilian *Mesta*, the state-supported cartel of migratory sheep owners treated in

---

[4] C. Given-Wilson, P. Brand, A. Curry et al., eds., *The Parliament Rolls of Medieval England* (Woodbridge, Suffolk and Rochester, NY: The Boydell Press, 2005; digital edition: Scholarly Digital Editions and The National Archives, Leicester, 2005; Internet version at www.sd-editions.com.ezproxy.library.yorku.ca/PROME, accessed 21 January 2008), membrane 2:369, Edward III, 1377 January, 50. XXXIII. M. Butturini, 'La pesca sul lago di Garda', *Archivio Storico Lombarda*, 6 (1879), 147–9.

chapter 5, may be thought a borderline case. Crown grants of jurisdiction to the cartel are recorded as having fiscal motives and economic intent, not grounded in the environmental relations they
certainly affected. Indeed they constitute a transfer of royal authority
to private interests rather than the reverse.)

Vestigial Frankish royal claims in the hands of early Capetian kings
and their great princely vassals likely provided the germ for gradual
construction from the twelfth and thirteenth centuries of French state
jurisdiction over woodlands, an evolution coincident with other
accretions of royal power there. Kings and their agents first built
from indigenous practices and later emulated Anglo-Norman administrative models. From the early twelfth century those overlords who
laid claim to public facilities, namely the counts, castellans, and the
like who would govern roads, rivers, markets, etc., were asserting
some analogous right called *gruerie* (*griera, gruaria*) over the disposition
of woodlands. The concept probably echoed or revived an obscure
Carolingian custom affecting land not in arable use, but by the late
1100s such territorial princes as the counts of Champagne, dukes of
Burgundy, counts of Anjou, and Capetians themselves in the royal
domain around Paris and Orleans were using it to limit, license, or
even prohibit first clearances, then wood sales, on lands of subject
seigneurs. A royal licence to cut cost a landowner in *gruaria* a third to a
half of the anticipated financial proceeds. The Norman customal
compiled in 1199/1200, when the province was still in John of
England's inheritance, required a ducal licence for any sale of wood
from strategic border areas. Shortly after Philip II seized Normandy in
1204, he extended this system of licensing wood sales to the entire
French royal domain, and in 1219 prohibited creation of new usage
rights in royal woodlands. From such exercise of superior authority
emerged in the next generation or so a legal distinction between
ownership of the ground (*fundus terre, treffonds, sol,* 'real estate') and
what was called its 'surface' or 'tonsure' (*superficia, tonsure*; later assimilated to 'moveables') over which princes claimed and consolidated
oversight. Of course in Champagne and elsewhere seigneurs for some
time resisted this imposition.

Enforcement of the overlord's claims and collection of his dues,
especially lucrative because paid in cash, was entrusted to district forest
officials, called variously *gruyer* (in the Île-de-France and Burgundy),
verdier (Normandy), or *garde* (in Languedoc, the southern region
added to the royal domain by 1272). These first reported to the

king's provincial governor, but from the mid- to late thirteenth century increasingly to supervisory *maîtres de forêts*. A hierarchy of local subordinates ranged down to local guards, 'sergeants', *garenniers* especially responsible for game management, and others, all meant to deter or capture violators of the overlord's customary rights. Late medieval court records and complaints by their very nature highlight malfeasance and corruption more than they do dutiful efficiency on the part of these local functionaries. Yet the very efforts to bribe or suborn low-level royal officers imply some genuine impact on how landowners and holders of common rights might otherwise exploit woodland resources.

The French woodland administration which had thus grown up piecemeal under the later Capetians was standardized and consolidated in Philip VI's 1346 Ordinance of Brunoy, which established four or five *maîtres des eaux et forêts* as the responsible officials across the realm. They were to hold regular enquiries in all forests and woodlands and regulate sales of wood and other uses so that 'the aforesaid forests may remain perpetually in good condition'. To this end no new usage rights were allowed and existing customs strictly enforced. The *maîtres* and their subordinates held sole judicial authority over all but hunting offences and arbitrated disputes between seigneurs and commoners. As France recovered from its early military disaster in the Hundred Years War, new legislation in the 1360s–1370s reiterated the substance of the 1346 ordinance, specified royal recognition of communal as well as private woodland, and set over the *maîtres* a single supervisory *souverain-maître* and, to receive the financial accounts, a single *receveur general*. By the close of the Middle Ages French royal officials, regulations, and licensing of uses had extended from the royal domain to cover most privately owned woodlands as well, even though other fiscal developments had sharply reduced their relative contribution to royal incomes. Under Louis XII (1498–1515) concerted efforts were made to write down hitherto largely oral customs and usage rights. At the start of the next reign Francis I officially confirmed royal inspection and control over private woodlands in a new ninety-two-article forest code which, for the first time, explicitly included hunting in the purview of his *eaux et forêts* administration. If enforced, state regulations curtailed the range of action in French woodlands of private seigneurs and subsistence peasants alike.

Princely governments along northern margins of the Alps from the Black Forest to the Vienna Woods took some notice of woodland

resources already in thirteenth-century charters for mining enterprises, notorious consumers of fuel. The main initiation of
Waldordnungen in this region dates, however, to 1470–1550, not
incidentally a period of renewed mining fever and output. In
Württemberg a rudimentary 'state' administration emerged from
the duke's household only towards the close of the fifteenth
century and took its first notice of woodlands in a general ordinance of 1495. This asserted short supplies of both fuel and timber
and instructed local officials to draft countervailing regulations in
consultation with the foresters. Fiscal motives likely played a secondary role here, as the government received little income from
the woods; resolution of local conflicts and display of state authority had greater weight. Not twenty years later popular rebels
accused ducal foresters of interfering in communal woodlands by
limiting pannage and cutting and by charging for use of pasture, as
well as being generally corrupt. Under Habsburg occupation in the
1520s Württemberg officials started to survey the duchy's woodlands, and followed up in 1532 with a clear regulatory regime,
organizing woods into managerial units (*coupes*), setting seasons for
cutting and clearing, and otherwise determining the framework for
use by both landowners and peasants. By the 1534 restoration of
Duke Ulrich the legitimacy of the state's regulatory role had
become accepted, but only if its officials reciprocated by drawing
on local expertise in its application.

Administrators for the prince-archbishop of Salzburg organized
their first formal *Waldordnung* of 1524 around energy supplies to the
salt works which produced that region's most valued export commodity. They, too, grounded their regulatory regime on reputed fuel
shortages and blamed their subjects' misuses of the resource and
disregard for prior local regulations. Centralized repetition reinforced
the legitimacy of the prince's authority. Standard elements in new
regulations plainly derived from the old: management by compartments to be cut in rotation; protection of new woods from grazing
livestock; monitoring sales; and continual increases in government
supervision rather than encouragement of technical or other innovation. Generally speaking, secular and ecclesiastical princes in the
Empire thus placed a premium on their woodlands supplying industrial and market needs. Their intervention reduced the role of local
governance, the access of peasant users, and the biodiversity of woodland ecosystems (see chapter 5).

Late medieval republican governments joined kings and lesser princes in asserting state authority over woodlands. Venice, since the eleventh or twelfth century an acknowledged sovereign city-state, consumed much wood for domestic and industrial fuel, ship timbers, and the tens of thousands of log pilings which still keep its buildings from sinking into the mud. None the less, up to the start of the fifteenth century the republic controlled no terrain for growing trees. When worried by occasional local shortages, the ruling Senate sought remedies in market mechanisms: its first legislation on wood in 1350 gave the Arsenal first refusal on timber brought to the city from mainly private but also some communal woodlands in the hills and river basins of northeastern Italy and Istria; in another generation officials were fixing the prices for both fuel and timber. A general concern for resource security at the turn of the fifteenth century then helped motivate Venetian conquest of the northeast (henceforth the *terraferma*) between 1404 and 1424. Although the Republic lost great power status a hundred years later, it long retained its independence and most of this territory.

Though now possessed of diverse woodlands scattered from the coastal plain to the Alps, Venetian elites clung to a mercantile and maritime orientation; their relative ignorance of woodland ecosystems reinforced the long-standing fear of siltation in the lagoon which had for centuries driven construction of levees and breakwaters. Even mid-fifteenth-century politicians worried by fuel shortages diagnosed the cause as silted waterways hampering the flow of laden rafts and barges to the city's markets and so proposed riparian plantings to secure the soil, not to grow wood. In part because Venetian common law lacked provisions to regulate use rights and in part for the sake of political stability, Venice long shrank from challenging the Roman law rights of mainland landowners. Only for the sake of water would the state before the sixteenth century confront private owners, who pushed back with lawsuits and other means, but in the late 1400s Venice did intervene in communal woodlands, already acknowledged as somehow public.

Venetian programmes to control woodland use were always framed in terms of public need, especially the strategic priority for naval timber. In 1471 the state took over thirteen communal woodlands of the Bosco del Montello north of Treviso as a public forest reserve and assigned management to the Arsenal. The Senate justified this unprecedented act by the traditional authority of the *res publica* to seize unclaimed resources for the public good, asserting that local people had been misusing the woods for lesser purposes. Under threat of severe penalties commoners' livestock was now banned, so too their coppicing, and their taking of firewood and leafy hay was permitted only under licence. By the mid-sixteenth century forty such state woodland reserves would dot the Venetian realm. General statutes to regulate all communal woods in the *terraferma* followed in 1476. These ordered that each woodland be divided into management parcels and coppice to follow a ten-year cycle; banned swidden, other uses of fire, and pastoral access; restricted the sale of firewood from licensed reserves; expanded the system of state fuel warehouses; forbade the sale of common land; and re-emphasized that the needs of the Arsenal always had first claim on resources. Only the measures against privatization might be thought to benefit, if secondarily, local peasant users.

Venice did not in the fifteenth century intervene in management of private land, but the pattern then set was slowly extended, especially to favour oak and beech, becoming more explicit in a post-war recovery situation after 1530. Construction of an elaborate and ever more knowledgeable bureaucracy followed. Well before 1500 Venetian state policy saw fuel and timber as the sole legitimate uses of woodland, and state security as the primary criterion for management decisions. The methods and impact of republican entry into the woods paralleled those of princely regimes elsewhere.

Collective concern for the waters of the lagoon so permeates Venetian history and mentality as to transcend interpretation as mere state intervention into distinctly environmental relations. Likewise Florentine and Milanese works to secure banks, channel, and drain flood plains along the Arno and Po fall in their mixes of private and public investment and purposes somewhere between the agricultural and urban developments treated in chapters 4–6 and the purposeful governmental incursions into hitherto private and 'economic' affairs here discussed. Communal Florence responded to the crisis of a devastating flood of the Arno in 1338 with essentially ad hoc emergency measures, not a programme to alter relations between society and the river.

A clearer instance of enlarged state ambitions in a programme of environmental management occurred in late fourteenth-century Roussillon, a then-autonomous county in personal union with the Crown of Aragon or its cadet line of Majorca. An eventually fruitless effort at large-scale flood control through river basin management highlights the triggers, justifications, and limits of a late medieval state responding to evident environmental hazards.

Neither the landscape nor written records from the northeastern end of the Pyrenees show any sign of rivers flooding between Gallo-Roman times and the late twelfth century. Large floods of the principality's three major rivers, Tech, Têt, and Agly, are then documented in, for example, 1264, 1307, 1316, 1322, 1332, 1419, 1421, and years after 1530. By the late thirteenth and early fourteenth century, low-lying riverside settlements were being abandoned. Structures of Roman and twelfth-century date there now lie beneath two to seven metres of alluvial sediment, the greater part of it dating to the 1300s. In retrospect woodland clearances, abandonment of arable, and climatic change (see chapter 9 below) together shaped a new hydraulic and erosion regime.

Local communities responded first to the new risk. In 1327 the city itself financed dykes and weirs to protect low-lying parts of Perpignan by way of special assessments on riparian landowners, and similar arrangements served in the 1330s to defend the dyers' riverside neighbourhood. But some villages and landholders opposed riparian structures and purposeful protective bank-side plantation of trees on grounds that the enlarged river bed diminished their properties.

Acknowledging the failure of site-specific measures, Prince Peter IV then tried to enlarge the scope of the protective programme. In 1362 he ordered a study into diversion of the beds of the Têt and Agly to prevent floods from destroying good land in the vicinity of Perpignan, and in 1378 the royal governor gained an agreement to realign the lowest three to four kilometres of the Têt below Perpignan and down to its confluence with the Agly. The new, wider, bed was to be bordered by plantings of trees. In 1382–3 the king revived and extended his earlier initiative, now proposing to reorder the courses of both the Agly and the Tech. He appointed local commissioners from Perpignan, but the bishop of Elne and others along the lower Tech, landowners and village communities alike, complained that the costs to them far outstripped the expected benefits. Although in 1384 the monarch ordered the project to go ahead 'for the common good', rising expenses and continued local resistance thwarted royal aims. In 1399 Martin I acknowledged the failure of his father's scheme and lamented the continual resultant losses of land and production. After the flood of 1419 Perpignan was again left trying to reorganize just its local drainage.

Though pushed by local victims and princely prestige and entrusted to figures from the regional elite, state intervention in the rivers of late medieval Roussillon failed in the face of local economic interests. Perhaps the scheme's narrow emphasis on flood control, channelling the rivers away from human structures, threatened more diverse uses of the river's bed and banks. There remain, however, signs of a proto-ecological awareness that riparian woodlands had a systemic and beneficial role like that voiced in Venetian debates a century later. Might closer exploration of procedural documents from other river-management and flood-control efforts find a broader consciousness among late medieval inhabitants of Mediterranean Europe?

State efforts to control exploitation of freshwater fisheries rank among the earliest well-documented interventions, with clearly ration-alized public regulatory regimes put in place during the mid- to late thirteenth century by self-governing Perugia and the French crown alike, and comparable measures being installed in, for instance, fifteenth-century Austria. Close parallels emerge on many levels with what has been seen in woodlands and along flood-prone watercourses.

While monarchs in Scotland and Sicily issued individual statutes to protect certain fish, the communal government at Perugia displayed precocious energy in taking charge of the fishery on Lago Trasimeno. Already from 1260 the city had been responsible for stocking the lake with fish, and with a series of ordinances and statutes from 1276, 1279, and thereafter, established a regulatory regime that lasted until a new papal governor asserted his authority in 1568. Legislation set minimum mesh sizes for nets, restricted use of enclosure traps, and banned netting of tench in September. The most important local fish, pike, tench, eel, and southern roach (*Rutilus rubilio*), were protected from 1 May to 31 August. Tench weighing less than four 'ounces', roach less than one, and small eel had to be returned to the water unharmed. From 1275, the 'seeding of pike, eel, and crayfish in the lake of Perugia' became an annual enterprise, carried out in spring and autumn, the latter especially with small eel procured from the river Chiana. From 1279 lakeside settlers were obliged every third October to place bundles of reeds and branches in shallows to shelter spawning and overwintering fish. A government-appointed cleric supervised the stocking and habitat improvement work; a special communal fisheries overseer, the *tencarame*, saw to enforcement, aided from 1490 by an armed patrol vessel. Violators could be fined as much as five hundred *lire*. Judicial records confirm arrests, convictions, and penalties. All this was 'so that in the city of Perugia there might be a large abundance of fishes' (the 1279 ordinance) and thus serve 'for the utility of the commune of Perugia' (in 1342).[5] Protecting the town's lucrative trade in fish throughout central Italy meant close municipal monitoring of individual activities and manipulation of natural elements, living and non-living, to this end.

Roughly contemporaneous with Perugia's active intervention, fisheries also attracted French royal interest, empowered by survival there of public jurisdiction over large navigable rivers. Already under Louis IX in the 1260s it was the royal governor of Paris who first recorded customary rules for fishing the Seine and Marne: fishers had to be licensed; fish for sale had to meet a minimum size; springtime closures protected spawning roach; use of certain gear was controlled along with the size of all mesh. King Philip IV's subsequent fisheries ordinance of April 1289 extended to all waters under royal authority because, he declared,

today each and every river and waterside of our realm, large and small, yields nothing due to the evil of the fishers and the devices of [their] contriving, and because the fish are prevented by them from growing to their proper condition, nor have the fish any value when caught by them, nor are they any good for human consumption, but rather bad, and further it happens that they are much more costly than they used to be, which results in no moderate loss to the rich and poor of our realm ...[6]

The theme of fish stocks destroyed by overfishing, wasteful capture techniques, and sheer human greed, with resultant loss to consumers and the community at large, which the monarch here introduced, would become a commonplace in subsequent French legislation to

---

[5] A. Scialoja, 'Statuta et ordinamento artis piscium civitatis Perusii (1296–1376)', *Bollettino della Regia Deputazione di Storia patria per l'Umbria* (1910), 817 note 1, and T. Biganti, 'La pesca nel lago Trasimeno: Sfruttamento et tutela delle risorse ittiche del lago di Perugia (seccoli XIII–XV)', in P. Carucci and M. Buttazzo, eds., *Gli archivi per la storia dell'alimentazione, Atti del convegno, Potenza-Matera, 5–8 settembre 1988*, Pubblicazioni degli Archivi di Stato, Saggi, 34 (Rome: Ministero per i Beni Culturali e Ambientali, Ufficio Centrale per i Beni Archivistici, 1995), 794. Translated by R. Hoffmann.

[6] H. Duplés-Agier, 'Ordonnances inédites de Philippe-le-Bel et de Philippe-le-Long sur la police de la pêche fluviale', *Bibliotheque de l'École des Chartes*, 14 (1852), 49–50. Translated by R. Hoffmann.

and beyond 1515. On those grounds Philip prohibited certain capture techniques and restricted the seasons and dimensions of others, put a closed season on some fish and size limits on others, and ordered royal bailiffs to seize and publicly burn illegal gear, fine the disobedient, and feed the illegally taken fish to the poor. One central official was named to oversee enforcement. Later statutes transferred oversight to the royal Master of Waters and Forests, occasionally modified the vocabulary of prohibited gear, and extended the system of seasonal closures and minimum size limits to more species.

Nor was this mere paper legislation, effective only within sight of the Louvre palace. Into the 1200s private holders exercised lucrative fishing rights in the Garonne at Toulouse without constraint and actual fishers needed only a licence from the count. By the 1360s, however, royal officers overseeing traps and weirs claimed as the king's prerogative any salmon or sturgeon from this public water. Of course local figures opposed and evaded this assertion, while other critics thought enforcement too lax. Yet at the close of the fifteenth century the king's Master of Waters and Forests was acknowledged to control all aspects of the fishery. Already in the 1420s royal attorneys in Paris had argued that the fishing privileges claimed by Saint-Magloire on the Seine were licences for use only, not commercial or regulatory concessions, and in another case brought charges against local fishers for illegal gear and retaining undersized fish.

Further suggestive parallels and differences marked intervention by later Habsburg princes of Austria into management of fisheries on their portion of western Christendom's longest river, the Danube. At the start of the fifteenth century Austrian communities and princes were together trying familiar small-scale remedies for a shared worry lest destructive practices deplete the region's resources. Viennese market regulations and a decree by Duke Albrecht V banned certain gear because of its harm to young fish. On the lower river Traun in 1418 thirty-two master fishers set out regulations which the duke's governor confirmed. In similar communal vein the city council at Tulln in 1469 approved regulations assembled by the local fishers' guild, which seasonally restricted certain techniques deemed hazardous. All this paralleled earlier practice elsewhere, with the state supporting local management.

As the fifteenth century drew to a close, state authority more firmly asserted itself. Grand Duke Emperor Frederick III (1440–93) issued for Upper and Lower Austria a general fisheries ordinance (not now

known to survive) and also in 1471 imposed a one-month morato-
rium on all fishing in the Danube 'so that the water again recovers its
fish'.[7] Then during the 1490s conflicts over fisheries' access on the
Traun gave the governor occasion to intervene directly. Following
instructions from Emperor Maximilian (1493–1519), to bring order to
the river so that its fish stocks were not depleted, in 1499 he solicited
the advice of the master fishers but himself issued the ordinance to
sharpen the rules enacted eighty years earlier. Small fish of named
species were protected by minimum legal sizes and generally by
regulation of mesh; certain gear was banned for blocking movement
of fish; and critical habitat was preserved by limiting diversion for
other purposes. The strong ideology and measures of the 1499 law
were, however, diluted when, a year later, Lambach monastery, a
major holder of land and fishing rights on the Traun, won exemption
from the prince.

Confronting such local resistance, Maximilian, whose personal
interest in fishing is well documented, changed approach. In 1506
he ordered local and guild authorities and holders of fishing rights to
join with officials in a new effort to protect and regulate the Danube
fisheries. These, he declared, naming seven valued species, had been
depleted by violation of existing laws and the use of gear harmful to
immature fish and hazardous to navigation. His new strategy removed
fisheries protection from the mandate of provincial governors and
assigned it to the first known imperial *Fischmeister* for Upper and
Lower Austria, Hans Wagner. Wagner was to consult with fisheries
organizations and local authorities and with their aid develop measures appropriate to local conditions. The policy extended what had
just been done on the Traun, as state authority supplanted and
absorbed older communal and corporate practice. Rules tailored to
localities, if socially and environmentally preferable, remained in
tension with the administrative uniformity sought by central officials.
Maximilian, however, stressed not substantive but jurisdictional
conformity, ordering all who exercised fishing rights to obey those
regulations which the *Fischmeister* would proclaim.

---

[7] Anton Mayer *et al.*, eds., *Quellen zur Geschichte der Stadt Wien*, I. Abteilung. *Regesten
aus in- und ausländischen Archiven mit Ausnahme des Archives der Stadt Wien*, 10 vols.
(Vienna: Verlag und Eigenthum der Alterthums-vereines zu Wien, 1895–1937),
vol. VIII, No. 16.102. Translated by R. Hoffmann.

Revised ordinances for the Traun and Vienna did come out in 1514 and 1516/17, but new full-scale legislative codes awaited Maximilian's successor, King Ferdinand, in 1537 for Upper Austria and in 1555 for Lower. In explicit service to 'the common good' (*gemainen nutz*), these reiterated the prince's concern for depletion, referred to the older legislation now superseded, and fine-tuned some specific provisions, while explicitly extending the competence of royal law and officials to all waters in the respective province. Although it then took ten years to bring the powerful parliamentary Estates of Upper Austria to agree, by the mid-sixteenth century Austrian river fisheries were the state's to manage.

From trees in France to rivers in Roussillon and fish in Perugia or Austria, the framework of state intervention is consistent. Authorities experienced a problem, resource shortage or environmental hazard, which they diagnosed as a *human* failure, the result of overexploitation, wastefulness, and disobedience (to existing law). Their programme for remedy was regulation and enforcement, which entailed licensing users, restricting the techniques to be used on the natural system, and rationing the time, location, and/or varieties to be exploited. Secondary considerations arose from more political conditions: fiscal motives had initial but less later importance; more common was a need, often voiced by subject users themselves, for conflict resolution in the resource area as in others (social violence, inheritance, etc.). Both the leading material dangers and the secondary more cultural ones fit comfortably into broader late medieval ideological programmes to establish or display the authority of the state and, to that end, to assert the importance of the 'common good'. But then the relative weight of environmental risk management, resource conservation, and the allocation of benefits among competing users is rarely accessible to the historian. As argued more generally by such modern writers as Jamie Scott, from early on state officials favoured more standard and more rational approaches over the varieties of local practice. The state's further tendency to prioritize single favoured uses (timber or fuel production, river navigation, etc.) gnawed away at traditional multiple uses and the diversity of natural ecosystems. Overall, and perhaps to no medievalist's surprise, state intervention proved more inimical to the resource access of peasants and their communities than to that of private landowners. The latter had to accept more limits and/or fiscal charges on their exploitation of what they thought belonged to them.

Cultural consensus in medieval western Christendom held the earth and things on it as made for humans, who in a world of sin and labour rightly possessed what was subject to their use. Characteristic possession was, however, of *rights*, not a whole and unbounded object or claim. Layering of property rights in the same natural object probably inhibited individual or collective possessors from some kinds of destructive overexploitation and certainly established the large cultural framework for resource conflicts of all sorts. Indeed the shape and courses of medieval disputes over the ownership and use of things of nature were little determined by particular qualities of the resource itself, its metabolic place, or the technologies used to colonize it. The same sorts of issues and protagonists came to the fore over *ager, saltus,* and *silva*, over waters deemed threatening or valuable, and over the animals to be taken from all sorts of habitats. Yet conversely, prevalent property rights regimes, products of larger cultural constructs and constellations of social power, did not themselves determine a priori the sustainability or destructiveness of medieval colonizations of the natural sphere. While the individual or collective quality of the decision-makers certainly partitioned social gains and losses from medieval exploitation of nature, it determined the destruction, depletion, or durability of a colonized ecosystem less than did the choices each actually made in an economic and ecological context. The Hardin theory simply fails to capture the conditions and outcomes of medieval resource use. Both medieval resource commons and exclusive private rights produced ecological disasters and long-stable adaptive systems. Hardin's 'tragedy' belongs in a historiographic museum, not the tool kit of an environmental historian.

Powers claiming public authority (the state) visibly entered resource conflicts from the thirteenth century on grounds of 'common utility', ostensibly to prevent depletion or to reduce risks to human life and property. The claim was not wholly specious, as late medieval societies generally did acknowledge a need for a degree of protective regulation, for all that each interest group preferred it be of someone else. On a case by case basis it can be difficult for a historian to untangle authentic pursuit of the public good from its use as a cover for partisan attacks on rivals or for self-serving aggrandizement and display of state power itself. But how critical or cynical ought historians be? There is solid prima facie evidence that late medieval authorities who presented themselves as 'public' enacted laws claiming to preserve and improve environmental conditions and therein frequently appealed to 'the common good'. This legislation has to indicate some 'constituency' aware of and wishing for the resolution of what would now be called environmental issues; it further implies that appeals to the general welfare resonated with politically significant groups in late medieval society. Also illustrated above were numerous occasions when at least some such enactments were enforced and so did infringe on the rights and punish, perhaps even alter, the behaviour of persons who claimed and/or used the resource in question. Does this make medieval polities any less concerned than are modern states for what they recognize as hazards and damage? What matters then and now for environmental outcomes has more to do with accurate diagnosis of problems and effectiveness of the solutions.

By the waning of the Middle Ages in the fifteenth and sixteenth centuries, the state had become an important determinant of what natural elements did belong to its subjects and what they could do with that possession. State intervention was not, however, notably productive of new or different uses of nature, or, on current reading of the evidence, of considering the environment as a value itself. Public thought and policy remained thoroughly utilitarian even when asserting broad social concerns. Environmental protection for its own sake had no meaningful role in official discourse.

Strong cultural forces thus greatly determined who established medieval programmes, who carried out the work, and who gained the rewards from deepening human colonization of Europe's natural sphere, but differences among human actors commonly failed to determine large environmental outcomes, notably the scale and sustainability of human actions in nature. On the contrary, as the next chapters demonstrate, all the prerogatives which medieval culture assigned to certain individuals, groups, or institutions remained subject to powerful forces from the natural sphere.

SUFFERING THE UNCOMPREHENDED:
DISEASE AS A NATURAL AGENT

———— • ————

Successive chapters have traced the interplay in medieval Europe between natural conditions that called for human adaptation and technological development on the one side and the environmental consequences of such cultural changes as landscape creation, cerealization, energy technologies, and urbanization on the other. But the interaction between human culture and the natural sphere has two dynamic elements, not just one: the natural sphere is always an autonomous actor, capable of initiating and altering human environmental relations, not merely part of the scenery or something that responds to whatever humans do. This chapter and the next show what natural forces and phenomena at both the smallest biological and largest planetary scales did in the Middle Ages. Microscopic pathogens of which medieval Europeans had barely an inkling afflicted, shaped, and ended human lives.

   Medieval European history is punctuated by acute and large-scale epidemic events which transpired against a shifting background of long-term endemic diseases. These experiences, both the epidemics and the patterns of endemic disease, resulted in a history of microbiological environments in medieval Europe. Parasites generated a history because the effects of biological processes on individual human bodies and society in general resonated in popular as well as learned thinking. The experience of a disease as represented in medieval culture led to programmes with material consequences arising from people trying to handle their situation. Much of what follows contrasts the present-day observer's knowledge, riddled with historical lacunae, with the understandings of contemporaries who could observe, however acutely, only superficial symptoms of what was happening to them and struggled in vain to understand, much less to manipulate, those natural forces.

PATHOGENIC DISEASE: INTRODUCTORY CONCEPTS

Pathogenic micro-organisms are as much a part of the human environment as are deer, weeds, a city, or the flow of solar radiation. Humans are likewise a part of the pathogen's environment. People engage in a reciprocal evolutionary relationship between parasites, hosts, and the environments both parties share. What medical professionals and laity call 'disease' is the patterned response of a host's body to the presence of a pathogen. Parasites that kill their hosts before they can get to another one are evolutionary failures. A host species that develops the ability to live with a parasite or survive and pass on an immunity to its attack has gained evolutionary advantage over others that succumb.

For an individual host, a disease is either *acute*, that is, a temporally limited attack which it either succumbs to or survives, or, at the other end of a spectrum, a *chronic* condition that invades the body and stays, carrying on its life cycle. In a host population a disease can be *endemic*, whereby there is a relatively low but continual incidence of cases within that population, or at the other extreme, it can be *epidemic*, with many simultaneous cases occurring episodically. Epidemics are most commonly also acute. Some pathogens share a mode of transmission that enables them to pass easily from one individual to another; they are called *contagious*. Others, though contagious, require long and intimate contact between a sufferer and someone else before the parasite moves to colonize the other individual's body. Still other parasites rarely pass directly from human to human or one member of a susceptible species to another, but rather move through a *vector*, most often but not always a specific insect or other arthropod that carries the disease, without exactly contracting it itself, from an infected individual to a susceptible individual of the same or of another susceptible species. If the vector carrying the parasite engages with a non-susceptible species, the disease is not transferred. Other pathogens, such as those which cause dysentery and typhoid fever, spread via inanimate *vehicles*, namely contaminated food and water.

Some pathogens spread over several host species which may react differently to the parasite. Thus the disease may be endemic in one species and so form a *reservoir* from which a vector or direct contagion can transmit it to some other species such as humans. Humans can contract tularemia from contact with infected rabbits and West Nile fever from a mosquito that fed on an infected bird.

Host, parasite, and any third species functioning as a vector or a reservoir all operate within broader environmental thresholds and tolerances. Lacking certain levels of temperature, humidity, or other conditions, for instance, a vector organism may not be able to live and thus carry the disease. Such environmental parameters are characteristic, even diagnostic, of certain diseases and vectors, but like all else in nature remain subject to random variation and evolutionary change over time. Neither disease organisms nor human organisms nor human cultural conditions and responses to disease are fixed in history. This operative understanding or principle must underlie discussion of disease in medieval Europe. Even when a present-day model exists, actual past behaviour must be inferred from historical evidence.

The historicizing of disease extends back to the origins of the human species, indeed probably to the origins of the hominid genus. The human groups who spread out of Africa in the Pleistocene already bore a burden of parasites, some of which fell away under different environmental conditions, while new ones took hold. Domestication exposed Neolithic humans to new pathogens of animal origin. Urbanization marked another key stage in the global evolution of humans and their diseases, notably those in which the parasite needs a large reservoir of hosts to keep going. This precondition was lacking until enough people lived close enough together to pass the disease on among them. Measles, for example, requires a susceptible population of a half million to become endemic, but varicella (chicken pox) only ten thousand. In populations below the self-sustaining threshold, such diseases will occur episodically as epidemics.

The spread of humans and acquisition of new diseases in different parts of the global land surface resulted in regional mutual adaptations between disease and human populations, creating what historian William McNeill referred to as 'disease pools'. These are associations between particular human populations and particular diseases that have evolved together over a significant period of time. A disease pool certainly emerged in eastern and central Asia, one or more in south Asia, and surely more than two in sub-Saharan Africa; the Mediterranean and Europe early probably comprised but one. The bulk of the New World developed one or more of its own. At the point of human history in which many diseases developed, next to no communication linked the various human communities, which was one reason disease pools emerged as temporal and spatial entities.

At the extreme end of disease pool formation comes mutual genetic adaptation to symbiosis. A prime example is the bacteria which inhabit every human gut; these started out as parasites and learned to live inside human bodies while the bodies learned to have them there. Travellers to parts of the globe where people have different gut bacteria still end up with intestinal and other ailments arising from competition between newly ingested micro-organisms and the earlier inhabitants. Similarly, childhood exposure to diseases that are ubiquitous, endemic, in a society, either kills the child or produces lifelong immunity. Hence certain diseases in certain pools evolved into childhood diseases with which virtually every adult is familiar, while the childhood diseases themselves attenuated over time. This was the Old World experience of measles and chicken pox.

The emergence during the Bronze Age and Iron Age of states and of reasonably long-distance trade between Old World communities resulted in the breakdown or merger of disease pools there, particularly the linkup of Eurasian and North African pools into one. It took close to a millennium for that merger to be completed and it came at the cost of heavy mortalities when unexposed populations were hit by a new parasite or, considered from the parasite's perspective, when it suddenly found a rich and vulnerable new host population to colonize. This situation is referred to as a 'virgin soil epidemic', in which a parasite enters a host population lacking prior experience of it. Virgin soil epidemics can produce massive mortalities. It may take a long time before a human population becomes accustomed to a new disease in the way that certain other human populations had already adapted for millennia. Probably by the time of the Persian Empire and classical Greece, and certainly throughout the Roman period and some while thereafter, pathogens flowed everywhere from east Asia to central Asia to the Black Sea and Mediterranean, including parts of western Europe. Relatively little connection was then established across the Sahara and likely little as well across the Indian Ocean to the south Asian pool(s). A barrier effect has to do with whether a disease occurs in a form that can be carried latent in the body of a host; if it is a form that kills quickly, a victim cannot survive to reach new host populations soon enough for the disease to come along.

BASELINE DISEASE CONDITIONS
IN PRE-INDUSTRIAL EUROPE

Host–parasite relationships ground discussion of baseline disease conditions in Europe during and after the Middle Ages. Three patterns were always part of the mix: normal mortality, intermittent mortality crises, and chronic debilitating conditions together shaped medieval human relations with the microbiological environment.

In medieval and early modern Europe a combination of endemic local respiratory, gastrointestinal, and childhood pathogens produced a characteristic pattern of 'normal' pre-industrial mortality. Most deaths were from disease; despite accidents, wars, and other violence, it always remained a vastly more important cause of death than were physical injuries. The average normal mortality in pre-industrial European society may be thought moderately high at 3 per cent per annum (compared with 1 per cent per annum in modern society). Much of that normal mortality was due to extremely high death rates among infants and children: in the first year of life – as indicated in fragmentary Carolingian and other medieval data and proved from the data-rich sixteenth century – between 150 and 250 of each thousand live births perished. Next, of a thousand children who had survived infancy, another 150–250 died by age seven. Only somewhere between four and seven of ten live babies survived into adolescence. This comprised a large part of the 3 per cent normal annual mortality. It was further built up by the high urban death rates mentioned in chapter 6. Mortality also related inversely to wealth. At any given time the richer were less likely to die or to die of disease, but rich people were so small a proportion of medieval society that they made little overall demographic difference.

Intermittent regional mortality crises were equally part of baseline conditions and characteristic of pre-industrial European demography (and probably elsewhere, too). Sudden surges in a year or even only three to five months pushed death rates to 6 per cent, 10 per cent, and occasionally even higher. Mortality crises are characterized by causes of death combining greater incidence and virulence of endemic diseases with an outburst of epidemic disease, a massive acute infection of one sort or another. Historic mortality crises were commonly linked to breakdowns in everyday social stability and security. They were often triggered by crop failure and/or war, both of which caused food shortages and refugees. Deprived of shelter, people who might have survived sickness at home died homeless. And further, people who might otherwise have contracted a disease, infected their families and neighbours, and died in their village so that the outbreak burnt itself out, were stirred up to carry the disease with them along roads and waterways. Add the fact that the unhoused, sick, mobile refugees lacked adequate food and an explosion of deaths in epidemics ensued. But for most people, even in a mortality crisis brought on by war or a great lack of food, the immediate cause of death was mainly disease. In both social and immunological terms people simply lost the ability to cope and the pathogens moved in and succeeded.

A third characteristic of baseline disease conditions in pre-industrial Europe did not directly impinge on mortality. Significant chronic debilitating diseases were endemic in medieval populations. Among the more important was malaria, to be examined below, but others included tuberculosis and such macroparasites as intestinal worms. Individuals suffering from them characteristically have limited physical strength, limited economic productivity, limited ability to bear children, and other kinds of fundamental disabilities. Victims are also more susceptible to deadly diseases, although the proximate cause of their death will not then be the leprosy, malaria, or liver flukes, but something else, more acute.

Medieval microbiological environments further included diseases of plants and animals, though only the latter are now beginning to draw serious historical attention. Incapacitating or deadly diseases of horses could affect major military campaigns and loss of draught oxen to an epizootic directly harmed agricultural production and thus human food supplies. Now best known is the cattle plague which swept from east to west across Europe north of the Alps during 1314–25 and may have killed half a million working oxen in England alone (a subject to which chapter 10 will return below).

Against the backdrop of conditions just surveyed, certain medieval encounters of Europeans with their parasites call for closer examination here. Reasonably well studied are five such experiences – the Justinianic epidemic of the sixth century; leprosy; the Black Death of the mid-fourteenth century; the 'English sweats'; and malaria – chosen both as informative cases and because it would be hard to specify others with greater overall significance for the course of medieval development or the lives of medieval Europeans.

THE 'JUSTINIANIC PLAGUE'

In some senses the Middle Ages began or classical civilization finally fell apart in a series of epidemics that started in the 540s but seem to have continued off and on up to 749–50. As briefly mentioned in chapter 2, historians name these collectively after the late Roman (Byzantine) Emperor Justinian, who ruled in Constantinople at the time of the initial outbreak and himself likely survived an attack of the disease. Thousands in his capital and probably hundreds of thousands in his empire did not. The epidemic began in the eastern Mediterranean, first, said contemporary witnesses, in Egypt's Nile delta in 541. It spread around the Levant to Constantinople, prevailed there through 541–2, and returned in a second wave in 558. Physicians described it as new, something outside their previous experience or knowledge. The epidemic then sprang up in or spread into North Africa in 549 and recurred there in 599–600. Meanwhile the Gallo-Roman bishop Gregory of Tours (539–94) and other western writers reported the presence of 'groin plague' (*lues inguinaria*), as they called it, in Gaul in 543, 571, 580, 588, and the early 590s. A much later Italian report puts it in Gaul and Italy in 565, 590, 593, 600, 654, and 680, the last being described as a severe pestilence which damaged the population and economy. Another outbreak hit Italy in 749–50. What is thought to be the same disease extended outside the former and contemporary Roman world to appear in Ireland in 544–5 and again in the 660s. It is described as being in England in 664–6 and 684–7. Absent any good ongoing records for Anglo-Saxon England prior to the mid-seventh century, and with Irish chronicles silent about British conditions, no earlier appearance there can be established. Such, then, are the recorded appearances of 'Justinianic' epidemics during the two centuries at issue.

Similarities in reports of epidemic symptoms, plus certain common time and space parameters, resulted in retrospective assertion by twentieth-century writers that all of these early medieval events were the same disease, a so-called 'First Pandemic' of bubonic plague. This rodent-based flea-borne infection by a bacterium now called *Yersinia pestis* was identified by medical scientists, particularly the Swiss Alexandre Yersin, working in eastern Asia during the 1890s. Researchers there encountered a disease not previously known to modern science and established its pathogen, vector, and primary host, the black rat. Humans are a secondary infection. *Y. pestis* will receive greater attention below. While all reported sixth- and seventh-century epidemics have not so far been ascertained as caused by the same pathogen, contemporary writers of diverse opinions and cultures all around the Mediterranean felt especially the first occurrences in their region as a heavy blow to society. The great mortalities in Ireland are said by some historians of religion to underlie the change from a territorial church run by bishops on the Roman pattern to an idiosyncratic 'Celtic' church of monastic networks led by charismatic abbots. However named or diagnosed, the sixth-century epidemics certainly rank among the key precipitants of those demographic, cultural, and settlement discontinuities which chapter 2 located between the world of antiquity and that of the Middle Ages.

So at the start of medieval history epidemic disease spread across the western parts of the more-or-less civilized world; it played an important material role; it reportedly had common descriptive features. It arose from the natural sphere. In the form of autonomous changes at the scale of microbiology, nature was a historical actor.

LEPROSY

The most prominent endemic feature of early and high medieval disease culture was leprosy, a chronic condition which became widespread in Europe during late Roman times. What is now medically identified under the name 'Hansen's disease' is caused by the parasitic bacterium *Mycobacterium leprae*. This is the slowest-growing bacterium known and very slowly contagious by direct human contact. After successfully establishing itself in a human individual, *M. leprae* remains latent for many years. The form of its eventual appearance is then largely determined by the human body's immune response. In one form it emerges as tubercular lesions in the lungs and very quickly kills the victim. More commonly it produces cellular deformity of nerves and other tissues and a gradual process of disfiguration of the 'leper', the person who has the disease.

Medieval texts clearly describe people whose symptoms perfectly match those of Hansen's disease. Modern studies of skeletal remains from cemeteries associated with medieval leprosaria also reveal distinctive leprous features, for the disease affects the bone as well as other tissues. Most recently palaeopathologists have identified distinctive *M. leprae* cells in tissues of some medieval corpses. Hence it can be said with confidence that in the Middle Ages there really was leprosy and people really had it, and not, as some historians once thought, that medieval society and physicians erroneously lumped together various other skin conditions. Progressive cellular deformity produces the horrifying and repulsive physical appearance that popular imagination still commonly associates with the disease. Probably also of historic cultural significance is leprosy's greatest and most visible success in well-fed people: *M. leprae* uses cholesterol as a primary growth element, so that meat-eating elites are more apt to display rampant physical leprosy than are undernourished people or those living primarily on cereals. No one in the Middle Ages knew that. This attribute generated records and much excitement about people like King Baldwin IV of Jerusalem and various noble men and women who were lepers. There was even a whole military-religious order of crusading warriors who were so diagnosed, the Knights of St Lazarus.

Medieval leprosy acquired great cultural importance in part because it appeared disproportionately among the elite, but more because western Christendom appropriated the Jewish Scriptures as its 'Old Testament' and those revered texts reflect massive abhorrence of this disease. Perhaps a contributing factor was leprosy's achieving endemic status in the western Roman world between the fourth and sixth centuries, just in time for Christians to associate it with their keen sense of cultural decay (see chapter 3). Leprosy was identified with moral pollution: in some way or another the individual suffering from leprosy was paying a price for immorality – not necessarily that individual's own immorality, for it might have been a parent or someone else. The affliction was understood as a physical manifestation of divine disgust. Despite this large cultural weight, medieval leprosy had no demographic significance at all. Had the disease been wiped off the medieval medical map, neither the number of people nor their collective patterns of mortality would have changed.

The symbolic cultural gravity of leprosy resulted in material cultural responses. Understanding the disease in a particular way generated programmes and action. In the first place it gave rise to a policy of isolation: the leper was to be removed from normal human society. This practice was already being suggested as a normal response in sixth-century ecclesiastical legislation from Gaul. The third Lateran Council confirmed this as the normative policy of the church in 1179 and English civil law concurred in 1220. Similar provisions appear in most of the great regional customary codes. Of course a person would be isolated from society only after careful investigation by knowledgeable men to ascertain that this individual really was a leper (and at least the skeletal evidence from leprosaria suggests the diagnoses were commonly correct). There followed a ceremony in which the person was declared to be socially and culturally 'dead', parted from ordinary society. The leper lost any rights to land or other property, was forbidden from engaging in commercial intercourse of any kind, and was banned from sexual intercourse with any but their spouse. In some places leprosy of a spouse was grounds for divorce, though the official church position opposed this. Nor were all of these limitations always enforced, especially upon persons whose wealth, rank, and power let them retreat to a secluded situation under their own control. Even as the leprous King Baldwin IV of Jerusalem (1161–85) became incapable of fighting he was still recognized as the king, though the politically influential were aware that his inability to sire an heir presaged future conflicts. He was not placed in an isolated institution.

An important response to leprosy, however, did create special places for lepers – leprosaria. Leprosaria were collective objects of massive charitable investment, which grew especially in twelfth- and thirteenth-century western Europe. These institutions arose in the great wave of religious reform and renewal associated with such monastic foundations as Cluny, with Pope Gregory VII, and then with new orders like the Cistercian monks and Premonstratensian canons. Moved to perform major charitable acts, wealthy people in the late eleventh century and notably the two hundred years thereafter founded leprosaria in the same spirit as they did religious convents. These quasi-monastic settings served the lepers and those who aspired to spiritual benefit from practising humility and social love by caring for repugnant human manifestations of immorality. France had in 1300 two thousand leprosaria. In England about two hundred foundations then housed probably in the range of two thousand lepers, and at any given time about as many victims lived outside such establishments. German and Spanish leper houses multiplied more rapidly in the thirteenth century than in the twelfth. So a substantial symbolic and material manifestation emerged from culturally mediated experience with a particular, long-acting, very slowly contagious disease.

Then during the later Middle Ages leprosy simply faded away from most of western Christendom. It was once argued that this must have happened because the Black Death killed all the lepers and left survivors immune to further infection. It is now evident that the disease had gone into steep decline before the 1347 appearance of the Black Death across most of the west. There is even some assertion that leprosy may have conferred a degree of immunity to the new epidemic – to the effect that some lepers were persecuted and killed on suspicion of propagating an illness which they seemed to defy. But the steepest decline does pre-date mid-century and remains unexplained. One medical theory is that the rise of a closely related bacterial disease, tuberculosis, conferred immunity to leprosy. A further clue may lie in the fact that European leprosy lasted longest, deep into the early modern period, in Scandinavia. There the winter conditions and housing customs meant that people lived very close together in unventilated situations for many months of winter, and this intimate contact could offer easier opportunities for the laggard *M. leprae* slowly to make its way from one individual to another. Scandinavian continuity could suggest that changes in residential patterns elsewhere in Europe may have disrupted the body to body transmission of leprosy. To anticipate issues from the next chapter, whether that shift occurred as early fourteenth-century Europe cooled down or more as a long-run consequence of the warm dry conditions thought common in the 1200s has not yet even been an object of scholarly speculation.

THE BLACK DEATH

The Black Death – only much later so-called – of 1347–52 comprised an abrupt and massive change in Europe's microparasitic environment. The largest ecological and demographic event in pre-modern European history is also likely the only such in present-day popular consciousness, even in part correctly. What follows sketches the course of events, outlines how historians have puzzled to diagnose what happened, and observes Europeans' cultural responses to their encounter with a new and deadly disease.

Some time in the 1330s a deadly epidemic erupted in central Asia. This is now known from travellers' reports and large cemeteries found in that area. By 1346 the epidemic had spread to the steppe zone along the northern Black Sea coast. An oft-repeated myth has it that a Mongol army besieging a city in Crimea, themselves struck by the disease, catapulted dead bodies of its victims into the city to infect their enemies. A historians' irony is that accepting the truth of such contagion would eliminate certain explanatory diagnoses of the disease and vice versa.

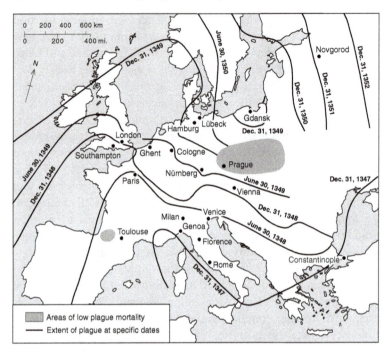

Map 8.1 The first epidemic of 'Black Death' in Europe, 1347–52

In any case, from infected Crimea, probably on Genoese trading vessels, the disease spread to Constantinople and thence, skipping around intervening land areas, appeared in Sicily, Sardinia, and Provence before the end of 1347. The now classic modern map of the spreading infection, here updated as Map 8.1, conveys both its remarkable speed and distinctive route. On a continent joined overland by plodding horses, ox-carts, and pedestrian humans, the epidemic crossed France in six months and took but a year to cover the British Isles, Low Countries, and Germany. Good grounds indicate that it did not enter interior Bohemia and southwestern Poland at this time. Some have asserted that it also spared certain parts of Flanders but that now seems incorrect. By the middle months of 1350 the pestilence was entering Scandinavia and reaching eastward along trade routes into the eastern Baltic to attack Muscovy in 1351/2. While Moscow is much closer to Crimea than to western Europe, the epidemic arrived not from there but by way of trade routes from the west. Indeed the map reveals a path conforming to prevalent commercial connections, first westwards along Italian Mediterranean shipping lanes, northwards across France and to its neighbours by roads familiar to mercantile pack trains, and finally turning east along the Hanseatic routes which joined the North Sea to the Baltic. The pattern held from Constantinople in 1347 around a great circuitous arc to Muscovy only four years later. The disease ravaged each locality for a period of some months and then burned out there.

The entire epidemic sweep across European Christendom thus lasted four, or barely five, years. It achieved very high morbidity – many people contracted the disease – and high and rapid mortality in both cities and rural areas. Credible recent estimates suggest that as many as 60–80 per cent of Europeans were infected and 75–90 per cent of those people died: by those figures, the disease killed somewhere between 45 and 72 per cent of the population. A new study taking a middle-of-the-road position calculates that up to two-thirds of London residents died in barely twelve months. Medieval physicians, well trained to observe symptoms, provide detailed descriptions. Many solidly prosaic record sources confirm vast numbers of dead. Entirely typical were villages where four out of five individually named tenants suddenly changed from one year to the next and others where half the households disappeared and were not replaced. Everything fits the model of a virgin soil epidemic.

Such 'pestilence', 'pest', or as Europeans also occasionally called it, 'plague' (*plaga*), faded after some deadly months and the catastrophe seemed past. Some sources suggest an upsurge in fertility. Then, just more than a decade later, the disease returned. The recognized second wave of 1361–2, by no means as carefully studied as the first, again covered most of the continent, this time killing principally children. The same disease came back in 1372. Thereafter the pestilence became an increasingly regional and urban phenomenon that would continue to crop up in one part or another of Europe for another four centuries, although intervals between local epidemics seem steadily to have lengthened. *Pest* became a typical, though not inevitable, element in recurring regional mortality crises. The last big, well-observed and well-reported urban 'plague' hit London in 1665, killing an estimated hundred thousand, one in five of the city's inhabitants. The last good-sized western European city to be struck was Marseilles in 1720, where infection in port quarters was clearly connected with the arrival of ships from the Ottoman Empire, where the disease remained endemic for another century or more. Western and central

Europe gained early respite in part because Habsburg authorities stationed on their Austro-Hungarian frontier with the Ottoman Balkans as many as 20,000 well-armed troops, who cleared a dead zone several kilometres deep where people lacking appropriate quarantine and licences could simply be shot.

The huge demographic effects of the Black Death initiated a collapse of European populations, plunging the continental trend into a steep downward curve that would not bottom out before the mid-fifteenth century (see Figure 4.1). While rapid surges in birth rates seem to have followed each major epidemic, for a long time none came close to restoring the losses. Rural–urban migration likely even dampened each temporary recovery. Despite the continual best efforts of lusty survivors, from somewhere above 70 million Europeans in 1346 there remained only about 50 million descendants a century later. Population levels from 1300 were not regained prior to the 1530s or even the 1550s, although many regions saw population growth set in by the early 1400s and gain speed from the 1450s.

So the story is quite clear in several respects: the disease is well observed, tracked in time and space, and its direct material consequences little in dispute. More problematic has been its identity. A 2002 essay by Sam Cohn Jr drew together and set out the fundamentals of a gathering attack on received diagnostic opinion which has not yet been fully refuted. Unproven diagnoses provide no grounds for deeper explanations.

Alexandre Yersin, the medical discoverer of 'bubonic plague' in late nineteenth-century east Asia, quickly asserted in correspondence with his family and subsequent publications that the disease he had just identified using correct modern medical science was also that of the mid-fourteenth and subsequent centuries in Europe and southwest Asia. Though possessed of a classical education, Yersin was no historian. Still, the declaration from a medical authority was picked up by historians and became ever more dominant, ever more detailed, in historical literature through most of the twentieth century. By the 1970s the Black Death was seen to initiate a 'Second Pandemic' of bubonic plague, dating from the 1330s into the early 1800s. By this account Yersin had found in eastern Asia a 'Third Pandemic', which subsequently expanded with the spread of certain rodent organisms to all the continents and remains today present and waiting for the horror story to resume. Or is it the same story after all?

Yersin's nineteenth- and twentieth-century disease has complex epidemiological features which reveal its deep links to local ecosystems. Bubonic plague is a disease of colonial rodents such as rats, gerbils, and prairie dogs, which are its preferred host. It was, as Yersin's French rival Paul-Louis Simond found in 1898, especially a disease of the commensal black rat (*Rattus rattus*). This timid animal likes to live in colonies very close to human beings, who offer sources of food and shelter. The disease is not, however, contagious among rats. The vector is a flea, mainly the rat flea *Xenopsylla cheopsis*, though others are also capable of transmitting the pathogen. The flea transmits the parasite by first taking a blood meal from an infected rat, thereby bringing live bacteria into its own digestive tract. The bacteria there continue to multiply, soon completely filling up the flea. The flea is now bloated and hungry but, full of bacteria, its gut can take in no food. The poor flea must vomit its gut content just before it takes a meal from its next victim, so placing the virulent bacteria right at the point where the blood flows from this newest host, which might be intraspecific, another rat, or, where rats are dying and fleas leaving the cooling corpses, fortuitously interspecific. An epizootic of *Y. pestis* in a black rat population kills many rats, the fleas abandon their dying hosts for conveniently nearby humans, and with their next bite carry the pathogen into a human body.

The first human manifestation of the disease was, in nineteenth-century clinical experience, very commonly a large black boil, a 'bubo', at the lymph node closest to the site of the bite. Few fleas jump very high and those that bite humans frequently do so on the leg, so most resultant buboes appear in the groin. A bite on the arm gave a bubo in the armpit. From the bubo, the successful pathogen expands into a general (and, absent antibiotics, deadly) infection of the human body, but it is not contagious between humans in this form. Rarely, in extremely intense epidemic circumstances, the disease may shift to become pneumonic (an infection lodged in the lungs) or septicaemic (in all bodily fluids). These even more mortal forms do seem to be contagious through expulsion of water droplets or contact with bodily fluids containing the pathogen, but are so acute and deadly as to limit their own spread and demographic impact. Generally speaking, then, bubonic plague is not contagious between rats, between rats and humans, or between humans, but rather is transmitted by the flea as a vector.

Bubonic plague produces fast and high mortality: 80–90 per cent of untreated victims die. There is no evidence that humans develop immunity to bubonic plague, understandable because this is not a disease of humans and the parasite in question gains no evolutionary advantage by becoming weaker and thus surviving longer in humans. The real business of *Y. pestis* is living in rats and other colonial rodents, at which it is successful. So the parasite was not adapting to humans who, in turn, only contracted it from 'outside'. Nor is human susceptibility to bubonic plague associated with malnutrition, although some debated indicators suggest that persons malnourished as children *might* later be more prone to contract it. This latter point is historically germane for potentially linking a disease-caused mid-fourteenth-century depopulation of Europe with a prior generation's experience of famine and malnutrition.

Present-day bubonic plague is seasonally associated with warm humid conditions, for fleas are then most active and mobile. Its incidence correlates negatively with cold dry or hot dry conditions, which exceed the tolerances of the essential vector. The spatial extension of bubonic plague is highly dependent on the movement of sick rats or the spread of the disease between what are stubbornly sedentary rat colonies. It might take weeks for a sick colony in one house to infect that next door. So the movement and diffusion of modern bubonic plague are measured in months and years. Yet Yersin, the prominent scientist who saw this disease and by experiment and observation in Hong Kong in 1894 identified the pathogen, declared it was just like the Black Death. Thus for almost a century students of history accepted the words of the medical expert and rested their interpretations of the Black Death on the epidemiology of bubonic plague.

In 1984 British zoologist Graham Twigg publicly challenged Yersin's diagnosis. Thereafter a number of scholars began to exhibit growing dissent and then debate on the subject. Objections rested largely on discrepancies between the nineteenth-century bubonic plague as described above and recorded medieval experience of the Black Death. Some of these discrepancies are more telling than others. In the first place the Black Death moved very fast: it seemed to move by a pattern that is typical of interpersonal contagion; it may even have been transferred by objects. It did not exhibit the patterns of spread that characterize rodent-borne diseases, of which there are several. Secondly, dissenters argued that after all there is no medieval or early modern evidence of many dead rats before people came down with Black Death. This reasoning would better convince were medieval sources to provide evidence of rats dying at any time. Black Death or not, however, medieval writers simply paid little attention to dead rats, while archaeological recovery of rat remains is rare and their dating elusive. More telling is that medieval physicians generally reported and worried about victims presenting symptoms of many spots, boils, perhaps 'buboes', all over their bodies, not just in the groin or armpit. And the medieval reports suggest that death took three to five days to arrive, rather than the one or two typical of bubonic plague. There are inconsistencies of seasonality – the Black Death was not confined to warm and humid times of year – and there are inconsistencies of pattern in that bubonic plague is a locally persistent endemic disease while the Black Death and its early modern successors came as decadal or longer recurrences. Questions also arise with respect to immunity. Fair amounts of evidence seem to suggest the Black Death produced acquired immunity among those who survived it. Certain disputed indicators may show a long-term decrease in mortality rates from the Black Death, particularly during the course of the fourteenth and fifteenth centuries. This is less clear regarding later local epidemics. Still, some grounds exist for seeing human biological adaptation to the Black Death, and no such indicate human biological adaptation to nineteenth- and twentieth-century bubonic plague.

Historical inconsistencies inspired various proposals that the Black Death was not bubonic plague but something else: influenza, anthrax, a mix of several diseases, some weird aerial contamination, or a whole list of other ideas. And in response counterarguments stressed the pneumonic and septicaemic forms of plague which are communicable between humans. Further counterarguments asserted that rats and fleas could move around more quickly if they were living inside sacks of grain or bundles of cloth or furs being transported by merchants.

Most recently palaeoscientific research on human remains in presumed burials of Black Death victims provided new information. Worth observing in this context is that, unlike leprosy and some other slow-killing or chronic conditions, plague leaves no physical traces on human skeletal remains. Hence besides contemporary written descriptions and records, palaeopathologists must rely on recovery of genetic material of the pathogen from bones and teeth of presumed victims. Both archaeological and laboratory technique must be impeccable so as to affirm the presence of the pathogen in a specific time and place. Some critics assert that once detected, the presence of the pathogen reveals no more than that, the pathogen in the

individual. These scholars hold that the marker of a particular pathogen in the DNA of a person unearthed in a pestilence pit is not
definitive proof that the pathogen caused the individual's death nor
is it proof that the pathogen caused the epidemic associated with
the pit. The identification of ancient DNA of *Y. pestis* in some
individuals from select 'plague' burials spread out over centuries is,
for these critics, hardly proof that this bacterium was the cause of the
Black Death or subsequent late medieval and early modern 'plague'
outbreaks.

Nevertheless, after several false starts and disputed efforts, a multi-
national team working in parallel in different laboratories under the
leadership of Stephanie Haensch did identify ancient DNA and protein signatures specific for *Y. pestis* in human skeletons from mid- to
late fourteenth-century mass graves in Hereford, Bergen op Zoom,
and Saint-Laurent-de-la-Cabrerisse (Languedoc), and from similar
early modern sites in Augsburg and Parma. The methodology seems
robust and the results convincing. Yet even if that identification of the
pathogen holds, many questions about the disease remain.

Later and more exacting genetic research on the mitochondrial
DNA of *Y. pestis*, using the part of the cell nucleus that preserves traces
of genetic change over time, indicates that a mutation occurred in
what is roughly thought to be the early 1300s. It can be speculated that
this may have increased the virulence of the pathogen and possibly
made it 'new' even to human populations in Europe and the
Mediterranean who had now distant prior experience of the
Justinianic plague, possibly also *Y. pestis*. It may be noted that in
addition to discoveries of *Y. pestis* in late medieval and early modern
human remains, two studies claim isolation of the bacterium in graves
dating to the 'First Pandemic', one in Bavaria (Aschheim) and thus
beyond the coverage of contemporary written sources.

Many disputants over retrospective diagnosis of the Black Death
cling to the notion that a disease organism must remain the same and,
except for its virulence, always behave the same. Therefore each
researcher looks at old descriptions and matches them up with that
disease or this one, always limiting options to an available inventory of
pathogens now known to medical science. But recent experience of
HIV/AIDS, SARS, Ebola, and antibiotic-resistant tuberculosis should
remind historians to acknowledge more possibilities in nature, including new diseases and evolutionary changes in the behaviour of existing
pathogens. Indeed the DNA of *Y. pestis* found in medieval victims

revealed two active strains of the bacterium, neither of them identical with those now present and one certainly now extinct. This reinforces the possibility that the behaviour of those historic pathogens may not be the same as that of those known today. In the absence of confirming historical evidence, it is fallacious to reason simply from present-day species-specific pathogen–host patterns to a past one. Understanding a past disease must take into account both genetic identification of the pathogen and the empirical observations of past witnesses to its behaviour in human bodies. In the case of medieval leprosy the diagnostic features, reported and material, do match up consistently; between the Black Death and bubonic plague they simply do not. It is prima facie true to say that the Black Death was not Yersin's 'bubonic plague', but this does not prove it was not *Y. pestis*. Nevertheless a researcher cannot validly take the pattern of how *Y. pestis* is supposed to work today and use it to fill the gaps and manipulate the evidence from the fourteenth century so it 'fits'. There is no longer any good reason to think that the Black Death had to behave that way. In particular, robust historical evidence indicates that the Black Death was somehow contagious, not rodent-borne, and exhibited a greater variety of symptoms than is reputed for modern bubonic plague. Such must be the starting points for further investigation.

Europeans responded to the Black Death within their culture and learned from their experiences. Immediate reactions to the unprecedented pandemic were dramatic and panic-ridden. People fled. Jews, lepers, and other human scapegoats suffered violent persecutions until observers began to wonder how these 'criminals' could be so clever as to poison other people yet so foolish as also to poison their own. Apocalyptic movements flourished, such as flagellants, who punished their bodies to ward off the evil. The learned and the faithful speculated about forces of planets and the anger of God. The great dying provoked cultural fascination with death, with morbidity, and also some degree of ambivalence.

At a longer perspective, despite the absence throughout the Middle Ages and entire pre-industrial period of anything resembling modern germ theory, there emerged empirical and pragmatic responses to Europe's new disease regime. From particularly 1361, the time of the second epidemic, onwards, physicians were compiling and writing plague tracts. In those works they rejected uninformed authorities from classical antiquity and called upon their own experience. They looked for preconditions: who contracts the *pest*? What social and environmental situations were involved? They tried to come up with prophylactics, mostly meant to avoid contagion from persons or from air perceived as carrying the poison. Doctors were very convinced that some contagious agent was at work. Civic responses turned to the kinds of religious petitions and community activities familiar to people faced with drought or floods, an invading enemy, volcanic eruptions, or swarms of locusts. By such means in the course of the later fourteenth and the fifteenth century they normalized *pest* into the way their culture handled other less than fully comprehended disasters.

Civic quarantine policies developed in the aftermath of the Black Death. Observers reasoned that if pestilence might arrive from some other place where it raged, travellers should be stopped and examined. In particular at Mediterranean ports in the course of the fifteenth century, ships arriving from places suspected of plague were forced to anchor at a distant part of the harbour for forty (Italian *quaranta*) days to give any infection time to burn itself out. All contact between ship and shore was blocked until persons carrying contagion would have died or recovered. Such quarantine policies were a most important part of the cultural response, culminating in the Habsburg military border in the Balkans. Governmental action may have helped the slow attenuation of this plague in Europe. Physicians, for all their clear observation, could offer no other effective prevention and no cure.

So the Black Death was a huge catastrophe, a great shock that medieval people tried to grasp as, in present-day terms, an environmental event with immense human repercussions. Over time they worked out ways to deal with it as something that was natural and increasingly thought to be understood. To an environmental historian the Black Death is a prime example of a highly successful parasite, whether diagnosed in modern medical terms or not. Some six centuries after the final episodes of the 'First Pandemic', this one arrived in late medieval Europe as a virgin soil epidemic, killed off many, many hosts, but managed to keep on going there for some four centuries. Human bodies and cultures were compelled to adapt to a new natural agent.

ENGLISH SWEATS

Not all new parasites succeed. *Sudor anglicus*, 'English sweats', exemplifies a new disease that failed to establish itself in medieval Europe. In summer 1485 an infectious condition suddenly appeared in southern England. It respected no social rank, but afflicted especially healthy males between the ages of fifteen and forty-five. Victims had difficulty breathing, began to sweat heavily, and within twenty-four hours either recovered or died; most died. English sweats killed some thousands of people and disappeared with the start of winter. Physicians took note. They recognized it again when it came back in 1507–8, then returned in 1517, 1528–30, and 1551, always in summer. The only time the disease occurred outside of England was in 1528: following the appearance of the epidemic in England, it cropped up in Hamburg, which had close commercial dealings with English east coast ports, and from there followed trade connections across a large area from Scandinavia to Poland-Lithuania to Switzerland. The sweats also in 1528–9 appeared in cities of the Low Countries, probably arriving directly from England. After 1551 this disease never returned in recognizable form anywhere.

Careful symptomatic descriptions by physicians made absolutely clear this was not the Black Death disease or any other they knew. Present-day retrospective diagnoses have hypothesized pulmonary anthrax, hantavirus, relapsing fever, a pulmonary virus, and every one of those is flawed. Each brings up a modern disease that somewhat resembles but fails to match with all that witnesses report about the sweats. This incongruity makes an important historical point: change is normal in the microbiological world as well as in the human. Did an organism in 1485 try and fail to parasitize humans? Were Englishmen confronted with an instance of cross-species colonization that ultimately did not work? Few, after all, do.

The story of the English sweats teaches historians extreme caution with retrospective diagnoses and with the very concept of diseases as fixed entities. Disease is a manifestation of the action of a parasite in a host. None of the parties necessarily remains exactly the same over time. Clearly English sweats did not succeed, falling to the bottom of the parasite class where the Black Death ranked near the top.

MALARIA

Throughout and beyond the Middle Ages Europeans were subject to the changing incidence and historical consequences of a major endemic disease, malaria. That name groups together several related pathogens, a whole genus of *Plasmodium* protozoans with very long experience parasitizing human beings. Much evidence reveals co-evolution between human communities and various *Plasmodium* species. Long-term shifts in the relationship of changing human and other environmental factors have occurred on several continents, including Europe.

Plasmodium is carried by mosquitoes of genus *Anopheles*, numbering dozens of species. The female mosquito picks up a blood meal from a malarial person, the parasite develops further in the mosquito, and with her next meal, the mosquito injects the next life stage into a susceptible host. If the mosquito is a species to which *Plasmodium* is not adapted or if a vector's next meal comes from an unsusceptible species, *Plasmodium*'s life cycle is broken. The parasite migrates to the liver, lodges and incubates there, and then infects the blood with active reproducing organisms which live off haemoglobin and are in turn picked up, ready to reproduce, by the next appropriate mosquito. The host's blood is infected in a multi-day rhythm set by the reproductive cycle of the *Plasmodium* organism, so malaria manifests itself as periodic fevers, every third day ('tertian ague') or every fourth ('quartan ague'). That applies to the milder forms of malaria, namely *P. vivax* or *P. malariae*. In the deadlier form, *P. falciparum*, the cycles of fever come with growing intensity and soon kill many victims. The survivors – and most survive the initial effects of vivax or malariae – may retain the disease in latent (non-reproductive) form. It can re-enliven itself and it is always present, producing chronic headache, anaemia, liver, kidney, and spleen damage, and general exhaustion. Those who fully recover from the initial infection acquire temporary partial immunity, which protects enough adults that most who die directly from the disease are children and newcomers. Nevertheless, in malarial areas early modern and nineteenth-century death rates were 25–50 per cent higher than in nearby areas without malaria. Few of those deaths were from malaria itself, because malarial debilitation makes its victims susceptible to other deadly infections, especially tuberculosis and pneumonia. The consequences of endemic malaria, therefore, are elevated death rates and a sharp reduction in human energy and the efficacy of human labour. Inhabitants of malarious regions gain reputations for torpor.

To survive in any location, malaria requires a reservoir of humans who have the disease and make it available for mosquitoes to transfer into new victims. It also needs a population of suitable mosquitoes, which turn out to have narrow habitat requirements of their own. This gives malaria a strong environmental dynamic in Europe.

Mediterranean Europe has a long history of vivax, with occasional more confined outbursts of falciparum. The latter is a late-evolving form from Holocene Africa which entered the Mediterranean only in classical antiquity. From long and deadly encounters, Africans have developed a genetic response to it: a recessive gene gives hereditary immunity at the cost of sickle cell anaemia in those individuals who inherit two such genes. Europeans have no such immunity to falciparum. While very clear evidence indicates its presence in early Roman times, it soon disappeared and returned to Mediterranean Europe only in the wet period of late antiquity when river mouths silted up and coastal marshes developed once more to provide the preferred habitat for the principal vector mosquito. This brought another virgin soil epidemic: recent studies of human remains from Italian sites of late Roman (fifth- to sixth-century) date show large numbers of people who died very quickly of falciparum malaria. So long as the water in the marshes remained fresh, the dominant vector was outcompeted by another species that can also carry malaria but prefers the blood of cattle, which do not contract the disease, thus limiting its spread. But when brackish coastal marshes reappeared, so too did evidence of recurring malaria between the fifth and the seventh century near Rome and around Ravenna. Falciparum became a deadly scourge in coastal Sicily from the thirteenth century, when lagoons were turned into marshes by the deposition there of soil eroded from overextended arable land. Italian populations show a high incidence of a gene called thalassaemia, again a recessive where a combination of two makes an individual anaemic, but a single one offers some protection against falciparum (not vivax). The survival of such risky genetic mutations in a human population proves the evolutionary value of resistance to a long-dangerous disease.

From the Roman Mediterranean malaria also entered lands around the North Sea. This was not falciparum, which northern temperatures prevent from reproducing in the mosquito, but vivax. Vivax even handles the absence of mosquito transmission during cold months by going dormant in the victim's liver and reactivating only when warming weather brings a new generation of vectors. It seems that people infected with vivax malaria came into the Rhine delta during Roman times, presumably from Italy and southern Gaul where it was endemic. The parasite proved capable of living in an indigenous mosquito, *A. atroparvus*, which then spread it into native populations, who may have suffered a virgin soil epidemic. *A. atroparvus* strongly favours brackish water and has a feeding range of less than three kilometres, so humans at greater distance from prime habitat remain uninfected. Telling allusions to ague occur in Anglo-Saxon texts by the ninth century, but for a long time the foothold of the disease seems tenuous. Adult mosquitoes had trouble surviving the northern winters and few people lived in the swamps. New people must move into the area to establish a reservoir for the parasite and build some structures where more mosquitoes could find winter refuge.

A major spread of vivax malaria occurred as agricultural drainage began to bring more permanent settlers into wetlands on both sides of the North Sea (see chapters 2 and 4 above). It became endemic in the Frisian area from the ninth century, when Carolingian writers refer to 'Italian fevers' along the Rhine. From the eleventh century onwards many sources along the coast trending northeast to Jutland refer to such fevers. They increased in the fourteenth century with greater flooding and marine incursions, which carried more salt water into the marshes and inhibited certain mosquito competitors of *A. atroparvus*. Warmer summers also seem to allow for longer incubation. Some Dutch natives in certain areas now show a genetic adaptation to vivax, suggesting past interactive co-evolution with what may for a time have been a more mortal threat to survival and reproductive success. But in the Netherlands and in Britain malaria remained highly localized. Popular recognition in the south of England was voiced in a proverb that a marsh dweller who married a woman from the hill would bury her within three years. Coming from outside the malarial zone, she would not have been exposed to malaria as a child and thus lacked acquired immunity or resistance. People of the wetlands, however, having survived repeated attacks, just moved with less speed and enthusiasm than those elsewhere.

Interior European wetlands also gained notoriety for fevers during the Middle Ages. A mythic tale of 'Saint Guinefort' from the poorly drained thirteenth-century Dombes, north of Lyon, imagined an evil creeping from stagnant pools to threaten especially children. Wherever established, endemic malaria drove large demographic and economic effects in contrast to the purely cultural consequences that flowed from endemic leprosy. From another perspective, slowly changing natural and cultural forces gave major endemic diseases a long-term, especially regional, significance comparable to that of the more wide-spread short-run surges in death rates brought by epidemics.

Natural processes are autonomous actors in human history. Pathogens pose ongoing checks to human efforts and drive adaptations both biological and cultural. Sometimes this is the structural situation of endemic disease. But pathogens also produce sudden shocks – epidemics – which may take much longer for a culture to assimilate. There is little to affirm that human agency, even inadvertent and at a distance, serves to explain the Justinianic or Black Death epidemics, or, indeed, the failure of the English sweats. But human agency was deeply involved in the ways in which societies reacted to these shocks. Consider the differences between what is known about the epidemics of the sixth century and those of the fourteenth and fifteenth, and compare medieval European responses to endemic leprosy, malaria, or other diseases.

By agents poorly known, even invisible, to medieval Europeans, forces of nature shaped human lives, regional cultures, and historical periods. The elucidation of all these phenomena provides a wide field of study for well-informed interdisciplinary historians.

AN INCONSTANT PLANET, SEEN AND
UNSEEN, UNDER FOOT AND OVERHEAD

·

'In the year of the Incarnation of the Lord 849,' wrote the learned
abbot of Reichenau, Walahfrid Strabo, 'a most great movement of the
earth took place (*terrae motus maximus factus est*) after the first cockcrow,
on April 20, a Saturday, and lasted several days. Afterwards others
came intermittently until the first of June of the same year, early in
the morning.'[1] Other sources corroborate what is thought to be
Walahfrid's personal experience of an earthquake and aftershocks
centred in the Swabian Alps to the east of his cloistered island in the
Bodensee. While by no means the first such event reported in
the Middle Ages, Walahfrid's rare personal witness conveys both the
precise observation and meagre social context all too common in
surviving records of the restless planet vexing its medieval inhabitants
with seismic, volcanic, and atmospheric catastrophes.

More forthcoming were chroniclers of the harsh northern Italian
winter of 1215–16, when the Po froze over in January so people could
walk, joust, and drive loaded wagons upon it. One contemporary said,
'It was so cold that bread, apples and pears, and all manner of food
froze solid and could not be cut or eaten until they had been warmed

---

[1] As quoted from the Latin of Stiftsbibliothek St. Gallen, Codex 878, fol. 305, and
translated in M. Gisler, D. Fäh, and V. Masciadri, '"Terrae Motus Factus Est":
Earthquakes in Switzerland before AD 1000: a Critical Approach', *Natural Hazards:
Journal of the International Society for the Prevention and Mitigation of Natural Hazards*,
43:1 (October 2007), 63–79 DOI 10.1007/s1069-006-9103-0.

up and thawed out at a fire.'[2] Another alleged needing an axe to hack lumps from frozen wine. These and other writers concurred that deep snow and terrible cold lasting two months caused the vines to wither and were accompanied by high cereal prices. Of course, some such tales may serve mainly dramatic purposes, but certain palaeoscientific records can test and verify seasonal weather as well as longer, less immediately perceptible trends of climate.

Strong forces from the non-living environment, like those of unseen living pathogens, exacted human tolls and called up socio-cultural responses in medieval Christendom. This chapter looks briefly at some exemplary tectonic events and their material and cultural consequences, identifies the methodological problems and interdisciplinary approaches common to both geologic and climatic history, and then sets out the narrative of long-term climatic change and short-term weather events with their impacts on human experience in medieval Europe.

SUBTERRANEAN VIOLENCE

Early medieval references to datable earthquakes are sparse, and still rarer is any specification of places affected, scale of damage, or societal response. Even Carolingian annals noting several strong and deadly earthquakes in the lower Rhine valley during 789–829, which geophysical records likely confirm, convey little information. By the early twelfth century, however, widespread monastic record-keeping allows present-day historical seismologists to rate the earthquake of 3 January 1117 as the strongest in northern Italy during historic times. This is thought to have comprised three separate seismic events: a pre-dawn shaking along northern slopes of the Alps felt across southern Germany; a stronger shock in mid-afternoon at an epicentre likely near Verona, therefore on the southern flank of the Alps; and probably a third, less well-reported evening event in the Tuscan Apennines. Besides more than two dozen chronicles compiled at locations between Prague and the central Rhine and south to Pisa and Cremona, physical and inscription evidence reveals collapse and subsequent extensive repair of major stone ecclesiastical buildings in, for instance, Cremona, Verona, Parma, Padua, and a convent beside

---

[2] As quoted in Vito Fumagalli, *Landscapes of Fear: Perceptions of Nature and the City in the Middle Ages*, tr. Shayne Mitchell (Cambridge: Polity Press, 1994), 112–13.

Modena. The fate of ordinary people and their houses, however, still lacked literate significance.

By the fourteenth century the better-recorded shakings convey meaningful details. Well-documented but fortuitously little-damaged Florence experienced at least seven quakes between 1300 and 1550. Less-favoured localities suffered grievous losses. Pending thorough collation of the medieval seismic record, only illustrative cases are appropriate. Noteworthy, though not equally massive or destructive, events shook bodies, material possessions, and minds in some widely separated parts of medieval western Christendom.

Church bells rang, it was said, without help of human hands before crashing to earth on the evening of 25 January 1348. They tolled for a now-estimated 10,000 dead and extensive damage reported from Pisa and Milan to northernmost Slovenia and eastern Carinthia, five hundred kilometres away. Centred in the Alps of Friuli, the quake was felt as far off as Munich and Prague. Francesco Petrarca later recalled the fear which broke off study in his library at Verona, the 'floor shaking under my feet . . . [and] the books tumbling upon one another from all sides'.[3] Florentine historian Giovanni Villani quoted compatriot merchants then in Udine, where the massive collapse of houses, palaces, churches, and castles caused fatalities. So terrified were local moneylenders that they begged debtors to come and retrieve the sinful usury customarily taken on loans. Further north, the quake dropped a large part of the Dobratsch mountain massif into the valley of the river Gail and temporarily formed a lake ten miles long. When the dam burst, the ensuing flood washed away the town of Villach, including an alleged five hundred people who had taken refuge in the parish church. Imagine the difficulties of rescue and restoration in the dead of winter in mountain country with the means then available. A generation later Venetians erected a memorial plaque in the Scuola Grande della Carità:

on January 25 on the feast of the Conversion of St Paul at about the hour of vespers there was a great earthquake in Venice and almost throughout the world and the tops of many bell-towers and houses and chimneys collapsed, as well as the church of San Basilio; and so great was the fear that almost everybody thought they were going to die, and the earth continued to shake for

[3] F. Petrarca, *Rerum senilium libri*, 10, 2, tr. A. Bernardo, S. Levin, and R. Bernardo in *Letters of Old Age* = *Rerum senilium libri*, 2 vols. (Baltimore: Johns Hopkins University Press, 1992), vol. II, 373.

about 40 days; and after this a great plague began and people died of various diseases and from various causes . . .[4]

Indeed the Black Death arrived in Venezia, Friuli, Tirol, and Carinthia so soon after the earthquake disaster that survivors and more distant chroniclers alike soon conflated the events into one terrible memory.

In the evening of 18 October 1356 what seismologists now assess as the most intense *intra*-plate European earthquake of the past ten millennia devastated Basel and its surroundings to a thirty-kilometre radius and was felt as far away as Zurich, Konstanz, and the Île-de-France. A first shock shortly after dusk drove frightened townsfolk from their homes to open spaces outside the walls and then at about 2200 hours a violent shaking brought down city walls, churches, and dozens of castles. Many wooden buildings remained erect, but shattered hearths and candles left burning by evacuees then ignited the ruins and nearly all within the walls was consumed. The first entry in the town council's new record book, begun early in 1357, declared that 'no church, tower, or house of stone in this town or in the suburb endured, most of them were destroyed'.[5] Early evacuation had, however, kept the death toll to a reported three hundred of roughly seven thousand inhabitants. Basel's cathedral was restored by 1363 and its town walls a few years later, but even into the sixteenth century visitors could identify and local antiquaries memorialize evident signs of damage and repairs.

Sometimes regional earthquakes come in waves. Between March 1373 and May 1448 the eastern Pyrenees, then wholly included in the Crown (kingdom) of Aragon, were hit by three major quakes and twice that many lesser ones, but thereafter the ground stayed stable into the seventeenth century. The first occurred in the midst of war with Castile and a dynastic struggle in the royal house, but still some hundred individual sources and archival series richly document it. Good administrative records kept by royal officials, Catalan towns, and churches display the whole sequence. The quake on 2 March 1373 was felt from Tortosa to Bordeaux and Avignon, and physical

[4] As translated in E. Guidoboni and J. Ebel, *Earthquakes and Tsunamis in the Past: a Guide to Techniques in Historical Seismology* (Cambridge University Press, 2009), 71.
[5] Original quoted in G. Fouquet, 'Das Erdbeben in Basel 1356 – für eine Kulturgeschichte der Katastrophen', *Basler Zeitschrift für Geschichte und Altertumskunde*, 103 (2003), 31–49. Translated by R. Hoffmann.

destruction of what might be thought the usual medieval sort is reported from Barcelona to the Ribagorza valley of upper Aragon (the only recorded fatalities) and also along the north slope of the mountains. The sensation alone prompted penitential processions in Tortosa, but normal social activities went on despite the damage and aftershocks: meetings of the Catalan *Corts* continued and so, too, a princely wedding. The most intense and deadly of the series came on the night of 2 February 1428, the culmination of a half-dozen quakes over the previous twelve months. Reported fatalities numbered in the high hundreds An episcopal survey in the Gerona diocese four years later identified more than thirty sites where ecclesiastical buildings had been totally destroyed and as many more with large or merely partial damage. The last big quake on the night of 24–25 May 1448 hurt and killed people and damaged structures across the entire kingdom, with special mention in several sources from Barcelona and Vic of the collapse of rural farmhouses. Inhabitants of Mataró, a town some forty kilometres up the coast from Barcelona, immediately obtained licence from their bishop to collect alms for the repair of the church of Santa Maria. Five years later, now claiming the earthquake had damaged two more churches and a hermitage, they cleverly extracted from Queen Maria certain fiscal privileges and greater municipal autonomy. Even disasters could be turned to use.

A quake centred in the Straits of Dover on 21 May 1382, though much less impressive than those just described, gained wide attention in contemporary chronicles, in part for its disrupting a church council at Blackfriars in London. Particulars are meagre. It was felt throughout England but damage – collapse of tall stone structures, etc. – was confined to the southeast. Long-term building projects at Christ Church, Canterbury halted for a decade as artisans were drafted in from surrounding counties to repair cracked stonework and broken walls. Even five years later the bishop of London was offering indulgences to fund repair of Paul's Cross, an outdoor preaching venue. While it was also felt in Flanders, Brabant, and much of northern France, driving panicked people into the streets of Ypres, for instance, only Bruges, Ghent, and possibly Liège report even moderate structural damage. The responsible bundle of intraplate faults beneath Kent and Artois, with links eastwards to the lower Rhine geological trench (Graben), would again produce a minor quake in 1449 and a more dangerous one with human casualties in 1580.

On 5 December 1456 southern Italian Campania, still today a region of high tectonic risk, was violently shaken, probably by four successive events. Best present-day estimates are approximately 12,000 fatalities. Personal experience of this event moved humanist Giannozzo Manetti (1397–1459) to compile the first-known European catalogue of roughly a hundred historic earthquakes. Manetti's treatise, *De terraemotu libri tres*, remained, however, in manuscript and unknown into the twentieth century, when wartime destruction of the state archive in Naples further deprived researchers of apparently extensive records of governmental response to the catastrophe.

Meanwhile, movements of the very Gibralter–Azores undersea fault that would trigger the infamous Lisbon earthquake of 1755 rattled the central Portuguese coast eight times in the fourteenth century and five in the sixteenth. The latter included a quake on 3 January 1531 whose estimated thirty thousand victims were the greatest human toll known to date from post-Roman lands of western Christendom.

Contemporaries clearly perceived the earth moving beneath their feet and the horrific effects of this. Their subsequent cultural representations were more ambivalent. Were these terrifying and destructive shakings supernatural manifestations and signs of the divine will, or essentially natural phenomena, perhaps inexplicable but part of normal earthly life? Not surprisingly the intentional written record is full of the former position: Gregory of Tours saw in the fatal breaking of a castle and later deaths of monks who had reoccupied it divine punishment for the victims' specific sins; prelates at the Blackfriar's council in 1382 first panicked that the trembling earth marked God's displeasure at their accusing John Wycliffe of heresy, then gratefully accepted Archbishop Courtenay's quick-witted reassurance that just as the earth lost its evil vapours, so would the church gain from expelling the wicked. Wycliffe himself declared the quake God's rejection of the decision. Communities struck by earthquakes quickly mounted penitential and propitiatory religious processions and, like Basel in 1356, legislated against sinful displays of luxury. Yet a pragmatic strain also surfaces: Icelandic chieftain Snorri *goði*, presiding in 1000 over the community's debate as to whether to accept Christianity, dismissed an earthquake as normal nature, not a message from any God or gods; Albertus Magnus hedged that some quakes might be divine signs and others just natural events; recent exhaustive study of extant sources for the earthquake of 1348 finds fewer acknowledging a divine punishment and more a terrible and unexpected but otherwise ordinary phenomenon. Certainly authorities religious and secular alike willingly undertook to support reconstruction with fund-raising campaigns (indulgences) and even occasional tax exemptions. Chroniclers a generation later credited citizens of Strasbourg, Freiburg im Breisgau, and other towns with sending emergency aid to shattered Basel.

Ordinary medieval people, for all their lack of present-day sensing devices, may have perceived such surprisingly widespread, if uncommon, occurrences as mild earthquakes more easily than those in the more boisterous present. Still, as today, seismic events then most often rattled Europe's Mediterranean margins where geologists now see the African continental plate pushing northwards and still creating the Alpine mountain system from the Pyrenees to the Balkans, including the Apennines. Iceland itself rests atop the active mid–Atlantic fracture zone. Basel and even more so sites on the great European plain were distinctly outliers for historic seismic risks and experiences.

Active volcanoes fit an even more limited territorial distribution inside that of earthquakes. Medieval Europeans could confront an eruption only in southern Italy or distant Iceland. Even so, Vesuvius remained largely quiescent during medieval centuries, while peasants colonized and worked the fertile soils above forgotten Pompeii and Herculaneum. Etna's habitual lava flows disturbed local land use along one slope or another an average of three times a century from 800 to the 1550s, while far from busy sea lanes Stromboli's continual small-scale display of pyrotechnics garnered little attention.

One of Iceland's thirty active volcanic centres probably inspired a tale in the Irish *Voyage of St Brendan* of subhumans hurling fiery rocks; dozens of recorded eruptions, one every four or five years on average, followed in the centuries after Norse settlers arrived in the late 800s. Most of these occurred beyond the horizon of continental awareness, but often forcibly reminded Icelanders of their hazards. For example, like many Icelandic eruptions, that of Öraefajökull in 1362 included lava flows from fissures beneath an ice cap as well as explosions of fiery ash. As monastic annals of Skálholt reported barely a generation later, the eruption, which lasted from early June into autumn, triggered a sub-glacial flood. Water, rocks, gravel, and mud swept violently across the whole coastal district of Litlhérad, killing the more than two hundred inhabitants of two obliterated parishes and turning a deep harbour into a plain. The plume of ash damaged pastures up to a hundred kilometres to the northeast while floating pumice blocked marine access. Litlhérad remained desolate for a century, haunted by legends of prescient escapes and innocent deaths, but eventually new settlers returned to use the now rich soil and forage.

Continental Christendom's first new volcano in some millennia, aptly called Monte Nuovo, burst into ephemeral life in the thermally active cluster of extinct volcanoes called the Phlegraean Fields to the west of Naples on 29 September 1538. Following several years of increasingly violent earthquakes around the fishing and market centre of Pozzuoli, the earth's surface bulged and fissures opened in the main street of Tripergole, a nearby spa village with a hospice and three flourishing inns. Inhabitants ran from the fountain of hot cinders; a day or so later volcanic bombs drove panicked neighbours from Pozzuoli. A fifty-metre cinder cone buried Tripergole. Then on 6 October the eruption stopped, but only after awakening thinkers in densely populated and well-connected Italy to questions of volcanic origins and import.

Minimal personal or even vicarious experience with volcanoes did not deter medieval writers from elaborate explication of their theological significance. Herbert of Mores, monk of Clairvaux and later an archbishop in Sardinia, compiled into his *Liber de miraculis* (*c.*1178) what he may have heard from an Icelandic bishop about the 1104 eruption of Hekla. This Herbert portrayed as 'an immense pit of Hell', which served to prove that eternal fire would torment the souls of sinners. His fellow Cistercians made much of this. Others closer to actual events, like the Skálholt annalist, expressed sheer amazement and horror, or else, as the Spanish viceroy of Naples who made an official inspection of Monte Nuovo, practical interest in the phenomenon and its implications. Were such impressive, often tragic, catastrophes *not* inexplicable manifestations of divine omnipotence (or perhaps other supernatural powers obedient Christians knew not to voice incautiously), medieval philosophers favoured a natural explanation they learned from Aristotle. In this view subterranean winds, driven variously by the earth's own heat, solar warming, or the natural property of elemental air to rise, agitated the earth to produce earthquakes and at times ignited or fanned subterranean fires of bitumen, sulphur, or other minerals which were then vented through volcanoes. Variants of this theory would remain dominant into the nineteenth century.

Catastrophic (i.e. abrupt and massive) events of tectonic origin hold a curious place in medieval human relations with European nature. No human agency, even unintentional, can reasonably be blamed for their occurrence. Some well-documented earthquakes had mostly cultural impact (e.g. Swabia 849, Dover Straits 1382), while others brought massive loss of human lives and material possessions. The latter sort differ from equally 'natural' great epidemics, which normally left physical capital and productive capacity unharmed and thus survivors in possession of greater per capita wealth. Present-day seismic disasters are acknowledged to have significant social construction: damages and loss of life are more severe in poorer and more densely populated areas and quakes tend to exacerbate prior poverty. Such questions have not been meaningfully raised in research on medieval events. While it appears that time of day affected mortality rates (night-time deaths of sleeping people compared with more likely escape by those awake), many reports tacitly indicate more damage to stone (i.e. elite) structures than to the less rigid dwellings of the poor. This matches present-day engineering assessments and historic proposals by Leonardo da Vinci and others for earthquake-resistant designs.

Eruptions and earthquakes were mainly discrete local or regional phenomena, devastating identifiable communities (socio-natural sites), yet leaving others unscathed. While historical epidemiologists debate what areas the Black Death missed, their seismological counterparts track the limits of damage and perception. But did the destruction and need to rebuild constitute any long-term drag on the well-being or development of these communities? Not on present historical knowledge: northern Italy, Catalonia, and southern Germany were scarcely disadvantaged or materially backward regions of sixteenth-century Europe. Some historians have, however, argued that, as capital goods and knowledge accumulation became more important in the run-up to modernity, Europe's relative immunity to large-scale natural disasters gave it an advantage over other advanced pre-industrial civilizations. While between 1000 and 1550 some twenty-four earthquakes are each recorded to have killed more than ten thousand people world-wide, only three of those occurred in western Christendom.

Some irony may now be felt that medieval thought so connected seismic and volcanic events with the air. While European earthquakes and eruptions, as seen, actually affected relatively few people across the medieval millennium, large eruptions elsewhere (including

Iceland), and well outside contemporary European awareness, are now recognized to have had great indirect impact on European lives by affecting atmospheric conditions at several scales. Volcanic dust in the atmosphere not only falls to earth with precipitation to leave traces in ice cores, its sulphur aerosols directly reduce solar radiation and throughout the modern era have consistently produced times of extreme cold. A shift in atmospheric conditions affects the way people live, die, eat, and survive. The much-discussed 'dry fog' of 536 with its detectable negative effects on solar irradiation, global temperatures, and plant growth is now convincingly linked to volcanic aerosols in well-dated Greenland and Antarctic ice cores, fallout of dust and chemicals blasted into the stratosphere by a near-equatorial volcano. Likewise eight of nine severely cold winters recorded between 750 and 950, which brought deaths from cold and famine, followed years when Greenland ice holds sulphates from volcanic eruptions. All ice core data sets indicate a massive such explosion somewhere near the equator early in 1258. European written sources, knowing nothing of volcanoes, depict a year of continual cloud cover, an abnormal cold spell in late winter and spring, crop failures in England, northern France, northern Italy, and southwest Asia, and then another remarkably cold winter in 1260–1.

Certainly more forces than volcanism drive the global atmospheric system and, as the rest of this chapter will show, its considerable short- and long-term effects on medieval Europe. Yet dynamic natural forces below and above the earth's surface share a further attribute, the inventory of interdisciplinary methods whereby their past manifestations are now identified and reconstructed.

RECAPTURING PAST PLANETARY VARIABILITY ABOVE AND BELOW GROUND

Different kinds of scientists study and seek to explain past tectonic and climatic events and changes. Their theories engage different aspects of the natural sphere. But from the perspective of a medievalist their common reliance on both naturally occurring data sets and the human cultural record deciphered by traditional historians brings them together. Certainly recent and authoritative methodological instructions for historical seismologists and climatologists have much in common, together indicating how connections between natural forces and medieval lives can be drawn.

Temperature, precipitation, and wind are the atmospheric variables collectively experienced as weather. Climate and weather label opposite ends of a continuum of atmospheric conditions and phenomena at different temporal and spatial scales. Weather happens in a short time in a delimited place. Climate happens over a large territory and/or a long period of time, conventionally thirty years. Climatic change refers to a shift in average conditions, in the frequency of phenomena, across such spans of time, always acknowledging that the atmospheric system is complex with important elements of chaos. This results in random but consequential variation. Atmospheric scientists predict and describe weather patterns, which are climate, for the past and the future, with a fairly high degree of precision.

Information about atmospheric conditions, past or present, can be conveyed in such indirect sources as verbal descriptions or the composition of such natural 'archives' as tree rings, ice cores, or annual deposit layers in a lake, or by direct measurement of temperature, precipitation, and wind. Direct observations, that is, scientific measurements, were taken for short periods of time in some European localities in the sixteenth century and for more and longer in the seventeenth. Systematic recording of atmospheric variables got underway in the eighteenth century and continued to develop in the nineteenth, so that from decades just before 1800 a long-term observational record can be worked out for many European areas. Scientific measurement of tectonic events is much more recent. In either case these systematic records provide the necessary baseline for comparison with the indirect evidence available at the same time and earlier.

Using records of climate-related phenomena that correspond with the period of scientific observation, historical climatologists seek to calibrate the indirect evidence and then read it backwards through a whole variety of data sets. Palaeoscientific proxy indicators also allow researchers to look back before recorded scientific observation. For example, just as sulphur compounds frozen in Greenland ice cores mark volcanic events, so too does the ratio of oxygen isotopes in the same annual layers of ice provide a clear proxy for sea surface temperature at the time that sea water evaporated to fall later as snow. The width of annual tree rings indicates primarily the moisture available during the growing season in the place where the tree grew; multiple tree-ring samples taken from whole stands of a species suggest regional conditions. Debris deposits and other signs of wave erosion well above a past coastline may mark a tsunami triggered by a quake offshore. Evidence of soil erosion and deposition with good relative or absolute dating can reveal periods of high precipitation, but also its absence in the case of wind-borne deposits. Many proxy indicators tell indirectly something about temperature, precipitation, or wind; fractured buildings or rock strata indicate the strength of an earthquake. Present values can be calibrated against observational records and earlier values then used to estimate those of the past. All such data sets result from modern-day scientists conducting palaeoscience; unlike the traditional historical record, past humans played no role in the creation or preservation of the relevant material from the past (see introduction).

Data sets about past climate are also derived from working with human documentation of natural proxies such as the written and dated record of ice forming on the lagoons of Venice, the start of the grape harvest in a particular area, or when certain plant species flowered locally. Each year's date of flowering by cherry trees at the royal palace in Tokyo (Edo) has been kept since the tenth century. This approach takes advantage of 'phenology', the consistent correlation of certain natural phenomena with temperature patterns, usually over some number of previous months. If human beings have kept a consistent record of these events, the result can stand for a scientific observation of the relevant atmospheric variable.

Finally, historians are able to learn about tectonic events and weather in times gone by from human narrative verbal descriptions, once these have passed critical scrutiny and are read systematically to recreate seasonal and monthly conditions or the strength and location of an earthquake shock. The systematic methodology was pioneered by Swiss climate historian Christian Pfister. It entails working with dozens, indeed sometimes hundreds, of written records over a defined area, establishing what each says, its precise date, that it was not copied from another source, etc., then using that verified information to tabulate whether a particular observer described a day, month, or a season as, for instance, extra wet, extra dry, or just nothing special. Assembled into a systematic timed and located data set, these become patterned reports of weather or a quake as experienced.

All of these different sources must be calibrated against observational records in a period of overlap to learn how they connect with one another. Each genre of palaeoscientific and historical data sets has a different degree of temporal and measurement sensitivity. Narrative stories about storms, extreme drought, or a volcanic eruption tend to be good about dates but to use fuzzy terminology. Ice cores provide precise proxy data but much less sharp dates. Both sets also present questions about regional definition – what area scale ought each measurement represent? Such are the kinds of data on which geological and climate history is studied for periods before systematic direct observation, including the entire Middle Ages.

Geological change mainly occurs at time scales too great for direct human perception; only the catastrophic events enter history at even a century scale. Not so for the atmosphere. Defining change, trends, or periodicity in palaeoclimatic data over time depends importantly on the kinds of questions being asked, for applicable temporal and spatial scales differ. What is needed to date a whole glaciation episode is irrelevant for understanding an individual human's lifetime. What matters for talking about the climate of the planet – the mean global temperature – helps little for learning regional responses to that planetary condition. Charting mean annual temperatures of a place says less about crop production than knowing if the growing season has been short or long. Further, temperature, precipitation, and storminess are three separate atmospheric parameters, not all the same thing. Statements about one bear no *necessary* relationship to values of another. Hence, many historical climatologists now prefer the term 'anomaly' to identify temporally defined clusters or specific types of events, especially as compared with some baseline period of the very recent past ('present'), which they use as a standard. Reading such material calls for awareness if the writer is, for instance, using as a baseline the whole of the twentieth century or rather a particular sub-period such as its middle decades, second half-century, or otherwise. Authors who refer to anomalies are really saying a particular set of phenomena appeared more or less often or strongly in the period being studied than it did during the baseline period. If various writers reference different baselines, confusion can ensue.

Defining a piece of the past as an anomaly has commonly been undertaken with respect to one or two variables only. Talking about that piece of the past as a period in the history of climate usually calls for it to be named. Like 'Middle Ages', all such names are retrospective, assigned by people of the twentieth and twenty-first centuries and never by people living through the times in question. As with other historical eras, the names placed on such climatic periods can catch only certain, perhaps not even the critical, features and they never refer to uniform conditions. Readers of terms such as 'medieval warm period' or 'Little Ice Age' must recognize them as labels, generalizations which cannot encompass everything that went on during the times so designated.

As implicitly shown at the start of this chapter, coherent historical treatment of human experiences with volcanoes and earthquakes needs reasonable familiarity with plate tectonics and its manifestations in regional geologies. So, too, must environmental historians collaborate with palaeoclimatologists and general climatologists. Yet the several disciplines' contributions and purposes regarding past environmental conditions may be thought intersecting interests, not coincident courses. Disciplinary paths from question to answer cross but rarely merge. Large matters of the causality of atmospheric phenomena are not issues that historical method or historians engage. Historians must be aware that the principal mechanism for weather and climate in Europe is the so-called North Atlantic Oscillation (NAO), but acquaintance with that mechanism does not mean that historians per se talk about what may have triggered it. Climatologists reasonably debate how much a particular shift in the NAO derived from a change in solar flux, arose as a consequence of volcanic activity, or might result from atmospheric chemistry changing concentrations, for instance, of greenhouse gases. Those are no more *historians'* issues than are the reasons why some *Anopheles* carry malaria and others do not. Historians should know about these scientific debates but not directly engage in them. What historians must do is verify claims about activities that are alleged either to be causes of climatic events or consequences of them. Also, historians must make use of the scientific data that help reconstruct past climate, weather, and geological phenomena in conjunction with traditional sources because historians are the ones best able to piece together and contextualize past conditions in the particular time and place being examined. Historians are more inclined to want to know about a particular time in a specific place or region and are discomfited if somebody presents evidence from, for instance, Italy, and would apply that to weather events in central Spain two years earlier. It is thus the historian's task to recover the parameters of climatic change in medieval Europe and the human response to it. This does not call for those parameters to be global conditions, nor for them to be explained at the level of atmospheric physics, although such explanations may reinforce the credibility of the descriptions. Historical scholarship needs to be able to infer European and regional conditions and their human effects. A medievalist is in some respects less interested in whether or not the Little Ice Age was a planet-wide phenomenon than in working with the evidence that people in Europe had to deal with, for example, certain seasonal temperatures different from those of their great-grandparents, whether they were conscious of this difference or not.

More than even the history of disease, that of climate is a rapidly evolving field. Its various approaches and purposes remain less than well integrated between the physical and the social and humane sciences. Since the 1990s worry over global warming has motivated large increases in research funding, first for the most recent millennium and later for that before 1000CE, but important new data sets are still slow to cross disciplinary boundaries, and obsolete or speculative assertions are too often treated as fact by impatient historians and climatologists alike. Students and researchers must carefully and critically assess differences between baselines for comparison, the territorial, temporal, and relative scale of measured variances, and the place of a publication in the recent development of the field before drawing conclusions about the potential and/or documentable material and cultural consequences of past climatic conditions and changes. Even if what follows meets the aspiration of a reasonably correct synthesis as of the early 2010s, new findings and debates may soon call for its revision.

<h3 style="text-align:center">MEDIEVAL EUROPEAN CLIMATES AT THE CENTURY SCALE</h3>

In the context just established, since the 1960s work of the pioneering English historical climatologist H. H. Lamb and his French counterpart, historian Emmanuel LeRoy Ladurie, scholars in general have distinguished two distinctive periods in the climate history of late pre-industrial Europe, a 'Medieval Warm Period' (henceforth MWP) and the 'Little Ice Age' (henceforth LIA). (These followed the Roman Optimum and Early Medieval Climatic Anomaly previously discussed in chapters 1 and 2 above.) By the second decade of the twenty-first century, however, climate scientists have come to prefer a global 'Medieval Climate Anomaly' (henceforth MCA) for the European MWP. Debate over the temporal boundary between the MCA/MWP and the LIA and over their regional manifestations has further led many scholars now to acknowledge an intervening transitional period distinguished by its very instability of climate from more stable conditions during MWP and LIA alike. So following the erratic

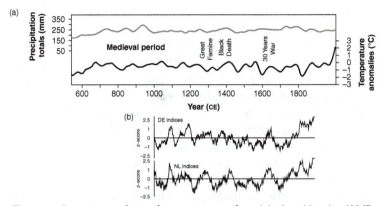

Figure 9.1 Long-term and annual temperatures and precipitation: (a) spring (AMJ) precipitation and summer (JJA) temperatures in central Europe, 600–1800; (b) winter temperatures in central Europe (DE) and the Netherlands (NL), 1000–1800

conditions of late antiquity or the earliest Middle Ages, medieval Europeans generally experienced some relatively warm centuries and then a time of instability as the climate cooled into the LIA.

The general pattern and some elements of its complex diversity are visible in Figure 9.1. This figure assembles and synchronizes four data sets published in the early twenty-first century. The selected time series derive collectively from two different methodologies used to reconstruct aspects of climate conditions in medieval west-central Europe. The top two graphs (Figure 9.1a) took the width of annual tree rings in 7,284 oak series in France and Germany to infer spring (April, May, June) precipitation (in millimetres) and in 1,546 series from high-altitude conifers in the Austrian Alps as proxies for summer (June, July, August) temperatures (shown as deviations from measured seasonal means, 1864–2003). The two lower graphs (Figure 9.1b) were created using the Pfister method of calibrating winter (December, January, February) temperatures from written records to show deviations from the mean for 1100–1950 in Germany (top) and the Netherlands (bottom). Figure 9.1 as a whole illustrates both important methods for climatic history and some representative regional-scale findings. Note both the timing and the amplitude of major climatic periods.

The LIA as a planetary cooling event prior to the industrial age has long been accepted by serious workers in this field. More recently and after some debate the consensus among climate scientists is that a global climate anomaly did occur earlier in the period between 900 and 1300, but important regional differences in time and space shaped local events and effects. One reason for the former disagreement was that some early estimates for the MWP in Europe were so high (annual averages as much as 4 °C warmer than in the twentieth century) as to bring into question the anthropogenic origins of planetary warming in the late twentieth and early twenty-first century. As described below, a generation of more recent studies like those in Figure 9.1 has much mitigated the amount of variance. All such periodizations also raise a taxonomic issue: to the extent that climatic conditions vary in wave-like fashion over time (as in the figure), is a 'period' located between peaks, between troughs, or as a uniform slope between points of change? More crucial when working at the century scale is to avoid an 'ecological fallacy', namely the error of reasoning from a descriptive generalization to specific phenomena within the generalized class. Just because a period is labelled an 'ice age' does not mean that its every moment was chilly: while the LIA does roughly encompass later medieval and all of early modern Europe, two important heat-loving crops, tomatoes and maize, spread across Europe during it. The rest of this chapter treats each of western Christendom's three principal post-Carolingian climatic phases in some detail (using much more evidence than that illustrated in Figure 9.1), before turning to selected cases at several scales where the interaction of medieval atmospheric conditions and human affairs can most clearly be seen.

EUROPE'S 'WARM' MEDIEVAL CLIMATE ANOMALY

When H. H. Lamb proposed an MWP during roughly 1000–1300 he principally used published British data to estimate a mean annual temperature then 1–2 °C above the British norm for 1931–60. Subsequent recalculation in 1997 of Lamb's figures following critical review and augmentation of his sources affirmed his chronology at the century scale. Comparable data sets for central Europe lag a bit from the British, with warming setting in during the late eleventh century and continuing into the first half of the fourteenth. The newer evidence reduces the variance to only 0.5 °C, but that is relative to a baseline of the entire twentieth century, which was warmer than the baseline used by Lamb.

Researchers working at the northern hemisphere scale in recent multi-proxy studies using calibrated and smoothed-out data offer a more complete understanding, which starts from recognition that radiation from the sun peaked during roughly 1080–1280. Among other effects, high solar irradiance sets a dominant 'positive' pattern to atmospheric circulation in the North Atlantic (the NAO) which favours a warmer and drier flow of air across Europe. Regional circulation and lags then come into play. Greenland ice cores indicate peak temperatures there *c*.800–1000, followed by very gradual cooling into the fourteenth century; annual high temperatures averaged more than 1 °C above those of 1881–1980. In Europe itself annual mean temperatures hit 0.3 °C above twentieth-century means during the late tenth and eleventh centuries and matched the twentieth-century figures during the twelfth century and much of the thirteenth (to 1260). For the growing season (April–September) in northern Europe, tree ring data shows the same or slightly greater warmth held during about 960–1250, followed by a sharp trough in the 1260s. The behaviour of major Swiss Alpine glaciers fits these findings. The largest, the Great Aletsch in Valais, had advanced considerably in the sixth and seventh centuries to a length of about twenty-three kilometres. Although minor advances did occur in the ninth century and around 1100, overall between 900 and 1300 its tongue retreated by two to three kilometres. In 1250 the glacier's front stood at an altitude higher than it would again occupy until after 1950.

The state of glaciers depends on temperature but also on precipitation. The retreat of ice in the Alps coincided with low levels during the tenth to the twelfth century in the mountain lakes of west-central Europe. Lake levels then rose *c*.1150–1280, only to fall again in the half-century following. That dry conditions overall were typical of Europe's MWP is confirmed by the growth patterns of trees in Scandinavia and the Alps and by datable sediment cores from lakes of eastern and estuaries of western Iberia, which reveal high evaporation and much flash flooding. In the latter case researchers found no coincidence with removal of tree cover and increase in cereal and crop pollens. Another methodology indicates that dry and warm conditions prevailed in the central Mediterranean between 1100 and 1270. Dominant southerly winds then picked up dust from the Sahara and deposited it in Sicily, southern Italy, and parts of Iberia and Greece. Such drying trends may also have been the norm on the plains of eastern Europe. Recent work further asserts that catastrophic droughts during the late tenth and eleventh century in southwestern and central Asia caused great social and political upheavals.

While the timing, duration, and scale of warmer periods during the tenth to the early fourteenth century certainly varied around the world, a positive North Atlantic Oscillation did make for relatively warm and relatively dry conditions across western portions of the Eurasian land mass. Across much of the northern hemisphere including Europe relatively stable seasonal patterns prevailed, characterized in the west by cold wet winters but mostly quite warm summers. Without worrying too much over what may be fuzzy temporal boundaries, historians can thus observe Europe's MWP in general contrast to previous and to subsequent regional climates.

This is not, however, to say that the MWP lacked local short-term variability. There were notably cold winters in 1118 and 1234 – frozen lagoons at Venice could bear a horse and rider – and distinctly warm ones in the 1180s, when trees in the Rhineland flowered in February. Short-term anomalies, commonly a hard winter followed by a cold, wet spring and summer, triggered crop failures and regional food shortages in northern Europe in 1005–6, 1043–5, 1099–1101, 1124–6, 1144–7, 1149–51, 1195–8, and 1224–6. However, summers in central Europe were especially warm and dry between 1261 and 1310 and in England from 1284 to 1310. Spring conditions essential for a good crop year were especially favourable between 1280 and 1300. A person born in the third quarter of the thirteenth century thus spent her or his working life in long and pleasant growing seasons and shared experiential truth that

> Sumer is icumen in,
> Lhude sing cuccu!
> Groweþ sed and bloweþ med
> And springþ þe wde nu.[6]

Certain widespread biological associations and general effects are visible. During these two or three centuries the tree line in the Alps climbed above the 2,000 metre mark, higher than in the twentieth century but not as high as it had been during the Bronze Age. The maximum altitude for successful grape production in the Rhineland rose by 200 metres compared with the early Middle Ages. Under

---

[6] Text from British Library, MS Harley 948, fol. 11v, published in A. Quiller-Couch, ed., *The Oxford Book of English Verse, 1250–1918*, new edn (Oxford: Clarendon Press, 1940), 1, and in Christopher Ricks, ed., *The Oxford Book of English Verse* (Oxford: Oxford University Press, 1999), 1.

MWP conditions inhabitants of England and southern parts of Scotland, Norway, and the Baltic coast also managed to produce their own wine. This may have lacked quality by medieval or modern standards and been driven significantly by religious ritual needs, but credibly fermentable grapes do indicate expectations of few severe summer frosts and a good deal of sunshine. Few vines and no serious viticulture were later to be found in any of those regions until the late twentieth century. Wheat culture shows a similar relationship. Between the tenth and the late thirteenth century the ceiling for its cultivation moved up by the same 200 metres in the Alps and in Norway, where it came to be grown as far north as Trondheim. Not surprisingly, with glacial retreat and other warm conditions, a rise of general sea level further characterized the period. As ocean levels crested in the course of the thirteenth century, storm tides cut new gulfs along central parts of the Frisian coast, creating whole new bays and basins in 1219 and again during 1277–87. These marine incursions were not particularly associated with heavy rains but with high normal sea levels and wind-driven high tides. But the world then changed.

TRANSITION TO A 'LITTLE ICE AGE'

Multi-proxy data sets now indicate falling mean annual temperatures as early as 1200, probably brought on by a cluster of volcanic eruptions and resultant peak global sulphur aerosols from the 1150s to 1260s. Solar activity then declined from the 1250s into what is now called the 'Wolf solar minimum', lasting until about 1380. What might in retrospect be thought a harbinger of things to come was the decade 1251–61, when much of northern Europe experienced wet and cold summers followed by crop failures. Regional food shortages again afflicted Britain, France, and central Europe. The 1250s have not, however, yet been studied comprehensively with the necessary inter-disciplinary focus on energy, atmospheric conditions, the productivity of agroecosystems, and food supply across western Christendom and its Mediterranean neighbours.

So as benign as late thirteenth-century weather may often have been in much of northern Europe, it calls to mind the northern hemisphere's month of August, when the atmosphere begins to cool well before swimmers and sunbathers are aware of a change. The late 1200s may still belong to the MWP but some balance had tipped. The 1300s followed with much and brutal climatic oscillation. Indeed some scholars see the entire fourteenth century and through to the mid-sixteenth as characterized by irregular cycles of climatic extremes, with concomitant regional bouts of catastrophic weather.

Fourteenth-century temperature regimes fluctuated wildly at the decade scale, showing nearly 1 °C variance in annual means even after smoothing with an eleven-year filter. Precipitation varied semi-independently, often but not consistently rising with cold conditions. One reading of chemical signatures in the Greenland ice cores finds an abrupt but temporary abnormality in Atlantic circulation between 1300/10 and the 1350s, which would integrate this changing weather into the NAO.

The century's second decade is a now familiar case in point, when the cold wet years of 1315–17 brought crop failures, a 'great famine', and many deaths to northwestern Europe. Already in 1314 unusually heavy summer rains in England and Germany reduced cereal yields and a severe winter meant food shortages. The following year, 1315, was wetter, with continual rains and floods setting in in April; all but unbroken cloud cover contributed to chilly summer conditions across all of northern Europe. Winter 1316 was so cold that ships were frozen into the Baltic ice ... and still the rains continued. Narrative and record sources alike report floods tearing away topsoil, waterlogged fields with sparse crops beaten flat, and 'unheard of sterility' on Cistercian farms in northern France. The rains tapered off in summer 1317, but that winter was the worst yet, described by a French writer as setting in by 30 November and continuing until the following Easter (23 April). Wheat yields on the southern English manors of Winchester cathedral and Westminster abbey fell anywhere from 13 per cent to 30 per cent below previous norms and sturdier barley and oats by almost as much. In 1316 and 1317 a priory near Paris lost half its dues in kind. Cold wet conditions meant grapes, too, failed to mature in both France and the Rhine Palatinate. By early 1316 all food reserves were exhausted and famine set in from Ireland to Silesia and Scandinavia to central France and Germany. Impacts differed by region, with waterlogged lowlands faring worst, and by social class, for the wealthy could access substitute supplies beyond the reach of the poor. In 1316–17 commercial Bruges suffered 5 per cent famine mortality and industrial Ypres 10 per cent as looms stopped for lack of customers with discretionary funds for fine fabrics. After generations of rising human numbers, northwestern population growth probably stopped. Livestock, too, debilitated by poor natural fodder and desperate humans competing for what normally fed cattle, fell victim to several epizootics. But chill and wet conditions do not harm all organisms: annual rings of oaks from Ireland, Hessen, Scandinavia, and the Alps show unusually good growth in precisely those awful years.

Weather inimical to humans and their possessions in fact continued past 1317 and far into the 1320s and 1330s. Storminess lasted into the early 1340s with the result that, as sea levels had barely receded, eastern England and the Low Countries suffered extensive coastal flooding, erosion, and loss of farmland. Local manorial lords even petitioned rulers to relieve their tenants from taxes on grounds that much of what had been village arable now lay beneath the waves. Central Europe experienced its own severe oscillations. Extreme drought in the late 1330s and early 1340s was broken by heavy snows in winter 1341–2, followed by violent runoff that began on 2 February. The ground became saturated with water while rains continued off and on throughout the spring. In early July the whole of the continent's midsection was hit by immensely heavy rains that peaked on 19 July and triggered violent floods in all of the rivers of central Europe. Unparalleled high water is everywhere recorded. The water mark in Frankfurt reached 7.85 metres above the normal level of the Main. The inundation was so remarkable that people kept track. At Hannoversch Münden, a small city at the edge of the central uplands where two small rivers join to form the Weser, 'the 19th of July in 1342 with immense waves, floods, and inundation' earned a near-contemporary memorial (Figure 9.2).

The plaque's place on the parish church stands two and more metres above a market square itself well over five metres above the rivers themselves. The natural record preserved on the ground from 1342 shows that single year produced seventeen times the annual erosion rate calculated over the past five thousand years. By comparison, annual erosion during notoriously rainy 1315–17 was but five times the mean. Uncounted numbers of people, cattle, and buildings, and unquantified social capital were simply wiped out as a consequence of these wild climatic fluctuations.

Warm dry summers returned in mid-fourteenth-century northern Europe, but the effects of changing climate in the Mediterranean followed a somewhat different rhythm. Repeated massive flooding of rivers on both slopes of the eastern Pyrenees during the first third of the century is reflected in local records, hence efforts to reduce the risk, and

Figure 9.2 Hannoversch Münden memorialized the Flood of 1342: (a) the memorial plaque at flood level; (b) location of plaque on the parish church; and (c) normal water levels at the junction of Fulda and Werra to form the river Weser, with the parish church on the hill in the middle distance.

reconstruction of ruined Catalan bridges at double their former length. South of the Alps and Massif Central, the years from 1320 to 1370 were noted for summer floods, rains, and cold winters. The hazards feared in Roussillon (see chapter 7) were not unique. At Florence, November 1333 began with five days of rain in the city and the upper Arno basin. This swelled the river over its banks to cover a vast rural area above the city, where weirs, ship mills, bridges, and the city's own new walls held back the flow. By the evening of 4 November the walls had begun to crumble, and for forty-eight hours the waters poured into the city, inundating some two-thirds of the walled area to depths of several metres. When the western fortifications finally burst, the flood roared on downstream, leaving behind it massive destruction and more than three hundred dead. Contemporaries then debated the relative roles of the divine will (to punish a heedless city), natural processes then understood in astro-meteorological terms, and human behaviour (neglect of a 1330 ban on fish weirs and mills, recent new constructions in the flood plain and river bed). Following up on intercessory religious processions, the communal government responded pragmatically with a wider and more severe ban on in-stream works, with disaster relief and reconstruction, and also with sumptuary laws to curb sinful luxury of dress and dining. Contemporaries attested to notably widespread rain in autumn 1345; continuing into the next spring, the wet conditions rotted the seed in the ground. The ensuing crop failure brought dearth and famine extending from Burgundy to Tuscany. Overall the early to mid-1340s were about as bad in terms of famine in the south as 1315–17 had been in the north. Both instances coincided with heavy and long-lasting precipitation. The north was less afflicted after the 1340s and the Mediterranean spared 1315–17, in so far as surviving records show. But Tuscany did suffer food shortages an average of one year in every five between 1282 and 1421, often in the context of unseasonable rain and cold. Ice layers from the 1340s contain more volcanic aerosols than any others between 1260 and 1450.

Italian climate researchers Franco Ortolani and Silvana Pagliuca, who work as geoarchaeologists, interpret the entire period 1270 to 1500 as transitional for the Mediterranean, with anomalous heavy rainfall that supported soil formation in Sicily while causing floods and erosion in the well-watered Po basin. That interval did not, however, feature the steady cold and damp that would characterize following centuries. So while using different methods, climate research on these issues in the Mediterranean concurs that conditions typical of the late thirteenth to the early sixteenth century shared with other regions a contemporary pattern of oscillations distinct from earlier and later times.

Oxygen isotopes in the ice cores from Greenland mark the fourteenth century as the coldest there for the previous seven hundred years, and 1343–62 the most frigid, averaging 10 °C below normal. In Switzerland the Great Aletsch and Gorner glaciers began to expand in the 1290s and reached maxima in 1360 and the 1380s respectively. Across the northern hemisphere general glacial readvance was underway before 1300 and peaked aroud 1350. While conditions in the last fourteenth-century decades were more favourable to people than to ice, some regions subsequently experienced early to mid-fifteenth-century cold so dry as to starve further glacial advance. Temperature anomalies in the Rhine–Meuse basins then exceeded 1 °C, while precipitation fell sharply. As strong variability spread eastwards, the 1430s became the coldest winter decade in central and western Europe up to the 1690s. But then 1450–1500 in central Europe and 1500–40 in the Netherlands became the longest runs of mild winters either would see again until the mid-eighteenth century. Regional summers were almost as benign. After these pauses, however, subsequent surges of glaciers are well dated in the 1560s–1680s and 1810s–1850s.

THE LITTLE ICE AGE

The behaviour of glaciers was Lamb's original reason for identifying a 'Little Ice Age'. Now a scholarly generation later, surging late medieval glaciers might be thought part of the chaos that marked a climatic transition or treated as the beginning of the LIA itself. Which choice has been made will affect how a writer speaks in general about the LIA, that is, which centuries are meant. The LIA in Lamb's long version runs from 1300 to 1850 and in the shorter version of later scholars from the 1560s to the 1840s. A definition based on changes in atmospheric circulation would start the LIA in the early 1400s, while another points to a new pulse of volcanism in the 1450s. Because glaciers need both cold and precipitation to grow and advance, glacial readvances imperfectly coincide with dates that other indicators identify as periods of the most extreme cold. In early modern Europe it is plain that 1560–1620 (labelled the 'Grindelwald Fluctuation') was unusually cold, but its nadir dated to the 1590s. Then the time from 1680 to 1720 (the 'Maunder Minimum', referring to a paucity of sunspots) was again more frigid, but reached its most awful depth during the 1690s. The age of Louis XIV is now well known for the terrible conditions suffered by ordinary French men and women.

The LIA was especially characterized by the *length* of its winters, which dragged on as much as two or three months longer than before. Springtime in Europe then came late and cold; autumns came early and cold. Over time the shortened growing season pushed trees, vines, and cereal grains back from the now environmentally marginal forward locations they had occupied during the MWP. Other signs likewise indicate shifts in basic ecological boundaries. Reports of wolves rise from the fourteenth century onwards in France and from the sixteenth century in the Alpine zone, culminating in well-documented eighteenth-century reports of large-scale wolf populations in central and northern France, all around the Alps, and much of central Europe. Predation on livestock and human fatalities are convincingly reported as never before. At another trophic level, a particular kind of scavenger bird, the bearded vulture (Lämmergeier, *Gypaetus barbatus*), with a beak too weak to handle frozen carrion, abandoned the central Alps in the course of the 1500s. Likewise across large areas of upland Britain the less demanding sheep replaced domestic cattle as the principal herd animal of large-scale pastoralists. The latter, of course, was a human response to shifting balances between productive capacities and market conditions.

While annual average and seasonal cooling by as much as 1–2 °C may also have affected Mediterranean Europe, the change was further manifest in shifting regional precipitation patterns. While parts of southern Provence, Languedoc, Lombardy, and Tuscany absorbed more rainfall, in certain areas of southern Spain, for example, lakes and wetlands diminished.

General and increasingly specific descriptors and labels are thus applied to successive multi-century periods in the climate of medieval and early modern Europe by comparison with the disrupted cold times of late antiquity and the warming trend of the most recent centuries. Medieval Warm Period, transition, and Little Ice Age are not sharply bounded like centuries, wars, or dynasties simply because that is not how atmospheric physics and biological and cultural adaptations work in the long run.

SOME CASE STUDIES OF CLIMATE, WEATHER,
AND MEDIEVAL CULTURES

To move from the general features and associations of historical climatic periods or phases to asserting particular links between atmospheric and cultural phenomena risks being trapped into simple-minded determinist thinking. Assertions such as 'Warm conditions meant the Norse expanded across the North Atlantic' or 'The LIA was cold, so people invented better stoves' are hard to escape when working at the very large scale, but also quite impossible to demonstrate in any robust way. Particular well-documented weather events, however, can trigger convincing material and cultural consequences, as, for example, did the floods of 1342. Long-term climatic change is more problematic because it is subtler, its results are more complex, and both seem comparatively slow in human terms. Such gradual alterations of natural phenomena tend to produce shifting human baselines. Each person has experience of weather and climate in his or her own lifetime (and place). Standards of comparison creep back and forth depending on each generation's own experience. When changes have been incremental, people lose memory of how things

An inconstant planet

once were different. Hence establishing and recognizing consequences of climatic change requires long-running record sources and precisely those are especially rare before 1350. Certain examples of short-run phenomena from the earlier and central Middle Ages do fall into Europe's MWP. What cannot so far be done is establish what it *meant* to be working through the transition from several centuries of late antique chill to more benign conditions. Cases can be cited from the short to the relatively long run, but the longer ones date mainly from the LIA.

Several fairly clear-cut instances have already been discussed, including the effects on production of reduced solar input during the climatic downturn of the second quarter of the sixth century (chapter 2) and the close association between volcanic aerosols, severe winters, dearth, and increased mortalities in well-recorded Carolingian times. In the latter, historian Michael McCormick and an interdisciplinary team including a geophysicist successfully combined ice core data with contemporary annals and chronicles. While the volcanic trigger was wholly beyond the ken of medieval monks and others, they were well aware that unusual cold and snow brought human deaths. A shift in atmospheric conditions affects the way people live, die, eat, and survive. Precisely who died under such climatic stress was, of course, strongly shaped by the distribution of wealth, status, and power in the affected society. At least some historians think that ninth-century Frankish peasants lived very close to a survival margin even at the best of times. The same is often said of the rural labourers who suffered the worst effects of the bad 1250s and the unemployed urban artisans who starved without access to what cereals remained undrenched in 1315–17.

Short-term events affected politics as well as subsistence. On 10 August 955 and in skirmishes over the next few weeks, collectively called the battle of Lechfeld from the main site beside Augsburg, the army of Otto I, king of Germany, defeated and destroyed a large force of tribal Hungarian raiders. Medievalists commonly acknowledge this combat to have ended fifty years of nomad attacks on central and western Europe and, in retrospect, the entire period of barbarian migrations into the Latin west. Otto's victory laid the basis for his intervention in Italy and revival of the Empire on a German base. Historian Charles Bowlus has established that the clash of armies itself took place on a day of extreme heat, but as soon as the Hungarians were driven from the field, the skies opened with heavy thunderstorms that continued for probably more than a week. This weather pattern of multi-day heavy rainstorms – a type well known to occur in late summer Bavaria – produces high water and floods in the rivers which flow north from the Alps into the Danube. Retreating Magyars had to cross a succession of these tributaries, whose banks are significantly composed of clay which becomes waterlogged and slippery. Close study of the written evidence shows that fleeing Hungarians were repeatedly trapped and killed attempting to cross rivers, drowned in the rivers, or slain trying to get back out of them. Contemporary sources attributed the greatness of the victory to miraculous interventions by bishop St Ulrich of Augsburg, whose subsequent cult celebrated his ability to command water and rivers. From today's perspective it appears that a congeries of atmospheric conditions added to the battle itself jointly constructed this momentous event.

Phenology, the correlation of certain recurring natural events with prior weather conditions, has already been introduced as an indirect measure of past climate variables. It can also point to their effects on human material life. One case involves the date of the *vendange*, the regional start of the harvest of the Pinot Noir grape in Burgundy. Pinot Noir is the source of the famous Burgundian red wines and the principal variety grown there since at latest the early 1300s. Each November's *vendange* is a key moment in the wine production cycle, offering good employment for large numbers of people and supplying vital material to the regional economy. Wine not only provided dietary calories and a fairly safe beverage, many peasants depended on the vines for their main cash crop.

French climate historians have established that in the Côte-d'Or region near Dijon, where the start of the harvest is precisely recorded from 1370 to the present, its dates are a precise proxy for the number of degree days (heat units) received in that area from April to November. The more heat built up in the course of the summer and early autumn, the earlier the date of the *vendange*. By this account Burgundy experienced warm summers in the 1380s, averaging 0.7 °C above the long-term mean; again in the 1420s at plus 0.6 °C; and in several more recent periods. It was, however, also hit by times of repeated cold summers as during 1435–60, when the mean summer temperature stayed half a degree below normal, and at the end of the seventeenth century. Both are periods for which other independent evidence also indicates extreme cold affecting the growing season. For so important a crop as wine, these fluctuations necessarily shaped yields, work opportunities, the incomes of producers, labourers, and merchants, and the well-being of their families.

Grain production less precisely mirrors seasonal growing conditions, but B. M. S. Campbell's compilation from dozens of English manorial accounts shows how the yield per seed suddenly crashed below the long-term mean in 1315 (down 39 per cent), 1316 (down 63 per cent), 1317 (down 10 per cent), and 1321 (down 33 per cent). Again during 1348–52 annual yield per seed averaged 40 per cent below the long-term mean. Both clusters of harvest failures sharply coincided with the bouts of terrible weather noted above, while otherwise English yield ratios remained high and indeed rose. (Seed–yield ratios, which measure biological productivity, are relatively independent of yields per hectare, a statistic not to be generated from medieval records, and of total output, which depends on the labour supply so savaged by the Black Death.) The crop failure of 1345 in Tuscany followed heavy rains and by 1346 famine stalked the land from there to Burgundy to Spain.

Weather and climate impacted human exploitation of nature further up the trophic pyramid, too. The medieval North Sea and western Baltic were home to large numbers of a small schooling fish, the herring (*Clupea harengus*). By the twelfth century herring fisheries had become a large seasonal industry in some areas, employing many people and yielding a protein source important during religious fasts, especially for poor people who could not afford a better meat substitute. Dense near-shore spawning concentrations were fished from mid-summer to late autumn, but most of that take was preserved for consumption in the coming early spring when Lent made meat taboo. These plankton-eating fish are highly sensitive to water temperature and chemistry, which affect the adult schools directly, their larvae, and the plankton on which they feed. Herring-like fish everywhere are thus subject to sudden and catastrophic population crashes resulting in failures of the fishery, as modern research world-wide and written evidence from medieval Europe in particular both affirm. In the times of interest here, the highly productive fishery off East Anglia, well known since the eleventh century, collapsed between 1360 and 1380, never to regain its former scale and volume. The greatest single herring fishery of the Middle Ages, that in the Danish Straits (Øresund), failed in the first few decades of the fifteenth century, rebounded slightly a human generation or two later, and fell terminally after 1520. Even the newer fishery off eastern Scotland fell on hard times during the mid-1400s, but revived before the century's end. Now research in climate history reveals the coincidence of each such collapse with particular periods of unusual cold or storminess. Modern fisheries scientists know that larval herring die under cold late winter and spring conditions, and historical climatology has found precisely those seasonal features during well-dated cold periods and the LIA in general. Like the grape harvest, decade-scale perturbations in near-shore herring catches reverberated through the whole late medieval economy, opening the market to Flemish and Dutch fishers who exploited different, less vulnerable, offshore stocks.

Climatic change and social failure to adapt are now conventionally blamed for the extinction of medieval Norse Greenlanders. By this account European settlers arrived at the least ice-covered southwestern shores of Greenland from the older Norse colony in Iceland in the late tenth century, luckily for them early in the MWP. They brought with them a subsistence strategy based on milk, meat, and fibre from cattle, sheep, and goats. They overwintered their essential livestock indoors on summer-cut hay and supplemented those primary resources through land-based capture of seals, seabirds, and caribou nearby. Norse Greenlanders obtained foreign goods in exchange for the ivory and hides of walrus and polar bear that they hunted on summer expeditions along the sea ice far to the north of their settlements. For some two centuries these adaptive strategies sustained a decent medieval standard of living in the colony.

But the cooling conditions now detectable after 1250 in Greenland reduced the time livestock could eat natural forage and the biomass available to cut and dry for winter storage. Animals had to be fed longer from smaller supplies of hay. At the same time falling average temperatures produced heavier sea ice that shifted seasonal concentrations of animals away from Norse settlements and closed off their routes to the north. Unwilling or unable to adapt to the fully marine hunting practised by their Inuit neighbours and rivals, the Norse abandoned their more exposed western (actually northern) settlement between 1341 and 1362, precisely the coldest period in Greenland's climatic record. They vanished from their southern farms later in the fifteenth century.

Norse Greenland has almost become a determinist cliché; late medieval Iceland with a hundred times more people on a land area larger than Ireland offers more realistic and thus complicated insight into variable human and planetary forces in multi-century interplay. Before Norse settlement, the uninhabited North Atlantic island harboured abundant seabirds and marine mammals while its grassy meadows and valleys of scrubby willows and birches supported many migratory waterfowl but of terrestrial mammals only mice and foxes. The whole ecosystem was necessarily adapted to violent volcanism, the presence of glaciers, and considerable short- and long-term fluctuation in its sub-arctic maritime climate.

The Norse who arrived, traditionally in 870 (their so-called *Landnam*), with experience of making a living along North Atlantic coasts, quickly spread their farms inland, though some upland valleys were still being newly settled into the early eleventh century. Their agropastoral economy grazed livestock and gathered winter fodder from natural meadows and the pastures which they created by burning woodland. Early settlers cultivated cereals, too: not temperature- and wet-sensitive wheat but more tolerant oats and barley. Seasonal fowling, fishing, and hunting of marine mammals completed the subsistence base and provided exchange for relatively few necessary imports. Even some iron could be smelted in bloomeries using local bog ores and wood fuel.

Icelanders and their animals inevitably transformed island ecosystems in a local variant of processes treated at length in chapters 4 and 5. By the twelfth and thirteenth centuries nearly all the scrubby valley woodlands had been destroyed and some areas in the more densely settled south were likely overgrazed to the point of erosion. Fuel wood had become scarce and timber supplies dependent on driftwood or imports. The resident walrus of the southwest coast were extirpated. The most recent research, however, draws attention to legal provisions and other evidence for successfully controlled grazing and sustainable use of wildfowl. It projects the dating of most serious episodes of erosion into early modern times. Without denying considerable impact from the Norse and their livestock, as elsewhere a 'tragedy of the commons' diagnosis fails in medieval Iceland.

Much as the mid-Atlantic ridge fractures Iceland geologically, its atmospheric conditions are controlled by century- and decade-scale shifts in the location and strength of the 'Icelandic Low' pressure zone in the North Atlantic. These variations (the NAO) mean the island's regional weather patterns have sometimes matched and sometimes worked reciprocally to those of Europe itself. In modern times the whole North Atlantic has been blessed with a dense and multidisciplinary network of climate scientists, proxy data sets, and historical sources, all of them possessing their own lacunae and critical limits. Taken collectively and with due caution, the verbal record and multiple palaeoscientific proxies now provide for Iceland a climate and weather narrative more nuanced than that for Greenland and illustrative of the important fluctuations masked by too close reliance on the generalizations of MWP and LIA.

Ice cores, sea-bottom probes, and other methods indicate climatic variation long before any humans reached Iceland: the centuries of the Roman Optimum were warmer there than any more modern period, but sharply colder times intervened before renewed warming shortly before arrival of the Norse. Scientific, archaeological, and later written records concur that generally mild conditions prevailed at and for a century following *Landnam*: sea ice remained rare or absent around the island; marine plankton adapted to warm water occur fleetingly in sea-bottom cores of that date; some early farms were established on sites later crushed by glaciers. This apparent idyll was, however, broken by cold and stormy weather between 975 and 1025 and at least unusually chilly summers continued for another hundred years or so. Some scholars point to moraines from glacial readvance of plausibly twelfth- or thirteenth-century date, which might, however, be connected to a cold and stormy spell from the 1180s to 1210. More generally, a warming trend that set in around 1100 lasted into the mid-thirteenth century, when oxygen isotopes in mollusc shells indicate summer maximum temperatures averaging 10 °C, the warmest in three centuries. After 1280 cooling set in and by 1320 all seasonal average temperatures had fallen by 2 °C, then by 1370 to the coldest summers since *Landnam*, averaging only 4.5 °C. Summer sea ice was generally severe, even reaching Iceland's shores in 1261 for only the second time in a century (and fifth ever recorded), but then it did so again in 1275, 1306, 1320, 1321, around 1350, and in 1374. The cold lasted into the 1420s. More than a century of warming followed, with dramatically increasing storminess but less sea ice (the written record is silent from 1430 to 1560, but some marine sediment cores indicate its presence). While the experience of medieval Iceland very roughly corresponded to the long high, then low, temperature regimes of the stereotyped MWP and LIA, deviations were large and influential.

Variations in Iceland's rather narrow temperature margins for cultivation and plant growth, sea ice blocking marine access and chilling the land, and storminess could massively affect life in Iceland. So, too, could local volcanic activity and the relative isolation of its population. As earlier noted, the 1362 eruption of Öraefajökull destroyed productive pasture and built structures for a human generation. Although the Black Death did not reach Iceland in 1347–51, two later epidemics were deadly. Despite the telling absence of rats from the island, what Icelanders called the 'Great Plague' lasted for eighteen months during 1402–4 (so across two winters) and killed an estimated 30–70 per cent of the population. It took two generations for human numbers to rebound, only to be ravaged as much again in the 'Last Plague' of 1494–5. As hinted by the repeated but well-separated heavy mortalities typical of virgin soil epidemics, the disease never became endemic in Iceland. Nor is it thought to have provoked abandonment of farms. In this setting of multiple natural hazards, particular impacts and responses in an evolving Icelandic culture may be difficult to trace.

Nevertheless several correlates and consequences do join Iceland's distinctively variable climate to the fate and behaviour of medieval Icelanders. Cold weather and food shortages are blamed for famine deaths related during the eleventh century and, with some disease, by the annalist of purportedly 2,400 deaths in northern Iceland alone in 1192. Shortened growing seasons provide one likely reason why farmers permanently abandoned cultivation of oats in the course of the 1100s and also then began a slower retreat from barley that was completed by 1500. That same cold spell curtailed the rearing of pigs and initiated a shift from primary dependence on cattle to more tolerant and omnivorous sheep. Longer winters or wet summers reduced the production and energy content of forage and hay, necessitating greater slaughter in autumn and, in a longer run, smaller herds oriented more to production of wool, a potential export commodity. Of course good economic reasons for such steps away from self-sufficiency coincided with those of agroecology.

Similar conjunctions after the mid-thirteenth century framed reorientation of Iceland's fisheries, since *Landnam* a subsidiary subsistence activity in waters both fresh (for salmon, trout, charr) and coastal (for the cod family). Rising European markets for preserved fish meant merchants in Bergen paid well for dried cod ('stockfish', *skreið*) from northern Norway, and Icelanders had long made and consumed the same product. Icelandic waters likewise held spawning concentrations of the largest arctic cod (*Gadus morhua*) and the cooling sea temperatures then setting in typically improve both reproductive success and growth rates of cod and kindred species. The presence of fish in food remains rose from a small share at early Icelandic sites to 25–40 per cent in late medieval centuries and 60–85 per cent thereafter. Bulk export of dried fish began during the 1290s and in the ensuing half-century replaced wool as the main earner of foreign exchange. Diversification to fish oil and other products occurred in the fifteenth century, but dried cod, which alone could be prepared without need for costly imported (or fuel-greedy) salt, remained dominant. The lucrative abundance of fish drew labour from the agricultural sector, with the first references to professional fishers appearing late in the fourteenth century. A law of 1404 (worth recognizing as the 'Great Plague' year), however, required fishermen to live as part of agricultural farmsteads, thus long preventing emergence of full-time fishing or the specialized coastal fishing villages then appearing elsewhere. When the economic potential further drew foreign, especially English, buyers and fishers to Iceland's shores, further legislation forbade their hiring local workers by the day, allowing only annual contracts which served to price these competitors out of the labour market. Certainly as the long cold spell gradually waned in the early fifteenth century, a dual economic order more in keeping with Iceland's chilly maritime situation had come to balance the agro-pastoral dominance established at *Landnam*.

Not all the effects of a colder sea could be turned to cultural advantage. The threat and presence of summer drift ice from the mid-thirteenth to the mid-fifteenth century had material negative effects. When near shore it lowered temperatures on land and further curbed the productivity of forage for livestock. The ice and accompanying fog along the coasts impeded or increased the risks of the fishery, the hunt for marine mammals, and even maritime communication and commerce. A mid-thirteenth-century Norwegian text, the 'King's Mirror', reports the deaths and loss of ships caused by this then-new environmental hazard.

Recent archaeological and anthropological considerations of medieval Icelanders' relations to an environment changing both autonomously and through their own impacts have stressed the loss of predictability for a society which lived close to various ecological margins. Both in the eleventh century and the fourteenth Icelanders possessed good social buffers against local or sectoral catastrophes and solid traditional awareness of the need to account for well-known climatic variability. But to do so successfully demanded reasonably accurate prediction of especially seasonal variables, such as when to move livestock from upland pastures or how early to attempt a trading or fishing voyage. Climatic thresholds are not easily perceived until transgressed, and both year to year and long-term changes in their timing or depth badly damage the ability to make the right decision. Successive difficulties with cereal or pastoral farming in the eleventh century, with sea ice and cold in the fourteenth – when bishops report food shortages – and with the storms of the fifteenth century all resulted from atmospheric processes shifting faster than human abilities to predict and counter them.

Long before well-known ferocious early modern demonstrations of the negative effects that cold, storms, and volcanoes could wreak upon Icelanders and their cultural practices in the natural world, long- and short-term planetary variability shaped a half-millennium of medieval life on the island. In this context it remains important to remember that past climate changes as now described are retrospective reconstructions of atmospheric processes, not objects of past human awareness, experience, or response. Especially in the absence of overarching scientific observations and reporting, people *feel* the experience of weather and on a day to day basis work from that. Over time cultures accumulate that experience into expectations and strategies for handling a normal range of seasonal and other variability. Even today these understandings evolve very slowly. From a historian's point of view the emphasis that climate scientists place on long-term turning points (inflections) and trends speaks little to recapturing how societies or even biota respond to weather conditions. Perceived crossing of experiential thresholds is therefore more important in periodizing and eventually explaining human consequences and responses to climate change than is the point at which solar radiation or atmospheric circulation may now be shown to have reversed direction. Notably at the regional level such as Iceland, the ability or inability to grow oats, feed a larger herd, or find schools of fish, all skills reliant on medium-term environmental consistencies, is where climate becomes a fact of history. What happens when weather events abruptly seem to transgress expectations in symbolic culture is another issue.

As detailed knowledge of past European weather and climate is extended back into the fifteenth and even the fourteenth century, a tantalizing linkage of changing atmospheric phenomena to cultural programmes and material efforts may be emerging. As observed in chapter 3, popular belief in the hidden powers of nature and the ability of certain people to manipulate those by occult means ('magic') prevailed throughout and beyond the Middle Ages. Sorcerers or 'witches' might notably control the air and storms for good or ill. While early medieval Christian authorities debunked such superstitions and reserved all such powers to God alone, thirteenth-century philosophers and theologians came to accept, for their own professional reasons, the presence of legitimate hidden powers in God's Creation and the existence of witches whose pacts with necessarily diabolical spirits granted them 'unnatural' influence over things of nature, especially the air. Earlier hints and allusions to maleficent weather-makers were codified in the 'Hammer of Witches' (*Malleus maleficarum*), a treatise published in 1484 by two inquisitors from the southwest Empire which provided early modern Europeans with a long-definitive template for large-scale official witchcraft persecutions.

On the evidence of anecdotal narrative sources and statistical correlation of large chronological data sets, Wolfgang Behringer and Emily Oster have argued for a close, indeed causal, connection between severe and 'unnatural' weather events and climatic stresses typical of the worst periods of the LIA and the temporally circumscribed, fiercest local witchcraft persecutions in sixteenth- and seventeenth-century Europe. After 1560 and again after 1680 local experiences of damaging storms and destructive cold and wet conditions across the continent brought crop failures, drove food prices up, and triggered local mortality crises. Seeking scapegoats, fearful communities demanded that higher authorities collaborate to root out the surely evil perpetrators. For example, a severe and damaging hailstorm widespread across much of central Europe in August 1562, immediately recognized as unfamiliar and thus 'unnatural', was shortly followed by local witch hunts. Where governments lacked the strength or ideological grounds to resist – secular explanations of weather prevailed in humanist-governed towns like Nuremberg, where no witches were killed – the cultural tension exploded. Witnesses against the (mainly) women accused mentioned hail and flood damage, spoilt crops, dying livestock, etc. as proof of evil actions. What some climatologists call 'LIA type events' triggered first ecological, then cultural processes, but did not determine them.

This line of enquiry has not, however, so far been extended to the climatic disasters of the early fourteenth century or the ensuing two hundred years of instability. The connection from natural events to material experience (crop failure, famine) to culturally mediated social response is plausible, but since most published research on witchcraft and witchcraft persecutions well pre-dates any precise scholarly awareness of a changing climate, the issue deserves thorough investigation by specialists on the later Middle Ages. Were such links to be found, they would parallel as a cultural response to atmospheric phenomena the attacks on Jews and others which occurred in some localities as a reaction to the altered microbiological environment in the Black Death.

Large-scale changes in atmospheric phenomena during the Middle Ages can therefore be generally observed to limit and on occasion to precipitate breakdowns in regional ways of life suited to the former conditions. It has been relatively harder for historians of societies *not* on an ecological and economic margin to pin down the consequences of medieval climatic change. The latter so far depends on recognizing short-term weather events where surviving records happen to reveal a convincing connection. Other creative approaches to test for cultural resonance of shifting, indeed deteriorating, late medieval weather conditions are to be encouraged. Yet negative events and disasters made for as good immediate 'copy' for medieval chroniclers as they do for modern media. Researchers need as well to probe more deeply for positive cultural adaptations to the experience of climatic catastrophes (dyke systems, etc.?) and of subtler climate changes (cropping practices, heating systems, ice vehicles?).

Multiscale atmospheric and tectonic phenomena result from their own dynamic. Even were some scientists' hypotheses of global temperature responding to pre-modern anthropogenic clearances and revegetation episodes shown to be true, climate change and weather remained as unexpected and outside human control as was the shaking of the very earth or a wave of epidemic deaths. They were not, however, outside human response, and the way each event or trend played out in a society depended on certain cultural antecedents. For peasant farmers living inland of a salt marsh, a particular set of high marine tides may have no consequence at all (ignoring for the moment indirect effects on malarial mosquitoes). But had colonists drained that marsh or lived exposed to the sea when high water came, colonized landscapes were destroyed and people had to adjust in other ways. Culture is always a part of the natural disaster, but need not be its initiator. Weak points in anthropogenic systems give way under stress, so when parameters shift and customary expectations fail, people withdraw from lands and activities that have become marginal. But such changes happen because nature is an active force to which humans respond. Humans are autonomous agents, too. The relationship of medieval cultures to the geological and climatic forces of the planet was not determinist; it fits into the interaction model.

A SLOW END OF MEDIEVAL
ENVIRONMENTAL RELATIONS

———————— • ————————

When is the end to an environmental history of medieval Europe? If the protracted transformation of late antiquity marked the advent of a new cultural entity with its own characteristic, if not all distinctive, ways of interacting with natural forces in a certain part of the earth's surface, what makes a comparable conclusion to this story? When it comes to periodization, multiple historical discourses, climatological, economic, sociological, epidemiological, cultural, and more, commonly talk past one another at best, each displaying its typical reductionism and determinism. Multiple perspectives on natural and cultural evolutions show autonomous and interactive changes playing out from the fourteenth century into the sixteenth.

ECOLOGICAL CRISIS? ANTHROPOGENIC OVERSHOOT, SLOW CHILL, SUDDEN NATURAL SHOCK

As just seen, climate in the form of the Little Ice Age and disease as manifest in the Black Death do provide bold historical markers with immediate effects in the curtailing of primary production and seasonal human activities and the magnitude of human deaths. Do these identify the end of the Middle Ages in environmental terms? Simple quantitative relationships of Europeans to their surroundings were surely recalibrated. Having reached some 75–80 million around 1300, their numbers fell by 30–60 per cent in the twenty years between the mid-1340s, which Christian Pfister has called the worst climatic conditions of the past millennium in central Europe, and the mid-1360s, with what the same expert has described as the coldest winter of the second millennium. At macrocosmic and microcosmic scales these rapidly catastrophic mid-fourteenth-century events invite juxtaposition with the climatic downturn associated with the 'dry fog' of 536 and the Justinianic plague of 540, both with centuries of alleged after-effects. Natural cataclysms appeal to audiences and writers who enjoy a past simply forged by natural forces.

Or would a better, less abrupt, defining chronology simply locate medieval environmental history more vaguely but realistically between comparable eras of climatic and epidemiological *instability*? To assert that medieval civilization was initiated by the harsh conditions of late antiquity, flourished in relatively benign times, and broke down in the first or successive waves of the Little Ice Age still smacks of a hard environmental determinism most historians would refuse to endorse.

A comparably abrupt and catastrophic but primarily anthropogenic break with the medieval past has been argued for a 'crisis of the fourteenth century'. One large body of historical scholarship has interpreted Europe's great famine and epidemic mortalities, population collapse, and widespread economic difficulties of the 'disastrous' 1300s as a broadly environmental crisis of human origin. This understanding arose from Malthusian explanations offered by mid-twentieth-century economic historians for the hard times they had observed to contradict older historical beliefs in continual material progress. In this view Europe's population growth and economic expansion of the eleventh to thirteenth centuries inexorably ran into the inherent limits of agricultural productivity (see chapter 5 above). In 1980, Charles Bowlus distilled this understanding into explicitly environmental terms. In an essay plainly attuned to the chorus of environmental concern then sweeping North America but at the time perhaps inadequately appreciated as a state-of-the-art historical synthesis, Bowlus laid out how the economists' findings could also be understood in ecological terms as culminating in a fourteenth-century 'ecological crisis' in Europe. Transcending simple Malthusian reasoning, he argued for genuinely ecological, i.e. interconnected, relationships among populations, clearances, and environmental stresses: 'The story ... is one of an economy that overexpanded relative to existing resources and available technology in the twelfth and thirteenth centuries ... Europe's natural resources ... were being rapidly depleted. In the fourteenth century nature foreclosed.'[1] Bowlus's interpretation was subsequently reiterated by, among others, J. Donald Hughes as an example of 'overshoot' and Jason Moore as 'socio-ecological contradictions' on the part of medieval society at large. Like Lynn White's Dominion thesis, it has become a commonplace of popular environmentalism.

In this view, and for whatever cultural reasons, high medieval Europeans so overexploited and overstressed their economy and ecosystem as to cause systemic breakdown and collapse. By around 1300 pressures of human demand were bringing about general resource shortages in fuel wood, timber, arable land, soil nutrients, and pasture; falling agricultural yields and biodiversity; rising prices of cereals, livestock, and fish; soil erosion and human immiseration; and an eventual die-off from famine and the Black Death. As previous chapters (4, 5, and 6) have observed, much specific local evidence – perhaps too much but by no means all from England – does point to ploughing up of land at altitudinal and latitudinal limits not otherwise reached; to thirteenth-century increases in food and fuel prices; to ever-smaller peasant family farms and more landless country people; to exiguous peasant livestock and access to pasture; and to mortalities from more frequent regional famines. Worried communities and authorities took measures to curb resource use, but in vain. Exhausted and insulted, nature broke down.

Bowlus's strong declensionist tone may now be thought to lack conceptual grounding and provide little depth on the cultural side, while scholarly understanding of certain key substantive issues has changed significantly – not just regarding climate and disease, but also on metabolic approaches to food, energy, and waste.

Does evidence of local depletion, decline, and destruction mean entire ecosystem limits (human carrying capacity under prevailing technologies) had been overreached? Results from research carried out since the 1970s often indicate otherwise. Earlier chapters here observed no general thirteenth-century decline of *land* productivity in case studies from well-documented England. Farmers on some marginal lands diversified their crop mix; others increased labour intensity. Innovation and rising output continued past 1300. Tuscan agriculture is likewise credited with productivity gains that largely compensated for the enormous rural–urban migration which much inflated the

---

[1] C. Bowlus, 'Ecological Crisis in Fourteenth Century Europe', in L. Bilsky, ed., *Historical Ecology: Essays on Environment and Social Change* (Port Washington, NY: Kennikat Press, 1980), 88 and 94.

population of Florence. Critically read complaints of wood shortage alert medievalists to how *local*, not general, energy supply problems drove some people to nibble at fossil fuel sources and others to undertake considerable improvements in the output of physical energy (wind, water power). Likewise the greatly accelerated production and use of metals, visible by the mid-1200s from Italy to Scandinavia, offered substitutes for organic and biomass materials to expand Europe's resource limits. Where new, non-agrarian sectors did complain of fuel shortages, they were also commonly associated with coppice management, a sustainable approach quite unknown to the mid-twentieth-century historians used by Bowlus and his followers. So, too, were arable and pasture production subjected to conservation measures commensurate with what centuries of experience with a stable natural world had established as normal risks and environmental variability.

Active researchers in economic history are now unwilling to interpret instances of resource shortage in thirteenth- and early fourteenth-century Europe as symptoms of agrarian regimes or of the culture as a whole paying a price for transgressing normal ecosystem limits. At least in relatively over-researched England, but also more broadly including Mediterranean Europe, knowledgeable scholars refer to a 'high-pressure' socio-ecological system prevailing at this time without detectable signs of breakdown even under heavy blows. Episodes of high grain prices before the 1340s in Aragon, Provence, Tuscany, or Sicily they diagnosed as regional accidents of an adolescent market network, not symptoms of general production failure, not least because consumers had access to alternative local foodstuffs which seigneurial and governmental records ignore. Deaths from the Great Famine had little evident larger effect: a maximum population and minimum standard of living remained stubbornly deadlocked from the 1280s to the 1340s. This was by no means an equitable regime but, in the view of B. M. S Campbell and others, no 'fatal or intrinsic flaw' made endogenous collapse or instability even retroactively predictable. The crash of human numbers came only at 1350. It may therefore require a firm causal connection between Black Death mortalities and antecedent malnutrition, famines, and other supply failures before a solidly convincing case can be made that Europeans' own overexploitation of their environment brought its wrath down upon them.

While an anthropogenic impetus for what happened in the fourteenth century is thus called into question, historians further exhibit growing unease with the concept of 'crisis' and more so 'ecological crisis' as tools for large-scale historical analysis. Critics note the simple term is a metaphor derived from medical discourse, where it denotes a point of decision when the patient either dies or recovers. While the medical analogy implies short temporal duration, environmental history knows the various time scales of politicians, individuals, human generations, even the planet. Common discourse now treats 'crisis' as a poor synonym for 'change' or for a distressing situation deserving greater awareness. Writers on the Middle Ages, Bowlus among them, have applied the term ambiguously to the situation *c.*1280–1350, seen as portending the mid-century population losses, referring to the mortalities themselves, and/or designating the tough agrarian and commercial conditions experienced by many people thereafter, which had their own environmental aspects (see below). Even the narrower 'ecological crisis' conceals ambivalence, referring variously to something happening within an ecosystem, arising from the environment to affect humans, or a human impact on an ecosystem. More careful users might confine the concept to conditions of *instability* preceding an abrupt change (as determined at the time or in retrospect). In no such case do hazards inherent in a system or evident precautions against those risks themselves constitute a system in crisis. Ecologists now prefer the more closely defined 'tipping point', as the moment at whatever scale when a system can no longer hold and passes over into something else. Did Europe experience a tipping point in the fourteenth century?

Equally germane to reassessing the 'ecological crisis of the fourteenth century' as an anthropogenic marker of a fundamental shift in European relations with the natural world are two often-reiterated historical points which an earlier generation of scholars could not fully grasp. First and simplest is awareness that even early medieval Europe was no pristine natural system as defined in a mythic New World past, but already fully marked by long human presence, learning, use, and adaptation of its ecosystems. At issue is not how conditions around 1300 measured against a human-free past but rather how they measured against patterns of resource use since the Neolithic and, most immediately, against more than five centuries of medieval practice. This acknowledges the inevitable, if variable, consequences of human colonization of the natural sphere. Human use, however, is not coterminous with a downward spiral of destructive destabilization. Environmental historians must distinguish between changes wrought by human use and a state of instability or collapse in colonized or fully anthropogenic ecosystems. Had medieval Europeans fractured ecosystem relations and services to the point of predictable failure? The answer now leans strongly to the negative.

An honest revisionism must further take into account the comparatively slim and now often obsolete knowledge available to mid-twentieth-century scholars regarding medieval natural phenomena, notably atmospheric but also with respect to disease. For this and for more discipline-based reasons, many social scientists and notably economic historians traditionally resisted or dismissed as irrelevant any role of 'exogenous' forces, meaning those originating outside the human economy. Likewise the prevalent assumption among older ecologists was a self-correcting natural balance subject to disruption only by human action. Both data and theory thus turned first to human activity as the origin of any change. This, too, no longer holds.

Two or more generations later not only have ecologists learned to view humans as participants in ecosystems, a new ecology of disturbance acknowledges that equilibria are not inevitable. At least two large classes of ecological changes may be posited, the one a gradual return to equilibrium following a disturbance of any origin and quality, and the other a sudden lurch to a new state after an abrupt shock. The latter is called 'punctuated change'. While not predictable a priori, punctuated change does occur in situations where the prior state lacks sufficient resilience, the ability mentioned in chapter 5 of a stable system to deal continually with stress and adapt without crossing critical thresholds. Perhaps ironically, a system robust enough to withstand gradual or limited stresses and maintain its previous state may be susceptible to large and dramatic shocks which quickly push it to a tipping point. Shocks arriving faster than the system's response time overwhelm its resilience. Only in the most recent decades have scientists, historians, and others learned the magnitude, mechanisms, and impacts of natural change at human temporal scales. New reference points complicate simple determinist verities.

Beyond the cultural, more especially economic, or the environmental determinist views of the fourteenth century a broader spectrum of explanations has now appeared. All concede a more distinct and autonomous role to natural systems in the large changes undergone in Europe. What might be called 'overshoot version 2' acknowledges that natural disasters, from epidemics and epizootics to floods, had autonomous natural precipitants but attributes their catastrophic effects to prior human destabilizing of productive economic and ecological relationships. Peak thirteenth-century populations and demand for energy, materials, and waste absorption left no room for normal natural fluctuations. Yves Lenoir has argued that effects of climate change (*recte* weather anomalies) overcame the normal safety margin of hitherto sustainable agricultural practices. Clearance of woodlands had removed natural buffering capacities. Drained Dutch peat soils sank dangerously below sea level. Complex long-distance food supply systems were susceptible to breakdown in any one stage and when operational helped propagate disease. Urbanization decoupled resource demand and cultural leadership from awareness of production conditions. Geomorphologist Hans-Rudolf Bork blames no human agents for the run of wet years in northwestern Europe from 1314 to 1317 or for the torrential downpour of 1342; the ensuing soil erosion beyond all past proportion he ascribes, however, at least equally to human reduction of central Europe's wooded cover to a mere 10 per cent of land area and to recent adoption of bare fallow meant to suppress all competition to cereal grains. Put more generally, the centuries-long trend towards cereal monocultures and the very socio-economic deadlock that enabled survival had reduced the resilience of an agroecosystem now faced with unexpected new hazards. The diagnosis is, of course, wholly in retrospect.

Worth emphasizing then, as B. M. S. Campbell has to his fellow economic historians, are the entirely 'natural' origins and quality of fourteenth-century disasters, which struck without relation to the condition of human socio-economic systems. In Campbell's view, cultural forces merely constructed and propagated the ensuing destruction and only thereafter shaped social responses. While initially ineffectual, these latter eventually set new directions for the future. Referring to much of the palaeoscientific research here reported in chapters 8 and 9, Campbell stresses the *extraordinary* behaviour of numerous natural variables in the century before the Black Death. The unprecedented harvest failures of 1315–17 in northern Europe were directly precipitated by a run of cold, wet weather during 1314–17 otherwise unparalleled in both British and central European records. This was triggered by abnormally warm North Atlantic sea surface temperatures that set in around 1300 and lasted until the early 1350s. While cereal grains suffered, western European oaks so enjoyed the wet conditions that their wide growth rings reversed the otherwise consistent correlation between trees of the Old World and the New. As remarkable was the cattle epizootic of 1314–25, which quickly spread from east-central Europe to Ireland and abruptly halved all herd sizes now recoverable. And at the end of the terrible half-century, another severe cold and wet spell around the North Atlantic reduced 1349–52 grain yields in England to less than half their long-term average – although disease-shocked contemporaries barely took notice. In Tuscany likewise, though not annually coincident with northern events, extreme weather peaked between 1305 and 1380, with many specific years of cold winters and wet summers bringing subsequent crop failures to reach a climax in 1345–7. At the planetary scale, a unique reversal of the radiocarbon decay curve during 1325–70 indicates sudden release into the atmosphere of long-stored carbon; geologists have commonly seen this as a symptom of large tectonic disturbance (presumably in this instance somewhere not then covered in the written record). Radiocarbon emissions, hemispheric patterns in tree growth, and oceanic temperature anomalies are not easily attributed to human behaviour, thus casting further doubt on human responsibility for simultaneous production failures and pathogenic triumphs.

Abrupt changes in autonomous atmospheric and microbiological conditions exceeded tolerances of agricultural production, supply of biochemical energy, and the human population itself. At small scale, losses of soil, crops, and livestock enabled regional famines; at large, new parasite–host relations killed Europeans in vast numbers. There is the tipping point, one not even retrospectively predictable from the prior European situation.

When parameters of the entire system so abruptly shifted, weak points in the anthropogenic regime gave way, whether in famine deaths or the post-1350 retreat from what had become marginal soils, lands, and even fossil fuels. What Hans-Rudolf Bork called a 'human–environment spiral' (*Mensch-Umwelt-Spirale*) might more largely be thought an environment–human–environment helix as each sphere responded successively to the other's changes. The European landscape on which these natural forces struck was, however, itself deeply configured by human colonization of earlier natural systems. Both material and symbolic cultural heritage thus strongly mediated immediate effects and longer outcomes of the natural shocks. Sudden shocks to a relatively stable baseline system of human–environmental relations turned into a new pattern of *in*stability on at least a generational scale. Problems of short-term resilience became long-term adaptability to and sustainability in a less predictable environment.

As compared with the vexed situation before the Black Death, scholars much less dispute the long-term consequences and changes which followed from the fourteenth-century loss of nearly half of Europe's humans. For all the differences in vocabulary and fierce conflicts over process, historians of all stripes do concur that the big decline in human numbers reset some central conditions for future developments. Within a generation of the first mid-century epidemic, and for more than a century thereafter, the human–land, land–labour, and, essentially, human–nature relationship all across Europe differed in essential features from what had earlier prevailed. At the otherwise undistinguished open-field village of Caldecote in Hertfordshire, for instance, the fifteen or sixteen farms of 1321 had become but six by the 1360s. The former economic gridlock of high populations, maximum arable emphasis, and minimum average living standards evaporated. Fewer people consumed less grain, ploughed less ground, and burned less fuel. Abandoned arable regained vegetative cover, grew more forage, and could, over time, return to a succession of woody plants and, perhaps, more diverse habitats and fauna. By the sixteenth century woodlands again covered 30 per cent of central Europe. To new experiences of fewer workers, greater per capita wealth and consumption levels, and relatively greater abundance of some (not all) resources, elites and peasants with variant cultural heritages responded differently. In retrospect their choices held large implications for the future balance of material, political, and symbolic innovation and leadership among European communities and states. If the events of the fourteenth century could not be predicted from the thirteenth, much that occurred after 1450 could not reasonably have been forecast from conditions in 1340 or even 1360.

However, in many normally diagnostic respects the fourteenth-century demographic disaster and late medieval economic depression and land-use 'restart' failed to alter long-term fundamentals in European environmental relations. Essential continuities prevailed from before the 1300s until well past the 1600s in most European regions and in the lives with nature of nearly all Europeans. The energy system remained firmly dependent on biomass production. Agriculture retained its ecological, economic, and social centrality. That the immanence of spirit in the natural world remained unbroken is plainly demonstrated both in late medieval and early modern persecutions for diabolical manipulation of occult powers in nature and in even longer centuries of rural priests and pastors everywhere lamenting the superstitions of their flocks. In so far as late medieval shocks and changes in material conditions were environmental in quality, Europeans survived and overcame them by 'normal' adaptive processes within existing patterns. That some of these short-run measures did subsequently eventuate in future transformations may be clear in retrospect, but bore little on their origins. The whole fourteenth century is hard to view as a 'collapse', and perhaps easier to approach as a response, sometimes fatally painful, to extraordinary disturbance in the longstanding regime of natural change and interacting material culture. From a fundamental metabolic perspective, therefore, much speaks for the unity of European experience with the natural world between the dissolution of classical Mediterranean civilization and the establishment of a fossil energy system during the late eighteenth and the nineteenth century. But other perspectives differ.

BY LONG-TERM CULTURAL EVOLUTION?

At some (if not total) remove from climatic cooling, disease events, demographic collapse and renewal, and economic reconfigurations, between the mid-fourteenth and the mid-sixteenth century Europeans did initiate and undergo seminal cultural developments which inflected basic ways they perceived and represented their experience of the natural world and then set plans and priorities for material action in it. Much had autonomous origins in a symbolic cultural sphere itself.

For a century or so on both sides of the Columbian voyages European cultural paradigms were shifting. While some departed from the medieval course, others continued projected medieval trends across critical thresholds. The period must be thought transitional in more than climate because in practice and not always consciously, Europeans were redefining their expectations towards the natural sphere. At least five such autonomous aspects of cultural evolution altered how they regarded the world around them: empiricism, quantification, the historic synergy between vernacular literacy and emerging print culture, Renaissance humanism, and ever-pressing claims from markets and from states over use of natural objects and materials.

European writing about nature in the course of the fourteenth through to the sixteenth century lent growing authority to empiricism and within it to quantification as tools for learning, thinking, and reporting about the natural world. The tendency was not wholly new. Frederick II and Gaston Phoebus had explicitly called on experience in composing their hunting manuals and so did Pietro de'Crescenzi in his early fourteenth-century handbook on agriculture. Some lawyers and surveyors treated thoughtfully the on-the-ground realities of property rights and boundaries. All of them pre-dated 1400 and presented natural phenomena understood at least in part by observation. This practice continued, indeed multiplied.

Empiricism grew in part as a general pattern of lay knowledge of the natural world acquired through respectful observation of it. The roll of empiricists might now include Leonardo da Vinci (1452–1519), who consciously and carefully investigated how nature operated. Leonardo reveals his process of enquiry and his results in drawings of, for instance, a pregnant womb, the precise articulation of a bird's wing, an olive press, and then an improved olive press that he had designed after such observation. A younger contemporary, the German philosopher, confidence man, physician, astrologer, and alchemist Paracelsus, wrote in the 1530s,

> God wants us to know the greater origin of things and not simply accept a created object as a creation but to research and learn why it has been placed there. Then we can investigate and establish what the wool on the sheep and the bristles on the backs of pigs are good for and assign each thing to its proper place . . .[2]

Humans were to view nature in order to figure out how it came to be where they found it.

This approach was especially followed by some northern humanists interested in natural history, who modelled their terrestrial observations on Pliny's *Natural History*, now recovered with other classics. In anatomy, therefore, Andreas Vesalius (1515–64) performed the first public human dissections since the Roman age. In botany and zoology efforts at accurate description prevailed and the new technologies of woodcut and engraving encouraged accurate illustration. Examples can now widely be examined in online editions and many reprints of

---

[2] T. Paracelsus [Theophrastus Bombastus von Hohenheim], 'Die Bücher von den unsichtbaren Krankheiten', in *Paracelsus: Essential Theoretical Writings*, ed. and tr. A. Weeks. Aries Book Series, Texts and Studies in Western Esotericism 5 (Leiden and Boston: Brill, 2008), 732–3, or otherwise in F. Klemm, *A History of Western Technology*, tr. D. Singer (Cambridge, MA: MIT Press, 1964), 144. Translated by R. Hoffmann.

works of Conrad Gessner (1516–65), a Swiss physician and polymath who published importantly on both plants and animals.

Empirical scholars turned their eyes from the earth's surface to the heavens as well. This process in celestial observation and understanding is exemplified in Copernicus (Mikołaj Kopernik, 1473–1543), a well-educated clerical humanist from Toruń on the Polish-Prussian border. From his home town gymnasium he went on to university in Kraków, and thence for postgraduate work to the school then best known for understanding natural history, Padua, in the Venetian state. There he studied writings by the second-century Greco-Roman geographer Ptolemy of Alexandria, whose *Almagest* described a geocentric universe. Back in provincial Poland for the next three decades, Copernicus puzzled over how such a system might work and, dissatisfied, pulled together contradictory heliocentric ideas, which he remained reluctant to publish. Thus only in 1543 did his *De revolutionibus orbium coelestium* ('On the Revolutions of the Heavenly Spheres') appear, positing a heliocentric theory of the universe. Copernicus advanced his new hypothesis in part for its more elegant mathematics. His observations of the heavens had nothing new, but he thought his formulae made more sense than the alternative.

Conceiving and expressing the world in terms of numbers, of uniform units, of quantification, was a growing aspect of the gradual transition to an early modern understanding of nature. This, too, had roots in the Middle Ages. Indeed from the eleventh century to the fourteenth Latin commentators on the recovered text of Aristotle's *Politics* had been trying to assess human numbers and balance those numbers against resources in a very quantitative kind of way. Without carrying out actual accounting, they thought about how this might work. The Arabic numerals (of actual Hindu origin), which make calculations easier and more accurate than working in Roman numerals, were most actively adopted in the thirteenth- and early fourteenth-century west not by intellectuals but by merchants, whose business needs routinely called for many calculations, especially as they began to develop financial accounts in double-entry format. Some historians now argue that the numerical, monetized, world apprehended by those merchants strongly influenced natural theologians and scientists at Oxford and elsewhere, who applied similar quantitative thinking to their observations particularly of light, but also of physical forces in the universe itself.

Representations of time and space took on quantitative form. Time is an inherently abstract dimension, not intrinsically segmented such that a universal unit begins when the sun comes up or ends when it sets. In place of the natural 'day', time construed as an abstract uniform element was first carefully articulated in scholastic music theorized and composed in early fourteenth-century Paris. Yet this conception of time as a quantity coincided with the invention and proliferation of mechanical clocks that do break it down into arbitrary units without regard to specific natural events. Cartographers likewise evolved ways to portray the uniform measurement of space. This culminated in the mid-fifteenth-century revival of Ptolemaic maps, modelled on works of the late antique geographer but now put to representing everything from the entire known world to specific continents, countries, and regions. All of these ways of thinking about and with numbers and quantities entered into how people encountered the natural world and represented what they experienced there.

Extension of innovative seeing and thinking was aided by vernacular literacy in tandem with development of a new print culture. Combination of popular languages with a new technology improved data storage and the abilities of more Europeans to share their experiences. The later Middle Ages had already seen an increased assertion and deepening of practical vernacular literacy, the ordinary use of written records not in Latin but in the spoken language. What began in secular government by about 1300 then spread downwards in society to estate management, town administration, business, family correspondence, and the like. By the closing decades of the fifteenth century and the start of the sixteenth, this practice had established a genuine 'middle class literacy'. While Danish merchants thus were keeping written accounts by the late 1300s, a century later even a blacksmith in Flensburg, a brick-maker named Per Teglslager on Langeland island, and villagers at Radsted on Lolland had their own invoices and ownership documents to produce in court. Around 1530 some 10–20 per cent of English men could read and 1–5 per cent of women. Comparable rates prevailed in Italy, the Low Countries, Germany, France, and Spain. Those proportions meant almost everyone at least knew someone who could read. It also meant demand for written literature to edify, inform, and entertain soon attained unprecedented scale. The demand was first met by adopting paper, a writing medium made from rags. This Chinese technology had been picked up by Arabs and transferred to Europe in the later Middle Ages. No longer were written texts dependent on skinning sheep, goats, and calves.

The greater response to late medieval European demand for written texts was the development and proliferation of printing with movable type. Its European manifestation seems an independent development, imitating older Asian practice only as an idea, if that. The technical breakthrough was accomplished by a Mainz metal-worker, Johannes Gutenberg (late 1390s–1468?), who was working on the problem already by the 1430s and in full production by the 1450s. Printing spread quickly: Gutenberg's native Empire had seven presses by 1470 and fifty by 1499; Italy, seventy-two presses by 1499; France thirty-nine; the Low Countries twenty-one; and England five or six. The printing revolution created more written materials. Each text could spread more widely; each reader had access to more texts. Print magnified the preservative power of writing. Print fixed texts, making of each a standard product. It allowed texts to be saved and accumulated more easily than did hand copying. Print stabilized texts and the languages in which they appeared. People could read a text and distinguish between what they already knew (having read it elsewhere) and what was newly learned and now to be grappled with. For all these reasons books became a normal part of everyday experience for readers and for those people who could be read to. Knowledge of the natural world could soon reach a growing literate community across Europe. Printed reports of Columbus's first voyage circulated in Italy and Germany within two years of his return. People could then pick up that information and make use of it.

As an overarching cultural construct Renaissance humanism probably affected human relations with nature less directly than surviving uncritical followers of the discredited Jacob Burckhardt are fully aware. Yes, with antique sources to hand anthropocentrism could be more fully articulated, but Renaissance intellectual preoccupations are no longer thought so greatly to depart from theocentric thinking. This is not to assert the absence of anthropocentrism, but to affirm the importance of religious considerations to Renaissance thinkers. Anthropocentrism is patent in such statements as Petrarch's 'man is the measure of all things' and manifest in the fashion for perspective drawing. This technique shows the world from the eye of a human beholder, abandoning overt attention to the allegorical importance of the objects. A king or saint portrayed at a distance is much smaller than a poor man in the foreground, an iconography no medieval artist would imagine or execute. Nature, however, the humanists consistently subordinated as an inferior foil and tool for humankind.

Simple anthropocentrism is less to be traced as a dominant strand through humanist thinking than is a strong sense of human abilities to study, to learn, and to master nature. As articulated by Paracelsus

The arts are all within man ... God has created nothing to perfection, but ordered Vulcan [allegorized man] to bring these things to completion ... The three Vulcans, the cultivator, the miller and the baker make of [grain] bread.[3]

One sense of the passage is descriptive: God set up the world but it is now transformed by humans. Another is teleological: God intends humans to master a nature created for that end. This is by no means a humble approach to the natural world, but rather a resource-centred view in which nature's human uses even included the plainly recreational. Career humanist Enea Silvio de Piccolomini (1405–64), since 1458 Pope Pius II, enjoyed garden walks at papal summer palaces in the hills behind Rome and rowing on a nearby lake. He took his cardinals on rural picnics rather than closing them in a stuffy consistory. The underlying attitude was not yet self-consciously manipulative science. It was, however, thoroughly ambitious and solidly foreshadowed the programmes later proclaimed by Francis Bacon, René Descartes, and Isaac Newton.

Balancing newly nuanced abstractions of professional thinkers was the unflagging thrust of commercialization, strengthening in the medieval economy since the twelfth century. The growing role of markets encouraged Europeans of all ranks to see and value natural organisms, objects, and materials in terms of their potential for exchange. Georg Agricola's path-breaking description of the world of early modern mining, *De re metallica* (1556), provides a good example. Agricola was well aware that mining destroyed woodlands, afflicted air and water quality, chewed up the ground surface, and endangered animal life. He argued, however, that the arable land and

---

[3] T. Paracelsus [Theophrastus Bombastus von Hohenheim], 'Labyrinthus Medicorum errantium', 7.4–7.5, in A. E. Waite, ed. and tr., *The Hermetic and Alchemical Writings of Aureolus Philippus Theophrastus Bombast of Hohenheim called Paracelsus the Great*, 2 vols. (London: J. Elliott and Col Co., 1894), vol. II:165–7, or, otherwise, in F. Klemm, *A History of Western Technology*, tr. D. Singer (Cambridge, MA: MIT Press, 1964), 145, and in *Paracelsus Essential Readings*, selected and translated by N. Goodrich-Clarke (Wellington, UK: The Aquarian Press, 1990), 103. Translated by R. Hoffmann.

metals obtained by clearance of woodlands and destruction of the land surface were worth far more than the trees or mountains they had replaced, while fish, birds, and animals could be purchased to replace those lost. Humans could see nature, make use of nature, and, if they disliked what had become of it, counterbalance loss with economic values gained.

Continued commercialization included general facilitating of European consumers' draw on distant resources. In many areas enhanced late medieval rural–urban migration meant city populations rebounded more quickly than did those in the countryside, so the proportion of people living from the market had increased. By 1460 westerners had revived their import of grain supplies from further east, which had ceased with the mid-fourteenth-century population crash. Each year during the 1460s approximately 10,000 tonnes of cereal grains, mainly rye from interior Poland, left the port of Gdańsk en route to the urban Low Countries. A century later Gdańsk was transferring 89,000 tonnes a year and in 1618 shipped 186,000. Western consumer demand pulled this mass about 1,500 kilometres along a roundabout route. Likewise, live cattle drives from Scotland to London, from Scandinavia to the Low Countries, and from Hungary to Germany and northern Italy, moved 10,000 head an average distance of 900 kilometres in 1400, as the new wealth of a diminished population encouraged more meat eating. The plodding herds became 85,000 head per annum by 1500 and 230,000 after 1574. If human numbers grew two- or three-fold, the movement of plant and animal biomass grew twenty-fold, a huge increase in the flow from the geographical centre of Europe to its western fringes. Apart from the ecological impact of so catering to the needs and demand of distant consumers, continued commercialization reset people's engagement with the natural world. More now ate what they had never seen alive.

Parallel transformations arose from the expanding activity of the state – or at least the expanding ambition on the part of the state – to manage natural resources in the interests of those who dominated the power structure of society. Like market-based exchange, the medieval state intervention examined in chapter 7 gained greater prominence in Europe itself and in Europeans' overseas ventures as the fifteenth century became the sixteenth. Officials for Louis XII (1498–1515) and Francis I (1515–47) codified and enforced the king's authority over timber harvests in royal *forêt* and on private seigneuries alike. Other ordinances regulated water quality and fisheries in navigable rivers by setting legal seasons, equipment, and conditions when the flow might be blocked. Against this background, the oft-cited French forestry ordinance of 1669 simply took older state claims to absolutist extremes.

Security concerns and post-war reconstruction gave republican Venice occasions to expropriate woodlands from some subject communes and set management practice on others in the 1470s. After 1530 the Senate extended the regulatory regime to privately owned woods. Groundwork was laid for creation of a professional forest bureaucracy. Indeed most Renaissance Italian states regularly issued and codified statutes to protect water quality for drinking and for fishing, to delimit hunting rights and methods, to regulate floating timber down rivers, and other such purposes. Simply articulating such regulatory measures became a key means for late fifteenth- to seventeenth-century German and Austrian princes to assert and extend their authority over local lords and municipalities.

All such government attempts to control nature, construed as natural resources, served practical or prestige purposes. Authorities saw themselves as either confronting a substantive issue or needing to assert their superiority over putative subordinates, which they did by claiming responsibility over use of the world of nature. Though commonly prefaced by worries over resource shortages or the common good, none of this state activity was visibly undertaken for the sake of the environment in a present-day sense. Poorly funded administration and enforcement always hobbled claims to state power and so did the recalcitrance of lesser authorities and users of the resources. They at times struggled as much against outside intervention as they did against the actual measures imposed. From the 1480s to 1630s, whenever the duke of Württemberg's government tried to set rules for managing woodlands, communities with large common woodlands resisted. While leading villagers and landlords agreed with the goals and measures the duke was proposing, they refused to adopt them on his say so. Tension occurred less over the actual treatment of the resource than over who had the right to determine it. State efforts are not therefore to be construed as achieving great success overall, but the state did seize an essential place in the process of handling resources in Europe and the progress and effects of early modern European expansion. What had been unusual during medieval centuries became a modern norm.

So within the large cultural sphere, construed by the interaction model as containing both the purely symbolic and hybrid material constructs, an autonomous shift of pattern was already under way by the early fourteenth century and continued deep into the seventeenth. It privileged empirical and quantified observation and the accumulation and spread of information through materials printed in vernacular tongues. It acknowledged a larger though vague idea of the natural world as it was meant to be handled, understood, and made use of by human beings. Older trends continued, commercializing more links between people and nature and enlarging the role of state power therein.

Other transformative cultural forces arose more directly from European experience of the material world. Notably with respect to technological change, a greater ability to transform nature is argued to have had at least reciprocal effect on how Europeans reflected upon it.

During the fifteenth and sixteenth centuries several of the incremental medieval technical adaptations noted in previous chapters crossed thresholds of effectiveness to achieve broad acceptance and far-reaching consequences. Having evolved in obscurity up to the mid-1400s, the blast furnace was thereafter widely adopted. Each such innovative replacement of a bloomery increased by a factor of ten the local capacity for iron production, while demanding only four times more charcoal fuel. In the mining sector a fifteenth- and sixteenth-century surge in European metal production kept up with rising demand through the use of larger and more complex mechanical draining and lifting devices which made more efficient use of muscles as well as water power. In Figure 10.1, a wood cut from Agricola's *De re metallica* of 1556, the person turning a crank has his power magnified by a series of gear connections to drive an endless bucket chain for lifting water from deep in the mine. Finally the full-rigged ship, also perfected during the fifteenth century, provided a larger, sturdier, vessel, both handier and capable of long oceanic voyages. This design shrank the size of the crew relative to the load it carried, but demanded more technical proficiency in navigation over long distances. These ships pulled more energy out of the wind to move what Europeans could not have moved before.

To such medieval continuities as already noted can be added four further assertions of European human power over the material world. The first mechanical clocks were a thirteenth-century European invention. Within two generations these devices were appearing widely in public urban settings, becoming a proud feature of each new town hall

Figure 10.1 Gaining mechanical advantage, 1556

or display structure, placed where all could witness local wealth and fashion. Clocks set twenty-four hours in a day, all of them equal in length and not, as monastic hours had been, shorter in the summer night than daytime and the reverse in winter. Made materially manifest by the hands of the clock, equal and quantified time set the rhythm for daily life. By the late 1400s town officials prescribed when employees were to open the gates in the morning and lock them in the evening on the basis of when the clock read a certain time. Time had been transformed. Clockwork also provided a model for regular mechanical movement, becoming an analogue for the movement of the earth in the universe as differently envisaged by Dante, who seems to allude to a mechanical clock, or by Copernicus, whose diagrammed orbital circles are reminiscent of gears and escapements. Clocks finally serve as evidence of Europeans' rising skill in the precise handling of materials. Though still mostly made of wood, key parts were of metal. A clock that can keep more or less accurate time for a week or two proves the pieces possess some degree of precision. The same quality can also be seen in the astrolabe, produced in greater numbers and used more regularly as the fourteenth century turned into the fifteenth.

Another device where materials were manipulated with growing accuracy was the printing press and movable type itself. As elaborate in its precision and its moving parts as were clocks, the press made relatively greater use of metal for, as distinct from the smoothly running clock, it had to exert force and absorb abrupt impacts. Wooden pieces wear nowhere near as well as metal. The metal craftsman Gutenberg, not a millwright or cabinet-maker, figured out how to carve the pieces of type from a hardened lead alloy suitable to be moved around for repeated use. Cheaper but fragile wood was relegated to the rarer large letters and illustrations.

Firearms became highly effective and important users of metal. The idea of an explosion propelling a projectile out of a tube was a European adaptation of the Chinese invention of gunpowder, which the inventors had used to propel the tube itself. After some generations of experiment, by the early 1400s Europeans had developed effective cannons and by that century's end made them more mobile and accompanied on the battlefield by small arms. Firearms in land combat contributed little to European expansion in the early modern period, but use of cannons on ships was critical. From an environmental perspective the ever-rising amount and sophistication of metal use has equal significance. Quantities of metal being used by European armies rose geometrically from the end phases of the Hundred Years War in the mid-fifteenth century through to the Italian wars and the Habsburg–Valois struggle of the sixteenth. Soaring capital and resource costs of war drove states to contrive ever more elaborate institutions and grounds to interfere in their subjects' relations with nature. New cannon-resistant defence schemes laid waste the immediate environs of cities. Early modern officials entered private cellars to scrape from the walls blooms of the saltpetre needed for more gunpowder. Pursuit of this natural resource meant seizing control over the geochemical process itself. Firearms not only enhanced the ability to kill humans and other organisms, they embodied a collective shift of cultural patterns. And most had to do with power.

Power was the primary attribute of water-driven machinery, the strongest terrestrial devices that early modern Europeans could control. Ever more complex water- (and to some degree wind-) driven machines served all sorts of resource extraction and heavy manufactures. In Figure 10.2, from a work on pyrotechnics printed at Venice in 1540, a water-wheel drives a shifting camshaft being used to draw wire. This force pulled a rod of metal through a hole in a sheet of heavier metal and thus made it a smaller wire. The brute task is no longer attempted or limited by the strength of a man or ox. Another illustration from Agricola's *De re metallica* (Figure 10.3) shows a bi-directional water-wheel with a diameter, judging by the scale of humans, in the range of ten metres. Closer study detects two sets of buckets and two feeder pipes, with controls for the operator to direct the wheel's rotation. The

Figure 10.2 Drawing iron wire with water power, 1540

Aber von den hasplen seye nuhn gnüg gsagt/jeßunder wil ich sagen von den
gezeugen/so wetter in die grübenn bringen/oder böses herauß zieh.,nt. So ein
schacht

Figure 10.3 Water power and mechanical control, 1556

entire mechanism drives a huge windlass that lifts water from a mine by means of a bucket made by stitching together five or six whole ox hides. Water power now did what neither people nor draught animals could earlier accomplish.

All these innovations – blast furnace, mine drainage, full-rigged ship, clocks, press, firearms, and water-powered machines – manipulated material surroundings. Europeans' self-evident ability to transform their physical world, it is argued, helped nudge their minds to separate themselves from nature well before any self-conscious formal pronouncements to that effect from the likes of Francis Bacon or René Descartes.

The distinction here drawn between self-generating cultural phenomena and those evolved from continual adaptation to the material world may be visible only in retrospect and for the sake of coherent discussion. Important to acknowledge is that far from merely being driven by such natural forces as climate, disease, or geographical relationships, late medieval European culture was actively transforming itself in ways that impinged directly on how humans experienced and worked in the natural world.

UNINTENDED CONSEQUENCES FROM AN
ANTHROPOGENIC SHOCK: THE COLUMBIAN
ENCOUNTER IN EUROPEAN PERSPECTIVE

At the end of the fifteenth century, if not without what can in retrospect be recognized as foreshadowing, still-medieval Europeans initiated the largest global ecological event in post-Neolithic millennia to date. The Columbian encounter reconnected continental (hemispheric) ecosystems sundered since tectonic forces had broken up Pangaea in the mid-Mesozoic era some 200 million years before. The global consequences of this reunion still reverberate in both spheres. Europeans initiated this upheaval – if without such intent or awareness – and thus, quite apart from its significance elsewhere, it is a major benchmark for European environmental history.

While, like so much in environmental relations, developments after 1492 were unforeseen, nevertheless Europeans were not unprepared for this momentous role. Global medium-run outcomes were even anticipated in the fifteenth-century eastern Atlantic. In the Canaries, which Europeans had rediscovered in the fourteenth century, Castilians struggled to dominate native Neolithic Guanches and eventually destroyed them more through European diseases than by military conquest. Conquerors and settlers introduced European cultivars, the exotic sugar cane, and later also enslaved Africans. After 1425 Portuguese settlement on the uninhabited archipelago of Madeira triggered massive clearances of primeval indigenous woodlands and the extermination of native animal species in the jaws of European domesticates (pigs), commensals (rats), and introductions (rabbits). New agroecosystems there produced and exported first wheat, then sugar, and eventually wine. The Genoese mariner Christoforo Columbo himself married into a Madeira Portuguese family and lived for some years on Puerto Santo, where farmers were already waging war against the rabbits.

The Columbian encounter changed the world. Though the doing of Europeans, its first primary impact occurred elsewhere. And what an impact it was! A huge demographic disaster for native American peoples played out over the ensuing three to four hundred years, but began massively in the sixteenth-century Caribbean and Mexico, where millions succumbed to disease and exploitation. Virgin soil epidemics of Eurasian 'childhood' diseases were followed by less selective pathogens of Eurasian and African origin: smallpox, malaria, and yellow fever. A reasonably estimated pre-Columbian population of 54±10 million (14 million in Mexico, 12 million in the Incan Andes) collapsed to a mere 5–6 million by the early seventeenth century. The American continents were emptied, creating what Europeans perceived as primeval wilderness where once had flourished anthropogenic landscapes shaped by hunter-gatherers, agriculturalists, and indigenous urbanizing cultures.

There followed a colonization of the natural realm in the New World and later parts of south Asia and Africa by Europeans and what historian Alfred Crosby called their 'portmanteau biota'. Caribbean islands, mining regions of Mexico and the Andes, and temperate North America were hard-hit early on. Conquest and settlement by Europeans and enslaved Africans imposed their own agroecosystems, landscape structures, and an ever-wider spread of introduced exotic mammals: cattle, horse, sheep, pig, rats. Elsewhere extraction of much-desired natural or cultivated resources – 'spices', precious metals, cod, furs, whale or seal oil – removed materials and shifted metabolic flows in colonized ecosystems. All went on with little evident worry about depletion or destruction, as if Europeans boarding their ships had left such ideas behind.

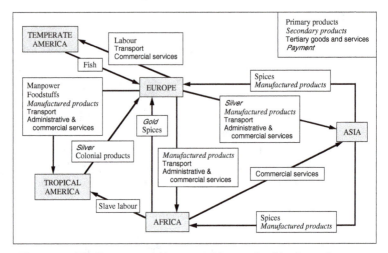

Figure 10.4 The European world commercial network of the sixteenth century

As a result, by the mid-sixteenth century there emerged a European world system, a globe-spanning commercial economy managed by Europeans, whose wind-powered ships linked most of the world's regions through oceanic trade in a limited array of goods. Europeans had learned which parts of the globe had complementary economic potentials and set out to control and gain from their exchange. Figure 10.4 provides a schematic representation. Europe, labour rich and technically adept, sought precious metals and other natural resources. Africa, also labour rich, wanted certain manufactures, even if in unequal exchange for its own people. Asia had resources and manufactures plus an apparently insatiable demand for precious metals. The Americas, rapidly bereft of human capital and with limited technical capacity, were resource rich. And thus the slaves sailed west; the cod, silver, and animal skins east; the silver especially even further east from Europe; and luxury consumables westwards out of Asia, all in European hulls and due in large part to European resourcefulness, remorselessness, and sheer luck. Massive transfers of biomass to Europe began with cod and then furs; sugar and cotton came a century and more later. This first genuine globalization began to transform distant economies and ecosystems in the interests of the dominant centre, whether through Portuguese, then Dutch, manipulation of spice production in the East Indies or wars Iroquois fought to control furs for trade to Europeans.

Barring a reversal of cultural trends comparable to that of late antiquity in Europe, the Columbian encounter had already by the 1550s shifted human impact on global environments to a new order of magnitude.

Even by the mid-sixteenth century, 'blowback' from this 'New World' on to Europe was already affecting the material lives of Europeans and, again in retrospect, deeper structures at the intersection of their natural and cultural worlds, both of which churned with change.

Experience of a 'New World' expanded European awareness of nature's diversities and possibilities. By using explicit and implicit comparisons of American biota to European counterparts, Columbus and other contemporary witnesses revealed their awareness of similarities and differences between prior experience and new observations. Even when the voyages caused blank spots on the globe to be reconceived from 'lands unknown' to 'lands not yet discovered', the larger culture remained slow to move from description to comprehension. While the first European writers were reluctant to assimilate the New World into a model of 'wilderness' (*deserta*), they generally did apply familiar Christian and classical models. Lawyers and theologians first debated, then acknowledged, the fellow humanity of newfound peoples. This brought an obligation to convert them to Christianity, an urge to use them for alternate visions of society (Thomas More's 1516 *Utopia* was set somewhere overseas), and common assertion of European cultural superiority. Awe and surprise caused witnesses to portray the entire landscape as the earthly paradise. The diversity of newfound flora and fauna made them incorporate the latter, though admittedly different, into Noah's ark (with intriguing speculation on how the American beasts had thereafter gone extinct in the Old World). Amerigo Vespucci early sounded a common note that such new knowledge meant his own moderns had surpassed the ancients. But all this sense of wonder mainly reinforced a teleological understanding of the world as a product of a divine plan for human benefit.

Following generations focused attention on practicalities of using new things of nature. While English-hired Venetian Zuan Caboto immediately saw the Grand Banks of Newfoundland as unlimited sources of dried cod, the tropical forest was represented as if a natural pharmacy. The need was to classify and order both the novelties and the familiar. By the 1560s Spanish physician Nicholás Bautista Monardes had catalogued medical uses of American plants in three published volumes, while others such as Ulisse Aldrovandi (1522–1605) in Bologna avidly sought specimens for their herbaria and botanical gardens. From the intellectual to the material, later authors came to believe – in a surely unknowing echo of some medieval attitudes – this profusion of 'wild' nature required civilized control.

Material consequences of the encounter more directly altered how Europeans lived in their own evolving ecosystems. The 'discoveries' and conquests gained some 60–80 million Europeans, hitherto confined to less than 6 million square kilometres of land, access to another 40–50 million square kilometres, a six- to eight-fold increase in potential resources. As a reserve to expand production or substitute for limited resources, this 'ghost acreage' has been labelled by economic historian Eric L. Jones 'a great ecological windfall for Europeans', who gained it when their own society was suffering little or no acute resource shortage. New materials were not 'free' but could be obtained at costs much below equivalent or substitute domestic production. Imports of American silver and fish forecast much more to come.

Arriving not as material imports but as genetic samples ready to be multiplied in Europe under the right cultural and environmental conditions were the exotic organisms from the New World introduced to sixteenth-century consumers and producers. Columbus's first voyage encountered maize (*Zea mays*), already a highly anthropogenic grass of Mesoamerican origin widespread in central and temperate parts of the Americas. Written descriptions from 1494 were followed by cultivation in Spain by the 1530s and Tuscany and the eastern Mediterranean by the 1550s. Maize proved to be a warm-weather crop with some tolerance of Mediterranean summer drought and suitable for animal fodder and human food. Peasants in the Venetian *Terra firma* adapted the exotic to customary European gruel/porridge and made *polenta*; their counterparts in the Balkans did likewise under names like *žganci, kačamak*, etc. The new crop's high yields per acre were most welcome, but as a dominant dietary staple maize, unlike wheat, left a vitamin deficiency condition, pellagra.

Other novel food crops followed. The potato (*Solanum tuberosum*), which Spaniards in what is now Colombia identified as an Andean staple in 1536, was adopted for shipboard use in European diets by the 1580s. Early Spanish and English cultivation is certain; conflicting tales obscure its introduction in Ireland. Cultural resistance to a member of the often-toxic nightshade family and problems of storage in humid Europe held back into the 1700s widespread adoption of this highly productive and nutritionally balanced plant. Potato and maize then fully emerged as major and calorie-rich substitutes for cereals. Another nightshade relative of Mesoamerican origin, the tomato (*Solanum lycopersicum* = *Lycopersicon esculentum*), with small fruits used in sauces and medicines in sixteenth-century Spain and Italy, took even longer to gain acceptance in maritime Europe, not aided by its warm-season needs during the Little Ice Age. When learned and adapted to European conditions, all these plants and more – capsicum peppers, some new genera of beans and squash – contributed to an increasingly diverse agricultural repertoire and diet.

Tobacco (*Nicotiana* sp.) had no dietary role. Columbus saw this plant and Cuban natives smoking its leaves in 1493. Reported and demonstrated to Europeans, a newly formed cultural 'need' and demand swept the continent and across the Mediterranean. By the 1550s tobacco was widely cultivated in Mediterranean and maritime Europe, despite its rapidly depleting soils and, in England, early governmental opposition on grounds first moral, then political (to protect the only export from the Virginia colony). While some writers, Monardes among them, alleged therapeutic benefits, tobacco's narcotic and recreational effects were plain and left fruitless the censure by other cultural authorities of the plant's moral and medical consequences. Tobacco presaged European adoption of other such psychoactive exotics as chocolate, coffee, and tea.

American animals, except the turkey, remained mere curiosities in sixteenth-century Europe. Before the 1800s not even invasive exotics caused a stir – with one probable exception. In 1494 Naples experienced a sudden epidemic of a ferocious 'new' disease. It began with rashes and ulcers of especially mucus membranes, fever followed, then bone pain and a quick or early death. The malady decimated an invading French army and spread, perhaps with the retreating troops, quickly across Europe. It soon acquired many popular names but physicians preferred *morbus gallicus*, 'the French disease'. By the 1510s–1520s, however, both medical authorities and veterans of the Spanish Caribbean were connecting its origins to Columbus's returning crewmen. Sexual transmission as a 'venereal' disease was recognized in 1527 and soon a quasi-literary discussion in 1530 concocted a mythic namesake, 'Syphilis', a shepherd whose amorous transgressions brought this punishment on humankind. Probably despite such harshly ineffectual cures as toxic concoctions of mercury, after mid-century its virulence seems to have attenuated, but syphilis remained a real point of interplay between a natural phenomenon and European cultural awareness.

Nineteenth-century medical scientists eventually identified the pathogen as a spiral-shaped protozoan, *Treponema pallidum*. Subsequent historical debate over its putative New World origin has become entangled in medical disputes over whether four distinct species of *Treponema* produce syphilis, yaws, pinta, and so-called 'endemic syphilis' respectively (the latter three being tropical ulcerative skin diseases transmitted by skin contact, not sexual relations), or one species has four distinct clinical syndromes. Both medical positions concur that sexually transmitted syphilis is the youngest evolved form. The 'unitary' theory sees sexual transmission as evolving in isolation in the New World; the non-unitary thinks it evolved from African yaws or the milder 'endemic' form in the port cities of the late fifteenth-century Mediterranean. Newer DNA research has found a *Treponema* ancestral to syphilis among native populations of deep interior Guyana, but also suggests sexual transmission was a sudden historic mutation which succeeded because Europeans wore clothing and thus offered the para-site less opportunity for other skin-to-skin contact. In either case, recognition that some non-human force had infiltrated the most inti-mate human physical relations provides a strong indicator of change in European relations with a newly reconfigured natural world.

Arguably, then, from natural as from human cultural agency, and as surely from some two centuries of interactions between the two autonomous classes of causalities, by the mid-1500s medieval European environmental relations irrevocably, if slowly and incompletely, gave way to something else.

AFTERWORD

———————— • ————————

Medieval Latin Christendom had an environmental history. How people engaged with nature had a bearing on their lives and their fate. This book means to show students, practitioners, and consumers of medieval studies and environmental studies this simple truth. The interaction of European nature and medieval culture writ large mattered then and says something of moment to those who would now listen. All three central themes of environmental history – environmental influences on human activity, human attitudes towards the natural world, and human impacts on the non-human – pertain to stories and outcomes interlaced through a millennium of Europe's past. Those narratives deal with problems of resource use, ecological balance, pollution, and values and equity in environmental relations. They illuminate similarities, differences, and diversities among past and present human experiences with natural processes and objects, whether those are now approached from a current analytical perspective or from as much as can be reconstructed of a medieval stance where central concepts were not as today's. Medieval environmental history also makes another contribution: its methods of drawing robust inferences about past events and conditions from surviving verbal and material artefacts and from traces preserved in nature constitute a call for enlarging interdisciplinarity in medieval studies. Respectful collaboration among medievalists, environmental scientists, and palaeoscientists is necessary to recapture lives, thoughts, and activities of medieval Europeans and the evolution of European nature in millennia before our own. By trying to exemplify what is

known or reasonably surmised and what might be worth
exploring, the present book advocates cooperation and shared learning among humane and scientific investigators, neophyte and veteran
alike.

The chapters of this book should have made plain that medieval
environmental history is not one story but many diverse stories operating simultaneously at different scales in time and space. Local and
regional drivers of change did not necessarily replicate continental or
cultural norms, while brief or catastrophic events could generate
responses unlike those resulting from generational or longer trends.
Different ecological and historical circumstances made England's 'New
Forest' a socio-natural site distinct from the ducal hunting parks of
Artois or Bavaria, even as all contributed to the medieval interplay of
elite recreation and wildlife ecology. The epic tale of the Black Death
does not supersede stories of plague in Iceland, diffusion of the blast
furnace, or choices of plough teams according to seasonal conditions of
local soils in eastern England. The microecologies that mattered around
the Mediterranean were smaller than their northern counterparts, but
each small-scale region was always where medieval people most
directly confronted their natural surroundings. This condition colours
but does not obscure generalization over greater time or space.

Examining flows of energy and materials between and among
medieval societies and their colonized ecosystems (their 'social metabolism') has been central to this discussion, highlighting ecological
and social linkages between driving forces, socio-natural sites, human
groups, and historical outcomes. Energy emerged as a key constraint
but also a potential tool of change. Members of an energy-poor
society had a different range of options from those where energy
was cheap and abundant. Massive medieval reliance on what are now
defined as biochemical sources set parameters for the whole culture,
whether contemporaries were aware of it or not. Tracing flows of
energy thus linked many aspects of arable farming, dietary practices,
exploitation of woodland, and eventual growth in production and use
of inorganic materials, notably metals. But the metabolic perspective
shrinks to insignificance when confronted with natural drivers of
environmental change. Epidemic disease and catastrophic tectonic
or climatic events abruptly altered conditions for social flows of
energy and materials. Medieval responses to rare and local geological
shocks help contextualize the more widespread impacts from disease
and weather events.

Metabolic flows, naturally and socially constituted, ground the notion of human society, its structures, and its artefacts as hybrids of nature and culture. They undergird use of an interaction model in a historical setting. They identify and exemplify the linkages from culturally defined values and wants to human work in the natural sphere, consequent ecosystem changes, and altered human experiences. This heuristic most notably served to frame and explicate the great clearances and other medieval colonizations of natural ecosystems, which by about 1300 had made larger areas of Europe into more thoroughly anthropogenic landscapes than ever before. Autonomous and deeply embedded natural processes set limits in the form of unintended consequences to these and other manipulations of nature. Thorough historical understanding of medieval cultural dynamics is thwarted by the recurring importance of the gap diagnosed in chapter 3 between this etic analysis and now invisible emic connections between people's experience and its cultural representation and between cultural programmes and human work. In many respects especially before the thirteenth century the absence of cogent cultural links between what medieval Europeans *experienced* in their natural surroundings and what they *did* there remains the greatest area of ignorance in medieval environmental history and in medieval studies as a whole. How much this arises necessarily from medieval cultural biases and how much from those of medievalists remains to be assessed. White's theory of Dominion explained little; can research into less abstract, more pragmatic thinking reveal more?

Plainly evident in the historical record are major medieval cultural adaptations, some with subsequent consequences for the natural sphere, which themselves arose from the impact of natural phenomena at large and small temporal and spatial scales. Even then natural processes and events did not necessarily set off cultural changes but could rather influence the way they played out.

Firstly, all who study medieval Europe are reminded that they explore a natural world neither stable nor pristine, but already subject for millennia to natural variability and co-evolution with human communities.

Large socio-cultural reconfigurations during late antiquity and the earliest medieval centuries, though mainly triggered by political and cultural instability in the Roman Empire, evolved under pressures of climate change and epidemic disease, with ensuing large losses of human numbers. These transformations were cumulatively much greater than occurred at the end of the Middle Ages, for they worked out over a longer period of time, though with less interregional synchronicity than occurred in the 1300s. Even taken together, exiguous cultural and palaeoscientific records poorly illuminate the processes at work. Notable climatic instability and the Justinianic plague make the second quarter of the sixth century a benchmark, but was it a tipping point? Or did local and regional changes follow other trajectories? At question here is how to fit indubitable natural events into a much longer socio-cultural dynamic. In any case, critical anthropogenic pressures on European nature changed fundamentally, leaving their net effect attenuated for some centuries. Meanwhile, newly emergent or resettled human communities between the Mediterranean and the North Sea were certainly learning how to live in initially unfamiliar landscapes.

A more open question is the extent to which the onset of climatic warming now detected in the late ninth or tenth century and the persistence, more or less, into the thirteenth century in many European regions of a Medieval Warm Period had demonstrable effect on medieval human activities independently of contemporary cultural programmes. Medieval records contain responses to climate change but nowhere ever acknowledge awareness of it. Given the slow emergence of marginally warmer and drier conditions relative to human time frames, the undoubted spread of European farming and pastoralism into altitudes and latitudes not previously or later so used is more convincingly to be understood as gradually learning and exploiting local opportunities rather than as conscious or direct responses to perceived change. So, too, a temporarily more benign North Atlantic might be thought permissive rather than constitutive of Norse expansion there. In any case, despite some fierce short-term events, atmospheric, tectonic, and pathogenic conditions long appear benign towards Europeans then purposefully enlarging their colonization of the biosphere.

Verbal and material records from the high Middle Ages onwards confirm pragmatic local responses to catastrophic events such as floods, earthquakes, storms, extreme weather, and mortality crises (epidemics and famines). In so far as medieval understandings and capabilities allowed, communities acted to recover, mitigate, and prevent future damages. Medieval Europeans were not passive victims, but it stretches credulity to think their incremental improvements in technology and material culture were primarily driven by natural pressures.

Transition of European weather to conditions typical of the Little Ice Age coincided in the first half of the fourteenth century with the first epidemic of Black Death. Climatic instability and incomprehensibly vast human mortalities drove general European relations with the natural environment to a plausible tipping point. Material and symbolic cultural responses and outcomes can be detected across multiple scales.

But the hybrid linkages between natural and cultural forces in medieval Europe were not deterministic. At the same times and over long periods, what might look from afar like analogous interactions had diverse outcomes. The fourteenth century did not reprise the fourth to the seventh century because the European world, social and natural, had changed. Simple concepts of crisis and collapse poorly capture the interplay between systemic hazards and stresses, exogenous shocks, and the working out in time of local resilience, adaptability, and reconstruction. Like slowly evolving natural forces, autonomous cultural changes in both attitudes and technical capacities shifted relations of Europeans with the environment. The Columbian imposition of Europe on the wider world arose from and reinforced that process.

Historic connections between medieval environmental experience and intentional actions are most visible around what would now be called sustainability, environmental awareness, and 'conservation'. Numerous practices and measures undertaken by communities of commoners, individual lords/landowners, and public authorities served to protect the usefulness of diverse kinds of natural resources. Some enactments made this purpose explicit, but none articulated concerns for a long-term future (no 'this is for the sake of our grand-children') or valued the natural world or its elements for their own sake. 'Environmental protection' as a concept or goal in its own right had no place or voice in medieval culture.

The present book has amply reviewed instances of local or sectoral overexploitation, depletion, pollution, and destruction, but even some such records themselves testify to contemporary recognition of the problem and its remedies. Of necessity actual users possessed solid traditional working knowledge of their resources, the limits, and the likely risks. Medieval communities had social mechanisms to prevent or respond to anthropogenic and natural environmental hazards and damage. As today, some measures for 'the common good' concealed special interests, some were effective at both rationing and conserving resources, and some failed from inadequate enforcement or knowledge. Neither the modern popular stereotype of a Middle Ages wallowing unabashed in filth nor the academic 'tragedy of the commons' corresponds to medieval realities. In many aspects of arable agriculture, pastoralism, woodland management, and use of wildlife, medieval practices could and did maintain exploitation at sustainable levels so long as surrounding environmental conditions varied within a familiar range. Some resource systems remained more flexible and resilient; others became more rigid over time. Even in relatively egalitarian resource commons, social equity had limited scope, and not just in the power of lords to diminish or abolish customary uses.

Over time a wider spectrum of influences, decisions, and consequences started to reshape medieval resource management, with effects resembling those now attributed to globalization. During early and central medieval centuries, elite demands had but rarely so transcended localities or regions as to impose exogenous priorities on local colonizations of the natural sphere. Charlemagne's ditch and William the Conqueror's forests come first to mind. From the high Middle Ages onward, however, claims of the market and of the state to override local interests expanded continually. Developing market exchange transmitted culturally driven demand for cereals, fuels, furs, fibres, and meats from centres of consumption to sometimes distant socio-natural sites, shifting the flow of energy and materials within and out of local ecosystems with little regard for local consequences. Flemish import of grain from the Elbe and Florentine import of that from Sicily were among the cases mentioned; so, too, consider Parisian courtiers in mantles lined with fur of Russian sable or citizens of Gdańsk in woollens from English sheep. Late medieval states played a more ambivalent role, at least when imposing on reluctant local owners and users of resources measures with the ostensible intent of conservation. The mêlée of parties and interests on the socio-cultural side makes historical assessment of human treatment of the medieval natural world as complex, even on occasion as surprising, as for the modern.

The hope of enlarging present knowledge and understanding of medieval Europeans in their natural world poses complementary challenges to environmental historians and medievalists. Environmental history as a subdiscipline has borrowed and developed its own paradigmatic questions and explanatory theories suitable for testing on past experiences. Some have helped make sense of events and the long term in a pre-modern past; others have not. Regarding the Middle Ages environmental historians confront several problems: ignorance of medieval life and culture, slim command of languages and genres of sources, and weak communication between historians, archaeologists, and natural scientists. Responsibility for the last rests with all three groups. While each disciplinary cluster makes indispensable contributions to knowledge of the past, environmental historians are especially suited to show present-day publics how the present situation is both special and derivative of prior human experience on the planet. Well-documented, much-studied medieval Europe provides whole cases of diverse successes, failures, and intermediate outcomes experienced by people coping with natural and anthropogenic change.

Medievalists need to open their already multidisciplinary field of study to pervasive aspects of medieval life they have hitherto ignored. Isolation among specialized cultural disciplines and a collective habit of medieval studies to treat material culture as an afterthought and the non-cultural as non-existent are no longer credible strategies for learning of greater consequence. Scholars and students capable of the greatest refinement in parsing a poem, deconstructing a diptych, or marking a meme can grant similar attention to the material and natural particulars of their protagonists and programmes. When this goes beyond clichés about the manual labour of monks, the Provençal sun, or the Little Ice Age, more branches of medieval scholarship will gain and provide insights into how medieval Europeans of all social sorts operated in their own worlds. Medievalists asking new kinds of questions and listening to a wider range of researchers in cognate fields will be able to turn their rich knowledge of medieval cultural artefacts to issues with wide-ranging resonance among other academics and a broader public.

A SAMPLER FOR FURTHER READING

————————— • —————————

Interested readers can learn more about topics covered generally in this book or its individual chapters. The selected references include items considered in preparing the book but by no means comprise a complete bibliography; among the selected serious scholarly works are some holding positions different from those adopted here. What have become obsolete works for a general audience are omitted where possible. Books in English were favoured, so scholarly and scientific articles are underrepresented; very limited selections in other languages aim to provide at least token coverage of regions not treated in English. Students should remember that, even as English becomes a more common means of scholarly communications, most history is published in the language of the country it describes.

INTRODUCTION AND GENERAL CONTEXT

Coates, Peter A. *Nature: Western Attitudes since Ancient Times.* Berkeley: University of California Press, 1998.

Delort, Robert, and F. Walter, *Histoire de l'environnement européen.* Paris: PUF, 2001.

Fischer-Kowalski, Marina, and H. Haberl, 'Tons, Joules, and Money: Modes of Production and their Sustainability Problems', *Society and Natural Resources*, 10 (1997), 61–85.

Fischer-Kowalski, Marina, and Helga Weisz. 'Society as Hybrid between Material and Symbolic Realms: Toward a Theoretical Framework of Society–Nature Interactions', *Advances in Human Ecology*, 8 (1999), 215–51.

Haberl, Helmut, Marina Fischer-Kowalski, Fridolin Krausmann, Helga Weisz, and Verena Winiwarter, 'Progress towards Sustainability? What the Conceptual Framework of Material and Energy Flow Accounting (MEFA) Can Offer', *Land Use Policy*, 21 (2004), 199–213.

Hughes, J. Donald. *What is Environmental History?* Cambridge: Polity Press, 2006.

Linehan, Peter, and Janet L. Nelson, eds. *The Medieval World*. London and New York: Routledge, 2001.

McNeill, John R. 'Observations on the Nature and Culture of Environmental History', *History and Theory*, 42 (2003), 5–43.

Pounds, Norman. *An Historical Geography of Europe*, 2 vols. Cambridge University Press, 1973–79.

Simmons, Ian G. *Interpreting Nature: Critical Constructions of the Environment*. London: Routledge, 1993.

  Global Environmental History 10,000 BC to AD 2000. Edinburgh University Press, 2008.

Winiwarter, Verena. 'Approaches to Environmental History: a Field Guide to its Concepts', in Jószef Laszlovszky and Péter Szabó, eds., *People and Nature in Historical Perspective*, 3–22. Budapest: Central European University, Department of Medieval Studies, and Archaeolingua, 2003.

Winiwarter, Verena, and Martin Knoll. *Umweltgeschichte. Eine Einführung*. Cologne, Weimar and Vienna: Böhlau, 2007.

Worster, Donald, ed. *The Ends of the Earth: Perspectives on Modern Environmental History*. Cambridge University Press, 1988.

CHAPTER 1 LONG NO WILDERNESS

Grove, A. T., and Oliver Rackham. *The Nature of Mediterranean Europe: an Ecological History*. New Haven: Yale University Press, 2001.

Horden, P., and N. Purcell, *The Corrupting Sea: a Study of Mediterranean History*. Oxford: Blackwell, 2000.

Hughes, J. Donald. *Pan's Travail: Environmental Problems of the Ancient Greeks and Romans*. Baltimore: Johns Hopkins University Press, 1994.

Robinson, Thomas M., and Laura Westra, eds. *Thinking about the Environment: Our Debt to the Classical and Medieval Past*. Lanham, MD: Lexington Books, 2002.

Sallares, Robert. *Malaria and Rome: a History of Malaria in Ancient Italy*. Oxford University Press, 2002.

Shipley, Graham, and John Salmon, eds. *Human Landscapes in Classical Antiquity: Environment and Culture*. New York: Routledge, 1996.

Stoddart, Simon, ed. *Landscapes from Antiquity*. Antiquity Papers 1. Cambridge: Antiquity Publications, 2000.

White, K. D. *Roman Farming*. Ithaca, NY: Cornell University Press, 1970.

Whittaker, C. R., ed. *Pastoral Economies in Classical Antiquity*. Cambridge Philological Society, Supplementary Volume 14. Cambridge Philological Society, 1988.

CHAPTER 2 INTERSECTING INSTABILITIES: CULTURE AND NATURE AT MEDIEVAL BEGINNINGS, *c*.400–900

Catteddu, Isabelle. *Archéologie médiévale en France. Le premier Moyen Âge (Ve–XIe siècle)*. Paris: La Découverte, 2009.

Cheyette, Frederic L. 'The Disappearance of the Ancient Landscape and the Climatic Anomaly of the Early Middle Ages: a Question to be Pursued', *Early Medieval Europe*, 16 (2008), 127–65.

Davis, Jennifer R., and Michael McCormick, eds. *The Long Morning of Medieval Europe: New Directions in Early Medieval Studies*. Aldershot and Burlington, VT: Ashgate, 2008.

Hamerow, Helena. *Early Medieval Settlements: the Archaeology of Rural Communities in North-west Europe, 400–900*. Oxford University Press, 2002.

Hooke, D. *The Landscape of Anglo-Saxon England*. Leicester University Press, 1998.

Little, Lester K., ed., *Plague and the End of Antiquity: the Pandemic of 541–750*. Cambridge University Press, 2007.

McCormick, Michael. *Origins of the European Economy: Communications and Commerce, AD300–900*. Cambridge University Press, 2001.

McCormick, Michael, Ulf Büntgen, Mark A. Cane, *et al*. 'Climate Change during and after the Roman Empire: Reconstructing the Past from Scientific and Historical Evidence', *Journal of Interdisciplinary History*, 43 (2012), 169–220.

Quirós Castillo, J. A., ed. *The Archaeology of Early Medieval Villages in Europe*. Documentos de arqueología e historia 1. N.p.: Universidad del País Vasco/Euskal Herriko Unibertsitatea, 2009.

Sonnlechner, Christoph. 'The Establishment of New Units of Production in Carolingian Times: Making Early Medieval Sources Relevant for Environmental History,' *Viator*, 35 (2004), 21–48.

Squatriti, Paolo. *Water and Society in Early Medieval Italy, AD400–1000*. Cambridge University Press, 1998.

   Landscape and Change in Early Medieval Italy: Chestnuts, Economy, and Culture. Cambridge University Press, 2013.

van der Leeuw, Sander, François Favory, and Jean-Jacques Girardot. 'The Archaeological Study of Environmental Degradation: an Example from Southeastern France', in Charles L. Redman, S. R. James, P. R. Fish, and J. D. Rogers, eds., *The Archaeology of Global Change: the Impact of Humans on their Environment*, 112–29. Washington, DC: Smithsonian Books, 2004.

Ward-Perkins, Bryan. *The Fall of Rome and the End of Civilization*. Oxford University Press, 2005.

Wickham, Chris. *Framing the Early Middle Ages: Europe and the Mediterranean 400–800*. Oxford University Press, 2005.

CHAPTER 3 HUMANKIND AND GOD'S CREATION
IN MEDIEVAL MINDS

Albertus Magnus [Albert the Great]. '*On Animals': a Medieval 'Summa Zoologica'*, tr. Kenneth F. Kitchell, Jr. and Irven M. Resnick. 2 vols. Foundations of Natural History. Baltimore: Johns Hopkins University Press, 1999.

Bratton, Susan P. *Christianity, Wilderness, and Wildlife: the Original Desert Solitaire*. University of Scranton Press, 1993.

    Environmental Values in Christian Art. Albany: State University of New York Press, 2008.

Cohen, Jeremy. '*Be Fertile and Increase, Fill the Earth and Master it': the Ancient and Medieval Career of a Biblical Text*. Ithaca: Cornell University Press, 1989.

Cunningham, Andrew. *The Identity of the History of Science and Medicine*. Burlington, VT: Ashgate, 2012.

Dutton, Paul E. *Charlemagne's Mustache and Other Cultural Clusters of a Dark Age*. New York and Basingstoke: Palgrave Macmillan, 2004.

Epstein, Steven A. *The Medieval Discovery of Nature*. Cambridge University Press, 2012.

Filotas, Bernadette. *Pagan Survivals, Superstitions and Popular Cultures in Early Medieval Pastoral Literature*. Toronto: Pontifical Institute of Mediaeval Studies, 2005.

Fumagalli, V. *Landscapes of Fear: Perceptions of Nature and the City in the Middle Ages*. Oxford: Polity Press, 1994.

Glacken, Clarence. *Traces on the Rhodian Shore: Nature and Culture in Western Thought from Ancient Times to the End of the Eighteenth Century*. Berkeley: University of California Press, 1967.

Gurevich, A. *Medieval Popular Culture: Problems of Belief and Perception*, tr. J. Bak and P. Hollingsworth. Cambridge University Press, 1988.

Herlihy, David. 'Attitudes toward the Environment in Medieval Society', in Lester J. Bilsky, ed., *Historical Ecology: Essays on Environment and Social Change*, 100–16. Port Washington, NY: Kennikat Press, 1980.

Houwen, L. A. J. R., ed. *Animals and the Symbolic in Mediaeval Art and Literature*. Groningen: Egbert Forsten, 1997.

Kleinschmidt, Harald. 'Space, Body, Action: the Significance of Perceptions in the Study of Environmental History of Early Medieval Europe', *Medieval History Journal*, 3 (2000), 175–221.

Rubin, Miri, ed. *Medieval Christianity in Practice*. Princeton University Press, 2009.

Salisbury, Joyce E. *The Beast Within: Animals in the Middle Ages*. New York: Routledge, 1994.

Salisbury, Joyce E., ed. *The Medieval World of Nature: a Book of Essays*. New York: Garland, 1993.

Santmire, H. P. *The Travail of Nature: the Ambiguous Ecological Promise of Christian Theology*. Philadelphia: Fortress, 1985.

Sievers, Alfred K. *Strange Beauty: Ecocritical Approaches to Early Medieval Landscape*. The New Middle Ages. New York: Palgrave, 2009.

Sorrell, R. *St Francis of Assisi and Nature: Tradition and Innovation in Western Christian Attitudes toward the Environment*. Oxford University Press, 1988.

Thomas, Keith. *Man and the Natural World: Changing Attitudes in England, 1500–1800*. London: Allen Lane, 1983.

White, Lynn T., Jr. 'The Historical Roots of our Ecologic Crisis', *Science*, March 10 1967. Reprinted in White, *Machina ex Deo: Essays in the Dynamism of Western Culture*, Cambridge, MA: MIT Press, 1968: and in White, *Dynamo and Virgin Reconsidered*, Cambridge, MA: MIT Press, 1971 (and later editions).

Whitney, E. 'Lynn White, Ecotheology, and History', *Environmental Ethics*, 15 (1993), 151–69.

CHAPTER 4 MEDIEVAL LAND USE AND THE FORMATION OF TRADITIONAL EUROPEAN LANDSCAPES

Abbé, Jean-Loup. *A la conquête des étangs. L'aménagement de l'espace en Languedoc méditerranéen (xiie–xve siècle)*. Toulouse: Presses Universitaires du Mirail, 2006.

Arnold, Ellen F. *Negotiating the Landscape: Environment and Monastic Identity in the Medieval Ardennes*. Philadelphia: University of Pennsylvania Press, 2013.

Barceló, Miquel, and François Sigaut, eds. *The Making of Feudal Agricultures?* Leiden: Brill, 2004.

Bavel, Bas van. *Manors and Markets: Economy and Society in the Low Countries, 500–1600*. Oxford University Press, 2010.

Bertrand, G. 'Pour une histoire écologique de la France rurale', in G. Duby and A. Wallon, eds., *Histoire de la France rurale, 1: La formation des compagnes françaises des origines au xive siècle*, 34–118. Paris: Seuil, 1975.

Bloch, Marc. *French Rural History: an Essay on its Basic Characteristics*, tr. J. Sondheimer. Berkeley: University of California Press, 1966.

Bourin, M., and S. Boisselier, eds. *L'espace rurale au Moyen Âge. Portugal, Espagne, France (xiie–xive siècle). Mélanges en l'honneur de Robert Durand*. Rennes: Presses Universitaires de Rennes, 2002.

Durand, A. *Les paysages médiévaux du Languedoc (xe–xiiie siècles)*. Toulouse: Presses Universitaires du Mirail, 1998.

Gardiner, Mark, and Stephen Rippon, eds. *Medieval Landscapes*. Macclesfield: Windgather Press, 2007.

Glick, Thomas F. *Irrigation and Society in Medieval Valencia*. Cambridge, MA: Harvard University Press, 1970.
Irrigation and Hydraulic Technology: Medieval Spain and its Legacy. Aldershot and Brookfield, VT: Variorium, 1996.

Green, S. W. 'The Agricultural Colonization of Temperate Forest Habitats: an Ecological Model', in W. W. Savage, Jr. and S. Thompson, eds., *The Frontier: Comparative Studies*, vol. II, 69–103. Norman: University of Oklahoma Press, 1979.

Hoffmann, Richard C. *Land, Liberties, and Lordship in a Late Medieval Countryside: Agrarian Structures and Change in the Duchy of Wrocław*. Philadelphia: University of Pennsylvania Press, 1989.

Howe, John. 'The Conversion of the Physical World: the Creation of a Christian Landscape', in J. Muldoon, ed., *Varieties of Religious Conversion in the Middle Ages*, 63–78. Gainesville: University Press of Florida, 1997.

Rackham, Oliver. *The History of the Countryside*. London: Dent, 1986 (and later editions).

Rippon, Stephen. *The Transformation of Coastal Wetlands: Exploitation and Management of Marshland Landscapes in North West Europe during the Roman and Medieval Periods*. Oxford University Press, 2000.

Sereni, E. *History of the Italian Agricultural Landscape*, tr. R. Burr Litchfield. Princeton University Press, 1997.

Squatriti, Paolo. 'Digging Ditches in Early Medieval Europe', *Past and Present*, 176 (August 2002), 11–65.

TeBrake, W. *Medieval Frontier: Culture and Ecology in Rijnland*. College Station: Texas A&M University Press, 1985.

Watson, A. *Agricultural Innovation in the Early Islamic World: the Diffusion of Crops and Farming Techniques*. Cambridge University Press, 1982.

White, Lynn T., Jr. *Medieval Technology and Social Change*. Oxford University Press, 1962.

Williamson, Tom. *Shaping Medieval Landscapes: Settlement, Society, Environment*. Macclesfield: Windgather Press, 2003.

CHAPTER 5 MEDIEVAL USE, MANAGEMENT AND SUSTAINABILITY OF LOCAL ECOSYSTEMS, I: PRIMARY BIOLOGICAL PRODUCTION SECTORS

Alfonso Anton, Isabel, ed. *The Medieval Countryside, vol. I. The Rural History of Medieval European Societies: Trends and Perspectives*. Turnhout: Brepols, 2007.

Almond, Richard. *Medieval Hunting*. Stroud: Sutton, 2003.

Bavel, Bas J. P. van, and Erik Thoen, eds. *Land Productivity and Agro-systems in the North Sea Area: Middle Ages–20th Century*. Turnhout: Brepols, 1999.

Bechmann, R. *Trees and Man: the Forest in the Middle Ages*, tr. K. Duncan. New York: Random House, 1990.

Beck, Corinne. *Les eaux et forêts en Bourgogne ducale (vers 1350–vers 1480). Société et biodiversité*. Paris: L'Harmattan, 2008.

Bork, Hans-Rudolf, Helga Bork, Claus Dalchow, Berno Faust, Hans-Peter Piorr, and Thomas Schatz. *Landschaftsentwicklung in Mitteleuropa: Wirkung des Menschen auf Landschaften*. Gotha and Stuttgart: Klett-Perthes, 1998.

Campbell, Bruce M. S., and Mark Overton, eds. *Land, Labour, and Livestock: Historical Studies in European Agricultural Productivity*. Manchester University Press, 1991.

Cooter, W. S. 'Ecological Dimensions of Medieval Agrarian Systems', *Agricultural History*, 52 (1978), 458–77 (with responses by R. S. Loomis and J. A. Raftis, 478–87).

Dam, Petra J. E. M. van. 'Sinking Peat Bogs: Environmental Change in Holland, 1350–1550', *Environmental History*, 6 (2001), 32–45.

Duceppe-Lamarre, François. *Chasse et pâturage dans les forêts du nord de la France. Pour une archéologie du paysage sylvestre (xie–xvie siècles)*. Paris: L'Harmattan, 2006.

Fox, H. S. A. 'Some Ecological Dimensions of Medieval Field Systems', in K. Biddick, ed., *Archaeological Approaches to Medieval Europe*, 119–58. Studies in Medieval Culture 18. Kalamazoo: Medieval Institute, Western Michigan University, 1984.

Hatcher, John., and Mark Bailey. *Modelling the Middle Ages: the History and Theory of England's Economic Development*. Oxford University Press, 2001.

Hoffmann, Richard C. 'Economic Development and Aquatic Ecosystems in Medieval Europe', *American Historical Review*, 101 (1996), 631–69.

Keyser, Richard. 'The Transformation of Traditional Woodland Management: Commercial Sylviculture in Medieval Champagne', *French Historical Studies*, 32 (2009), 353–84.

McNeill, John R., and Verena Winiwarter, eds. *Soils and Societies: Perspectives from Environmental History*. Stroud: White Horse Press, 2006.

Pluskowski, Aleksander. *Wolves and the Wilderness in the Middle Ages*. Rochester, NY, and Woodbridge, Suffolk: Boydell & Brewer, 2006.

Pretty, J. 'Sustainable Agriculture in the Middle Ages on the English Manor', *Agricultural History Review*, 38 (1990), 1–19.

Rackham, O. *Ancient Woodland: Its History, Vegetation and Uses in England*. London: E. Arnold, 1980.

Semmler, Josef, ed. *Der Wald im Mittelalter und Renaissance*. Studia Humaniora, Düsseldorfer Studien zu Mittelalter und Renaissance 17. Düsseldorf: Droste Verlag, 1991.

Sweeney, Del, ed. *Agriculture in the Middle Ages: Technology, Practice, and Representation*. Philadelphia: University of Pennsylvania Press, 1995.

Vera, F. W. M. *Grazing Ecology and Forest History.* New York: CABI Publishing, 2000.

Woolgar, C. M., D. Serjeantson, and T. Waldron, eds. *Food in Medieval England: Diet and Nutrition.* Oxford University Press, 2006 [many chapters on cereals, animal husbandry, and wildlife].

CHAPTER 6 MEDIEVAL USE, MANAGEMENT AND SUSTAINABILITY OF LOCAL ECOSYSTEMS, 2: INTERACTIONS WITH THE NON-LIVING ENVIRONMENT

Bork, Robert, ed. *De Re Metallica: the Uses of Metal in the Middle Ages.* AVISTA Studies in the History of Medieval Technology, Science and Art 4. Aldershot and Burlington, VT: Ashgate, 2005.

Burnouf, J. *Archéologie médiévale en France. Le second Moyen Âge (xiie–xvie siècle).* Paris: La Découverte, 2008.

Cavaciocchi, Simonetta, ed. *Economia e energia secc. xiii–xviii: Atti della 'Trentaquattresima Settimana di Studi' 15–19 aprile 2002,* 585–98. Istituto Internazionale di Storia Economica 'F. Datini', Prato: Serie ii: Atti delle 'Settimane di Studi' e altri Convegni 34. Florence: Le Monnier, 2003.

Classen, Albrecht, ed. *Urban Space in the Middle Ages and the Early Modern Age.* Berlin and New York: Walter de Gruyter, 2009.

Durand, A., ed. *Jeux d'eau. Moulins, meuniers et machines hydrauliques, xie–xxe siècle. Études offertes à Georges Comet.* Aix-en-Provence: Publications de l'Université de Provence, 2008.

Fossier, Robert, *The Axe and the Oath: Ordinary Life in the Middle Ages,* tr. Lydia G. Cochrane. Princeton University Press, 2010.

Gimpel, Jean. *The Medieval Machine: the Industrial Revolution of the Middle Ages.* New York: Holt, Rinehart and Winston, 1976; 2nd edn 1992.

Guillerme, André E. *The Age of Water: the Urban Environment in the North of France, AD 300–1800.* College Station: Texas A&M University Press, 1988.

Hoffmann, Richard C. 'Frontier Foods for Late Medieval Consumers: Culture, Economy, Ecology', *Environment and History,* 7 (2001), 131–67.

'Footprint Metaphor and Metabolic Realities: Environmental Impacts of Medieval European Cities', in Paolo Squatriti, ed., *Natures Past: the Environment and Human History,* 288–325. Comparative Studies in Society and History book series. Ann Arbor: University of Michigan Press, 2007.

Jørgensen, Dolly. 'Cooperative Sanitation: Managing Streets and Gutters in Late Medieval England and Scandinavia', *Technology and Culture,* 49 (2008), 547–67.

'Local Government Responses to Urban River Pollution in Late Medieval England', *Water History,* 2 (2010), 35–52.

Landers, John. *The Field and the Forge: Population, Production, and Power in the Pre-Industrial West.* Oxford University Press, 2003.

Langdon, John. *Horses, Oxen, and Technological Innovation: the Use of Draught Animals in English Farming from 1066 to 1500.* Cambridge University Press, 1986.

Mills in the Medieval Economy: England, 1300–1540. Oxford University Press, 2004.

Malanima, Paolo. *Pre-Modern European Economy: One Thousand Years (10th–19th Centuries).* Leiden and Boston: Brill, 2009.

Padberg, B. *Die Oase aus Stein. Humanökologische Aspekte des Lebens in mittelalterlichen Städten.* Berlin: Akademie Verlag, 1996.

Pleiner, Radomír. *Iron in Archaeology: the European Bloomery Smelters.* Prague: Archeologický Ústav AVCR, 2000.

Roux, Simone. *Paris in the Middle Ages,* tr. Jo Ann McNamara. Philadelphia: University of Pennsylvania Press, 2009.

Smil, Vaclav. *Energy in World History.* Boulder, CO: Westview Press, 1994.

Smith, Elizabeth B., and Michael Wolfe, eds. *Technology and Resource Use in Medieval Europe: Cathedrals, Mills and Mines.* London: Ashgate, 1997.

Squatriti, Paolo, ed. *Working with Water in Medieval Europe: Technology and Resource Use.* Leiden: Brill, 2000.

Zupko, Ronald E., and Robert A. Laures. *Straws in the Wind: Medieval Urban Environmental Law – the Case of Northern Italy.* Boulder, CO: Westview Press, 1996.

CHAPTER 7 'THIS BELONGS TO ME . . .'

Appuhn, Karl. *A Forest on the Sea: Environmental Expertise in Renaissance Venice.* Baltimore: Johns Hopkins University Press, 2009.

Ault, Warren O. *Open-Field Farming in Medieval England: a Study of Village By-laws.* London: George Allen and Unwin; New York: Barnes and Noble, 1972.

Dahlman, C. J. *The Open Field System and Beyond: a Property Rights Analysis of an Economic Institution.* Cambridge University Press, 1980.

Garnsey, Peter. *Thinking about Property: From Antiquity to the Age of Reason.* Cambridge University Press, 2007.

Grant, R. *The Royal Forests of England.* London: Alan Sutton, 1991.

Kaijser, Arne. 'System Building from Below: Institutional Change in Dutch Water Control Systems'. *Technology and Culture,* 43:3 (2002), 521–48.

Reynolds, Susan. *Before Eminent Domain: Toward a History of Expropriation of Land for the Common Good.* Chapel Hill: University of North Carolina Press, 2010.

Stevenson, Glenn G. *Common Property Economics: a General Theory and Land Use Applications.* Cambridge University Press, 1991.

Warde, Paul. *Ecology, Economy and State Formation in Early Modern Germany*. Cambridge University Press, 2006.

Wood, Diana. *Medieval Economic Thought*. Cambridge University Press, 2002.

CHAPTER 8 SUFFERING THE UNCOMPREHENDED: DISEASE
AS A NATURAL AGENT

Arrizabalaga, J., J. Henderson, and R. French. *The Great Pox: the French Disease in Renaissance Europe*. New Haven: Yale University Press, 1997.

Benedictow, Ole J. *The Black Death 1346–1353: the Complete History*. Rochester, NY and Woodbridge, Suffolk: Boydell & Brewer, 2004.

Cohn, Samuel K. 'The Black Death: End of a Paradigm', *American Historical Review*, 107 (2002), 703–38.

  The Black Death Transformed: Disease and Culture in Early Renaissance Europe. London: Arnold; New York: Oxford University Press, 2002.

Demaitre, Luke. *Leprosy in Premodern Medicine: a Malady of the Whole Body*. Baltimore: Johns Hopkins University Press, 2007.

French, Roger. *Medicine before Science: the Rational and Learned Doctors from the Middle Ages to the Enlightenment*. Cambridge University Press, 2003.

Haensch, Stephanie, Rafaella Bianucci, Michael Signoli *et al*. 'Distinct Clones of *Yersinia pestis* Caused the Black Death', *PloS Pathogens*, 6:10 (October 2010), 1–8.

Herlihy, D. *The Black Death and the Transformation of the West*, ed. S. Cohn, Jr. Cambridge, MA: Harvard University Press, 1997.

Jakob, Tina. *Prevalence and Patterns of Disease in Early Medieval Populations: a Comparison of Skeletal Samples of the 5th–8th Centuries AD from Britain and Southwestern Germany*. BAR International Series 1959. Oxford: John and Erica Hedges, 2009.

Little, Lester K. 'Plague Historians in Lab Coats', *Past and Present*, 213 (November 2011), 267–90.

McNeill, William H. *Plagues and Peoples*. Garden City: Anchor/Doubleday, 1976.

Newson, Linda A. 'A Historical-Ecological Perspective on Epidemic Disease', in William Balée, ed., *Advances in Historical Ecology*, 42–63. New York: Columbia University Press, 1998.

Nutton, Vivian, ed. *Pestilential Complexities: Understanding Medieval Plague*. London: Wellcome Trust Centre for the History of Medicine at UCL, 2008.

Rawcliffe, Carole. *Leprosy in Medieval England*. Rochester, NY and Woodbridge, Suffolk: Boydell & Brewer, 2006.

Roberts, Charlotte A., Kerth Manchester, and Mary E. Lewis, eds. *The Past and Present of Leprosy: Archaeological, Historical, Palaeopathological and Clinical Approaches*. BAR International Series 1054. Oxford: Archaeopress, 2002.

Sallares, Robert. 'Role of Environmental Changes in the Spread of Malaria in Europe during the Holocene', *Quaternary International*, 150 (2006), 21–7.

Scott, Susan, and Christopher J. Duncan. *Biology of Plagues: Evidence from Historical Populations*. Cambridge University Press, 2001.

CHAPTER 9 AN INCONSTANT PLANET, SEEN AND UNSEEN, UNDER FOOT AND OVERHEAD

Behringer, Wolfgang. 'Climatic Change and Witch-Hunting: the Impact of the Little Ice Age on Mentalities', *Climatic Change*, 43 (1999), 335–51. *A Cultural History of Climate*. Cambridge: Polity Press, 2010.

Bennassar, B., ed. *Les catastrophes naturelles dans l'Europe médiévale et moderne*. Actes des XVes Journées Internationales d'Histoire de l'Abbaye de Flaran, 10, 11, 12 Septembre 1993. Toulouse: Presses Universitaires du Mirail, 1996.

Bowlus, C. 'Ecological Crisis in Fourteenth Century Europe', in Lester J. Bilsky, ed., *Historical Ecology: Essays on Environment and Social Change*, 86–99. Port Washington, NY: Kennikat Press, 1980.

Brazdil, Rudolf, Christian Pfister, H. Wanner, H. van Storch, and J. Luterbacher. 'Historical Climatology in Europe – the State of the Art', *Climatic Change*, 70 (2005), 363–430.

Brown, N. *History and Climate Change: a Eurocentric Perspective*. New York: Routledge, 2001.

Büntgen, Ulf, W. Tegel, K. Nicolussi *et al.* '2500 Years of European Climatic Variability and Human Susceptibility', *Sciencexpress*, 13 January 2011, 1–4: 10.1126/science.1197175.

Fréchet, Julien, Mustapha Meghraoui, and Massimiliano Stucci, eds. *Historical Seismology: Interdisciplinary Studies of Past and Recent Earthquakes*. Modern Approaches in Solid Earth Sciences 2. Dordrecht and London: Springer, 2008.

Glaser, Rüdiger, and Dirk Riemann, 'A Thousand-Year Record of Temperature Variations for Germany and Central Europe Based on Documentary Data', *Journal of Quaternary Science*, 24:5 (2009), 437–449.

Guidoboni, Emanuela, and John E. Ebel. *Earthquakes and Tsunamis in the Past: a Guide to Techniques in Historical Seismology*. Cambridge University Press, 2009.

Jones, P. D., K. R. Briffa, T. J. Osborn *et al.* 'High-Resolution Palaeoclimatology of the Last Millennium: a Review of Current Status and Future Prospects', *The Holocene*, 19:1 (2009), 3–49.

Jordan, William C. *The Great Famine: Northern Europe in the Early Fourteenth Century*. Princeton University Press, 1996.

Lamb, H. H. *Climate, History and the Modern World*. 2nd rev. edn. London: Routledge, 1995.

LeRoy Ladurie, Emmanuel. *Histoire humaine et comparée du climat, vol. I: Canicules et glaciers (XIIIe–XVIIIe siècle)*. Paris: Fayard, 2004.

Luterbacher, Jürg, Elena Xaplaki, Carlo Casty *et al*. 'Mediterranean Climate Variability over the Last Centuries: a Review', in P. Lionello, P. Malanotte-Rizzoli, and R. Boscolo, eds., *Mediterranean Climate Variability*, 27–148. Amsterdam: Elsevier, 2006.

McCormick, Michael, Paul Edward Dutton, and Paul A. Mayewski. 'Volcanoes and the Climate Forcing of Carolingian Europe, AD 750–950', *Speculum*, 82 (2007), 865–95; available online at www.medievalacademy.org/pdf/Volcanoes.pdf.

McGovern, Thomas H., Orri Vésteinsson, Adolf Fridriksson *et al*. 'Landscapes of Settlement in Northern Iceland: Historical Ecology of Human Impact and Climate Fluctuation on the Millennial Scale', *American Anthropologist*, new series, 109 (2007), 27–51.

Oppenheimer, Clive. *Eruptions that Shook the World*. Cambridge University Press, 2011.

Oster, Emily. 'Witchcraft, Weather and Economic Growth in Renaissance Europe', *Journal of Economic Perspectives*, 18 (2004), 215–28.

Perdikaris, Sophia, and Thomas H. McGovern. 'Codfish and Kings, Seals and Subsistence: Norse Marine Resource Use in the North Atlantic', in Torben C. Rick and Jon M. Erlandson, eds., *Human Impacts on Ancient Marine Ecosystems: a Global Perspective*, 187–214. Berkeley: University of California Press, 2008.

Rohr, Christian. 'Man and Natural Disaster in the Late Middle Ages: the Earthquake in Carinthia and Northern Italy on 25 January 1348 and its Perception', *Environment and History*, 9 (2003), 127–50.

Schenk, Gerrit J. '"… prima ci fu la cagione de la mala provedenza de'Fiorentini …" Disaster and Life World Reactions in the Commune of Florence to the Flood of November 1333', *Medieval History Journal*, 10 (2007), 355–86.

Stothers, R. B. 'Climatic and Demographic Consequences of the Massive Volcanic Eruption of 1258', *Climatic Change*, 45 (2000), 362–74.

CHAPTER 10 A SLOW END OF MEDIEVAL
ENVIRONMENTAL RELATIONS

Abulafia, David. *The Discovery of Mankind: Atlantic Encounters in the Age of Columbus*. New Haven: Yale University Press, 2008.

Bourin, Monique, John Drendel, and François Menant, eds. *Les disettes dans la conjoncture de 1300 en Méditérranée Occidentale*. Rome: École Française de Rome, 2011.

Bowlus, Charles R. 'Ecological Crisis in Fourteenth Century Europe', in Lester J. Bilsky, ed., *Historical Ecology. Essays on Environment and Social Change*, 86–99. Port Washington, NY: Kennikat Press, 1980.

Campbell, Bruce M. S. 'Nature as Historical Protagonist: Environment and Society in Preindustrial England (The Tawney Memorial Lecture 2008)', *Economic History Review*, 63 (2010), 281–314.

'Physical Shocks, Biological Hazards, and Human Impacts: the Crisis of the Fourteenth Century Revisited', in Simonetta Cavaciocchi, ed., *Le interazioni fra economia e ambiente biologico nell'Europa preindustriale. Secc. XIII–XVIII / Economic and Biological Interactions in the Pre-Industrial Europe from the 13th to the 18th Centuries*, 13–32. Istituto Internazionale di Storia Economica 'F. Datini', Prato: Atti della XLI Settimana di Studi, 26–30 aprile 2009. Florence: Florence University Press, 2010.

'Panzootics, Pandemics and Climate Anomalies in the Fourteenth Century', in Bernd Herrmann, ed., *Beiträge zum Göttinger Umwelthistorischen Kolloquium 2010–2011*, 177–216. Göttingen: Universitätsverlag Göttingen, 2011.

Crosby, Alfred W. *The Columbian Exchange: Biological and Cultural Consequences of 1492*. Westport, CT: Greenwood, 1972.

Fraser, E. D. G. 'Can Economics, Land Use, and Climatic Stresses Lead to Famine, Disease, Warfare, and Death? Using Europe's Calamitous 14th Century as a Parable for the Modern Age', *Ecological Economics*, 70:7 (2011), 1269–79.

Jones, Eric L. *The European Miracle: Environments, Economies, and Geopolitics in the History of Europe and Asia*. 3rd edn. rev. Cambridge University Press, 2003.

Long, Pamela O. *Artisan/Practitioners and the Rise of the New Sciences, 1400–1600*. Corvallis: Oregon State University Press, 2011

Richards, John F. *The Unending Frontier: an Environmental History of the Early Modern World*. Berkeley: University of California Press, 2003.

Schlesinger, Roger. *In the Wake of Columbus: the Impact of the New World on Europe, 1492–1650*. 2nd rev. edn. Wheeling, IL: Harlan Davidson, 2007.

Smith, Pamela H., and Paula Findlen, eds. *Merchants and Marvels: Commerce, Science, and Art in Early Modern Europe*. New York: Routledge, 2002.

INDEX

·

Guadiana, 178
Gulf of Bothnia, 27
Gutenberg, Johannes, 355, 361
Guthlac, 95

Hainault, 236
Hamburg, 236, 299
'Hammer of Witches' (*Malleus maleficarum*), 339
Hannoversch Münden, 121, 325
Hanseatic merchants, 189
Hanseatic routes, 291
Hardin, Garret, 241–3, 247, 261, 277
Harz, 216, 218, 222
hay, 175, 250, 270, 333, 336
hazards, *see* risks
hegemonic cultural norms, 79, 83
    see also Christianity: hegemonic cultural
        norms
Hekla, 311
hemp, 226, 230, 264, 265
Henry II, king of England, 253
herds/herding, 22, 28, 47, 58, 66, 124, 130,
        140, 164, 174–9, 248
    see also pastoralism
Hereford, 296
Herlihy, David, 94
Herrad of Hohenbourg (Landsberg), 209
Hertfordshire, 350
Hessen, 325
high Middle Ages, 119, 127, 146, 169, 172,
        173, 175, 179, 220, 246, 249, 263, 302,
        322, 332, 376
Highland Scots, 140
Hohenstaufen, 254
Holland, 114, 136, 138, 167–8, 181, 232,
        237, 260
Holocene, 22, 23, 24, 25, 26, 27, 29, 30, 32,
        202, 301
households, 81, 82, 157, 158, 169, 175, 192,
        200, 247, 289, 291
Howe, Nicholas, 153
Hugh Capet, king of France, 254
Hughes, J. Donald, 171, 239, 344

human bodies, 115, 198–9, 232, 234–5, 265,
        279, 280, 282, 286, 293, 295, 297, 298,
        300, 301
human species, 22, 29, 281
human waste, 235
humanism, 96, 102, 309, 351, 352, 353,
        355, 356
humans and nature (relationship), 30, 61, 79,
        86, 107, 110, 118, 237–9, 240, 243–4,
        283, 286, 300, 302, 312, 337, 343, 346,
        349, 350, 355–6, 359, 364, 371
    see also environmental impact;
        environmental influence;
        environmental modification;
        environmental perception
humoral theory, 39, 109, 115, 215
    see also medicine, medieval
Hundred Years War, 267
Hungarians, *see* Magyars
Hungary, 26, 101, 179, 181, 185, 189, 357
    see also Pannonia
Huns, 57, 58, 75
hunting 29, 40, 98, 107, 109, 110, 189,
        190–2, 251, 252, 253, 254, 255, 267,
        337, 352, 358
Huntingdonshire, 248
hydrology, 149, 150

Iberia, 38, 42, 57, 60, 144, 189, 208, 213, 257,
        259, 321
    see also Portugal; Spain
Ibero-romans, 95
ice cores, 69, 313, 314, 316, 321, 327, 330, 335
Iceland, 4, 153, 310–11, 313, 333–8
Île-de-France, 67
incastellamento, 169
Innocent III, pope, 96
instability, 54–6, 70, 172, 173, 238, 283, 319,
        337, 340, 343, 346, 349, 373, 375
    natural shocks, 52–4, 324, 325, 347,
        348–9; *see also* ecological crisis;
        ecosystem: collapse; ecosystem:
        instability